The **Rough Guide** to

Seattle

written and researched by

JD Dickey and Richie Unterberger

ROUGH
GUIDES

NEW YORK • LONDON • DELHI

www.roughguides.com

Contents

Coffee culture insert
following p.112

Green (& blue) Seattle
insert following p.240

◄◄ Monorail at the Experience Music Project ◄ Washington Park Arboretum

Introduction to

Seattle

**The sparkling waterside city of Seattle is one of America's
most attractive metropolises, laced with parks and lakes,
and almost perfectly sited between rugged mountains and
sylvan islands at the northwest corner of the lower 48
states. The city is defined by striking hills overlooking its
shorelines, boats from kayaks to ferries cruising its scenic
waterways, and winding streets leading through historic
districts rich with public artworks and outdoor markets.
Its central Downtown core, narrowly saved from the
wrecking ball by popular outcry, has been converted into a
thriving hub for some of the city's best arts, shopping, and
nightlife.**

Before the modern rise of the high-tech economy,
Seattle spent many decades as an enterprising port
town, first relying on the timber trade for its
well-being, then the aerospace industry and federal
military contracts. The notable World's Fair of 1962
– highlighted by its theme-park-like monorail and its
Space Needle icon – gave much of the world its first
look at this remote American jewel, known as "The Emerald City." After
that the city made few headlines until the early 1990s, when key local companies like Starbucks and Microsoft led a controversial vanguard of global
American capitalism, and Seattle-bred grunge music fueled the meteoric
rise of alternative rock bands such as Nirvana and Pearl Jam.

In the late 1990s it seemed that the good times might never end, and that
this once-obscure city in the Pacific Northwest would finally challenge San
Francisco and LA for West Coast prominence. But a new century brought
trouble in the form of natural disasters (a devastating 2001 earthquake),
the bursting of the dot-com bubble, and a national recession; and the city's
fortunes began to resemble its winter weather – dark and dreary. However,
Seattle has since stopped its freefall, rebounding with small but growing
optimism despite continuing economic struggles. More importantly for

visitors, the countless museums, shops, galleries, cafés, and hotels that were built on the wave of the 1990s remain in place – and are quite affordable compared to their California counterparts.

For all its arriviste character, Seattle is neither a chaotic urban funfair nor 24-hour party zone, and those expecting the throbbing pulse of a New York or Tokyo will definitely be underwhelmed. While its **museums** are enjoyable, its **theater** scene vibrant, and the pervasiveness of its **café culture** unmatched in the US – offering social

> **Seattle is best experienced on an itinerary that emphasizes nature hikes, neighborhood strolls, and ferry rides as well as traditional sightseeing and untamed nightlife**

centers where coffee-drinking, avant-garde decor, and lively performances meld in one artsy pot – the mood of the city is decidedly low-key. In fact, Seattle is best experienced on an itinerary that puts as much emphasis on nature hikes, neighborhood strolls, and ferry rides as it does on traditional sightseeing and untamed nightlife.

What to see

The city of Seattle has roughly an hourglass shape: skinny in its central section and wider to the north and south, with water on the sides. To the west is Puget Sound, a huge waterway that extends about a hundred miles from its northern entry on the Pacific Ocean down to its southern tip. Downtown Seattle lies on the Elliott Bay portion of

Rock in Seattle

In the 1990s the music world became aware of Seattle's importance to the rock scene with the release of Nirvana's *Nevermind* album. The grunge era of the first half of that decade was characterized by slow, grinding beats, guitar distortion, downbeat lyrics, and a surfeit of flannel. Seattle-area groups such as Pearl Jam, Mudhoney, Soundgarden, Alice in Chains, and Screaming Trees quickly became household names, inspiring plenty of imitators but also helping to shine a light on local artists who dominated the scene before them. Examples include 1960s pioneers the Sonics, Ventures, and Wailers, as well as Jimi Hendrix and arena rockers Heart – whose guitarist Nancy Wilson is married to Cameron Crowe (who did his part to immortalize local music culture with his 1992 film *Singles*). For more on alternative rock in the city, see p.297.

the Sound, while further west are such fetching islands as Vashon, Bainbridge, and Whidbey. Seattle is separated from its eastern suburbs by Lake Washington, which is connected to Puget Sound by the Lake Washington Ship Canal, a narrow waterway that, at various points, widens into Portage Bay, Union Bay, and Lake Union. Boats of all sorts – and salmon – exit the canal into the Sound through the Hiram M. Chittenden Locks, at the western edge of Salmon Bay.

Downtown contains many of the city's top attractions, particularly Pike Place Market, the best urban agora in the US; the waterfront, with its prime views of the Sound; the worthwhile Seattle Art Museum; and the eye-popping architecture of the New Central Library. Just south of Downtown is **Pioneer Square**, Seattle's most historic district and a lively place to hang out at night or sample the local art scene, and the **International District** – aka Chinatown – which is also home to significant numbers of pan-Asian immigrants and some excellent ethnic diners. North of Downtown is **Belltown**, a former hipster neighborhood now awash in upscale restaurants and boutiques; the **Seattle Center**, a large complex of theaters, sports arenas, and museums, as well as the Space Needle; and the stately mansions of **Queen Anne**, a genteel area that also holds some decent cafés and restaurants.

The I-5 freeway divides Downtown on the east from **Capitol Hill**, the neighborhood with the best combination of cafés, shops, and nightlife, along with the fine Washington Park

Arboretum and a handful of classic mansions. North from here, the Montlake Bridge leads across the ship canal to the **University District**, or U District, dominated by the campus of the University of Washington, home to several enjoyable museums and gardens. On the opposite side of town, west and northwest of Queen Anne are **Magnolia**, featuring one of Seattle's best green spaces, Discovery Park, and **Ballard**, known primarily for the Hiram M. Chittenden Locks, but also good for its architecture, street fairs, and taverns. Continuing east toward the U District, **Fremont** is the city's most unpretentiously bohemian corner, with its funky public art and freewheeling atmosphere, and **Wallingford** is a pleasant neighborhood enlivened by the towers of Gasworks Park. Further north, the Woodland Park Zoo makes for an excellent family outing, as does nearby Green Lake, and adjacent **Greenwood** appeals for its cafés and antique stores.

On the edge of Capitol Hill, the western border of **Lake Washington** runs through some of Seattle's prettiest areas, from Madison Park down to Seward Park, and offers excellent biking terrain, too.

Waterfront seafood restaurant

Suggested itineraries

Seattle can be experienced in many different ways, depending on your focus – ferry trips to islands, nature hikes, art museums, and so on. The following itineraries are designed around the key sights and include suggestions for where to have lunch. Of course, if any of the days seem too sight-oriented for you, don't be afraid to skip the sights and just wander – or bicycle – around.

Two days
• Pioneer Square; waterfront; Pike Place Market (lunch); Capitol Hill; Washington Park Arboretum
• Belltown; Seattle Center (lunch); Experience Music Project or Pacific Science Center; Queen Anne

Four days
As above plus . . .
• Discovery Park; Hiram M. Chittenden Locks; central Ballard (lunch); Fremont; Gasworks Park
• Woodland Park Zoo; Greenwood (lunch); Green Lake; University District

One week
As above plus . . .
• Tacoma and Olympia, or Bellevue and Marymoor Park, or Museum of Flight and West Seattle/Alki Beach
• Ferry trip to Vashon, Bainbridge or Whidbey islands (or three-day trip including Port Townsend and San Juan Islands)
• Mount Rainier or Mount St Helens

On the lake's eastern side are Seattle's most prominent **suburbs**, the most worthwhile of which is **Bellevue**, with a few interesting museums and parks. In Seattle's southern industrial section is the first-rate Museum of Flight, while Alki Beach, on the peninsula of **West Seattle**, is the sandy location where the city was officially born in 1851.

To get the most out of a lengthier visit to Seattle, you have to get on a ferry and explore some of **Puget Sound** – any of its islands makes for a good excursion, though the San Juans are justly renowned as some of the most scenic spots in the Pacific Northwest. Inland daytrip options include the cities of **Tacoma**, highlighted by the Museum and Bridge of Glass, and **Olympia**, Washington state's capital, while longer drives bring you to **Mount Rainier** and **Mount St Helens**, two of the most spectacular mountain parks in the country.

When to go

Seattle tourist authorities proudly note that the town ranks but 44th among US cities in annual rainfall, somewhat belying its reputation as the country's cloud capital. However, Seattle's soggy

Liquid sunshine

The Pacific Northwest – and Seattle most of all – is famous for its rain. Even though places like Hawaii, or, for that matter, the western side of Washington's Olympic Peninsula, get much more precipitation (up to 275 annual inches for the latter), Seattle still gets pegged as America's wettest place. Averaging about 33 inches per year, the city's rainfall is not huge, though it is constant throughout the winter – and, oddly enough, quite aesthetically appealing in the spring.

From March to June, the region is prone to scattered, rain-bearing clouds, but not always fully overcast. When the sun's rays slant through at a low angle – which happens frequently this far north – a strange result can occur: the cool, driving sheets of rain are illuminated by sunlit radiance, making for a dramatic effect when set against glittering Elliott Bay and a verdant backdrop of mountains. Visitors not accustomed to this striking effect may experience some cognitive dissonance, but the natives scarcely even notice.

renown is mostly deserved – not for the quantity, but the regularity. In the fall and winter, drizzly days can pile upon one another endlessly, and when it's not raining, it's often overcast.

Despite this, Seattle is never really that cold, even in the dead of **winter**. **Summers** are quite lovely here – the average monthly rainfall in July and August hovers around just one inch, and the skies are often sunny, but the temperatures are almost never scorching. For this reason, you should consider defying conventional traveler wisdom about peak season: midsummer may be the most crowded time of the year, but it's also undeniably the most enjoyable, both for the good weather and the numerous festivals. Accommodation can be scarce, but with enough advance planning you should be fine. If you want a bit more elbow room, May, June, and September are all

recommended, although the weather won't be quite as warm, or as dry. Outside of these parameters, you risk getting caught in one of the city's wet spells – though even in the colder months there's still plenty going on to keep you occupied, particularly when there's a steaming mug of coffee in front of you.

Seattle's climate

	Jan	Feb	Mar	Apr	May	Jun	Jul	Aug	Sep	Oct	Nov	Dec
Average daily maximum temperature												
°F	46	50	53	58	64	70	75	76	70	60	51	46
°C	8	10	12	14	18	21	24	24	21	16	11	8
Average daily minimum temperature												
°F	36	37	39	42	47	52	55	56	52	46	40	36
°C	2	3	4	6	8	11	13	13	11	8	4	2
Average rainfall												
in	5	4	4	3	2	2	1	1	2	3	6	6
mm	130	104	97	66	46	38	20	25	41	81	150	142

23

things not to miss

It's not possible to see everything that Seattle has to offer in one trip, so what follows is a selective taste of the city's highlights: hip cafés, first-rate museums, exciting festivals, breathtaking scenery, and more. They're arranged in color-coded categories, which you can browse through to find the best things to see and experience. All entries have a page reference to take you straight into the text, where you can find out more.

01 **Splashing in the International Fountain** Page **87** ● Get drenched by powerful jets of water that spurt high in the sky – a great way to cool off in the summertime.

02 **Strolling along Alki Beach** Page **137** • Enjoy a walk along the city's best beach, with an impressive view across the bay.

04 **Coffeehouses** Page **153** • Admire quirky artworks, take in a music jam or poetry slam, noodle around on the Internet, or order a pastrami sandwich or simple cup o' joe at these bonafide bastions of high and low culture.

05 **Port Townsend** Page **253** • Take a trip to this nicely preserved Victorian hamlet on the west side of Puget Sound, chock-a-block with elegant mansions, restaurants, and boutiques.

03 **Snoqualmie Falls** Page **273** • *Twin Peaks* fans will recognize this 270ft waterfall, which spews from the heights of a solid bedrock gorge.

06 Seafood Page **162** • Gorge on fresh and tasty seafood, from raw oysters to good old fish-and-chips, along the waterfront docks.

07 Fremont public art Page **120** • Keep an eye out for some of the city's most striking and bizarre public artworks scattered around this eminently bohemian and free-spirited district.

08 Gasworks Park Page **122** • A wondrous conversion of an old industrial plant into a grassy spot featuring rolling hills, kite-flying kids, and looming gas towers.

09 Washington Park Arboretum Page **98** • This lush greenspace, with a fine Japanese Garden, provides access to Foster Island and is one of Seattle's best spots for a leisurely walk.

10 **Browsing at Elliott Bay Book Company** Page **219** • Seattle's finest fix for bibliophiles is an emporium of left-of-center books, good poetry readings and lectures, and assorted magazines.

11 **Burke-Gilman Trail** Page **208** • Follow the curve of the ship canal and its lakes – on bike or on foot – for a marvelous journey between Shilshole Bay and Lake Washington.

12 **Discovery Park** Page **109** • Experience this striking spot's engaging hikes and memorable bayside vistas, as well as its signature lighthouse that's one of the region's finest.

13 **Bumbershoot** Page **204** • Venues across the city host Seattle's most freewheeling festival, encompassing music, food, theater, dance, and countless other diversions.

14 **Mount St Helens**
Page **279** • The notorious peak that erupted on May 18, 1980 is one of the state's best places to go for a hike or a climb.

16 **Hiram M. Chittenden Locks** Page **112** • Watch boats big and small rise up and plunge down, while native salmon do the same below the waterline.

15 **Smith Tower** Page **65** • Check out the views from the 35th-floor observation deck of this 1914 terracotta icon of old Seattle.

18 **New Central Library** Page **59** • This Rem Koolhaas masterpiece of canted glass walls and staggering geometry is easily the most important piece of modern architecture in the Northwest, if far from the most conventional.

17 **Pike Place Market** Page **49** • Take in the sights and smells at this frenetic bazaar, loaded with fish vendors, produce stalls, fancy restaurants, fun cafés, and just about anything else you can think of.

19 Museum and Bridge of Glass Page **237** • Witness Dale Chihuly's masterworks in Tacoma, which feature crystalline blue towers, sparkling seashells, vivid flowers in vases, and a gamut of colorful shapes and oddities – all made of glass.

21 Experience Music Project Page **83** • A Frank Gehry–designed, Paul Allen–funded temple to all things with a backbeat, as well as one of Seattle's more inventive museums – if you can call a place that lets you rock out to your favorite songs a "museum."

23 Museum of Flight Page **135** • It's worth the trek south of Seattle to see this prime collection of classic aircraft, military fighters, commercial jets, and an early version of Air Force One.

20 Solstice Parade Page **202** • Expect to see belly dancers, cartoon robots on stilts, human-powered floats, and a phalanx of nude bicyclists at this legendary Fremont event, where local eccentricity is at its best.

22 Harbor cruises Page **36** • One of the best ways to really experience the city, either on a high-priced pleasure cruise or a much cheaper ferry to the islands in Puget Sound.

Basics

Basics

Getting there

Tucked up in a remote corner of the US, Seattle is not easily accessible from most of North America, so unless you happen to live in the Pacific Northwest, the quickest and best way of getting there is to fly. While alternatives certainly exist – a long freeway slog, or longer train ride – there's little question that for most people, their first view of the Emerald City will be from above.

If flying is not an option, **rail travel** may be an alternate choice, though there are few options save for Amtrak, the ailing US train system – which really won't save you that much money for all the added travel time. The cheapest way is to go by **bus**, but it's also the least comfortable and by far the most time-consuming. Similarly lengthy (unless you live nearby), a **car** ride to Seattle will most assuredly devour your vacation time, and with rising US gas prices, is no longer the cost-saving bargain it once was.

Shopping for air tickets

Airfares always depend on the season, with the highest during summer and around Christmas; you'll get the best prices during the **low season**, mid-January to the end of February, and October to the end of November, excluding the days around Christmas, Thanksgiving and New Year's Day, when prices are hiked up and seats are at a premium. **Shoulder seasons**, where prices hover between the low- and high-season averages, cover the rest of the year.

It's worth calling the airlines directly to inquire about their fares, though you'll likely save yourself a lot of time, and often cut costs, by going through a **specialist flight agent** – either a **consolidator**, who buys up blocks of tickets from the airlines and sells them at a discount, or a **discount agent**, who, in addition to dealing with discounted flights, may also offer special student and youth fares and a range of other travel-related services such as rail passes, car rental, tours and the like.

Online booking agents and general travel sites

Many airlines and discount travel **websites** offer you the opportunity to book your tickets online, cutting out the costs of agents and middlemen; as a result, prices are usually cheaper. Good deals can also often be found through discount or auction sites, as well as through the airlines' own websites.

Ⓦ **www.cheapflights.com,** Ⓦ **www .cheaptickets.co.uk,** Ⓦ **wwwcheaptickets.ca,** Ⓦ **www.cheaptickets.com.au** Flight deals and packages (listed by country of access), and good links to relevant destination sites.

Ⓦ **www.ebookers.com** Low fares on an extensive selection of flights.

Ⓦ **www.etn.nl/discount** A hub of consolidator and discount agent links, maintained by the nonprofit European Travel Network.

Ⓦ **www.expedia.com,** Ⓦ **www.expedia.co.uk** Discount airfares, all-airline search engine and daily deals.

Ⓦ **www.flyaow.com** "Airlines of the Web" – online air travel info and reservations.

Ⓦ **www.hotwire.com** Bookings from the US only. Last-minute savings of up to forty percent on regular published fares. Travelers must be at least 18 and there are no refunds, transfers, or changes allowed.

Ⓦ **www.lastminute.com** UK site offering good last-minute holiday package and flight only deals.

Ⓦ **www.opodo.co.uk** Popular and reliable source of low UK airfares. Owned by, and run in conjunction with, nine major European airlines.

Ⓦ **www.orbitz.com** Comprehensive Web travel source, with the usual flight, car hire and hotel deals but also great follow-up customer service.

Ⓦ **www.priceline.com,** Ⓦ **www.priceline.co.uk** Name-your-own-price websites with deals around forty percent off standard fares.

Ⓦ **www.skyauction.com** Bookings from the US only. Auctions tickets and travel packages to destinations worldwide.

Ⓦ **travel.yahoo.com** Incorporates some Rough Guides material in its coverage of destination countries, with information about places to eat and sleep, etc.

Ⓦ **www.travelocity.com**, Ⓦ **www.travelocity .co.uk** Destination guides with deals for car rental, lodging and airfares.

Ⓦ **www.travelzoo.com** Great resource for news on the latest airline sales, cruise discounts and hotel deals. Links bring you directly to the carrier's site.

From the US and Canada

The best means of getting to Seattle from most places in North America is to **fly**, as many airlines offer daily service – both nonstop and connecting – across the US and Canada. Another plus is that if you book your ticket three weeks or so in advance, flying isn't much more expensive than rail or bus travel, especially when you factor in how long Amtrak and Greyhound can take when coming from far away.

By plane

The main airport for domestic arrivals into Seattle is **Sea-Tac Airport** (☎1-800/544-1965, Ⓦwww.portseattle.org/seatac), fourteen miles south of Downtown and centrally located for both Seattle and Tacoma – hence the name.

The cheapest round-trip prices generally start at around $250 from New York, $270 from Chicago, $300 from Miami, $200 from LA, $230 from San Francisco, $400 from Toronto, or $470 from Montreal.

Travelers **from Canada** may find that, with less competition on these routes, fares are higher than flights originating in the US. If you're coming to Seattle from an eastern Canadian city, you may often find that it's worth getting to a closer US city first and flying on from there. And if you don't mind an out-of-the-way stopover (say, via Phoenix when going from Toronto to Seattle on America West), you can save up to $100 on certain routes.

Airlines

Air Canada ☎1-888/247-2262, Ⓦwww .aircanada.ca
Alaska ☎1-800/252-7522, Ⓦwww.alaska-air .com
America West ☎1-800/235-9292, Ⓦwww .americawest.com
American ☎1-800/433-7300, Ⓦwww.aa.com
Continental domestic ☎1-800/523-3273,

international ☎1-800/231-0856, Ⓦwww .continental.com
Delta domestic ☎1-800/221-1212, international ☎1-800/241-4141, Ⓦwww.delta.com
Frontier ☎1-888/241-7821, Ⓦwww .frontierairlines.com
Hawaiian ☎1-800/367-5320, Ⓦwww .hawaiianair.com
Horizon ☎1-800/547-9308, Ⓦwww.horizonair.com
JetBlue ☎1-800/538-2583, Ⓦwww.jetblue.com
Northwest/KLM domestic ☎1-800/225-5252, international ☎1-800/447-4747, Ⓦwww.nwa.com or Ⓦwww.klm.com
Song ☎1-800/359-7664, Ⓦwww.flysong.com
Southwest ☎1-800/435-9792, Ⓦwww .southwest.com
Sun Country ☎1-800-359-6786, Ⓦwww .suncountry.com
United domestic ☎1-800/241-6522, international ☎1-800/538-2929, Ⓦwww.ual.com
US Airways domestic ☎1-800/428-4322, international ☎1-800/622-1015, Ⓦwww.usair.com

By train

The national passenger rail line, **Amtrak** (☎1-800/USA-RAIL, Ⓦwww.amtrak.com), is a leisurely but expensive option. Although financially precarious for years, the company has managed to keep running, though rarely ever on time. The trains themselves vary in style, amenities, and speed, so it's worth checking ahead to see what type of train services your intended route.

Amtrak's newest trains are on its regional **Cascades** line, which runs four times per day between Seattle and Eugene, Oregon, and once-daily between Seattle and Vancouver, BC; the older trains on the once-daily **Empire Builder** line travel west from Chicago across the Rocky Mountains and Great Plains. Perhaps the most memorable route is the **Coast Starlight**, which runs between Seattle and LA every day (with a connection to San Diego), passing by some of the most appealing scenery anywhere, from coastal whale-watching between San Luis Obispo and Santa Barbara to an evening trip around Mount Shasta or a journey through the wooded terrain of the Cascades Mountains.

One-way cross-country fares can be as low as $125 during the offseason on the Empire Builder or $83 on the Coast Starlight, or twice that much during peak periods.

On the Cascades line, business seating (for only $10–15 more) should be booked when available: spacious seats, overhead TVs, and fewer children provide for a much more enjoyable ride. However, while Amtrak's basic fares are a good value, the cost rises quickly if you want to travel more comfortably: sleeping compartments, which include small toilets and showers, start at around $300 for one or two people, but can climb as high as $600, depending on the class of compartment, number of nights, season, and so on. These options include three meals per day, making up somewhat for the high price. Another option is to buy a **rail pass**, with varying options for domestic and foreign travellers – contact Amtrak or visit their website for further details on the various options as well as locations of where rail passes can be purchased internationally.

By bus

Bus travel is a slow, often agonizing way to get to Seattle, and in the end you won't really save that much money over train or air travel. **Greyhound** (☎1-800/231-2222, ⓦwww.greyhound.com) is the sole long-distance operator servicing Seattle, and will cost you a minimum of $200 round-trip, purchased at least seven days in advance, from major cities like New York, Chicago, or Miami.

The main reason to take Greyhound is if you're planning to visit other places en route; the company's domestic **Discovery Pass** (ⓦwww.discoverypass.com) is good for unlimited travel within a set time: 7 days of travel costs $249; 15 days, $369; 30 days, $429; and 60 days, $689; passes for overseas travelers run about five percent less. Other variants cover Canada and the US, for 15 ($449) to 60 days ($739) of travel, or the West Coast of both countries, for 10 ($309) and 21 days ($409). Passes are valid from the date of purchase, so it's a bad idea to buy them in advance; overseas visitors, however, can buy passes before leaving home, and they will be validated at the start of the trip.

By car

For many Americans in the western US, getting to Seattle **by car** is still the pre-eminent transportation option. If you don't already have a vehicle, you can **rent a car**, though this usually isn't the best option: rental prices aren't cheap (neither is gas), and many companies won't rent to those under 25, for insurance reasons. Contact info for the major US car rental companies is listed below.

The **freeway choices** to Seattle are straightforward: there's I-90 from the east, either through Spokane or via a bypass from I-84 in Oregon, or I-5 from the south or north. However, be forewarned that connecting to the southbound I-5 from Canada is a tedious process, often resulting in hours of waiting time at the border while drivers are grilled about drugs, weapons, and the like.

Car rental companies

Advantage ☎1-800/777-5500, ⓦwww.arac.com
Alamo ☎1-800/462-5266, ⓦwww.alamo.com
Avis ☎1-800/230-4898, ⓦwww.avis.com
Budget ☎1-800/527-0700, ⓦwww.budgetrentacar.com
Dollar ☎1-800/800-3665, ⓦwww.dollar.com
Enterprise ☎1-800/325-8007, ⓦwww.enterprise.com
Hertz ☎1-800/654-3131, in Canada ☎1-800/263-0600, ⓦwww.hertz.com
National ☎1-800/962-7070, ⓦwww.nationalcar.com
Payless ☎1-800/729-5377, ⓦwww.paylesscarrental.com
Thrifty ☎1-800/847-4389, ⓦwww.thrifty.com

Travel agents

Airtech ☎212/219-7000, ⓦwww.airtech.com. Standby seat broker; also deals in consolidator fares.
Educational Travel Center ☎1-800/747-5551, ⓦwww.edtrav.com. Low-cost fares worldwide, student/youth discount offers, car rental and tours.
STA Travel US ☎1-800/329-9537, Canada ☎1-888/427-5639, ⓦwww.statravel.com. Worldwide specialists in independent travel; also student IDs, travel insurance, car rental, rail passes, and more.
Student Flights ☎1-800/255-8000, ⓦwww.isecard.com/studentflights. Student/youth fares, plus student IDs and bus passes.
TFI Tours ☎1-800/745-8000, ⓦwww.tfitours.com. Well-established consolidator with a wide variety of global fares.
Travel Cuts US ☎1-800/592-CUTS, Canada ☎1-888/246-9762, ⓦwww.travelcuts.com. Popular, long-established student travel organization, with worldwide offers.

Travelers Advantage ☏ 1-877/259-2691, ⓦ www.travelersadvantage.com. Discount travel club, with cash-back deals and discounted car rental. Membership required ($1 for 3 months' trial).

Specialist tour operators

A number of US companies specialize in overland **adventure trips** and **sightseeing tours**. TrekAmerica, for one, offers a fourteen-day LA-to-Seattle "Pacific Crest" trip, starting with Disneyland and the movie studios, then heading up to Big Sur, Yosemite, San Francisco, and the coastal range up to Mount Rainier and Olympic national parks; prices from $883–1019. See below for more options.

American Express Vacations ☏ 1-800/346-3607, ⓦ www.americanexpress.com/travel. Flights, hotels, last-minute specials, city-break packages and specialty tours involving Seattle.

Amtrak Vacations ☏ 1-800/YES-RAIL, ⓦ www .amtrak.com. Train or Amtrak Air Rail trips on the West Coast, along with hotel reservations, car rental, and sightseeing tours in the Pacific Northwest, including guided treks through Seattle.

Collette Vacations ☏ 1-800/340-5158, ⓦ www .collettevacations.com. Packages include eight-day visits to the Pacific Northwest ($1349) and four-day cruises along the coast of Oregon, Washington and British Columbia ($1029).

Globus Journeys ☏ 1-866/755-8581, ⓦ www .globusjourneys.com. Aside from numerous trips elsewhere in the US, the Northwest option is a ten-day, San Francisco-to-Seattle "Pacific Coast Adventure" ($2039).

Suntrek ☏ 1-800/SUNTREK, ⓦ www.suntrek.com. One- to thirteen-week journeys around the West Coast and the rest of the US, from $500 to $6000.

TrekAmerica US and Canada ☏ 1-800/221-0596, ⓦ www.trekamerica.com. Seattle is the jumping-off spot for several two- to four-week trips, ranging from the Pacific Northwest to the American West, with a broad set of options and prices ($827–2040). Aimed at 18- to 38-year-old travelers.

United Vacations ☏ 1-888/854-3899, ⓦ www .unitedvacations.com. Wide range of chain and boutique hotel accommodation, car rental and other options for visits to Seattle, and the rest of the Pacific Northwest.

From the UK and Ireland

Flying from the **UK** to Seattle, you'll most likely have to stop over in one of the major hubs – Chicago, New York, or Atlanta – and expect about 14–16hrs of travel time. British Airways does offer a nonstop route (for a minimum cost of £540), taking about ten hours from London Heathrow, though you can expect to pay about £100 more than the cheapest one-stop route from the UK. Because of the time difference between Britain and the West Coast (eight hours most of the year), flights usually leave Britain mid-morning and arrive in Seattle in the late afternoon or early evening of the same day. Return tickets start at £300 in low season and £425 in high. Prices are for departures from London and Manchester and do not include a UK airport tax of £40–50.

There are no nonstop **flights from Ireland** to Seattle, though British Airways and Aer Lingus do offer service from Dublin (12–15hrs), usually with a stopover in London and possibly another in the US, for around EUR600 in low season and EUR800 in high season. KLM/Northwest offers similarly priced service, with at least one stopover in Amsterdam and possibly another in the US.

Package deals

Package deals – fly-drive, flight/accommodation, and guided tours (or a combination of all three) – can work out cheaper than arranging the same trip yourself, especially for a short stay. The obvious drawbacks are the loss of flexibility and the fact that most operators use hotels in the mid-range bracket; that said, there is a wide variety of combinations to choose from. High-street travel agents have plenty of brochures and information detailing the various options.

Fly-drive deals, which give inexpensive (sometimes free) car rental when buying a transatlantic plane ticket, always work out cheaper than renting on the spot and give especially great value if you intend to do a lot of driving. On the other hand, you'll probably have to pay more for the flight than if you booked it through a discount agent. Competition between airlines and tour operators means that it's well worth phoning to check on special promotions. Watch out for hidden "extras" in the price, such as local taxes and "drop-off" charges (which are sometimes unavoidable), and be sure to get Collision Damage Waiver insurance. Remember, too, that while you can drive in the States with a British license, some companies, for insurance reasons, won't rent vehicles to those under 25.

Airlines

Aer Lingus ☎ 01/886 8844, ⓦ www.aerlingus.ie
Air Canada ☎ 1-888/247-2262, ⓦ www.aircanada.ca
American ☎ 1-800/433-7300, ⓦ www.aa.com
British Airways ☎ 1-800/247-9297 or ☎ 0845/77 333 77, ⓦ www.ba.com
Continental ☎ 1-800/231-0856, ⓦ www.continental.com
Delta ☎ 1-800/241-4141, ⓦ www.delta.com
Lufthansa ☎ 1-800/645-3880, ⓦ www.lufthansa.com
Northwest/KLM ☎ 1-800/447-4747, ⓦ www.nwa.com or ⓦ www.klm.com
Scandinavian ☎ 1-800/221-2350, ⓦ www.scandinavian.net
United ☎ 1-800/538-2929, ⓦ www.ual.com
Virgin Atlantic ☎ 01293/747 747, ⓦ www.virgin-atlantic.com

Travel agents

McCarthy's Travel Ireland ☎ 021/427 0127, ⓦ www.mccarthystravel.ie. Established Irish travel agent now part of the Blackpool chain, featuring flights, short breaks, and group holidays.
North South Travel ☎ 01245/608 291, ⓦ www.northsouthtravel.co.uk. Discounted fares worldwide – profits are used to support projects in the developing world.
STA Travel ☎ 0870/1600 599, ⓦ www.statravel.co.uk. Worldwide specialists in low-cost flights and tours for students and those under 26, though other customers welcome.
Trailfinders ☎ 020/7938 3939, ⓦ www.trailfinders.com, Ireland ☎ 01/677 7888, ⓦ www.trailfinders.ie. Well-informed and efficient agent for independent travelers.
Usit Ireland ☎ 0818/200 020, Northern Ireland ☎ 028/9032 7111, ⓦ www.usit.ie. Specialists in student, youth and independent travel – flights, trains, study tours, and visas.

Specialist tour operators

AmeriCan Adventures ☎ 01295/756 200, ⓦ www.americanadventures.com. Small-group camping adventure trips throughout the US and Canada, including jaunts across the American West and Pacific Northwest. Now part of TrekAmerica.

British Airways Holidays ☎ 0870/442 3820, ⓦ www.baholidays.com. Using British Airways and other quality international airlines, offers an exhaustive range of package and tailor-made holidays to North America and elsewhere.
Europa Travel ☎ 044/2890 623211, ⓦ www.europatravel.com. Belfast-based operator for sports and leisure packages; provides connections to American cities on KLM.
Martin Randall Travel ☎ 020/8742 3355, ⓦ www.martinrandall.com. Small-group cultural tours with experts on art, archeology, or music. Notable for its Seattle tour focusing on Wagner's *The Ring* opera cycle.
North America Travel Service ☎ 0207/499 7299 ⓦ www.northamericatravelservice.co.uk. Tailor-made flights, accommodation, car hire, and so on.
Premier Holidays ☎ 0870/889 0850, ⓦ www.premierholidays.co.uk. Flight-plus-accommodation deals to Seattle, with trips to national parks and central Washington's wine country.
Thomas Cook ☎ 0870/5666 222, ⓦ www.thomascook.com. Long-established one-stop 24-hour travel agency for package holidays or scheduled flights, to Seattle and many other US cities.
United Vacations ☎ 0870/606 2222, ⓦ www.unitedvacations.com. City breaks, customized trips, and fly-drives; Seattle options include stays at any of seven major hotels.
Virgin Holidays ☎ 0870/220 2788, ⓦ www.virginholidays.co.uk. Packages to a wide range of destinations; packages include a pair of hotels in Seattle, along with regional tours and cruises.

From Australia and New Zealand

Getting to Seattle from **Australia** or **New Zealand** will most likely require a stopover via LA or San Francisco; the travel time between Auckland or Sydney and Seattle is 17–22 hours.

From **Australia**, there are daily flights from Sydney on American, United, Air New Zealand and Qantas for around A\$1650 in low season (or A\$300 more in high season); options for connecting flights to Seattle average around A\$325 in low season, and \$40-60 more in the high; the total price (from A\$2000) is about the same when traveling on Air Canada with a stopover in Vancouver, BC. Similar rates apply for stopping over in New Zealand via Auckland, or in Honolulu, Fiji, Tonga, or Papeete.

From New Zealand, the best deals are out of Auckland on Qantas, American, United, or Air New Zealand, with low-season deals around NZ$1800 (or NZ$2500 in high), both with stopovers in LA. Japan Airlines offers the best fares via Asia, starting at NZ$1800/2150 for low and high seasons, with a transfer or stopover in Tokyo, while Korean Air via Seoul costs from NZ$2000.

Airlines

Air New Zealand Australia ☎ 13 24 76, New Zealand ☎ 0800/737 000, ⓦ www.airnz.com
America West Australia ☎ 02/9267 2138 or 1300/364 757, New Zealand ☎ 0800/866 000, ⓦ www.americawest.com
American Australia ☎ 1300/130 757, New Zealand ☎ 0800/887 997, ⓦ www.aa.com
British Airways Australia ☎ 1300/767 177, New Zealand ☎ 0800/274 847 or 09/356 8690, ⓦ www.britishairways.com
Cathay Pacific Australia ☎ 13 17 47 or 1300/653 077, New Zealand ☎ 09/379 0861 or 0508/800 454, ⓦ www.cathaypacific.com
Continental Australia ☎ 1300/361 400, New Zealand ☎ 09/308 3350, ⓦ www.continental.com
Delta Australia ☎ 02/9251 3211 or 1800/500 992, New Zealand ☎ 09/379 3370, ⓦ www.delta-airlines.com
Japan Airlines Australia ☎ 02/9272 1111, New Zealand ☎ 09/379 9906, ⓦ www.jal.com
KLM/Northwest Australia ☎ 1300/303 747, New Zealand ☎ 09/309 1782, ⓦ www.klm.com
Korean Air Australia ☎ 02/9262 6000, New Zealand ☎ 09/914 2000, ⓦ www.koreanair.com.au
Lufthansa Australia ☎ 1300/655 727, New Zealand ☎ 0800/945 220, ⓦ www.lufthansa.com
Malaysia Australia ☎ 13 26 27, New Zealand ☎ 0800/777 747, ⓦ www.malaysia-airlines.com
Qantas Australia ☎ 13 13 13, New Zealand ☎ 09/357 8900, ⓦ www.qantas.com
Singapore Australia ☎ 13 10 11, New Zealand ☎ 09/303 2129, ⓦ www.singaporeair.com
United Australia ☎ 13 17 77, New Zealand ☎ 09/379 3800 or 0800/508 648, ⓦ www.unitedairlines.com
Virgin Atlantic Australia ☎ 02/9244 2747, New Zealand ☎ 09/308 3377, ⓦ www.virgin-atlantic.com

Travel agents

Budget Travel New Zealand ☎ 0800/808 480, ⓦ www.budgettravel.co.nz. Travel services for New Zealand; part of the Gullivers Travel Group.
Flight Centre Australia ☎ 13 31 33, ⓦ www.flightcentre.com.au, New Zealand ☎ 0800 243 544, ⓦ www.flightcentre.co.nz. Rock-bottom fares worldwide.
New Zealand Destinations Unlimited New Zealand ☎ 09/414 1685 ⓦ www.holiday.co.nz. Packages, tours, and flight scheduling.
STA Travel Australia ☎ 1300/733 035, New Zealand ☎ 0508/782 872, ⓦ www.statravel.com. Worldwide specialists in low-cost flights, overlands and holiday deals. Good discounts for students and under-26s.
Student Uni Travel Australia ☎ 02/9232 8444, ⓦ www.sut.com.au, New Zealand ☎ 09/379 4224, ⓦ www.sut.co.nz. Great deals for students.
Thomas Cook Australia: Sydney ☎ 02/9231 2877, Melbourne ☎ 03/9282 0222, New Zealand ☎ 09/307 0555, ⓦ www.thomascook.com. One-stop travel agency for package holidays or scheduled flights, to Seattle and many other US cities.
Trailfinders Australia ☎ 02/9247 7666, ⓦ www.trailfinders.com.au. One of the best-informed and most efficient agents for independent travelers.

Specialist tour operators

Adventure World Australia ☎ 02/8913 0755, ⓦ www.adventureworld.com.au, New Zealand ☎ 09/524 5118, ⓦ www.adventureworld.co.nz. Agents for a vast array of international adventure travel companies that operate trips to every continent.
Australian Pacific Touring Australia ☎ 1800/675 222 or 03/9277 8555, New Zealand ☎ 09/279 6077, ⓦ www.aptours.com. Package tours and independent US travel.
Canada and America Travel Specialists Australia ☎ 02/9922 4600, ⓦ www.canam.com.au. Wholesalers of Greyhound Ameripasses, plus flights and accommodation in North America.
Silke's Travel Australia ☎ 1800/807 860 or 02/8347 2000, ⓦ www.silkes.com.au. Gay and lesbian specialist travel agent, helping provide US accommodation and air transit.
Sydney Travel Australia ☎ 02/9299 8000 or 1800/251 911, ⓦ www.sydneytravel.com.au. US flights, accommodation, city stays, and car rental.
United Vacations Australia ☎ 1300/887 870, ⓦ www.unitedvacations.com.au. Tailor-made city stays or wider American holidays, with departures available from several Australian airports.

Entry requirements

Keeping up with the constant changes to US entry requirements since 9/11 can sometimes feel like a hopeless task. Several times a year the American government announces new, often harsher, restrictions on foreign entry into the country, adding considerably to the red tape involved in visiting it. Nonetheless, there are several basic rules that apply to these requirements, which are detailed (and should be frequently checked for updates) on the US State Department website ⓦtravel.state.gov.

As of 2005, under the **Visa Waiver Program**, if you're a citizen of the UK, Ireland, Australia, New Zealand, most Western European states, or other selected countries like Singapore, Japan, and Brunei (27 in all), and visiting the United States for less than ninety days, you need an onward or return ticket, a **Machine Readable Passport** (MRP), and a visa waiver form. The MRP requirement is a recent manifestation (November 2004) of America's security clampdown, and requires certain high-tech protections built into the passport against fraud and counterfeiting, including a security chip and digital photograph of the passport holder. It is up to the various countries covered by the Visa Waiver Program to provide such passports to its citizens; for more information, inquire at American embassies or consulates (see below). The **Visa Waiver Form** (an I-94W) will be provided either by your travel agency, or by the airline during check-in or on the plane, and must be presented to Immigration on arrival. The same form covers entry across the US borders with Canada and Mexico. If you're in the Visa Waiver Program and intend to work, study, or stay in the country for more than ninety days, you must apply for a regular visa through your local US embassy or consulate. UK citizens must apply in person at the US Embassy in London (see below) and have "British Citizen" stated on their passports. (To stay up-to-date on these issues visit ⓦwww.dhs.gov/us-visit.)

Canadian citizens, who have not always needed a **passport** to get into the US, should have their passports on them when entering the country. If you're planning to stay for more than ninety days, you'll need a visa, which can be applied for by mail through the US embassy or nearest US consulate. If you cross the US border by car, be prepared for US Customs officials to search your vehicle. Remember, too, that without the proper paperwork, Canadians are barred from working in the US.

Citizens of all other countries should contact their local US embassy or consulate for details of current entry requirements, as they are often required to have both a valid passport and a **non-immigrant visitor's visa**. To obtain such a visa, complete the application form available through your local American embassy or consulate, and send it with the appropriate fee, two photographs, and a passport – valid for at least six months from the end of your planned stay. Beyond this, you can expect additional hassles to get a visa, including one or more in-depth interviews, supplemental applications for students and "high-risk" travelers, and long delays in processing time. Visas are not issued to convicted criminals or those with ties to radical political groups; complications also arise if you are HIV positive or have TB, hepatitis, or other communicable diseases. Furthermore, the US government now fingerprints all visitors to the US from countries not covered by the Visa Waiver Program, and applies spot background checks looking for evidence of past criminal or terrorist connections.

For further information or to get a visa extension before your time is up, contact the nearest **US Citizenship and Immigration Service office**, whose address will be at the front of the phone book, under the Federal Government Offices listings, or call ☏1-800/877-3676. You can also contact the

National Customer Service Center at ☎1-800-375-5283. Immigration officials will assume that you're working in the US illegally, and it's up to you to prove otherwise. If you can, bring along an upstanding American citizen to vouch for you, and be prepared for potentially hostile questioning. Under no circumstances are visitors who have been admitted under the Visa Waiver Program allowed to extend their stays beyond ninety days.

US embassies and consulates

For a more complete list around the world, check ⓦusembassy.state.gov. Details of foreign consulates in Seattle are given in Chapter 21, "Directory."

Australia Moonbah Place, Yarralumla, Canberra, ACT ☎02/6214 5600, ⓦusembassy-australia .state.gov

Canada 490 Sussex Drive, Ottawa, ON K1P 5T1 ☎613/238-5335, ⓦwww.usembassycanada.gov

Ireland 42 Elgin Rd, Ballsbridge, Dublin 4 ☎01/668-7122, ⓦdublin.usembassy.gov

New Zealand 29 Fitzherbert Terrace, Thorndon, Wellington ☎04/462 6000, ⓦwww.usembassy .org.nz

UK 24 Grosvenor Square, London W1A 1AE ☎020/7499 9000, visa hotline ☎09068/200290, ⓦwww.usembassy.org.uk

Tourist information

For information about Seattle, a good place to start looking is Seattle's Convention and Visitors Bureau (see below), which has hundreds of free brochures on Seattle and Washington state, plus copies of basic maps, alternative weeklies, and complimentary magazines geared toward the tourist trade. There's also a wall full of free bus maps in the hall outside the bureau.

Located inside the Washington State Convention and Trade Center, Seventh Ave at Pike St (daily 9am–1pm & 2–5pm; ☎206/461-5840, ⓦwww.seeseattle.org), the Bureau's **Citywide Concierge Center** has a friendly staff that can help with accommodations. Still, it's best to arrange where you'll stay for the first night or two in advance instead of just turning up. The free official travelers' guide, *Washington State Lodging and Travel Guide* (call ☎1-800/544-1800 for a copy, or visit ⓦwww.tourism.wa.gov), has a comprehensive list of the state's accommodations.

Insurance and health

Although not compulsory, international travelers should have some form of travel insurance. The US has no national health care system, and it can cost an arm and a leg (so to speak) having even minor medical treatment. Many insurance policies are adaptable to reflect the coverage you want – for example, sickness and accident benefits can often be excluded or included at will. If you do take medical coverage, verify if benefits will be paid during treatment or only after your return home, and whether there is a 24-hour medical emergency phone number. If you need to make a claim, keep receipts for medicines and medical treatment. Also, if you have anything stolen from you, you must obtain an official statement from the police.

A typical **travel insurance** policy provides coverage for the loss of baggage, tickets, and a certain amount of cash or travelers checks, as well as the cancellation or curtailment of your trip. Most policies exclude so-called dangerous sports unless an extra premium is paid; in the US, this can apply to rock-climbing, whitewater rafting, and windsurfing. Therefore, if you're visiting Seattle as part of a wider trip and planning to do water sports or similar activities, you'll most likely have to pay extra.

Before buying travel insurance, check that you're not already covered. Credit card companies, home insurance policies, and private medical plans sometimes cover you and your belongings when you're abroad. Most travel agents, tour operators, banks, and insurance brokers will be able to help you, or you could consider the travel insurance

offered by Rough Guides (see box). Remember that when securing baggage insurance, make sure that the per-article limit – typically under $800/£500 – will cover your most valuable possession.

Health matters

For **emergencies** or ambulances, dial ☎911. If you have medical or dental problems that don't require an ambulance, most hospitals will have a walk-in emergency room; for the nearest hospital, check with your hotel or dial ☎411. Should you need to see a **doctor**, lists can be found in the *Yellow Book* under "Clinics" or "Physicians and Surgeons." A basic consultation fee is around $60–130, and medications aren't cheap either – keep all your receipts for later insurance claims. Many minor ailments can be remedied by items available in **drugstores**. Foreign visitors

Rough Guides travel insurance

Rough Guides has teamed up with Columbus Direct to offer **travel insurance** that can be tailored to suit the needs of individual travelers, who can choose from many different products, including a low-cost backpacker option for long stays; a short break option for city getaways; a typical holiday package option; and many others. There are also annual multi-trip policies for those who travel regularly, with variable levels of cover available. Different sports and activities (trekking, skiing, etc) can be covered, if required, on most policies.

Rough Guides travel insurance is available to the residents of 36 different countries with different language options to choose from via our website – ⓦ www .roughguidesinsurance.com – where you can also purchase the insurance. Alternatively, US citizens should call ☎1-800/749-4922; UK residents should call ☎0800 083 9507; Australians should call ☎1 300 669 999; and all other nationalities should call ☎+44 870 890 2843.

should bear in mind that some pills available over-the-counter at home need a prescription in the US, and local brand names can be confusing; ask for advice at any drugstore's pharmacy.

For **other medical issues**, Planned Parenthood of Western Washington, 2211 E Madison, Capitol Hill (☎206/328-7700, ⓦwww. ppww.org), has reliable clinical services and reproductive health education and information, while the Aradia Women's Health Center, 1300 Spring St, Capitol Hill (☎206/323-9388, ⓦwww.aradia.org), is a feminist clinic open to all women. For emergencies, the Rape

Crisis Line (☎206/632-7273) is open 24hrs a day; other relevant phone lines for women are listed at ⓦwww.metrokc.gov/dchs/csd /Women/Hotlines.htm.

In **Canada**, provincial health plans usually provide partial cover for medical mishaps while outside the country. In addition, holders of official student/teacher/youth cards in Canada and the US are entitled to meager accident coverage and hospital in-patient benefits. Students will often find that their student health coverage extends during vacation periods and for one semester beyond the date of last enrollment.

Costs, money, and banks

Given the historically low value of the American dollar, there's rarely been a better time for foreign travelers to visit the US, and Seattle is no exception. For all visitors, the city is less expensive than, say, San Francisco or New York, and has plenty of good deals if you search for them. Indeed, with a minimum of effort you can find plenty of bargains and reasonably priced goods and services, though of course you won't lack for choice should you want to splurge at one of the city's swankier restaurants or trendy bars.

Average costs

Seattle's economy is slowly recovering from the recession at the turn of the twenty-first century, caused by the bursting of the high-tech bubble. Visitors can still find numerous options for cheap amenities and amusements, along with many bargains and affordable costs for goods and services. Keep in mind, though, that added to the cost of most items you purchase is an 8.8 percent **sales tax**, and 9.3 percent on food and beverage sales in restaurants and bars. Additionally, the city of Seattle tacks on a **hotel tax** of around 16 percent, which can drive up accommodation costs dramatically. For attractions in the main part of the *Guide*, prices are quoted for adults, with children's rates listed if they are more than a few dollars less; at some spots, kids get in for half-price, or for free if they're under 6.

Unless you're staying in a hostel, where dorm beds cost from $18–20, **accommodation** will be your greatest expense while in Seattle. Adequate lodging is rarely available for under $50, and a marginally decent room will run anywhere from $70–90, with fancier hotels costing much, much more – upwards of $300 in some cases. Of course, **camping** in the region is an alternative, but only if you're staying in more remote areas like the islands in Puget Sound, where you can get into a campground for around $15–21 per night; see Chapter 23, "Puget Sound," for more details.

Unlike accommodation, prices for good **food** range widely, from espresso carts to chic restaurants. You could get by on as little as $15 a day, but realistically you should aim for around $50 – and remember, too, that Seattle has plenty of great spots for a splurge. Beyond restaurants, the city has many **bars**, **clubs**, and **live-music venues** to suit all tastes and wallets. For **transportation**, you may wish to rent a car from any of the rental outlets around the airport, though the region's **public transit** is quite affordable and effective, even considering the area's traffic congestion.

Finally, you should figure in costs for **tipping** into your travel budget. Expect to tip about 15 percent of the bill before tax to waiters in most restaurants (unless the service is truly wretched), and 20 percent for particularly good service. In the US, this is where most of a waiter's income comes from, and not leaving a fair amount is seen as a big faux pas. About 15 percent should also be added to taxi fares; round up to the nearest 50¢ or dollar, as well. A hotel porter should get $1 per bag; chambermaids $1–2 a day; and valet attendants $1.

Banks and ATMs

Bank hours are generally from 9am to 4pm or 5pm Monday to Thursday, and from 10am to 6pm on Friday; the big local names are Wells Fargo, Washington Mutual, and Bank of America. For banking services – especially currency exchange – outside normal business hours and on weekends, try major hotels or Travelex outlets (see Chapter 21, "Directory").

With an **ATM card**, you'll be able to withdraw cash just about anywhere in Seattle, though you'll be charged $2–4 per transaction for the privilege of using a different bank's network. Foreign cash-dispensing cards linked to international networks, such as Plus or Cirrus, are also widely accepted – ask your home bank or credit company which branches you can use.

Travelers checks

US **travelers checks** are the safest way for overseas visitors to carry money, and the better-known checks, such as those issued by American Express and Visa, are treated as cash in most shops. The usual fee for travelers check sales is one or two percent, though this fee may be waived if you buy the checks through your home bank.

Credit and debit cards

Credit and **debit cards** are the most widely accepted form of payment at major hotels, restaurants, and retailers, even though some smaller merchants still do not accept them. You'll be asked to show some plastic when renting a car, bike, or other such item, or to start a "tab" at hotels for incidental charges; in any case, you can always pay the bill in cash when you return the item or check out of your room. Most major cards issued by foreign banks are honored in the US. Visa, MasterCard, American Express, and Discover are the most widely used.

Wiring money

Having money **wired** from home is never cheap, and should be considered a last resort. If you must, the quickest way is to have someone take cash to the nearest

US money: a note for foreign travelers

At the time of writing one pound sterling will buy $1.70–1.90, a Euro $1.15–1.35, a Canadian dollar 70–85¢, an Australian dollar 65–80¢, and a New Zealand dollar 50–70¢ – all of which makes visiting Seattle an attractive budget vacation.

US currency comes in bills of $1, $5, $10, $20, $50 and $100 **denominations**. All are the same size, though denominations of $10 and higher have in the last few years been changing shades from their familiar drab green. These days such bills offer more colorful pastels of faint red, yellow, and blue, and other embedded inks and watermarks – all to deter would-be counterfeiters. The dollar comprises one hundred cents, made up of combinations of one-cent pennies, five-cent nickels, ten-cent dimes, and 25-cent quarters. Quarters are useful for buses, vending machines, parking meters and telephones, so always carry plenty.

Emergency numbers for lost cards and checks

American Express cards ☏1-800/528-4800, ⓦwww.americanexpress.com
American Express checks ☏1-800/221-7282
Citicorp checks ☏1-800/645-6556, ⓦwww.citicorp.com
Diners Club ☏1-800/234-6377, ⓦwww.dinersclub.com
Discover ☏1-800/DISCOVER, ⓦwww.discovercard.com
MasterCard ☏1-800/826-2181, ⓦwww.mastercard.com
Thomas Cook/MasterCard checks ☏1-800/223-9920, ⓦwww.travelex.com or
ⓦwww.thomascook.co.uk
Visa cards ☏1-800/847-2911, ⓦwww.visa.com
Visa checks ☏1-800/227-6811

American Express Moneygram office (call ☏1-800/543-4080 for locations; also available at participating Travelex branches) and have it instantaneously wired to you, minus a ten-percent commission that varies according to the amount sent – the entire process should take no longer than ten minutes. For similar, if slightly pricier, services, **Western Union** also has offices in Seattle (information at ☏1-800/325-6000 in the US; ☏0800/833 833 in the UK; and ☏1800/649 565 in Australia; ⓦwww.westernunion.com), with credit card payments subject to an additional $10 fee.

If you have a few days' leeway, sending a postal **money order**, exchangeable at any post office through the mail, is a cheaper option. The equivalent for foreign travelers is the international money order, for which you need to allow up to seven days in international airmail before arrival.

Arrival

All points of arrival into Seattle, whether by airplane, bus, or train, are fairly convenient to the city center – Sea-Tac airport is a bit outside of town, but there are plenty of cheap and easy ways to make it into Downtown from there. If you're coming by car, be prepared for heavy traffic and a tough time parking.

By air

Seattle Tacoma International Airport, almost always known as **Sea-Tac** (☏206/433-5388 or 1-800/544-1965, ⓦwww.portseattle.org /seatac), is fourteen miles south of Downtown near the I-5 freeway. Baggage claim is on the lower level of the main terminal, and there's a small **visitor's information booth** in front of baggage carousel 8. With the recent expansion of Sea-Tac's Central Terminal, the construction dust has settled and the airport is much easier to navigate than before – along with being suitably modernized.

From Sea-Tac, there's a handful of options for **ground transportation** to Seattle. Several **car rental** firms (see p.21 for contact info) have counters in the baggage claim area, with pick-up and drop-off on the first floor of the garage across from the main terminal; other companies with off-airport branches provide courtesy van service to their pick-up points. **Buses** to Seattle leave from the north end of the baggage claim area. The cheapest option is Metro bus #194 ($1.25, $2 during peak hours Mon–Fri 6–9am & 3–6pm), a 30-minute trip that deposits you

Downtown at the Convention Center; bus #174 plies a similar route for the same cost, but takes an extra fifteen minutes.

The Gray Line Airport Express bus (daily 5.30am–11pm every 30min; $10.25, $17 round-trip ☎206/626-6088 or 1-800/426-7532, ⓦwww.graylineofseattle.com) drops off at eight major hotels in the Downtown area, including the *Hilton* and *Westin*, with connector services to 25 other hotels in the area from 5.30am to 9pm, for $2.50 extra; reserve at least one hour in advance for these connections at ☎206/255-7159. Shuttle Express has door-to-door service (daily 4am–midnight; ☎206/622-1424 or 1-800/487-RIDE, ⓦwww.shuttleexpress.com) for $24.25 to Downtown, with the return trip about $3 less. **Taxis** charge $35–40 for the airport–to-Downtown route, and leave from the third floor of the parking garage; call ☎206/246-9999 for pick-up once you arrive.

By train

Trains arrive at the **Amtrak** terminal in unlovely King Street Station at Third Avenue and Jackson Street, near the International District (☎206/382-4125 or 1-800/872-7245, ⓦwww.amtrak.com). It's about a dozen blocks from here to the city center; just to the east along Jackson Street, the International District Station is a hub for frequent Metro buses going Downtown. Also nearby is the southern terminus of the **waterfront streetcar** (see p.32), which takes a tourist-friendly route along the bay – though it's not much good if you're loaded down with luggage and want to reach your accommodation quickly.

By bus

Greyhound buses (☎206/628-5526 or 1-800/231-2222, ⓦwww.greyhound.com) arrive at Eighth Avenue and Stewart Street, on the eastern edge of Downtown, just a fifteen- or twenty-minute walk from most Downtown accommodation, as well as at King Street Station, at Third Avenue and Jackson Street – convenient if you need to connect to an Amtrak train.

By car

If you're **driving** into Seattle, you'll most likely arrive on I-5, the main north–south artery connecting California through to Canada. Major north- and southbound exits include Seneca Street (for central Downtown), Mercer Street (Seattle Center), and Dearborn/James streets (Capitol Hill). Coming in from the east, you'll probably arrive via I-90, which runs from central Washington to Seattle, coming into town in south Seattle. I-90's Downtown exits (164–167) come quickly from both sides of the freeway; keep alert for off-ramps onto Stewart or Union streets for Downtown. See p.35 for info on parking.

City transportation

There are a number of good options for getting around Seattle – though Downtown is easy enough to cover by walking alone, as are adjacent neighborhoods such as Belltown and Capitol Hill. Beyond this, buses are frequent and well run, and most of the more interesting destinations are pretty close to one another. However, some areas are not well served by public transportation, especially at night. Thus, you may well need to take a car or, in some cases, a ferry.

Whatever your mode of transportation, it's essential to understand the logic of **navigating the city** and to familiarize yourself with a few basics of Seattle's streetplan. To begin with, most addresses are preceded or followed by a direction (eg, NW 67th St,

Directional tags for city neighborhoods

The following directionals applied before or after an address will most likely place the site in one of the following areas. The absence of any such tag usually signifies a place around Downtown.

N Fremont, Green Lake (also E), Greenwood

S International District, Mount Baker, Columbia City

E Capitol Hill, Madison Park, Madrona

W Magnolia, Queen Anne (also N)

NW Ballard

NE Wallingford (also N), University District , Kirkland

SW West Seattle

SE Mercer Island, Bellevue (also NE)

or 13th Ave E). These tags do not indicate the directional position of an address *on* a street, as they do in most American cities, but rather the position the *entire street* holds in relationship to the city's center. Consequently, Second Avenue W and Second Avenue S are two different streets, and the location of something on Second Avenue W might be a good five miles or so from an address on Second Avenue S. Furthermore, some streets, particularly in Downtown Seattle, are not tagged with a direction at all.

Think of Downtown as the center of a compass used to plot out the city's coordinates. Thoroughfares running east–west are usually designated as streets, with the section of the city in which it lies placed at the beginning of the address (eg, 500 N 36th St, since this part of 36th Street is north of Downtown), while those running north–south are usually designated avenues, with the section of the city in which it lies following the address (eg, 5000 22nd Ave NE, since this part of 22nd Avenue is northeast of Downtown). There are also Ways, Places, Courts, and so on, most of them marked with similar directional tags. Be careful when you ask directions, too: natives have a habit of casually referring to a street address without directionals, so the 15th Avenue address you were heading to in Capitol Hill may actually be in the University District, depending on if it's 15th Avenue E or 15th Avenue NE.

If all else fails, see the box for the loose parameters of city neighborhoods and their respective directional tags.

Metro

Seattle's mass transit system, the **Metro** (☏206/553-3000, ⓦtransit.metrokc.gov), runs buses throughout the city and King County, extending into the Eastside suburbs across Lake Washington and south to Sea-Tac Airport. On the whole, the Metro is efficient and pleasurable, with frequent service between Downtown, Capitol Hill, and the University District, and, to a lesser extent, Fremont and Ballard. **Customer service stations** are available at Westlake Station (Mon–Fri 9am–5.30pm) and at King Street Station, 201 S Jackson St (Mon–Fri 8am–5pm); both offer maps and schedules, and are the most reliable places to buy daily passes on weekdays. You can also purchase passes online at ⓦbuypass.metrokc.gov, a useful site that provides a list of some sixty Seattle-area vendors of bus passes (mostly markets and pharmacies).

The Metro's best feature is its **Downtown Ride Free Area**, bounded by Battery Street, S Jackson Street, Sixth Avenue, and the waterfront. From 6am to 7pm daily, bus trips beginning and ending within this zone are free, a system initiated in 1973 when Downtown merchants subsidized the service to boost business. Keep in mind that the free scheme does not apply to the waterfront streetcars running from Pier 70 to the International District, and, unlike buses on other routes, those in the Free Area don't permit the loading of bicycles.

Until summer 2007, Seattle's streets will be even more congested since the 1.3-mile **Metro Tunnel** – built for running buses on underground streets – will be undergoing renovation to allow for light-rail tracks. Therefore, several dozen once-subterranean routes will clog Downtown streets, with many aboveground lines being slightly re-routed to accommodate them. Check the Metro website or visit a customer service station to inquire about the latest updates on the project.

Outside of the Ride Free Area, **fares** for adults are $1.25 off-peak, $1.50 peak (Mon–Fri 6–9am & 3–6pm) and a mere 50¢ for kids under 18; if you're taking a "two-zone" ride that takes you outside the city limits (for instance, from Downtown to the airport), the peak price rises to $2. If you board within the Downtown Ride Free Area and get off outside of the free zone boundaries, you pay when you get off, not when you get on. (Bus operators routinely drive in the Ride Free Area with their hand covering the collection box to prevent accidental

Major bus routes

From Downtown

#1, 2, 3, 4 Seattle Center and Queen Anne (#2 and 3 also to Madrona)

#5, 26, 28 Fremont (all three) and Greenwood (#5 and 28 only)

#7, 34, 39 International District, Columbia City

#10 Capitol Hill, along Pine St and 15th Ave E

#11 Madison Park, along E Madison St

#12 Capitol Hill, along Madison and 19th Ave E

#15, 18 Ballard, via Seattle Center and Queen Anne

#16, 26 Wallingford and Green Lake

#17 Ballard and Fishermen's Terminal

#19, 24, 33 Magnolia and Discovery Park

#25 University District, via Eastlake

#27 Madrona, including Lake Washington Blvd, Leschi Park, and Colman Park

#37 Alki Beach, via Harbor Ave and Alki Ave, then through West Seattle along Beach Drive to Lincoln Park

#39 Beacon Hill and Seward Park

#43 University District, via E John St, 23rd Ave E, and 24th Ave E in Capitol Hill

#51, 55, 56, 57 West Seattle (also Alki Beach on #56 and 57), through Pioneer Square

#71, 72, 73 University District, via Eastlake

#118, 119 Vashon Island, through ferry terminal

#252, 257, 260 Kirkland

#256, 261, 550 Bellevue

Other routes

#8 Capitol Hill to Seattle Center and Queen Anne

#9 Capitol Hill to Columbia City

#31 Magnolia to University District, via Fremont and Wallingford

#44 Ballard Locks to University District, via Wallingford

#45 Seattle Center to University District, via Queen Anne

#46 University District to Ballard, via Fremont and Wallingford

#74 Seattle Center to University District, via Fremont and Wallingford

#99 Waterfront streetcar, from the International District through Pioneer Square to Pier 70

#167 University District to Bellevue and Renton

#174, 194 Sea-Tac Airport to Downtown (Museum of Flight in Tukwila en route)

payment.) If you board outside a free zone, simply pay as you get on, whether or not Downtown is your final destination. Transfers are valid for about one hour after they're issued. **Visitor passes** for $5 are available only from customer service centers (or other vendors noted above).

Bus **maps** and **schedules** are available at the Citywide Concierge Center (see p.26), libraries, shopping centers, and Metro-approved vendors. The customer service offices also dispense free copies of the large *Metro Transit System Map*, although this is such a densely packed grid that you're better off picking up the pocket-sized schedules of the routes you plan to travel frequently.

PugetPass

If you'll be in town for a while, you may want to pick up a **PugetPass**, good for use on a variety of mass-transit options in the region. Passes are available in one-month, three-month, and twelve-month varieties; the monthly pass costs $54 (one-zone peak), $72 (two-zone peak), and $45 (one- and two-zone off-peak), or a flat $18 for kids under 18. The PugetPass can also be used on Pierce Transit (serving areas south of Seattle), Community Transit (serving areas north of Seattle), Sound Transit (commuter trains), and some Washington State Ferry routes. If your ride costs more than the value shown on the front of the

Major Puget Sound ferry routes

As steep increases in fuel prices have led to ever-rising **fares** on ferries, the one-way fees below should be considered minimum rates, with price hikes usually planned for late spring. Peak season refers to the summer months (June–Sept), and extra passengers in vehicles (beyond the driver) are charged at the foot passenger rate.

Downtown Seattle to Bainbridge Island Departs from Pier 52 approximately hourly from 5.30am to 1.35am; 35min journey length; foot passengers $6.10 (collected westbound only in peak season); vehicle and driver $10.60 non-peak, $13.30 peak season.

Downtown Seattle to Bremerton Departs from Pier 52 approximately hourly from 6am to 12.50am; 60min journey length; foot passengers $6.10 (collected westbound only); vehicle and driver $13.30 peak and non-peak season.

Downtown Seattle to Vashon Island (passenger ferry only) Three per day Mon–Fri 7.30am–6.10pm, no weekend service; 35min; $8.10 peak and non-peak (collected westbound only).

Fauntleroy (West Seattle) to Vashon Island Around 33 sailings daily 5.20am–2.10am; 20min; foot passengers $4; vehicle and driver $13.60 non-peak, $17 peak. All fares collected westbound only.

Point Defiance to Tahlequah, Vashon Island Around 18 sailings daily 6am–10pm; 15min; foot passengers $4; vehicle and driver $13.60 non-peak, $17 peak. All fares collected at Point Defiance only.

Mukilteo to Clinton, Whidbey Island Departs Mukilteo, about thirty miles north of Seattle; 42 sailings daily 5am–2am; 20min; foot passengers $3.60 (collected westbound only); vehicle and driver $6.30 off-peak, $7.90 peak.

Port Townsend to Keystone, Whidbey Island 16 sailings daily, 6.30am–8.30pm; 30min; foot passengers $2.35; vehicle and driver $8.20 non-peak, $10.30 peak.

Anacortes to San Juan Islands Ten routes daily (5.30am–12.15am): to Lopez (40min), Orcas (60-80min), and Friday Harbor on San Juan Island (70min). Fares are $11–12.20 for foot passengers in peak season, $9–10 non-peak. With car during peak season: $30–33 to Lopez, $35–40 to Orcas, $41–47 to San Juan Island; with car non-peak: $22–24 to Lopez, $35–39 to Orcas, $31-35 to San Juan Island; all vehicle fares collected westbound only. For inter-island travel, fares are free for passenger trips (for cars $13.90 non-peak, $17.40 peak; collected westbound only).

pass, you can add cash to pay the difference. You can also get a book of ten or twenty tickets, but it doesn't save you anything except time. Passes and ticketbooks are sold at Metro customer service offices and most Bartell Drug stores. For more information call ☎206/624-PASS or visit ⓦwww.pugetpass.org.

The monorail

Built for the 1962 World's Fair, the **monorail** that connects Seattle Center with the Westlake Center shopping mall Downtown is not currently of much use unless you need to get from Downtown to Seattle Center (or vice versa) in a flash. Then, it's very useful, though you shouldn't gear up for a thrilling or particularly scenic high-tech ride: with no stops on the route, the journey takes just two minutes or so from start to finish. Trains run every ten minutes (Mon–Fri 7.30am–11pm, Sat & Sun 9am–11pm; one-way fares $3.50, or $1.50 for kids); further details can be had at ⓦwww.seattlemonorail.com. See the box on p.58 for information on the monorail's possible expansion into a more functional transit system.

Taxis

It's been reported that one of the biggest cab companies in Seattle has some two hundred **taxis** on duty, and delivers nearly three million passengers a year – though visitors will have a hard time believing it. Taxis are usually hard to find, and have comparatively high fares. Nonetheless, there are times when you'll want to use them, particularly if you're out clubbing in Downtown areas that can get a bit dicey after midnight, or in a neighborhood where bus service becomes infrequent or nonexistent after the early evening. The more reliable companies include Graytop Cab (☎206/282-8222) and Yellow Cab (☎206/622-6500). Fares have standardized at $2.50 for the meter drop, and $2 for each mile or 50¢ per minute. Be wary of unmarked, unregulated private cabs, which can rip you off badly.

Driving

A **car** isn't vital in Seattle. Traffic on the freeways is usually a nightmare, and sometimes streets become one-way or lanes become right-turn-only with practically no warning. Still, if you're going to be hopping around to far-flung locations, having a vehicle can be useful.

It's difficult to find cheap **parking** Downtown, with virtually all of the spaces metered ($1–2 per hour) from 8am to 6pm (except on Sunday and holidays), and $30 tickets routinely imposed after your time runs out. Capitol Hill and the University District are not as heavily metered, but space is still at a premium. In residential neighborhood blocks, parking is a lot more manageable – but even there, weekday restrictions apply, dictating how long you can leave your vehicle in one spot (usually two hours). Downtown garage rates start at about $3–5 for the first hour, and can rise to as high as $20/day.

Ferries

If you do any traveling outside of the city, particularly into Puget Sound, you'll likely be using **ferries** quite often; access points are listed where applicable throughout this guide. Most routes are run by Washington State Ferries (☎206/464-6400 or 1-800/84-FERRY, ⓦwww.wsdot.wa.gov/ferries), and tickets are available at the departure points or from Pier 52, Colman Dock, Downtown. **Schedules** are available on the piers and at many places throughout town, usually at the same locations that carry racks of Metro bus schedules. Timetables and fares vary by season, and sailing times vary between weekdays and weekends, so it's best to pick up sailing/fare schedules before making plans.

If you're traveling at a peak time of the week or year – typically heading away from the city at the beginning of weekends and holidays, and returning toward it at the end – make sure to account for **waiting time** to get on ferries, especially if traveling with an automobile. In such circumstances, it's not unheard of to wait a mile away from the dock in a ferry queue, on the shoulder of the road, for up to three hours. Luckily, at non-peak times the waiting time is less than a half-hour, sometimes just a few minutes if you time it right.

City tours

Seattle offers a good number of walking, boating, flying, and biking tours, sometimes organized according to a specific theme, such as cultural tours of Chinatown or World War II history jaunts. If you're looking to take to the water for an organized cruise, consider that pretty much the same view of the Seattle skyline and Puget Sound can be had for much less money on the local ferries.

While not exactly a tour, the **Seattle City-Pass** ($42, kids $25; good for nine days; Ⓦcitypass.com) can act as a good sort of "self-guided" option. It covers admission to the Seattle Aquarium, Pacific Science Center, Space Needle, Museum of Flight, and Woodland Park Zoo, and includes an Argosy harbor tour as well, costing half of what it would to visit all attractions at regular prices. The CityPass can be purchased at the first such sight visited.

Bus, biking, and walking tours

Bicycle Adventures ☎1-800/443-6060, Ⓦwww.bicycleadventures.com. Intense, four- to eight-day spring and summer bike tours that incorporate hiking, river and sea kayaking, and/or whale watching into the mix, featuring terrains from the Cascades to the San Juan Islands, including options for camping and dining at local restaurants. $1044–2688.

Chinatown Discovery Tours ☎425/885-3085, Ⓦwww.seattlechinatowntour.com. Wide-ranging culinary and cultural tours of the area lasting 90min to three hours, taking in familiar and lesser-known parts of the International District; also with added options for lunch or dinner at local restaurants. $17–44, kids $11–24.

Discover Tours ☎206/667-9186, Ⓦwww.seattlearchitecture.org. Walking tours past the architectural highlights of several Seattle neighborhoods, as well as themed tours of theaters, skyscrapers, and the like. Sponsored by the Seattle Architecture Foundation, lasting two to three hours. April–Oct, Sat 10am; $10.

Gray Line ☎206/626-5208 or 1-800/426-7532, Ⓦwww.graylineofseattle.com. One- to three-hour narrated bus tours of Seattle's most well-known attractions ($17–30), with a six-hour Land & Water Tour ($54), on buses and ships, on offer from spring to summer. Also has trips to the Boeing plant ($39), and mounts Rainier ($54) and St Helens ($79).

MOHAI History Tours ☎206/324-1126, Ⓦwww.seattlehistory.org. Summertime walking and bus tours of sites and neighborhoods integral to Seattle history, from Ballard to Columbia City, sponsored by the Museum of History and Industry (see p.99). Usually begins at the given site at Sat 11am; $25. Save $5 by reserving ahead.

See Seattle ☎425/226-7641, Ⓦwww.see-seattle.com. Half-day walking tours of Downtown, strolling by the major sights from Pike Place Market to the International District; also does specialist tours for prearranged groups, as well as walking-inspired scavenger hunts around town (all tours $20 per person).

Terrene Tours ☎206/325-5569. An impressive range of biking, skiing, hiking, and snowshoeing tours, plus customized outings covering the Seattle region, from neighborhoods to island tours and four-day jaunts; $25–1000.

Cruises and ferry tours

Argosy Cruises ☎206/623-4252, Ⓦwww.argosycruises.com. Offering year-round tours through most local waters, including a harbor cruise of Elliott Bay (1hr; $13.75, $17.25 summer), lake cruise in Lake Washington and Lake Union (2hr; $21, $25.75 summer), and locks cruise (2hr 30min; $25, $32 summer). Also with brunch ($39) and dinner ($65) trips.

Cruise the Locks ☎206/626-5208 or 1-800/426-7532, Ⓦwww.graylineofseattle.com. Year-round tours of Elliott Bay and the Ballard Locks from the deck of a Gray Line cruise ship, lasting two to three hours. Departs from Pier 56 on the Downtown waterfront. $27–35.

Emerald City Charters ☎206/624-3931 or 1-800/831-3274, Ⓦwww.sailingseattle.com. Sailboat trips from Pier 54 (May to mid-Oct; $25–40), from 90min to 2hr 30min, including sunset departures.

Ride the Ducks ☎206/441-3825 or 1-800/817-1116, Ⓦwww.ridetheducksofseattle.com. Land-and-sea tours in a conspicuous World War ll amphibious landing craft, starting at the Space Needle, then going into Lake Union for a ride around Portage Bay (April–Dec leaves every half-hour 10am–6pm; 90min; $23, kids $13).

Victoria Clipper ☎206/448-5000, ⓦwww.victoriaclipper.com. Eye-opening trips to Friday Harbor on San Juan Island (April–Sept only; $60 round-trip, kids $30) or to Vancouver Island in Canada (year-round; $110–133 round-trip, kids $55–66), leaving on the high-speed, passenger-only *Victoria Clipper* from Seattle's Pier 69.

Specialty tours

Discover Houseboating ☎206/322-9157, ⓦwww.discoverhouseboating.com. Get a nice glimpse of Seattle's famous floating homes, including plenty of history and lore, throughout the houseboat-heavy inlets of Lake Union and Portage Bay (daily 10am; $35).

Private Eye on Seattle ☎206/365-3739, ⓦwww.privateeyetours.com. Van tours of the scenes of lurid crimes in Capitol Hill and Queen Anne, plus a "Seattle Ghost Tour" of various allegedly haunted sights (2hr 30min–3hrs; $25).

Seattle Seaplanes ☎206/329-9638 or 1-800/637-5553, ⓦwww.seattleseaplanes.com. Twenty-minute flights of various routes over Seattle, for $67.50/person, including options for hydroplane and dinner rides.

Washington Wine Tours ☎1-877/869-TOUR, ⓦwww.washingtonwinetours.com. Weekly to monthly trips to the well-regarded vineyards of suburban Woodinville, with transportation provided to and from Downtown Seattle (Sat noon–4.30pm; $59). Also offers private day-tours to the nationally renowned wineries of the Yakima Valley, in central Washington ($120).

 # Communications

Even more than most major US cities, Seattle has an excellent communications infrastructure, with countless high-tech links to the rest of the country and the world. Although some areas are better hooked up than others – Downtown, for example – most communication services are more than adequate throughout the region, especially telephone service and the Internet; the US mail is comparatively slow, if usually quite reliable.

Telephones

For placing **telephone** calls, the general Seattle region has four major **area codes**: 206, for the city itself, plus Mercer, Bainbridge, and Vashon islands; 425, for the Eastside suburbs from Everett to Renton, and as far east as Snoqualmie Falls; 253, for the southern areas including Tacoma; and 360, for all outlying zones such as the San Juan Islands, Port Townsend, Whidbey Island, Mount Rainier, and Mount St Helens. (Cell phones may use these or their own unique area codes.) A **local call** on a public phone usually costs 50¢. For detailed information about calls, area codes and rates in the local area, consult the front *White Pages* of the telephone directory.

Calling from your **hotel room** will cost considerably more than if you use a pay phone, as hotels often charge a connection fee of at least $1 for all calls, even if they're local or toll-free. Also, beware of making an international call from your hotel room – it will undoubtedly cost a small fortune. If you need to call back home from abroad, you'd do well to get a good calling card (see below).

Many major hotels, government agencies, and car rental firms have **toll-free numbers** that are recognizable by their ☎1-800, 866, 877 or 888 prefixes. Some of these numbers can only be accessed nationally, outside the state of Washington, and many are inaccessible from abroad – dialing is the only way to find out. Numbers with a ☎1-900 or 976

Useful telephone numbers

Emergencies ☎911 for fire, police, or ambulance

Police ☎206/625-5011 for non-emergencies

Operator ☎0

Local directory information ☎411

International calls to Seattle Dial your country's international access code + 1 for the US + area code + phone number.

International calls from Seattle ☎011 + country code of country you're dialing (see below) + phone number

Country codes Australia ☎61, Ireland ☎353, New Zealand ☎64, United Kingdom ☎44. For all other codes, dial the operator or check the front of the local *White Pages.*

---

prefix are **toll calls**, typically sports information lines, psychic hotlines, and phone-sex centers, and will cost you a variable, though consistently high, fee for just a few minutes of use. Even worse, swiping a regular **credit card** at a public phone can incur astronomical charges for long-distance service, including a mysteriously high "connection fee" – with the total amount as much as $7 a minute.

Telephone charge cards

In the **US** and **Canada**, most long-distance companies enable their customers to make calling-card calls while away from home, billed to their home number. Call your company's customer service line to find out if they provide this service, and if so, what the toll-free access code is.

In the **UK** and **Ireland,** it's possible to obtain a free **BT Chargecard** (☎0800/800 838), from which all calls made overseas can be charged to your quarterly domestic account. AT&T (dial ☎0800/890 011, then 1-888/641-6123 when you hear the AT&T prompt) has the Global Calling Card, a charge card that can be used in more than 200 countries; while the Mercury Calling Card (☎0500/100 505) can be used in more than sixty countries abroad, including the US, though the fees cannot be charged to a normal phone bill.

To call **Australia** or **New Zealand** from overseas, telephone charge cards such as Telstra Telecard or Optus Calling Card in Australia and Telecom NZ's Calling Card can be used to make calls while abroad, which

are charged back to a domestic account or credit card. Apply to Telstra (☎1800/038 000), Optus (☎1300/300 937), or Telecom NZ (☎04/801 9000).

An alternative to telephone charge cards is cheap **pre-paid phone cards** offering cut-rate calls to virtually anywhere in the world. Various stores in Seattle sell them; look for signs posted in shop windows advertising rates (which can vary dramatically, so be sure to check the fine print to make sure you're getting a good deal). Some cards, through the use of a unique PIN number, allow you to add time to them as their minutes run out, while others may only have a set number of minutes available. Pre-paid calling-card companies may change their rates, policies, or deals on a month-to-month basis, or go out of business altogether, so if you're buying such a card make sure to use it within a reasonable amount of time, lest you end up with a piece of useless plastic.

Cell phones

If you're **from the US or Canada** and want to use your cell phone, it should work in Seattle, though the cost of the call can vary widely depending on your provider and plan. Some phones, when used outside the area code in the phone number, will incur steep "roaming" charges; others are on nationwide plans and don't differentiate between calling from New York or within Seattle.

If you are visiting Seattle **from overseas**, your mobile phone probably won't work, unless you have one of the **tri-band** variety.

For details on which types of phones work in the US and which don't, contact your service provider; alternatively, check out ⓦwww .telecomsadvice.org.uk/features/using_ your_mobile_abroad.

Mail

Post offices are usually open Monday through Friday from 9am to 5pm, and some are open on Saturday from 9am to noon or 1pm, as well. Ordinary mail sent within the US costs 37¢ for letters weighing up to an ounce, while standard postcards sent within the US cost 23¢. For mail sent to anywhere outside of the US (except Canada), airmail letters weighing up to an ounce cost 80¢, while postcards and aerogrammes cost 70¢; to Canada, postcards are 50¢, airmail letters 60¢, and aerogrammes 70¢. Airmail between the US and Europe may take a week, or twelve to fourteen days to Australia and New Zealand. If you already have stamps, you can drop your mail off at any post office or in the blue **mailboxes** you'll find on street corners throughout Seattle. If you don't have stamps, you'll have to buy these from a post office first.

You can have mail sent to you c/o **General Delivery** (known elsewhere as **poste restante**), Seattle, WA 98101. Letters will end up at the main post office Downtown at 301 Union St (Mon–Fri 7.30am–5.30pm; ☎206/748-5417 or 1-800/275-8777), which will hold mail for thirty days before returning it to the sender – so make sure whoever's sending you mail puts a return address on the envelope. For other area post offices, see Chapter 21, "Directory," or see ⓦwww .usps.com for further information.

If you want to send **packages** overseas from Seattle, check the front of telephone directories for packaging requirements. You'll need to fill in a green **customs declaration form**, which is available from post offices. International parcel **rates** for items weighing less than a pound run from $13 to $17, depending on the package's size and destination.

The Internet

Email is often the cheapest and most convenient way to keep in touch with friends and family back home. **Cybercafés** are found throughout Seattle, as are regular cafés with a computer or two; rates are usually around $6 per hour (see Chapter 11, "Cafés," for a few of these). Additionally, many public libraries have computers that provide free **Internet access** for a limited time period – though you may have to put your name on a waiting list and sit patiently for fifteen minutes up to an hour.

If neither of these options fit the bill, or if you just need a fast machine with assorted peripherals, then find a commercial photocopying and printing shop (look under "Copying" in the *Yellow Pages*). They'll charge around 25¢ a minute for use of their computers, but you're guaranteed fast access. Most upscale hotels also offer email and Internet access – though at a steep price, often beginning at 20–40¢ a minute.

The media

Although Seattle is well-known for its emphasis on computers and the Internet, the familiar standbys of the old media are also present, with a smattering of good choices for printed news and information, and a less inspired selection of radio and TV stations.

Newspapers and magazines

Seattle's daily papers pale in comparison with the best ones on the East Coast; fortunately, the city is home to a handful of good alternative tabloids and arts magazines, most of them free. The city's two daily **newspapers** are the *Seattle Post-Intelligencer* (Ⓦ seattlepi.nwsource.com), which is simply called "the *P-I*" by locals, and the *Seattle Times* (Ⓦ seattletimes.nwsource.com), both published in the mornings. In summer 2005, a longstanding agreement to jointly operate the papers ended, and the survival of the *P-I* has been put in doubt – so it may or may not be on news racks when you come to town. At the moment, each paper publishes entertainment supplements on Friday (the "Ticket" section in the *Times*, the "What's Happening" section in the *P-I*) that include comprehensive listings. Better and considerably more independent are the free alternative weeklies *The Stranger* (Ⓦ www.thestranger.com) and *Seattle Weekly* (Ⓦ www.seattleweekly.com), both of which are available throughout the city in cafés, bookstores, and newsboxes on the street.

Seattle cafés and bookstores offer community and arts **magazines**: some of the better ones include the *Seattle Press* (Ⓦ www.seattlepress.com), a biweekly covering many neighborhood issues; *Seattle Gay News* (Ⓦ www.sgn.org), with good features and listings; and *Eat the State* (Ⓦ eatthestate.org), a lively "forum for anti-authoritarian political opinion, research, and humor."

Radio stations in Seattle

AM

KNEZ 530 Traffic reports
KVI 570 Right-wing talk radio
CBU 690 Canadian public radio
KIRO 710 News, talk, traffic
KIXI 880 Oldies

KJR 950 Sporting events, sports talk
KOMO 1000 Talk
KKNW 1150 CNN Headline News affiliate
KKDZ 1250 Radio Disney

FM

KPLU 88.5 National Public Radio (NPR), jazz, blues
KEXP 90.3 Alternative, independent, eclectic
KBCS 91.3 World music, jazz, blues, folk
KUBE 93.3 Pop, soul, rap
KMPS 94.1 Country
KUOW 94.9 National Public Radio (NPR), talk
KJAQ 96.5 Eclectic pop
KBSG 97.3 Oldies

KING 98.1 Classical
KWJZ 98.9 "Smooth jazz"
KISW 99.9 Hard rock and metal
KQBZ 100.7 Talk, shock jocks
KPLZ 101.5 Retro-pop from the 1980s and 90s
KZOK 102.5 Classic rock, AOR
KMTT 103.7 Alternative-leaning pop and light rock
KFNK 104.9 Alternative rock
KNDD 107.7 Current and retro indie rock

Radio and television

The most interesting **radio** programs in Seattle are found on the non-commercial stations at the left end of the **FM** dial, as they are in every American city. KUOW (94.9 FM; ⓦwww.kuow.washington.edu), the local National Public Radio affiliate, has excellent public affairs and news programming, while KPLU (88.5 FM; ⓦwww.kplu.org) is strong on both news and jazz, as well as blues on weekends. For the best and most intelligently programmed music in Seattle, check fellow non-commercial stations KEXP (90.3 FM; ⓦwww.kexp.org), which broadcasts all sorts of alternative and independent sounds, and also streams its programs over the Web. Unfortunately, but for news and traffic reports, **AM** radio is bleak enough that you might have to resort to dialing in the Canadian public radio affiliate, CBU "Radio One," broadcast from Vancouver but powerful enough to be heard in Seattle.

The major **television** channels in Seattle are KOMO (ABC, channel 4), KING (NBC, channel 5), KIRO (CBS, channel 7), KSTW (UPN, channel 11), KCPQ (Fox, channel 13), and KTZZ (WB, channel 22) – one good alternative is the public station KCTS, channel 9; see ⓦwww.kcts.org for a list of its programs. Most motel and hotel rooms are hooked up to some form of **cable TV**, though the number of channels depends on where you stay. See the daily papers for channels, schedules, and programs. CNN, MSNBC, and Fox News have round-the-clock news, while ESPN is your best bet for sports. HBO and Showtime present big-budget Hollywood flicks and excellent TV shows such as *The Sopranos*, while Turner Classic Movies take its programming from the Golden Age of cinema.

Many major **sporting events** are transmitted on a pay-per-view basis, and watching an event like a heavyweight boxing match will set you back at least $50-100, billed to your motel room. Most hotels and motels also offer a choice of **recent movies** that have just finished their theatrical runs, at around $8–10 per film.

Opening hours and public holidays

The opening hours of specific Seattle attractions – including museums, theme parks, public offices, and homes open for tours – are given throughout the guide. It's always worth checking ahead on opening hours, though, especially if you're planning to visit sights far from central Seattle. Some points of interest have dramatically reduced hours, or are completely closed, during certain public holidays and festivals. A rundown of festivals and events taking place throughout the year can be found in Chapter 17.

Opening hours

As a general rule, most **museums** are open Tuesday through Saturday (occasionally Sunday, too), from 10am until 5 or 6pm, with somewhat shorter hours on the weekends. Many museums will also stay open late one evening a week – usually Thursday, when ticket prices are sometimes reduced. Government **offices**, including post offices, are open during regular business hours, typically 8 or 9am until 5pm, Monday through Friday (though some post offices are open Saturday morning until noon or 1pm). Most stores are open daily from 10am and close at 5 or 6pm, while specialty stores can be more erratic, usually opening and closing later in the day, from noon to 2pm until 8 to 10pm, and remaining shuttered for two days of the week. **Malls** tend to be open from 10am until 8 or 9pm daily, though individual stores may close before the mall does.

While many diners stay open around the clock, the more typical **restaurants** open daily around 11.30am for lunch and close at 9 to 11pm. Places that serve breakfast usually open early, between 6 to 8am, serve lunch later, and close in the early or mid-afternoon. Dance and live-music **clubs** often won't open until 9 or 10pm, and many will serve liquor until 2am and then either close for the night or stay open until dawn without serving booze. **Bars** that close at 2am may reopen as early as 6am to grab bleary-eyed customers in need of a liquid breakfast.

Public holidays

On the **national public holidays** listed below, banks, government offices, and many museums are liable to be closed all day. Small stores, as well as some restaurants and clubs, are usually closed as well, but shopping malls, supermarkets, and department and chain stores increasingly remain open, regardless of the holiday. Most parks, beaches, and cemeteries stay open during holidays, too.

Official national holidays

January
1 New Year's Day
third Monday: Dr Martin Luther King Jr's birthday
February
third Monday: Presidents' Day
May
last Monday: Memorial Day
July
4: Independence Day
September
first Monday: Labor Day
October
second Monday: Columbus Day
November
11: Veterans' Day
last Thursday: Thanksgiving
December
25: Christmas

Crime and personal safety

When it comes to crime, Seattle is a relatively safe place, and violent crime, usually of paramount concern to most travelers, is low in the Pacific Northwest. Other, non-violent, types of crime occur in the city, from pickpocketing to vehicle theft, and con men typically gravitate to tourist zones like the Pike Place Market to ply their trade. Beyond petty larceny in the popular areas, though, there are a number of districts that have a reputation for more serious kinds of crime, and it's worth knowing about these before you set out.

For the most part, Seattle's **highest-crime neighborhoods** tend to be well off the familiar tourist route and offer few attractions to lure visitors astray. They include places like the Central District, the Rainier Valley in the far southeast part of town, and around I-5 in the industrial zone south of Downtown. However, there are a few neighborhoods which offer some appeal to more intrepid travelers, and which have their dicier elements as well. Parts of Mount Baker and Columbia City, for example, were until the last decade considered off-limits to casual visitors, but have since rebounded with restored historic architecture and a growing number of small boutiques – still, the fringes of these districts can be sketchy at times, and things get worse the further southeast you go.

For more **centrally located areas**, the International District and Pioneer Square have their risky parts, especially apparent at night; it's worth taking a daytime visit first before you go wandering in search of nightlife. Similarly, Belltown has its unpleasant side during the evening (more toward Fourth and Fifth avenues than First and Second), although it's quickly diminishing in the wake of high-priced restaurants and condos and an enhanced police presence. Furthermore, much of Downtown's financial district shuts down at night, and should be avoided unless you have a firm destination in mind. Beyond these areas, the main neighborhoods, from Capitol Hill to Fremont, are generally safe.

Mugging and theft

If you're unlucky enough to get **mugged**, just hand over your money; resistance is not a good idea. After the crime occurs, immediately report it to the police (see box, p.232 for phone numbers) so you can later attempt to recover your loss from an insurance provider – unlikely, but worth a try. Also, keep **emergency numbers** for credit cards and travelers' checks handy, so they can be canceled after the crime occurs (see box, p.38).

Always be careful when using **ATMs**, especially in non-tourist areas. Try to use machines near major hotels, shops, or offices, and during the daytime. If the worst does happen, it's advisable to hand over your money and afterwards find a phone and dial ⊕**911**, or go to the nearest police station. Here, report the theft and get a reference number on the report so you can claim insurance and/or travelers check refunds. Call the local Travelers Aid (see the

"Directory," p.232) for practical advice about hospitals and emergency services.

If your **passport** is stolen (or if you lose it), call your country's consulate and pick up or have sent to you a passport application form, which you must submit with a notarized photocopy of your ID and a reissuing fee, often around $30. Because the process of issuing a new passport can take up to six weeks, you should also spend an extra $10 or so to have the consulate fax record departments back home.

Finally, a few **simple rules** to keep yourself safe are worth remembering: don't flash money around, don't leave your wallet open or count money in public, and don't look terrified, even if you are.

Hotel room theft

To avoid being the victim of a **hotel room theft** – a more frequent problem for lower-end establishments, though even the elite hotels are not immune from it – lock your valuables in the room **safe** when you leave, and always keep doors locked when you're in the room. Don't open the door to suspicious individuals, and if a questionable visitor claims to be a hotel representative, phone the front desk to make sure of it.

Car crime and safety

Crimes committed against tourists driving **rental cars** have decreased in the last decade, but there are certain precautions you can take to keep yourself safe. In major urban areas like Seattle, any car you rent

Breaking the law

Aside from **speeding** or **parking violations**, one of the most common ways visitors bring trouble on themselves is through **jaywalking**, or crossing the road against red lights or away from intersections. Although such laws are mainly enforced if your actions are blatant (charging across a divided highway or right in front of a police officer), fines can still be stiff, and the police will most assuredly not take sympathy on you if you mumble that you "didn't think it was illegal."

Other infringements include **insulting a police officer** (ie, arguing with one), and **riding a bicycle at night** without proper lights and reflectors. **Alcohol laws** provide another source of irritation to visitors, particularly as the law prohibits drinking liquor, wine, or beer in most public spaces like parks and beaches. Note too that liquor is officially off-limits to anyone under 21. And although possessing small amounts of **marijuana** is a misdemeanor in Washington, it may get you thrown out of the country if you're a foreigner – or into jail for larger amounts.

should have nothing on it – such as a special license plate – to distinguish it as a rental car. When driving, under no circumstances should you immediately stop if you are "accidentally" rammed by the driver behind you; instead, drive on to the nearest well-lit, busy spot and phone the police at ☎911. Keep doors locked and hide valuables out of sight, either in the trunk or the glove compartment, and leave any valuables you don't need for you journey back in your hotel safe.

Should a relatively uncommon "**carjacking**" occur, in which you're told to hand over your car at gunpoint, you should flee the vehicle as quickly as possible, get away from the scene, and then call ☎911. If your car **breaks down** at night while on a major street, activate the emergency flashers to signal a police officer for assistance, or, if possible during the day, find the nearest phone book and call for a tow truck. Should you be forced to stop your car on a **freeway**, pull over to the right shoulder of the highway – never the left – and activate your flashers. Wait for assistance either in your vehicle, while strapped in by a seat belt, or on a safe embankment nearby.

Women's safety

Generally, going into **bars** and **clubs** throughout Seattle should pose no problems, as women's privacy is usually respected, especially in dance and rock clubs. However, sexual harassment is more common for single women in country-and-western clubs, and in nightspots in the outlying rural parts of the region. If in doubt, gay and lesbian bars are generally trouble-free alternatives (see p.198 for some of these).

As a rule, women (or men, for that matter) should **never hitchhike** anywhere in the city. This mode of travel leaves you open to every thug and would-be rapist motoring down the highway; if you're driving, avoid hitchhikers just as steadfastly. Also on the danger list is **walking** through desolate, unlit streets at night; if you feel at all unsafe, you're better off taking a cab to your destination, even if it's just for a few blocks.

One option for women travelers in the US that's unavailable in most European countries is **pepper spray** or **mace**, which comes in a small canister that you can carry in a purse or pocket. Upon contact with an attacker's eyes, the spray causes terrible, temporary pain – giving you the opportunity to flee the scene and alert the police (see box, p.232, for emergency phone numbers). Keep in mind that you should never enter an airport with the spray, and always get rid of it before you return home.

Travelers with disabilities

Like other large American cities, Seattle has reasonable accommodations and facilities for travelers with disabilities. With a little planning, accessing all the city's major attractions, hotels, and transit options shouldn't be too difficult.

Because of the passage of the 1990 **Americans with Disabilities Act**, all public buildings must be wheelchair-accessible and have suitable toilets. Most hotels and restaurants, especially those built within the last fifteen years, also have adequate accommodations for wheelchairs, though movie theaters have been slower to change their ways, and in some venues you may end up near the front row with a skewed view of the screen or stuck in an alcove off to the side.

Free copies of *Access Seattle*, a guidebook for disabled persons that covers accommodations, restaurants, public transportation, and the like can be ordered from the Easter Seals Society of Washington, 157 Roy St,

Seattle, WA 98109 (☎206/281-5700, ⓦwa
.easterseals.com). The Washington Coalition
of Citizens with Disabilities, 4649 Sunny-
side Ave N, Suite 100, Seattle, WA 98103
(☎206/545-7055, ⓦwww.wccd.org), is
another prominent organization for information and services.

Transportation

American **airlines** must by law accommodate those with disabilities, and some even
allow attendants of those with serious conditions to accompany them on the trip for a
reduced fare. Similarly, almost every **Amtrak
train** includes one or more cars with accommodation for disabled passengers, along
with wheelchair assistance at train platforms,
adapted on-board seating, free travel for
guide dogs, and fifteen-percent discounts
on fares, with 24 hours' advance notice.
Passengers with hearing impairment can get
information by calling ☎1-800/523-6590 or
checking out ⓦwww.amtrak.com.

That said, traveling by **Greyhound** and
Amtrak Thruway bus-connection service is
often problematic. Buses are not equipped
with platforms for wheelchairs (although
intercity carriers are required by law to
provide assistance with boarding, and disabled passengers may be able to get priority
seating). Those unable to travel alone, and
in possession of a doctor's certificate, may
receive two-for-one fares to bring a companion along. Call Greyhound's ADA customer
assistance line for more information (☎1-
800/752-4841, ⓦwww.greyhound.com).

Passengers with disabilities can travel
on **Washington State Ferries**, and many
other regional transportation options, for half
the regular fare by presenting a **Regional
Reduced Fare Permit** or other proof of
disability. The permit is also good for **Metro
buses**, around eighty percent of which are
wheelchair-accessible, with drop-down
entry ramps and detached seating to allow
for wheelchair access. A free transit system
pamphlet, *Accessible Metro*, includes a
useful map detailing both the accessible and
non-accessible routes throughout Downtown; call ☎206-553-3060 or check ⓦwww
.metrokc.gov/kcdot for more information.

Seattle's major **car rental** firms can provide
vehicles with hand controls for drivers with

leg or spinal disabilities, though these are
typically available only on the pricier models.
Parking regulations for disabled motorists
are now uniform: license plates for the disabled must carry a three-inch-square international access symbol, and a placard bearing
this symbol must be hung from the car's
rearview mirror. A good resource, the *Handi-
capped Driver's Mobility Guide*, is published
by the American Automobile Association
(☎206/448-5353, ⓦwww.aaawa.com).

Disabled access

The major hotel and motel chains are your
best bet for accessible **accommodation**. At
the higher end of the scale, Embassy Suites
has been working to comply with new standards of access that meet or, in some cases,
exceed ADA requirements, involving building
new facilities, retrofitting older hotels and
providing special training to all employees; see
p.149 for a review of the company's Bellevue
location. To a somewhat lesser degree, the
same is true of Hyatt Hotels – see p.146 for a
review of its Downtown Seattle branch – and
the other big chains in town.

Citizens or permanent residents of the US
who have been medically determined to be
blind or permanently disabled can obtain the
Golden Access Passport (ⓦwww.nps.gov/
fees_passes.htm), a free lifetime pass to
federally operated parks, monuments,
historic sites, and recreation areas that
charge admission fees. The pass must
be picked up in person, from the sites
described; it also provides a fifty-percent
discount on fees charged at facilities for
camping, boat-launching, and parking.
Furthermore, the Washington State Parks
and Recreation Commission offers a free
annual **Disability Pass** that allows for half-
priced camping and boat-launching fees at
state parks. The commission also publishes
information online about accessible accommodation and travel to regional parks – visit
ⓦwww.parks.wa.gov/ada-rec.

Resources

Major US **organizations** for the disabled
include the Society for Accessible Travel &
Hospitality (SATH) and Mobility International.
Easy Access to National Parks, by Wendy
Roth and Michael Tompane, explores every

national park from the points of view of people with disabilities, senior citizens, and families with children, and *Disabled Outdoors* is a quarterly magazine focusing on facilities for travelers with disabilities who wish to get into the countryside.

Organizations

Access-Able PO Box 1796, Wheat Ridge, CO 80034 ℡303/232-2979, ⓦwww.access-able.com. Information service and network that assists travelers with disabilities by putting them in contact with other people with similar conditions.
Directions Unlimited 720 N Bedford Rd, Bedford Hills, NY 10507 ℡1-800/533-5343 or 914/241-1700. Tour operator with customized tours for people with disabilities.
Easy Access Travel 5386 Arlington Ave, Riverside, CA 92504 ℡1-800/920-8989, ⓦwww.easyaccesstravel.com. Travel consulting services with tour packages.

Mobility International USA PO Box 10767, Eugene, OR 97440 ℡541/343-1284, ⓦwww .miusa.org. Answers travel questions and operates an exchange program for the disabled. Annual membership ($35) includes quarterly newsletter.
Society for Accessible Travel & Hospitality (SATH) 347 Fifth Ave, #610, New York, NY 10016 ℡212/447-7284, ⓦwww.sath.org. Nonprofit travel industry group comprising travel agents, tour operators, hotels, airlines, and travelers with disabilities.
Twin Peaks Press Box 129, Vancouver, WA 98666-0129 ℡360/694-2462, ⓦhome.pacifier .com/~twinpeak. Publishes the *Directory of Travel Agencies for the Disabled*, listing more than 370 agencies worldwide, as well as a general guide, *Travel for the Disabled*.
Wheels Up! ℡1-888/38-WHEELS, ⓦwww .wheelsup.com. Online service that provides discounted airfares, tour, and cruise prices for disabled travelers, and publishes a free monthly newsletter.

The City

The City

Downtown Seattle

From a distance **Downtown Seattle** offers a tidy pocket of skyscrapers set perfectly against a glistening bay and surrounding mountains, a picturesque setting for the unquestioned commercial and financial hub of the Pacific Northwest. Despite its importance, though, Downtown isn't Seattle's most exciting quarter, and offers the same proliferation of chain stores and fast-food vendors found everywhere else in the US – many independent businesses have left in recent years because of escalating rents and the lure of hipper districts nearby, such as Capitol Hill. Nonetheless, from the waterfront, Downtown's **skyline** is still quite compelling, with the office blocks reflecting off the bay and providing a dramatic backdrop for ferries, pleasure cruisers, and tugboats passing by. And, of course, the entire cityscape is overlooked by the Space Needle (see p.82), Seattle's most memorable building.

Downtown's borders are most easily defined by the transit system's **Ride Free Area** (see p.32) – a small area that holds most of Seattle's mainstream tourist sights and stretches from Jackson Street to the south, Battery Street to the north, Sixth Avenue to the east, and along the waterfront. The old favorite **Pike Place Market** is the first destination for just about everyone, and still a great place to eat and shop, while west and downhill the **waterfront**, home to the **Seattle Aquarium**, is a good spot for a stroll. South of the market, the otherwise staid Business District is home to the sizable **Seattle Art Museum** and elegant **Benaroya Hall**, which have bolstered the city's cultural reputation, but perhaps not as much as the new Rem Koolhaas-designed **Central Library**, a spectacular icon of glass geometry. The rest of the district holds only scattered appeal – and mostly for architecture fans – with the darkly looming **Bank of America Tower**, the Northwest's tallest building, and the oddly curved base of the **Rainier Tower** among the few high points.

Sights aside, you'll still probably spend a fair amount of time around here, as it's where many of the city's chain **hotels** can be found (see p.145). Fortunately, the area itself is compact and easily covered on foot; a brisk walk or a short bus ride away are the more colorful neighborhoods of Belltown, Pioneer Square, and Capitol Hill, as well as the Seattle Center.

Pike Place Market

There are few better urban agoras than **Pike Place Market** (Mon–Sat 9am–6pm, Sun 10am–5pm; ☎206/682-7453, ⓦwww.pikeplacemarket.org),

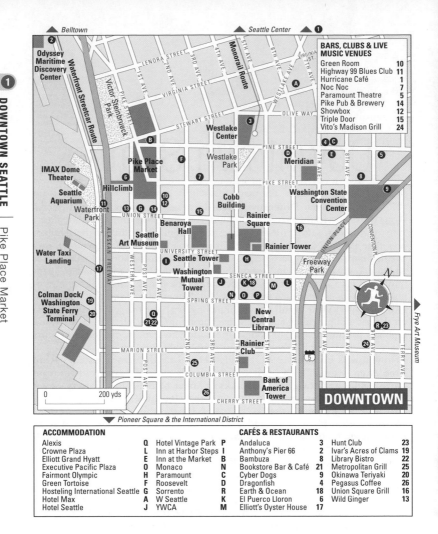

BARS, CLUBS & LIVE MUSIC VENUES

Green Room	10
Highway 99 Blues Club	11
Hurricane Café	1
Noc Noc	7
Paramount Theatre	5
Pike Pub & Brewery	14
Showbox	12
Triple Door	15
Vito's Madison Grill	24

ACCOMMODATION

Alexis	Q	Hotel Vintage Park	P	
Crowne Plaza	L	Inn at Harbor Steps	I	
Elliott Grand Hyatt	E	Inn at the Market	B	
Executive Pacific Plaza	O	Monaco	N	
Fairmont Olympic	H	Paramount	C	
Green Tortoise	F	Roosevelt	D	
Hosteling International Seattle	G	Sorrento	R	
Hotel Max	A	W Seattle	K	
Hotel Seattle	J	YWCA	M	

CAFÉS & RESTAURANTS

Andaluca	3	Hunt Club	23
Anthony's Pier 66	2	Ivar's Acres of Clams	19
Bambuza	8	Library Bistro	22
Bookstore Bar & Café	21	Metropolitan Grill	25
Cyber Dogs	9	Okinawa Teriyaki	20
Dragonfish	4	Pegasus Coffee	26
Earth & Ocean	18	Union Square Grill	16
El Puerco Lloron	6	Wild Ginger	13
Elliott's Oyster House	17		

whose splendid retro-neon clock and sign make it one of the most recognizable public places in the western US. As you stroll through the entrance at First Avenue and Pike Street – within easy reach of most Seattle buses passing through Downtown – you get a sense of how huge the place is: thirteen buildings on a triangular lot covering nine acres, with more than three hundred produce and fish vendors, bakeries, craft stalls, and small retailers dealing in everything from tacky trinkets and boutique-wear to left-wing books; for reviews of the best stores in the market, see "Shops and galleries," p.218. Best of all, the market is owned, managed, and patronized by locals, not just by out-of-towners, making for a good opportunity to mix with city denizens.

Along with ubiquitous seafood, much of Seattle's tastiest and least expensive **ethnic food** can be found here; you can also dine at one of several restaurants offering sweeping views of Puget Sound. The **Main Arcade** – where every business must either grow or make whatever they have for sale – is the key attraction for most people, whether for sipping java or snacking on fresh fruit and veggies. A spectacle in its own right, the central **Pike Place Fish Company**, right through the front entry, is packed tight with tourists vying to watch the late-morning ritual: raucously shouting signals like football quarterbacks, fishmongers behind a counter heave huge slabs of trout and salmon at a "fish-catcher" in the thick of the crowd. Getting a picture taken with the airborne catch-of-the-day is sure to be a highlight.

Not surprisingly, the market can get unbearably crowded on weekends and summer days, when parking can be especially difficult. With the exception of some restaurants and bars, the market largely shuts down by 6pm. If you can stand the crowds and are in town around Memorial Day, check out the annual **street fair**, which features live music, children's activities, and even more food vendors.

Some history

Although nowadays an essential sight on Seattle's tourist circuit, and as intrinsic to the city as the Space Needle, Pike Place Market began as a much less celebrated venue. Established in 1907 as a way for local farmers to sell their products directly to consumers, the market was simply a thick warren of itinerant stalls and fruit wagons, long before any permanent masonry was built. Years later, the place became a helter-skelter array of snaking alleys, sloping terraces, and jumbled geometry when the present buildings were shoehorned into an Escher-like maze.

While the market's quirky, erratic character may endear it to current visitors, the place was considered enough of an eyesore by dogmatic modernists in the 1950s and 1960s that it was slated for demolition – its dilapidated condition not helping matters. Nonetheless, local architect **Victor Steinbrueck** headed a campaign in the 1960s to save it (along with Pioneer Square), both for its early twentieth-century buildings and to ensure that lower-income Seattleites had a place to buy affordable groceries. As a result of Steinbrueck's efforts (commemorated in an adjacent park named after him), a "**Keep the Market**" initiative was approved by voters in 1971, paving the way for its restoration with the establishment of a Market Historical District in 1974. This, in turn, led to the market's unused upper-floor space being converted into five hundred units of low-income housing for the elderly.

Today, no one talks about tearing down the market, but political conflict continues to hover around the edges. There's concern that increased traffic from nearby development (particularly along the waterfront) might overload the capacity of the market, undermining its charm considerably. Even so, it's difficult to imagine its commercial and cultural viability being seriously threatened any time soon.

Inside and around the market

Inside the market there's an **information booth** on the traffic island at the First Avenue entrance on Pike Street, and stacks of the free monthly *Pike Place Market News* (www.pikeplacemarketnews.com), which includes a decent map, are piled liberally throughout the buildings. Historical, one-hour tours of the complex begin at the **Market Heritage Center**, 1531 Western Ave (Wed–Sun 11am & 2pm; $7; reserve 24hrs in advance, or by Fri 4pm for

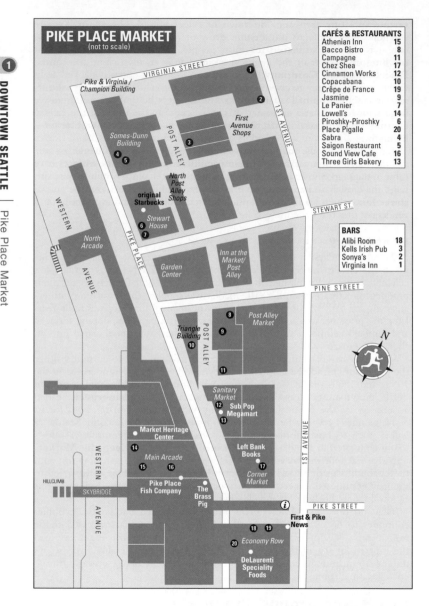

PIKE PLACE MARKET
(not to scale)

CAFÉS & RESTAURANTS

Athenian Inn	15
Bacco Bistro	8
Campagne	11
Chez Shea	17
Cinnamon Works	12
Copacabana	10
Crêpe de France	19
Jasmine	9
Le Panier	7
Lowell's	14
Piroshky-Piroshky	6
Place Pigalle	20
Sabra	4
Saigon Restaurant	5
Sound View Cafe	16
Three Girls Bakery	13

BARS

Alibi Room	18
Kells Irish Pub	3
Sonya's	2
Virginia Inn	1

Map labels: VIRGINIA STREET; Pike & Virginia / Champion Building; First Avenue Shops; 1ST AVENUE; POST ALLEY; Somes-Dunn Building; North Post Alley Shops; original Starbucks; Stewart House; STEWART ST.; WESTERN AVENUE; North Arcade; PIKE PLACE; Garden Center; Inn at the Market/Post Alley; PINE STREET; Triangle Building; POST ALLEY; Post Alley Market; Sanitary Market; Sub Pop Megamart; Market Heritage Center; Main Arcade; Left Bank Books; Corner Market; 1ST AVENUE; HILLCLIMB; SKYBRIDGE; WESTERN AVENUE; Pike Place Fish Company; The Brass Pig; PIKE STREET; First & Pike News; Economy Row; DeLaurenti Speciality Foods; N

weekend tours, at ☎206/774-5249), though the best way to experience the market is to wander through it at your own pace. A favorite meeting place is the **brass pig** in front of the Public Market Center sign – not a sculpture but rather a piggy bank, with receipts going to various charities. Beyond the pig, the multi-story **Main Arcade** sprawls out down the hillside, and a map is helpful here if you don't want to get lost. The weekly **Organic Wednesdays**

(June–Oct 10am–4pm, also "Summer Sundays" June–Sept 10am–4pm) gives you the opportunity to buy organic produce under canopies set up on the cobblestones of Pike Place itself. Along this stretch you'll find the *Athenian Inn* (see p.161), one of the prime shooting locations for the movie *Sleepless in Seattle*, and the Woodring Orchards stall, which offers tasty, freshly bottled cherry and raspberry juice.

On the south end of Pike Place Market, **Economy Row** features the Italian and Mediterranean delicacies of DeLaurenti Specialty Foods, and has an enormous international newsstand as well. To the north, the **Corner Market** is home to countless produce vendors and the collectively run Left Bank Books, which stocks various political and feminist manifestos, experimental fiction, and the usual conspiracy rants. This area and the nearby **Sanitary Market** have most of the market's top bakeries, too, among them the oldest vendor at the site, the Three Girls Bakery, serving up baked goodies since 1912. Further north the geometry of the market becomes somewhat jumbled within the buildings, but the larger structures themselves are separated by **Pike Place** proper – which essentially separates the Main Arcade from everything else – and **Post Alley**, known for its street musicians and sidewalk cafés, as well as better restaurants such as *Café Campagne*.

The crowds can get particularly dense as you head to the narrower, arts-and-crafts-dominated **North Arcade**, thick with dealers in jewelry, silk-screened shirts, and wooden carvings. Directly across Pike Place, at no. 1912, in the **Stewart House** building, you'll find the original location of the *Starbucks* chain (see box), which, true to form, is pretty much like every other of the company's coffeehouses – except for the topless mermaid logo of old.

Starbucks in Seattle: fertile coffee grounds

Long before it was a globe-straddling behemoth doling out mass-marketed java under an anodyne green logo, **Starbucks** began as a humble shop in Pike Place Market in 1971, named after the coffee-swilling first mate in Herman Melville's *Moby-Dick*, and advertised with a bare-chested mermaid. Since then, its explosive growth has been fueled by good luck, timely expansion, and the monopolistic practices of American multinational corporations in the 1990s, leading the company to achieve annual revenues of more than $4 billion and spread out to thousands of locations worldwide.

It all started when the company's marketing director **Howard Schultz** (who now controls both *Starbucks* and the Seattle Mariners), inspired by a trip to Italy, decided to see if espresso-bar culture could catch on back home. No one foresaw just how successful his sales pitch would be. As his empire swelled, so too did the company's guidelines for selecting, roasting, grinding, and brewing beans – today, employees are required to take **Coffee 101**, a class that gives instruction on the proper way to correctly serve up the industrial brew.

Neither located atop a skyscraper nor housing the infernal lair of Dr Evil (as in the first *Austin Powers* sequel), *Starbucks* **corporate headquarters** can be found south of Downtown, but it's off-limits to the caffeinated masses. For diehard fans of the chain, there's still the original outpost in the Stewart House building of the Pike Place Market, where, as in many *Starbucks* joints, you can not only knock back a frappuccino, but also purchase mugs, coffeemakers, and caffeine-themed trinkets. Additionally, these days you can sample the music of Bob Dylan, the 1960s folk hero who has given the corporate giant the exclusive right to market his latest record until 2007.

The waterfront

Despite what the tour brochures might tell you, it's not essential on a short trip to visit Seattle's **waterfront** – specifically, the Puget Sound edge along Elliott Bay – and lakes Union to the north or Washington to the east offer their own worthwhile, scenic activities. Nonetheless, visitors usually head to the bayside waterfront, set on a downward course on the outdoor stairway known as the **Hillclimb**, directly behind (ie, west of) Pike Place Market.

Provided you actually find the Hillclimb (after roaming through several corridors and stairwells inside the market), you're not likely to come across much here other than a few snack vendors and cafés. Beyond this you cross under the towering, double-decked **Alaskan Way Viaduct** and reach the bayfront proper, home to ferry landings, trinket stalls, and chic hotels, along with a handful of attractions. Around piers 57–59, **Waterfront Park** is pleasant enough for its views, though a far cry from what it was at the turn of the last century, when its docks were the embarkation point for countless masses of gold-hungry prospectors headed up to Alaska's Klondike in hopes of striking it rich. A lucky few came back wealthy, though many more ended up broke or destitute, or simply frittered away their meager earnings in saloons, gambling halls, and brothels. Heading north, the stretch from the ferry docks to Myrtle Edwards Park (see p.55) makes for a nice stroll, though the din of freeway traffic from Alaskan Way provides a rather unwelcome soundtrack.

One of the best ways to see the area is to use the **waterfront streetcar** (Metro route 99; daily 6.30am–11.30pm; $1.25, $1.50 peak, seniors 25¢, kids 50¢; ⓦtransit.metrokc.gov), though this route is not part of the Downtown Ride Free Zone (every passenger pays a fare, and transfers permit you to get on and off at any of the nine stations for a period of ninety minutes). Streetcars from Melbourne, Australia, built in 1927, were imported especially for this service when the line began operation in 1982.

The streetcar runs its twenty-minute route from Jackson Street in the International District north through Pioneer Square, and then from Pier 48 to Pier 70/Broad Street, running three times an hour. Like San Francisco's cable cars, this service isn't exactly speedy – if you're in a hurry, you could probably walk the distances just as quickly – but it is a touristy indulgence worth enjoying at least once.

Alternatively, at Pier 55 you can hop aboard the **water taxi** (May–Sept one-way fares $3) that takes visitors twelve miles across Elliott Bay to the Seacrest Park dock on the eastern side of the West Seattle peninsula. It's an attractive journey, especially on the glistening north side of the boat (away from the industrial zone of south Seattle), even if the Seacrest destination offers little to keep you for more than a half-hour of relaxed bay watching. Most of West Seattle's sights are on the other side of the peninsula, making for a very lengthy hike, though Metro bus #53 or shuttle #773 provide easy access.

The Seattle Aquarium

The main reason for heading down to the waterfront is the **Seattle Aquarium** on Pier 59, just across the street from the Hillclimb (daily June–Aug 9.30am–7pm, rest of year 10am–5pm; $12, kids $8; ☏206/386-4320, ⓦwww .seattleaquarium.org). With around four hundred species of fish, birds, plants, and marine mammals, the Aquarium boasts a spacious, easily navigable layout, part of which is outdoors near the shore. Along with a 400,000-gallon underwater dome that re-creates life in Puget Sound, the highlights include black-tip sharks, electric eels, octopi, a functional salmon hatchery and fish ladder, which displays the life cycle of the threatened Pacific salmon, and a hands-on **Discovery Lab** allowing visitors to touch tidepool specimens. The sea otters are the true show stealers, ceaselessly backpaddling to the delight of onlookers; this was the first aquarium in the world in which the aquatic scamps were successfully bred, born, and raised to adulthood.

Keep in mind that until autumn 2006, the Aquarium is being remodeled and partially reconstructed, with the onsite IMAX Dome theater closed in the interim. Most other sights and exhibits should be open, though you might want to check ahead if there's a particular shark or lumpsucker you simply have to see on your trip.

South to Colman Dock

The area between Pier 59 and the ferry terminals to the south is riddled with souvenir shops and bland diners, an exception being **Ivar's Acres of Clams**, Pier 54 (☎206/624-6852, ⓦwww.ivars.net), the waterfront's most notable restaurant (see p.55), which has its own "Clam Central Station" stop on the streetcar, and is the main branch of a citywide chain. It's also excellent for its streetside **fish bar**, open until 2am, where you can grab a bowl of clam chowder or a helping of cod-and-chips if you get the late-night munchies.

A few yards to the south is Pier 52, where **Colman Dock** is the terminal for Washington State Ferries (see "City transportation," p.34), taking you to spots like West Seattle and Bainbridge Island; Pier 50, just to its south, handles foot passengers between Seattle and Vashon Island. The best views of the boats can be found on the elevated platforms running alongside the terminal – though you get a better overall view of Elliott Bay from the observation platforms on Pier 66.

North to Myrtle Edwards Park

North of Pier 59, the waterfront has few real sights before Pier 66 (aka the Bell Street Pier), home of the industrially oriented **Odyssey Maritime Discovery Center**, 2205 Alaskan Way (Wed & Thurs 11am–3pm, Fri 11am–4pm, Sat & Sun 11am–5pm; $7, kids $5; ☎206/374-4000, ⓦwww.ody.org), which presents nearly fifty interactive exhibits devoted to trade and transport in Puget Sound. Although kids might get a kick out of a simulated sea kayak journey, the working models of shipping boats and propellers, or the computer game that lets you play crane operator, most adults will find the experience interminable, unless you have an especially strong zeal for reading up on port-management studies and intermodal cargo transport.

Just to the right of the center's entrance, a staircase leads to the **Bell Street Bridge** and a series of secluded platforms and free-use telescopes, which offer the best views of Elliott Bay along the waterfront. A few blocks north of Pier 66, past the last stop on the streetcar line, **Myrtle Edwards Park** features a bike and pedestrian path that winds along the shore for several miles and continues through adjoining Elliott Bay Park before terminating near Magnolia Bridge. It's an excellent place to look out on the bay and the Downtown skyscrapers from a distance, especially at sunset. Shadowing the paths are the famed rotating globe atop the **Seattle Post-Intelligencer** building, 101 Elliott Ave W (reading "It's in the P-I"), and a renowned **grain terminal** at Pier 86, whose mammoth tubes load ships at 3000 tons per hour. At the south end of the park, the developing 8.5-acre **Olympic Sculpture Park** is an ongoing project by the Seattle Art

Museum, highlighted by Richard Serra's five undulating steel panels, known as *Wake*. The park, however, will not be open to the public until mid-2007, and is aimed mainly at fans of hulking, metallic modern sculpture, with works by Mark Di Suvero, Tony Smith and Alexander Calder among the other highlights.

The Business District

Between Second and Seventh avenues, east and south of Pike Place Market, most of Downtown is given over to the steel-and-glass office towers of Seattle's **Business District**. If you're using mass transit, it's almost inevitable that you'll cross through here at some point, as many bus lines have hubs on the avenues. Like countless other corporate enclaves in US cities, the area offers limited amusement, and is nearly deserted at night and on weekends. Moreover, the region's two most celebrated economic powerhouses, Boeing and Microsoft, are not even located here, but are firmly ensconced in the suburbs.

Other than a few large, local enterprises with flagship stores (including REI and Nordstrom; see "Shops and galleries," p.218), plus the usual array of enclosed malls, the resident cultural attractions are few, except for the **Seattle Art Museum** and **Benaroya Hall**, home to the **Seattle Symphony**. If it's architecture you're interested in, though, there are a number of intriguing and quirky offerings, most prominently the shiny angles of the **Central Library** and the Pacific Northwest's tallest building, the **Bank of America Tower**.

The Seattle Art Museum

The section of First Avenue between Pike Place Market and Pioneer Square features an assortment of galleries, pawn shops, and diners, as well as one of the top cultural institutions in the region, the **Seattle Art Museum**, 100 University St (Tues–Sun 10am–5pm, Thurs closes at 9pm; $7, kids $5, free first Thurs of month; some exhibits may cost $3–5 extra; ☎206/654-3100, ⊛www .seattleartmuseum.org). Visually unmistakable for the giant, inset letters on its facade, the museum, designed by Robert Venturi and completed in 1991, is perhaps most well-known for Jonathan Borofsky's *Hammering Man* kinetic sculpture, a 48-foot black-steel and aluminum marvel pounding away in front of the entrance, the slow repetitive motion of the figure's arm complemented by the deep groan of its electric motor. One of five such sculptures around the world, the metallic titan is among the best pieces at the museum, and is viewable for free. The museum also hosts a full schedule of **concerts**, **films**, **lectures**, and other **special programs**, detailed in the quarterly program guides available in the lobby, and there's a **fine arts bookstore** just inside the entrance. If used within a week, admission tickets to the museum are also good for entrance to the Seattle Asian Art Museum (see p.95) and, presumably, the Olympic Sculpture Park (see p.55), once it opens in 2006. Finally, entire levels or sections of the museum may be **closed** to the public at various times through 2007, as the institution undergoes an expansion and renovation that promises to allow more space to show its considerable collection.

The collections

Although the museum's **collections** hardly equal those found in the biggest American cities, there are more than enough worthwhile pieces to keep you busy for a few hours. From the lobby, a grand staircase winds to the second floor, where temporary exhibitions cover everything from Chinese porcelain, European modernist painting, and twentieth century American photography to works by Louis Comfort Tiffany and Isamu Noguchi. The third floor features a variety of **international art**, including traditional and modern works from Japan, China, Korea, Indonesia, the Andes, and the Near East, with an especially large section of indigenous art from the Northwest Coast. Especially notable are the **Native American** totem poles, rattles, and canoes, along with colorful headdresses, masks, baskets, and woven fabrics. Contemporary and traditional **African art** is on display as well, with surprising pieces like *Mercedes-Benz Shaped Coffin* by Ghana's Kane Kwei, a jarring blend of postmodern style and traditional design.

Regional modern art gets the biggest section of the top floor, with rotating exhibits giving exposure to budding Pacific Northwest talents. Elsewhere, there are small, unimpressive selections of eighteenth- and nineteenth-century works, as well as pockets of Baroque, Medieval, Renaissance, and ancient Mediterranean designs. But the main attractions are the monumental **nineteenth-century American** works by landscape masters Frederic Church and Albert Bierstadt and notable **twentieth-century works** like Andy Warhol's *Double Elvis*, the sixteen photographic tunnels of Gilbert & George's *Coloured Shouting*, Bruce Nauman's neon wall-piece *Double Poke in the Eye II*, Roy Lichtenstein's cartoonish *Study for Vicki!*, and Robert Arneson's provocative pun *John With Art*.

Benaroya Hall

One of the most impressive recent additions to the Business District is the graceful **Benaroya Hall**, home of the **Seattle Symphony** (see p.191; ☏206/215-4747, ⓦwww.seattlesymphony.org/benaroya), which occupies an entire city block just east of the Seattle Art Museum, bounded by Union and University streets and Second and Third avenues. The hall's massive, curving glass-curtain wall in the Grand Lobby affords views of Elliott Bay, while the Robert Rauschenberg mural and chandeliers by local glass titan Dale Chihuly are just a few of the decorative highlights. Tours of the complex (Tues & Fri noon & 1pm; free) begin in front of the Grand Lobby entrance; if you're lucky, you might even see part of a concert rehearsal or hear the hall's impressive house organ at full blast. Otherwise, you can visit the Hall's own **Soundbridge**, at Union and Second (Tues–Sun 10am–4pm; $7), something of a showpiece for classical instruments and music-making – the smaller, highbrow equivalent of the Experience Music Project. Aimed more at kids and those with only a sketchy knowledge of European art music, this music center lets you play conductor with a phantom orchestra, listen to the great works and warhorses of the canon, and bang away at pianos and drums like a true avant-garde modernist.

Westlake Center and around

Another familiar stop on most tourist routes, the **Westlake Center**, 400 Pine St (daily 10am–9pm; ⓦwww.westlakecenter.com), is a giant, four-story enclosed mall several blocks east of Pike Place Market; it's most notable, however, for being the southern terminus of the 1.3-mile **monorail** (Mon–Fri 7.30am–11pm, Sat–Sun 9am–11pm; one-way fare $3.50, kids $1.50; ⓦwww .seattlemonorail.com). For the moment, this elevated route has only two stops

Seattle transit: the Magic Kingdom solution

Created for the Seattle World's Fair of 1962, the **Seattle Monorail** was built as a private enterprise to showcase the high-technology designs of the time, including towering concrete pylons, smoothly efficient pneumatic rubber wheels, 700-volt electric power from the side rails, and a quiet overall operating noise. Three years after the fair, the system was turned over to the city for $600,000 – about a sixth the amount it cost to create – and debate soon began as to whether the elevated train was worth keeping at all. Although some in the community were concerned over its operating cost, political feasibility, and alleged visual blight over Downtown, a majority of the residents favored its continued existence, and for the next few decades the system was regarded as a charming throwback to the New Frontier, shuttling tourists between a shopping center and the Seattle Center without too much ado.

Perhaps surprisingly – with the purpose of alleviating traffic congestion – Seattle voters in 2002 began approving a series of **ballot measures** that called for the expansion of the monorail system from a pleasant Disneyesque diversion to an actual mass-transit solution. Surprising still, several successful measures actually created and validated a monorail-fund **taxing authority**, costing Seattlites $140 per every $10,000 of assessed value of their automobiles – this in the famously anti-tax state of Washington. Thanks to this voter support, one wouldn't think that miserly politicians or planning curmudgeons would wish to stop the project, yet they keep trying – indeed, bureaucratic delays and dubious accounting have in 2005 once again put the project in jeopardy. It's hard to keep track of the number of times the monorail plan has been pronounced "dead," only to be resurrected in a different form.

Assuming the monorail system ever does get built, the fourteen-mile route (at last review) will connect West Seattle to Ballard through Downtown's main sights via twenty rail stations. If you have a particular desire to check the monorail's progress (or lack thereof), see Ⓦ www.elevated.org for details.

(the northern one is at Seattle Center), but may be expanding in the coming years thanks to a successful ballot measure (see box). You can hop on the train for a two-minute ride, departing every ten minutes from the loading point on the mall's top floor, where you'll find plenty of tourists to keep you company. The adjacent **Westlake Park**, on Fourth Avenue between Pike and Pine, is a much livelier spot than the mall, hosting occasional lunchtime concerts and the odd political rally near its distinctive water-wall fountain.

The only other unique park in the area, **Freeway Park**, about a third of a mile southeast of Westlake Park at Eighth Avenue, is one of the strangest municipal landscape projects in the US, featuring fountains, small waterfalls, and gurgling channels flowing over concrete ramps and down geometric terraces, all built directly over the path of an interstate highway. The sloping paths and stairways make for an interesting refuge, especially as the watery racket tends to drown out the rest of the urban clamor, partially masking both the drab appearance and grinding drone of I-5.

Rainier Tower and around

South from the parks and Benaroya Hall, the main attractions are aimed at architecture buffs with a taste for the unusual. Few skyscrapers are indeed quirkier than **Rainier Tower**, at Fifth and University, a 1979 office block famed for its narrowly tapering base, which gives the structure an uneasy, top-heavy appearance. Occupying only 25 percent of its footprint at the base, the tower is called "the wine glass" by locals, and was designed to cash in on the gravity-defying look popularized by New York's Citicorp Center in the mid-1970s.

In the shadow of the Rainier Tower, **Rainier Square** is a rather standard-issue shopping center that features the Seattle Architectural Foundation's appealing **Rainier Square Gallery**, 1333 Fifth Ave, level 3 (Mon–Fri 8am–5pm, also May–Oct Sat 9am–1pm; free; ☎206/667-9184, ⌨www.seattlearchitecture.org), which hosts the ongoing exhibit "Blueprints: 100 Years of Seattle Architecture." Employing detailed text and numerous vintage city photos, it's a fairly exhaustive display that also includes models, artworks, sketches, and, of course, blueprints from Seattle's urban-design history. Architecture enthusiasts may also enjoy the foundation's periodic lunchtime salons, relating to topics of current concern among local architects, or embark on any of nineteen **walking tours** that are offered throughout the year (see p.36). Within a few blocks of Rainier Square is an interesting pocket of antique piles highlighted by the **Cobb Building**, off University Street at Fourth Avenue, a 1910 terracotta curiosity decorated with "Indian head" reliefs, supposedly representing the faraway Iroquois tribe. Across University Street, the **Seattle Tower** is one of the finest of the city's early-modern structures, its facade decorated with 33 different shades of brick, which progressively lighten in tone from the building's dark, wide base to its pale Art Deco crown. Also appealing are the floors in the building's lobby and on various other levels that feature marble quarried from three European countries and five American states.

Just around the corner, at 1201 Third Ave, the **Washington Mutual Tower** is a landmark of the postmodern style, a 1988 skyscraper presenting an array of glittering, convex glass paneling and gradual setbacks (as in the Zigzag Moderne of the 1920s), rising up to a striped triangular roof – an odd effect that has led some locals to dub the building "the spark plug."

Northeast of Rainier Square, conspicuous consumerism is the sole attraction of the **Meridian** complex, Sixth Avenue and Pike Street, a colossal retail enterprise that houses familiar chain stores, but is best known as the site of the 1999 **anti-WTO demonstrations**, when it was besieged by a sizable mob of anti-corporate protestors.

The New Central Library to the Bank of America Tower

Once you venture **further south** of the Financial District's main cache of buildings and malls, you come to the highlight of Seattle's crop of modern buildings: the **New Central Library**, 1000 Fourth Ave (Mon–Wed 10am–8pm, Thurs–Sat 10am–6pm, Sun 1–5pm; ⌨www.spl.org), a colossal Rem Koolhaas creation that resembles few other libraries in America. With a facade composed of brilliantly reflective glass panels, unexpected angles, and cantilevered stories looming high above, the library will amaze at street level alone, long before you enter. Inside, the complex is equally astounding, especially on the **concourse level**, which resembles a huge greenhouse for books, with a pitched ceiling, windows on a massive triangular grid, and sunlight cutting through to create arch shadows among the stacks. From here an escalator can take you up to the **mezzanine**, where the computer terminals are located and the interior views are especially striking. Unfortunately, the upper levels, collectively known as the **Spiral**, are less inspired, being much harder to navigate with their myriad ramps,

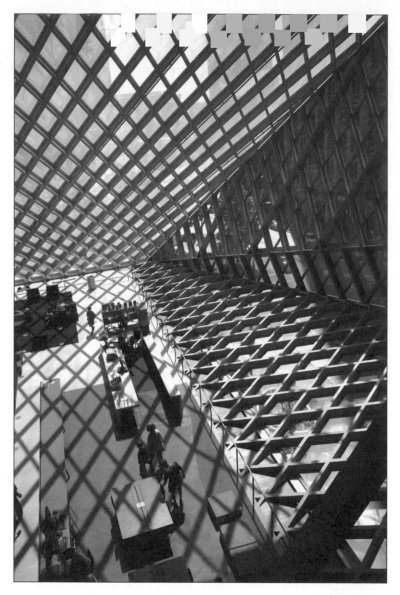

△ New Central Library

escalators, and cramped geometry. Before you go, though, make sure to walk through the bizarre corridor where the **conference rooms** are located, north of the concourse: this eerie, blood-red tunnel more closely resembles something out of *The Shining* than it does a public library. (General library tours Mon–Sat 10am & 3pm, Sun 2pm; architectural tours Mon & Wed 5.30pm, Fri 12.30pm,

Sat 11.30am & 1.30pm, Sun 1.30pm; first-come, first served; information at ☎206/733-9609.)

It's hard to get the library out of your mind as you venture toward Seattle's highest, but much less inspired, building, the Bank of America Tower. Before you reach the Tower, though, along Fourth Avenue you'll find the fancy **Rainier Club**, at no. 820 (⊚www.therainierclub.com), a snooty spot built in 1904 where only Seattle's "best people" were admitted. Not surprisingly, the building's meticulous brickwork can only be admired from the outside, as the unmarked structure – easily mistaken for a swank hotel or apartment complex – is still a private enclave, with a select membership that, until recently, was strictly an (old) boys' club.

One block south of the Rainier Club, the darkly looming **Bank of America Tower**, nicknamed "the BOAT," stands out with three concave walls that give the structure an oddly curving silhouette. Nearly a thousand feet high, it's the tallest building west of the Mississippi River by number of stories (76), though not the tallest overall (that honor goes to LA's Library Tower). Inside, it's a rather ordinary corporate affair, but you can still get a good panoramic view of the surrounding area on the 73rd-floor **observation deck** (Mon–Fri 8.30am–4.30pm; $5, kids $3).

2

Pioneer Square and the International District

S outh of Downtown Seattle, **Pioneer Square** and the **International District** occupy a section of the city that, to newcomers at least, might be best known for its sports facilities: **Safeco Field** and **Qwest Field**, where the city's baseball and football teams play. Along with their good food and nightlife, Pioneer Square and the "ID" offer some of the richest social and cultural history in the Pacific Northwest.

The entire zone, which begins a few blocks south of the Bank of America Tower, has been, at various times, home to Seattle's **underclass**: from **Jackson Street** for African-Americans, to **King Street** for Chinese immigrants, to **Pioneer Square** for white prospectors bankrupted by the Gold Rush, the streets and parks of the area are thick with the history and lore of tough times faced by a local working class of all races and nationalities. Even today, long after such memories have faded for many, the influx of **new immigrants** from Korea, Vietnam, and elsewhere in Asia has ensured that the historic character of the area will be preserved for coming decades.

Pioneer Square

Located just east of the city's southern waterfront (which is more accessible here than Downtown), **Pioneer Square** is a once-dilapidated nineteenth-century district that's been cleaned up and somewhat gentrified, and thus it gets its share of tourists. However, unlike the sanitized historical zones of nearby cities (such as Gastown in Vancouver, BC), Pioneer Square hasn't lost all its old-time grime and squalor – note the assortment of panhandlers and drug addicts in spots – making it a more "real" experience than the usual array of chain retailers lurking behind Victorian storefronts and lace curtains found elsewhere.

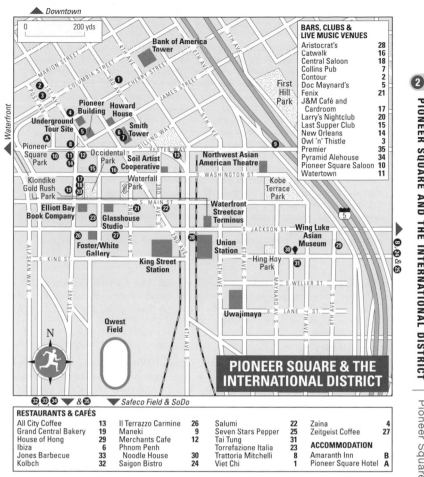

▲ *Downtown*

0   200 yds

PIONEER SQUARE & THE INTERNATIONAL DISTRICT

Bank of America Tower
First Hill Park
Pioneer Building
Howard House
Underground Tour Site
Smith Tower
Pioneer Square Park
Occidental Park
Soil Artist Cooperative
Northwest Asian American Theatre
Klondike Gold Rush Park
Waterfall Park
Kobe Terrace Park
Elliott Bay Book Company
Glasshouse Studio
Waterfront Streetcar Terminus
Wing Luke Asian Museum
Foster/White Gallery
Union Station
Hing Hay Park
King Street Station
Uwajimaya
Qwest Field

N

▼ Safeco Field & SoDo

Waterfront

BARS, CLUBS & LIVE MUSIC VENUES

Aristocrat's	28
Catwalk	16
Central Saloon	18
Collins Pub	7
Contour	2
Doc Maynard's	5
Fenix	21
J&M Café and Cardroom	17
Larry's Nightclub	20
Last Supper Club	15
New Orleans	14
Owl 'n' Thistle	3
Premier	35
Pyramid Alehouse	34
Pioneer Square Saloon	10
Watertown	11

RESTAURANTS & CAFÉS

All City Coffee	13	Il Terrazzo Carmine	26	Salumi	22	Zaina	4
Grand Central Bakery	19	Maneki	9	Seven Stars Pepper	25	Zeitgeist Coffee	27
House of Hong	29	Merchants Cafe	12	Tai Tung	31	**ACCOMMODATION**	
Ibiza	6	Phnom Penh Noodle House	30	Torrefazione Italia	23	Amaranth Inn	B
Jones Barbecue	33	Saigon Bistro	24	Trattoria Mitchelli	8	Pioneer Square Hotel	A
Kolbch	32			Viet Chi	1		

There are plenty of fine **restaurants**, **bars** and **galleries** here, as well as many excellent examples of early-modern architecture. Typically faced with elegant brick, terracotta, and stone, these remodeled offices and workshops from the 1880s and 90s now hold all manner of smart **boutiques**, **bars**, and **bookstores**. **Live music** is also a big draw, with blues, rock, and jazz bands on the bill at a handful of top-notch clubs. Meanwhile, the frenetic taverns draw the sports crowds from nearby Safeco Field, making for a lively mix of revelers that adds an element of debauchery to the historic surroundings. (See "Bars," p.173, and "Clubs and live music," p.180, for entertainment options.)

Once a month, highbrow culture and hedonism find a place at Pioneer Square: the **Gallery Walk** (first Thurs of month 6–8pm; free) showcases nearly forty local art dealers holding simultaneous openings, while **Art in the Park** (3–9pm; free) features a broad range of visual and performance-art pieces in Occidental Park. Both events occur on "**First Thursday**," when the area's ongoing gentrification is most openly on display, with well-heeled yuppies and

Skid Road

There's no certain answer as to whether the term "Skid Row" originated with the Seattle street once known as **Skid Road**. When Henry Yesler built his steam-powered lumber mill in Pioneer Square in the 1850s, this was the route upon which cattle dragged timber down to the mill from the forest above town, the logs literally "skidding" down the road. Later renamed Mill Street, then Yesler Way (its current moniker), the road marked the division of property between feuding town-founders **Arthur Denny** and **David "Doc" Maynard**, resulting in streets that still twist around Yesler Way like mismatched jigsaw pieces.

When **Klondike Gold Rush** fever hit in the 1890s, roustabouts invaded Pioneer Square in force, turning it into a thriving scene for gambling, drinking, and prostitution. Gold mania didn't last long, though, and after it ended, many luckless fortune-hunters remained, even as the focus of Seattle's commercial activity moved northward. Pioneer Square was left to decay, populated only by the destitute and unemployed. Although the original Skid Road was long gone, the term "Skid Road" now referred to the area in general (as in "men on the skids"), and, in theory, through the example of Seattle and other cities with a similarly rough area of their own, "Skid Row" became common parlance for any such down-and-out area in the US.

middle-class bohemians rubbing shoulders with the square's still-formidable number of homeless people. Even with the flood of new money in recent decades, the hard-knocks environment that may have given rise to the term "Skid Row" is still evident (see box).

Some history

Upon Seattle's first white settlement in the mid-1800s, the twenty or so square blocks of what would become Pioneer Square were no more than a tidal mud flat below steep, tree-laden cliffs. Despite this, the area was much more hospitable than the initial site favored by settlers, Alki Beach (see p.137), and by 1890, Seattle's population – most of whom lived around the area – had increased to more than 40,000, many of them residing near what is now Yesler Way and triangular Pioneer Place Park.

Commemorated by a small plaque on the post office at the corner of First and Madison, the **Great Seattle Fire of 1889** (see box on p.67) destroyed much of Pioneer Square's original wooden buildings. But within five years, sturdier brick structures, many designed by noted local architect Elmer Fisher, had been erected to take their place in a neo-Romanesque style – unusual for the West Coast, since these monumental forms were most identified with academic and religious architecture in New England. However stalwart they looked, the buildings' survival was hardly assured, as the neighborhood was in decline through much of the twentieth century, leading to an urban renewal plan in the late 1960s to raze the district and create more parking for Downtown. The grim, gray parking structure (disparaged by locals as "the Sinking Ship") opposite the Pioneer Square Building at James and Yesler – a site formerly occupied by the elegant *Hotel Seattle* – is just a hint of the design horror that might have been visited upon the area.

Thanks to the efforts of concerned citizens like **Victor Steinbrueck** (better known for saving Pike Place Market), Pioneer Square became a **historic preservation district** in 1970, with many of its sights granted landmark status – though it's really only since the 1980s that the area has begun to thrive, with the rise of a vibrant nightlife and "poetry slam" scene and quality art galleries and related events. This renaissance is most visible along First Avenue between Yesler and Jackson, which boasts quaint street lamps and a tree-lined median, reminiscent of the old townsite if you can look past the presence of the tour buses and club-hoppers. Ironically, amid all the classic buildings once slated for demolition – previously labeled as "outmoded" and "irrelevant" by modern architects – is the 1904 **Heritage Building**, at 111 S Jackson St, home to NBBJ, the second largest architectural firm in the US (though it's due to move in 2006), and creator of such high-modern structures as the Pacific Science Center and 505 Union Station.

Smith Tower and around

The tallest of the area's early-modern buildings is the gleaming-white, 42-story **Smith Tower**, 506 Second Ave at Yesler Way. With its terracotta trim and pyramidal peak, it was the tallest building west of the Mississippi when it opened on Independence Day, 1914, displacing the elegant, 14-story Alaska Building, Second Avenue at Cherry Street. The 462-foot Smith Tower has since been superseded, height-wise, by the Bank of America Tower and plenty of other, less appealing West Coast skyscrapers.

Built by corporate magnate Lyman Smith – best known for making typewriters (Smith-Corona) as well as guns (Smith & Wesson) – the building has a 35th-floor **observation deck** (Nov–April Fri–Sun 11am–4pm, May–Oct daily 10am–8pm; $6; ⊛www.smithtower.com) and plenty of modern, renovated office space. Make sure to step inside to look at the carved Indian heads in the elegant lobby and take a ride on one of the eight old-fashioned brass elevators, still manually operated after ninety years. The King County municipal art organization, **4Culture**, has its headquarters here, but its newly relocated public **gallery** – where you're apt to see anything from the latest abstract paintings to oddball performance works – is now open a block east of the tower, at 101 Prefontaine Place S (Mon–Fri 8.30am–4.30pm; free; ☎206/296-7580, ⊛www.4culture.org), near Third Ave and Yesler Way. Also, a block north of Smith Tower, the **Howard House**, 604 Second Ave (Tues–Sat 10.30am–5pm; free; ☎206/256-6399, ⊛www.howardhouse.net), one of Seattle's best-regarded alternative galleries, combines the usual media like painting and photography with sculptural work in ceramics, glass, and metal, all of it with a strong avant-garde or conceptual bent.

Pioneer Square Park

One long, triangular block west of Smith Tower, the smaller triangle of **Pioneer Square Park**, between James Street and First Avenue, marks the place where Henry Yesler's sawmill first processed logs in the 1850s. Decades later, the site was to come under the shadow of the adjacent **Pioneer Building**, a massive pile of stone cladding, rocky columns, and rough-hewn arches and towers, highlighted inside by an elegant atrium and vintage gated elevators. Designed by Elmer Fisher, this grand 1892 structure owes much to the influence of H. H. Richardson, whose East Coast interpretation of the Romanesque had a surprising influence as far away as Seattle. With Fisher having designed many of the park's surrounding structures, the strong air of Richardsonian Romanesque is palpable, making for a rigid, forbidding look intended to resemble a medieval church or fortress.

Down in the Pioneer Building's basement, the **Pioneer Square Antique Mall**, 602 First Ave (Mon–Sat 10.30am–5.30pm, Sun noon–5pm; free;

△ Tlingit totem pole

@www.pioneersquareantiquemall.com), occupies what was once a street-level business. It now features all sorts of old-fashioned gadgets, equipment, and furnishings, much of it dating from the same era when the street was buried under ten feet of earthen fill (and looking like it, too). Outside the building, on the south edge of the park, the glass and iron **pergola** has been a visual landmark of the neighborhood for many years. Here, businessmen and transients hid from the rain, architects and designers admired its elegant form and detail, and history buffs imagined the grand marble bathrooms that once were accessible below-ground. A disastrous encounter with a tractor-trailer truck in early 2001 nearly destroyed the pergola, but it's since been reconstructed and re-installed, with its original 1909 fixtures.

Nearby stands a modest bust of the town's namesake, **Chief Sealth** (also honored at Tilikum Place in a full-body statue; see p.79), while in the middle of the park towers the **Tlingit totem pole**. The monument that stands today is a replacement for an earlier totem pole, which was acquired in 1899 after local members of the Chamber of Commerce broke into an Alaskan native village and stole it without apology or recompense; the men were fined $500 for their actions, but the city was allowed to keep its booty. In 1938, an arsonist burned the original pole, and the city commissioned the Tlingits to carve a replacement, which their native artists did – after receiving $10,000, which paid for both the first, stolen pole and the replica. From the top, the figures on the pole relate to legends about a raven, a frog, a mink, another raven, a killer whale, and, at the base, the King of All Birds, with a curved beak and downward-pointing, multicolored wings.

The Underground Tour

Promising "Dirt!…Corruption!…Sewers!…Scandal!" Bill Speidel's **Underground Tour** (hours vary by month, usually leaving daily on the hour 11am–4pm, sometimes until 6pm; $11, kids $5; ☎206/682-4646, @www .undergroundtour.com) is one of the familiar stops on any visitor's itinerary,

The Great Seattle Fire

The **Great Seattle Fire** of 1889, which caused more than $15 million worth of damage and devastated Downtown, was in many ways an unexpected blessing for Seattle. After the fire, the city was forced to rebuild with a safer infrastructure, which helped to modernize its business district and gave rise to many of the buildings that lend Pioneer Square its historic character today.

The fire occurred on June 6, 1889, when one John Back was melting glue on a stove in a basement carpentry shop. The glue pot overheated, starting a blaze that quickly spread to the streets, igniting about fifty tons of ammunition in nearby hardware stores. As more than ninety percent of the buildings in the central business district were wooden – with both streets and buildings on stilts to keep them out of the mud – much of Seattle was wiped out overnight, though no lives were lost,.

When Mayor Robert Moran addressed several hundred businessmen the next day, citizen Jacob Furth presciently remarked, "The time is not distant when we shall look upon the fire as an actual benefit. I say we shall have a finer city than before … in eighteen months." Indeed, while businesses operated from makeshift tents, the wooden structures were replaced by brick ones, streets were straightened and widened to make them more conducive to commerce, and Seattle gained 17,000 residents over the next year alone. When Pioneer Square's streets were elevated a full story to construct a new sewer system – a process that took about thirty years to complete – the city also gained an array of subterranean passages, now seen in Bill Speidel's Seattle Underground Tour. Storefronts at the original level continued to do business for years, with customers actually descending by ladder to conduct transactions.

though whether it merits as much attention as it gets is open to question. It departs from the east side of Pioneer Square Park at *Doc Maynard's* pub, 610 First Ave, for a ninety-minute look at the subterranean history of the area. After rising tides repeatedly backed up sewage drains and caused flooding, street levels were elevated by an entire story in the 1890s, and the original businesses soon became underground in more than one sense of the word. Operating amid narrow passageways, creaky ladders, and dark stairways, the legitimate merchants continued to hawk their wares until the subsurface zone was officially closed in 1907, even as shady operations like speakeasies, burlesque houses, and brothels were still accessible via subterranean corridors well into the twentieth century.

The value of the Underground Tour largely depends on whether you have any interest in seeing musty, interconnected chambers in an advanced state of decay, or hearing legends of the vices and corruption of old-time Seattle. The visual highlights are mainly dusty old storefronts and semi-preserved interiors featuring assorted antiques and junk. The tour guides, many of them self-styled comedians, maintain a constant, jokey patter while herding visitors around rotting walls and pipes, remnants of saloons and bordellos, and the odd scurrying rat. The tour only covers a few sections of three blocks reopened to the public in the 1960s, a small fraction of the 33 blocks that constitute the entire underground; for a free look at some of the rest, check out the basement galleries and antique stores in the underground arcades along First Avenue.

Klondike Gold Rush National Historical Park

A few blocks south of *Doc Maynard's*, Pioneer Square's other top tourist draw can be found at **Klondike Gold Rush National Historical Park**, 117 Main St (daily 9am–5pm; free; ☎206/553-7220, ⓦwww.nps.gov/klse), where a small museum houses a few exhibits on the 1897 stampede to find gold in the Klondike of northwestern Canada. Although far from Seattle itself, the goldfields had a considerable impact on the city's development, as thousands of eager prospectors passed through town on their way up north. The crush of gold-seekers – including the mayor, who resigned to organize an abortive mining expedition – swelled so rapidly that each settler bound for the Yukon was required by the police to bring a year's supply of food, tools, and clothing to sustain himself, which profited local vendors enormously. As a result, the economic depression that had begun with the national Panic of 1893 was ended, and Seattle was transformed from a small lumber and sawmill town into a manufacturing and shipping powerhouse.

As for the **museum** itself, the equipment, photos, and memorabilia vividly depict the hard life of the mining migrants, many of whom had been lured into expeditions by fabulous tales of easy fortunes made in the Yukon, and very few of whom struck it rich. The museum also runs a few short documentary films on request, the best overview being the half-hour *Days of Adventure, Dreams of Gold*. Between mid-June and the first week of September, the park rangers also give free daily, one-hour tours of Pioneer Square at 10am, as well as periodic gold-panning demonstrations.

Occidental Park and around

Although it's not quite as appealing as Pioneer Square Park, **Occidental Park** is the center of Pioneer Square art activities on the First Thursday of the month (see p.63), and it does have a handful of sights if you find yourself in the area. This tree-lined, cobblestone plaza is ringed by shops and cafés (and inhabited by homeless people), and prominently displays four of native artist Duane Pasco's **totem poles**, carved with various figures from regional Native American legends. The centerpieces are the **Tsonoqua**, a pair of squatting wooden giants with darkly looming bodies reaching out to each other, their dignified forms somewhat undercut by the pigeon droppings allowed to collect on their heads. The park's other striking icons include the four masked, bronze figures of the **Seattle Fallen Firefighters Memorial**, honoring the 31 local firemen who have lost their lives in the line of duty since 1889, the memorial's strewn granite slabs symbolizing the job's difficult conditions (such as chaos and collapsed buildings). On the west, Occidental Park is linked with the 1889 **Grand Central Arcade**, 214 First Ave S, a glassy, two-level route (part of it subterranean) that's a prime location for restaurants and boutiques, originally built as part of an opera house and hotel.

Waterfall Park and nearby galleries

A block east of Occidental park, **Waterfall Park** includes a 22-foot cascade built in 1977 with a wall of rough-hewn boulders and surrounding foliage, and commemorates the delivery company UPS, which began operation here in the early twentieth century. It's worth a rest stop as you make your way to more aesthetic pursuits. South of Occidental Park, pedestrianized **Occidental Avenue** holds the greatest concentration of Seattle's **galleries**, the most noteworthy of which is Foster/White, 123 S Jackson St (Tues–Sat 10am–6pm; ⊛fosterwhite.com), which showcases contemporary artists from the Pacific Northwest working in a variety of media, among them glass-blowing heavyweight Dale Chihuly. Nearby at the Glasshouse Studio, 311 Occidental Ave S (Mon–Sat 10am–5pm, Sun 11am–4pm; ⊛www.glasshouse-studio.com), you can watch less-heralded, but no less appealing, artists busy with their own creations.

One long block east of Waterfall Park, those with a taste for edgy, postmodern pursuits can drop in on the **SOIL Artist Cooperative**, 112 Third Ave S (Thurs–Sun noon–5pm; free; ☎206/264-8061, ⓦwww.soilart.org), which is well-regarded for its compelling, sometimes shocking, displays of contemporary artworks, among them elegant porcelain sculptures of snub-nosed revolvers and a "Last Supper" featuring Ronald McDonald. A recent "performance" piece, *They Will Be The Judge Of That*, featured an ink drawing and two live gerbils, who, according to the museum, were "at liberty to chew and shred their way through the artwork."

Elliott Bay Book Company

A block southwest of Occidental Park, the former *Globe Hotel*, an 1890 Romanesque pile that has survived an array of fires, earthquakes, and explosions, houses **Elliott Bay Book Company**, 101 S Main St (Mon–Sat 9.30am–10pm, Sun 11am–7pm; ⓦwww.elliottbaybook.com), one of the city's literary highpoints and an essential stop if you're in the area. With a selection of 150,000 volumes on three levels, the store is great for browsing, meeting other book-minded friends, or listening to a nightly reading downstairs in the underground level. The free *Discovering Pioneer Square Map & Guide*, which covers basic highlights of the neighborhood's history and architecture, can be picked up at the bookstore's main entrance.

The International District

Like many neighborhoods named by municipal bureaucracies, the so-called **International District** is a charmless moniker for what was once called **Chinatown**. In truth, that name is outmoded these days, since the area hosts a broad array of thriving Asian communities. Indeed, this diverse urban area just southeast of Pioneer Square has in recent years welcomed immigrants from all over Southeast Asia, along with more longstanding generations of blacks and Asian-Americans originally hailing from Japan and China. The number of these groups has fluctuated wildly in the last 120 years, depending on the relative tolerance, hostility, or downright racism shown by white Seattle residents to their presence.

If you're interested in exploring the cultural highlights and not the usual tourist draws, the district's dozen or so blocks – bordered by Second and 12th avenues (east–west) and Washington and Weller streets (north–south) – can be covered on foot in a few hours. Dominated by eateries, groceries, and other small businesses catering to the community, the most active local scene is found between Fifth and Eighth avenues on Jackson and King streets. There's not much in the way of museums, architecture, or other such sights, but the agreeable number of markets, parks, and restaurants more than compensates. One great place to sample the local flavor is at the huge pan-Asian supermarket/ general store **Uwajimaya**, 600 Fifth Ave S (daily 9am–10pm, Sun closes 9pm; ☎1-800/889-1928, ⓦwww.uwajimaya.com), now part of a growing Pacific Northwest chain, which also serves as a community center. The place offers not only a giant array of foodstuffs from its excellent Food Court, from spicy seasonings to the prized geoduck ("gooey-duck") clam, but also a wide range of handcrafted Asian gifts such as scented candles and origami paper. You can even take sushi-making classes.

Union and King Street stations

On the west side of the International District, and originally built by a Union Pacific subsidiary in 1911, **Union Station**, Fourth Ave at Jackson St (Mon–Sat 9am–5pm; free; closed during special events), is a sparkling complex that has maintained the allure of old-fashioned rail travel while changing step for a new era. Its splendid centrepiece, the **Great Hall**, is a barrel-vaulted Beaux Arts jewel whose ceiling rises to eighty feet, and whose walls feature ornate glass windows and *trompe l'oeil* detailing that gives the impression of classical stone construction. Today, it's a public/private complex that features a mix of old and new buildings that serve widely different purposes. Much of the space is currently being used by the online retailer Amazon.com, as well as by Sound Transit, a government agency responsible for handling the region's transportation problems – quite a difference from the old days of the 1980s, when Union Station was rented out as a concert venue that hosted fiery shows by Nirvana and other bands.

While the architecture of the main part of Union Station is Neoclassical, other buildings on the site are strikingly modern; this is particularly true of **505 Union Station**, the headquarters of Microsoft co-founder Paul Allen's Vulcan corporation. An eye-popping curiosity, the front of the building features a heavily slanted glass curtain wall that lunges out toward traffic, as a sweeping pane of green glass envelopes the side of the structure like a giant, transparent tongue.

Around the turn of the twentieth century, Union Station competed with **King Street Station**, the Northern Pacific Railroad's 1906 entry into the transit scene, a block west of Union Station at 303 S Jackson St. Despite its iconic clock tower (supposedly modeled after that of St Mark's in Venice), the station is – unlike its neighbor – dreary and unrestored and not much to look at. Nonetheless, you'll get a good view of it if you arrive by train, either via Amtrak (see p.31) or Sounder commuter rail from Tacoma (see p.237).

For a different kind of transportation experience, head back two blocks east of King Street Station to access the southern terminus of the **waterfront streetcar**, a line more suited for casual sightseeing.

Wing Luke Asian Museum

Four blocks east of King Street Station is the district's main cultural institution, **Wing Luke Asian Museum**, 407 Seventh Ave S (Tues–Fri 11am–4.30pm, Sat–Sun noon–4pm; $4, $2 kids; ☎206/623-5124, ⓦwww.wingluke.org), named for the first Asian-American elected official in the Northwest. Portraying two hundred years of Asian and Pacific Island immigration, from the first Hawaiian settlers to more recent newcomers from Southeast Asia, its several small rooms are easily covered within an hour or two. The museum holds old photographs, ceremonial garments, oral and written histories of individual immigrants, and various intriguing artifacts, the most eye-catching of which are the hand-painted kites that hang from the rafters. Many of the other displays trace the changing demographics of Seattle, as well as the sometimes brutal discrimination faced by minorities (see box, opposite). For example, a walk-through replica simulates the assembly center of "**Camp Harmony**" in Puyallup, Washington, where thousands of American-born Japanese from Seattle were incarcerated during World War II.

The museum has **special exhibits** on Asian-American parades, celebrations, and other enjoyable fare. Those with an especially strong interest in Japanese-American history should check out the museum's **Densho Project**

The rise and fall (and rise again) of an ethnic enclave

In the late nineteenth century, thousands of **Chinese immigrants**, many of whom had worked building the railroads of the American West, came to Seattle to earn a living in the city's canneries and mills. However, economic depression fueled anti-Chinese **riots** in the Northwest in the 1880s; in one case, many Asian immigrants were expelled from nearby Tacoma and sent down to Portland. In Seattle a few months later, an anti-Chinese "committee" forcibly delivered Chinese residents and their possessions to a dock, where a steamer was about to depart for San Francisco. The ship refused to accept them as passengers unless their fares were paid, and a surrounding mob quickly coughed up the dough. The Chinese were belatedly offered governmental protection from armed guards, but quite a few chose to leave town anyway. This legacy of racism and xenophobia was hardly unique to the area, and found an unfortunate echo throughout many Western American cities in the late nineteenth-century.

From the nineteenth to the mid-twentieth century, the number of Chinese and **Japanese immigrants** in the district see-sawed, often depending on which group bore the brunt of local hostility at any particular time. When the Chinese were at their most persecuted (at one point their population dwindling to a few dozen), many Japanese newcomers – even though they only constituted a small minority of residents – picked up the slack and created a highly visible, active presence in the city's cultural and economic affairs.

Any delusion of social acceptance was shattered, though, once World War II began, when the local Japanese – many of whom were American citizens – were shipped off to **internment camps**. Not only did this cause incalculable damage to the Asian-American community, it also negatively affected the Seattle economy, as local Japanese businesses were shuttered or run badly by others in their owners' absence. At the same time, though, Chinese immigration had rebounded, bringing new life to the district.

After World War II ended, the situation settled down again, with more new immigrants moving to the area. In turn, the 1960s heralded the beginning of visible, active **ethnic identity movements**, the members of which began to take political and social action to challenge the abuses of the present and try to rectify those of the past. Lately, however, this has occurred against the background of the most recent change to the district: namely, the ongoing arrival of new waves of immigrants from Asia – especially Vietnam, Laos, Korea, and the Philippines – who in fleeing the unstable economic conditions of the old countries have done much to preserve the vitality of Seattle.

Archive, in which photos and hours of taped interviews are presented on interactive computer terminals, documenting Japanese-American life over the last hundred years.

Hing Hay and Kobe Terrace parks

With its ornate pagoda and large, somewhat faded dragon mural, **Hing Hay Park**, across from the museum, at the corner of King and Maynard streets, is the nominal center of the International District. Although it's pleasant enough, you're better off heading three blocks north, taking a steep hike up to the top of Washington Street to enter the far greener **Kobe Terrace Park**, where a 200-year-old, 8000-pound, four-legged stone lantern graces the entrance. Here, narrow paths wind down through gardens on the park slope, cherry trees add to the splendor, and the sweeping views can be inspiring when it's not raining,

Jazz on Jackson Street

You'd never suspect it now, but the strip of **Jackson Street** that runs through the International District was, during the Swing era of the 1930s and 1940s, a center of vice as well as a hotbed for after-hours **jazz clubs**. Back then, Seattle's musicians' union was segregated, and this was the place for its black musicians to find work, at such colorful spots as Basin Street, Black Elk's, and the Bucket of Blood. Teenagers Quincy Jones (later to produce Frank Sinatra and Michael Jackson, among many others) and Ray Charles (who moved to Seattle briefly after growing up in the South) both came here in the late 1940s, although neither truly got on the path to stardom until they left town shortly afterwards.

In those days, the hepcat scene was at its most frenetic around Twelfth and Jackson, where swinging clubs and low-rent dives played host to some of the bounciest sounds in the Pacific Northwest, attracting not only locals but also more than a few white music-lovers from outside the neighborhood. By the 1960s, though, with the end of official segregation and "restrictive covenants" that kept blacks from buying property where whites lived, the old Jackson strip was on its way out, a fun but faded relic of another era. Today, jazz of any sort is long gone from the area, and few relics remain, except at the intersection of Twelfth Ave, where an official sign commemorates the Jackson jazz scene – which the city finally got around to recognizing in October 2005.

with Puget Sound spreading out to the west and the upper stories of the Bank of America Tower just visible above the treeline.

Contiguous with Kobe Terrace Park, **Danny Woo Community Gardens** is a pleasant enough spot where residents are allowed plots to grow their own vegetables. Although fairly lacking in visual excitement or stunning horticulture, the garden lanes are tidy, the elderly gardeners friendly, and the entire scene a good image of the neighborhood's civic commitment and industrious spirit. If you've had your fill of greenery, take a visit to **Nippon Kan Theatre**, also known as the **Northwest Asian American Theatre**, nearby at 628 S Washington St (☎206/340-1445, ⊛www.nwaaff.org), a historic four-hundred-seat venue built in 1909 that plays host to a wide variety of cultural events, but is especially worthwhile for its film offerings, notably the Northwest Asian American Film Festival in January.

Jackson Street

In recent years, Jackson Street has become the axis of a new community of **Vietnamese immigrants**, many of whom either fled the wars with the US and China during the 1970s or the oppressive Communist government that still rules Vietnam. At the corner of Twelfth and Jackson, you'll see busy residents buying supplies at corner groceries, eating spicy, homestyle soups at area diners, or shopping at mini-malls. Though the area may be called **Little Saigon**, it's unquestionably associated with the modern lifestyle of Greater Seattle, and is mainly worth a visit for its excellent, authentic Southeast Asian cuisine at cheap prices.

The Stadium District and SoDo

At the southern edge of the International District lies the **Stadium District**, a rather bland zone of sports bars and chain diners in the shadow of the town's sports complexes. Perhaps the most beloved is **Safeco Field**, First Ave at Atlantic St, the **Seattle Mariners**' baseball stadium (tickets at ☎206/346-4001, ⊛seattle .mariners.mlb.com), which hosted its first game in July 1999 after a $517 million construction project. The resulting ballpark is a much better place to watch baseball than was the now-demolished Kingdome: its retractable roof allows most games to be played in outdoor weather, though it can always be closed if it rains. Baseball aficionados may find it enjoyable to take an hour-long **tour** (April–Oct usually daily 10.30am & 12.30pm; Nov–March Tues–Sat 12.30 & 2.30pm; $7, kids $5), which admits visitors into some otherwise off-limits areas, including the dugouts, the clubhouse, and the press box. For everything you could ever want to know about this half-billion-dollar colossus, check out the assorted photos and minutiae at ⊛seattlepi.nwsource.com/safeco.

Another prominent sports venue, **Qwest Field** (tickets at ☎1-888/NFL-HAWK, ⊛www.seahawks.com), formerly known as **Seahawks Stadium**, is just north of Safeco Field, at 800 Occidental Ave S, and hosts Seattle's football franchise. Paul Allen made sure this $425 million, 67,000-seat facility, with a profile that resembles gaping steel jaws, was funded mostly through public expenditure by paying the cost of a voter referendum himself, and outspending his opponents in the campaign by nearly $5 million – a controversial tactic that left many taxpayers livid. For an up-close, behind-the-scenes look at this stadium, 90-minute **tours** are available (June–Sept daily: 12.30pm & 2.30pm; Oct–May Thurs–Sat same hours; $7; ☎206/381-7582, ⊛www.qwestfield.com).

SoDo

In the vicinity of and south of the Stadium District lies the area once known, accurately, as the **Duwamish Industrial Zone**. It's since been rechristened as **SoDo**, first standing for "South of the Dome" after the now-extinct Kingdome, and currently meaning "South of Downtown," which pretty much describes everything in the area. Whatever you call it, SoDo is the bleeding edge of gentrification in Seattle, with yuppies and real-estate moguls lustily eyeing the cheap industrial sites for redevelopment into condos, boutiques, and upper-end restaurants. There's been some resistance to this scheme, though, especially with the prospect of even more working-class jobs being eliminated to make way for low-paid service work. The waterfront to the west, centered on the **container port** at Pier 46, is hardly tourist-friendly, but other sites around and south of the stadiums do have their appeal.

Between the sports facilities, the **Qwest Field Events Center** hosts trade and consumer shows and mainstream concerts, and there's also a plethora of burger joints and sports bars here – perhaps most notably **Pyramid Brewing**, 1201 First Ave S, a bar and diner that has the benefit of its own microbrewing facility and produces a mean Apricot Ale – which you can sample on a free public **tour** (Mon–Fri 5.30pm, Sat & Sun 2 & 4pm; free; ☎206/682-3377, ⊛www.pyramidbrew.com). The district, too, has a longstanding community of actual starving (and well-fed) artists, who occupy lofts and occasionally appear for gallery shows. You can get a glimpse of the creativity lurking in these old piles by dropping by the **Bemis Building**, a block from Safeco Field at 55 Atlantic Ave S (information at ☎206/381-8457, ⊛www.ouchmyeye.com), which hosts some thirty artists' studios and puts on regular shows every month or two, as well as participating in the First Thursday Gallery Walk (see p.63), otherwise based out of Pioneer Square.

Finally, if you just can't resist, you can take a gander at the (private) corporate headquarters of the **Starbucks** empire, a mile south at 2401 Utah Ave S, based in a 1915 brick complex with two million square feet of space. The structure is crowned with a graceful clock tower, above which lurk the eyes of the familiar green mermaid in a manner reminiscent of *1984*.

3

Belltown

Situated just north of Pike Place Market, extending a mile north toward Seattle Center, **Belltown** is Seattle's prime faux-bohemian zone. In the 1980s, after several decades of shuttered storefronts and general decay, this became home to many underground galleries and slacker-friendly coffeehouses, as well as cheap diners and vintage-clothes merchants. The neighborhood's success in attracting a creative, if underemployed, class proved to be its undoing, though, as the old edginess has been sapped in the last fifteen years with the arrival of chain stores and high-priced condos – and the masses of generic, latte-sipping neo-yuppies who occupy them. Still, Belltown has its grungy edge in spots (and many down-and-outers remain), and there's a handful of interesting **art galleries** here, along with diverse **live music** venues, quality **bars**, and good, if über-fashionable, **eateries**.

Some history

Belltown is spread across the **Denny Regrade**, created when the steeply sloped Denny Hill was flattened at the turn of the century to make way for "urban progress." An earth-removal project of massive proportions, the regrading took several decades, and resulted in the once-towering district being reduced to flattened avenues and alleys – though a hint of the slope of the old neighborhood can be seen on the north side of Pike Place Market, where streets like Stewart still climb dramatically for a block or two.

As with the physical restructuring of Belltown at the beginning of the twentieth century, the **social alterations** at the end of it have been just as jarring. From decaying inner-city wasteland to the lair of rockers and bohemians to the home of upper-crust poseurs, Belltown's transformation has been remarkable, though not always necessarily for the better.

By the mid-1980s, many of the storefronts in Belltown were shuttered and neglected by both city planners and property developers. This situation changed considerably when the neighborhood became a focus of Seattle's youth music and arts scene in the latter part of the decade, offering local bands places to play and local audiences cheap places to hear them. Perhaps most notably, **Sub Pop**, Nirvana's original record label, was born here. By the 1990s, though, the "Haight-Ashbury" effect set in: shiny high-rise housing sprung up beside funky brick flophouses, upscale restaurants muscled in on low-rent diners, and overpriced boutiques materialized where there'd once been only thrift stores. These days, despite the ongoing presence of the homeless and the odd addict wandering about, whatever else remains of the zone's old-style funkiness and off-kilter mirth are increasingly buried under a slew of colorless commercial developments.

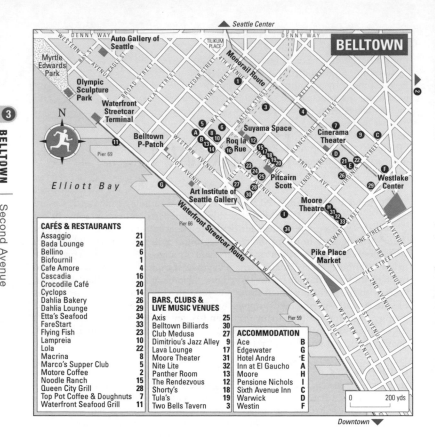

▲ *Seattle Center*

BELLTOWN

Auto Gallery of Seattle — Myrtle Edwards Park — Olympic Sculpture Park — Waterfront Streetcar Terminal — Belltown P-Patch — Pier 69 — *Elliott Bay* — Suyama Space — Cinerama Theater — Roq la Rue — Pitcairn Scott — Westlake Center — Art Institute of Seattle Gallery — Moore Theatre — Pier 66 — Pike Place Market — Pier 59

Downtown ▼

CAFÉS & RESTAURANTS	
Assaggio	21
Bada Lounge	24
Bellino	6
Biofournil	1
Cafe Amore	4
Cascadia	16
Crocodile Café	20
Cyclops	14
Dahlia Bakery	26
Dahlia Lounge	29
Etta's Seafood	34
FareStart	33
Flying Fish	23
Lampreia	10
Lola	22
Macrina	8
Marco's Supper Club	5
Motore Coffee	2
Noodle Ranch	15
Queen City Grill	28
Top Pot Coffee & Doughnuts	7
Waterfront Seafood Grill	11

BARS, CLUBS & LIVE MUSIC VENUES	
Axis	25
Belltown Billiards	30
Club Medusa	27
Dimitriou's Jazz Alley	9
Lava Lounge	17
Moore Theater	31
Nite Lite	32
Panther Room	13
The Rendezvous	12
Shorty's	18
Tula's	19
Two Bells Tavern	3

ACCOMMODATION	
Ace	B
Edgewater	G
Hotel Andra	E
Inn at El Gaucho	A
Moore	H
Pensione Nichols	I
Sixth Avenue Inn	C
Warwick	D
Westin	F

0   200 yds

Second Avenue

Having been dramatically reduced in the last ten years, the hip core of Belltown is now more or less confined to a three-block area of **Second Avenue** between Lenora and Battery streets. Here, the strip's remaining cafés, bars, vintage clothing outlets, record stores, and offbeat galleries cater to those local students and artists who haven't yet moved on to less-gentrified turf in Capitol Hill and Fremont. Nevertheless, there are still worthy establishments boasting compelling entertainment and diverse crowds to be found here: one of the best is the **Crocodile Café**, 2200 Second Ave (☎206/441-5611, ⊛www.thecrocodile.com), the hottest rock joint in Belltown and a solid place to chow down on eggs, waffles, sandwiches, and other diner fare, while you stare at the quirky junk art on display (such as alligator heads, neon signs, and monkey posters); see p.165 and p.182 for full reviews.

The hub of Belltown's **gallery scene** can be found along Second Avenue as well. What's on display around here is sometimes uneven, but is broad enough in scope to reward a visit. **Suyama Space**, at no. 2324 (Mon–Fri 9am–5pm; ☎206/256-0809, ⊛www.suyamapetersondeguchi.com/art), has challenging avant-garde and conceptual installations, much of it bizarre or simply inexplicable, such as computer-operated Victorian coffee tables and small, wood-frame building replicas. Since the space is located in an architectural office, you'll have to buzz the front door to get in for a look.

Much more light-hearted is **Roq La Rue**, at no. 2312 (Thurs & Sat 1–6pm, Fri 1–7pm, or by appointment at ☏206/374-8977; free; ⓦwww.roqlarue.com), presenting a flashy parade of brightly colored, often outlandish works with themes taken from pop culture and mass entertainment, and styles that often involve grotesque caricature or satiric visual puns. If you prefer your art a bit more on the conventional side (if only a bit), try **Pitcairn Scott**, at no. 2207 (Tues–Sat 11am–6pm; ☏206/448-5380, ⓦwww.pitcairnscott.com), which, despite its brooding color studies and mixed-media assemblages, is just about as close to the mainstream as Belltown gets.

A few blocks south, the classic old **Moore Theatre**, no. 1932 (☏206/467-5510, ⓦwww.themoore.com), sits between Downtown and Belltown, and hosted many alternative bands in the grunge era, and still does so, along with everything else: kids' shows, Broadway musicals, and political and cultural lectures. Built in 1907, the theater is Seattle's oldest, and well worth a look for its restored design, loaded with grand classical columns and arches, and an old-fashioned wooden interior with marble touches, that's still redolent of the pre-cinema era when the theater mainly presented vaudeville acts.

Around Second Avenue

The streets in the vicinity of Second Avenue, though less densely populated by commercial ventures, also offer a few interesting spots for exploration. A major accretion of chic eateries (and a few hotels of varying quality), on **First Avenue** between Lenora and Vine, has been underway since the 1990s, making this the most upscale stretch of Belltown. As elsewhere, mixed-media establishments combining art, food, and music remain a trademark: modern sculpture and furniture from the 1950s adorn many of the bars and dining spots, underground rock and techno boom from the clothing stores and galleries, and mild-mannered cafés transform into lively music venues at night. For reviews of good restaurants in and around the area, see p.165; for reviews of some of the best watering holes, see p.175.

Cinerama and Sub Pop Records

Further east, one entertainment venue that shouldn't be missed is Paul Allen's grandly restored **Cinerama**, 2100 Fourth Ave (tickets $10; ☏206/441-3080, ⓦwww.seattlecinerama.com), with state-of-the-art sound and picture quality and a storied history that goes back to the massive, three-projector films of the early 1960s. With both a modern 70mm screen for showing the latest blockbusters and a massive 90-by-30-foot screen with two thousand vertical panels for experiencing classic epics like *How the West Was Won* and *2001: A Space Odyssey*, this is one of only two such moviehouses still in existence anywhere in the world. Whether or not you're a fan of the latest Hollywood product, the theater is well worth a look for its refurbished retro-modern details such as mohair seats and Italian tilework, not to mention its impressively colossal viewing space.

Just as important (to some, even pilgrimage-worthy), **Sub Pop Records**, famous for its promotion of the alt-rock scene with early releases by Nirvana, Mudhoney, and Soundgarden, was born on the edge of Belltown, where it still

3

The Sub Pop story

No Seattle label has had a greater impact upon rock music and popular culture than **Sub Pop Records**, which grew out of a fanzine – *Subterranean Pop* – and record-cassette club begun in the early 1980s by DJ, rock critic, and record-store owner **Bruce Pavitt** that covered the burgeoning Seattle alt-rock scene. By 1986 local musician and club booker **Jonathan Poneman** had joined the Sub Pop team, and they popularized the now-legendary **Sub Pop Singles Club**, a subscriber service that mailed out new rock songs every month to members. The label quickly became recognized for recording and promoting a distinct style of music that fused punk with pop and metal. Characterized by distorted guitars, dirge-like riffs, blackly ironic lyrics and an attitude that was even more sour and cynical than either metal or punk, this type of rock became famously known as **grunge**. Soundgarden, Mudhoney, Screaming Trees, Tad, Green River, Alice in Chains and, of course, **Nirvana** were some of the leaders of the movement.

Though Nirvana left for major label Geffen before *Nevermind* propelled the band to stardom, the buy-out deal gave a small percentage of the seminal album's sales to Sub Pop, allowing the label to remain afloat for the time. While its glory days were effectively over by the early 1990s, a strong back catalog and quality releases by new indie acts such as the White Stripes and Sleater-Kinney (as well as financial backing via part-ownership by Warner Brothers) have kept things moving nicely since then. See "The Rise of Alternative Rock," p.297, for a brief history of the local music scene.

remains, at 2514 Fourth Ave (⊛www.subpop.com). Their tiny retail store, the **Sub Pop Megamart**, was formerly around the corner, but has now moved into digs at Pike Place Market, 1514 Pike Place #14 (daily 10am–6pm, Sun opens noon; ☏206/652-4356), where you can buy records from the label's old and new bands, and pick up irreverent t-shirts and alt-flavored knickknacks.

Elliott Avenue

West of Second Avenue, a few spots along **Elliott Avenue** offer isolated points of interest, though the avenue isn't inherently appealing. One of these spots, the **Art Institute of Seattle**'s small **gallery space** at no. 2323 (open during regular events; info at ☏1-800/275-2471, ⊛www.ais.edu), highlights work in various media, from fashion design and film to sculpture and even culinary artworks, including, but not limited to, pieces by AIS students and faculty.

Down the road at no. 2520 is the **Belltown P-Patch** (☏206/441-7702, ⊛www.speakeasy.org/ppatch), a small community garden dotted with folk-art designs and sculptures, including a solar-powered water fountain and a Gothic-styled entry gate. The three adjacent **cottages** are the last remaining examples of the Denny Regrade neighborhood's architecture as it appeared in the early 1900s, and are the focus of an ongoing renovation to turn them into living quarters for visiting artists.

Northeast of Belltown

On the **northeast** side of Belltown, the area's colorful vibe begins to dissipate, but there are several sites you can visit if you're on your way to the Seattle

Center. Most notably, at the oft-deserted **Tilikum Place** – where Fifth Avenue, Cedar, and Denny intersect – you'll find the forlorn statue of **Chief Sealth**, the Native American leader who befriended the city's white founders and managed to keep his tribe out of the region's Indian Wars in the mid-1850s. The settlers decided to name their new home in the chief's honor, though with a bit of a twist, finding "Seattle" easier to pronounce. Strangely, the copper likeness of

△ Statue of Chief Sealth

this important figure, with his arm raised and gaze firmly in the distance, now presides over water-dribbling bear heads and a bronze plaque of two fish biting a clamshell.

The other noteworthy spots in the vicinity are a trio of interesting galleries. Just west of Tilikum Place, at 3025 First Ave, is the **Auto Gallery of Seattle** (Mon–Sat 10am–7pm; free; ☎206/448-1247, ⊛www.autogalleryseattle.com), which doubles as a showroom for upper-end used cars and an exhibition space for local artists, strong on painterly and photographic realism – with a few of the subjects, naturally, being automobiles. Even more worthwhile, north of Tilikum Place at 407 Dexter Ave N, is the underrated **Wright Exhibition Space** (Thurs & Fri 10am–2pm, or by appointment; free; ☎206/264-8200), which has three rooms of contemporary art on rotating display from the holdings of collectors Virginia and Bagley Wright, a former real estate developer who had a hand in the creation of the Space Needle, including rarely seen works by artists such as Andy Warhol, Julian Schnabel, Jeff Koons, Claes Oldenburg, and Eric Fischl. Art of a more irreverent sort is on view at the **Center on Contemporary Art**, or **CoCA**, across the street at 410 Dexter Ave N (Wed–Sun noon–5pm; $5 suggested donation; ☎206/728-1980, ⊛www.cocaseattle.org); its small space is given over to constantly rotating exhibits of work that's more risqué than what you'll see in the Seattle Art Museum's contemporary galleries. Nam June Paik, Survival Research Laboratories, and Lydia Lunch are some of the artists who received their first major exposure in the Northwest through CoCA's eye-opening exhibits, which still maintain their compelling, aggressive, experimental, and sometimes-polemical character.

Seattle Center and Queen Anne

The irregular polygon of the **Seattle Center** – just across Denny Way, at the northern tip of Belltown – is home to a number of the city's essential sights, none more famous than the Space Needle, the unquestioned symbol of Seattle. This small but tightly packed area – the equivalent of about seventeen square city blocks – is not a neighborhood but a large entertainment/cultural complex that offers a wealth of theaters, museums, and venues for cultural and sporting events.

Spreading out northwest from the Seattle Center is the charming, well-heeled hillside district of **Queen Anne**. Up a steep slope ascended by Queen Anne Way, the neighborhood's main artery, you'll be able to see the entire city from marvelously sweeping vistas, especially at Kerry Park. With the Space Needle in the foreground, this view from Queen Anne makes for an irresistible Emerald City picture-taking opportunity.

Seattle Center

The **Seattle Center** (ⓦwww.seattlecenter.com), along with the **monorail** that leads to it, grew out of the 1962 World's Fair, and, then as now, the two provided many visitors with their first impression and experience of the city. Unlike the early days, though, when the Center was a temporary showpiece for American industrial and commercial products, the 74-acre complex has since been transformed into a busy sports and cultural hub, highlighted by such varied institutions as the **Pacific Science Center**, the **Seattle Children's Theatre**, the **Experience Music Project**, and, of course, the **Space Needle**. In addition to these attractions, there are also venues for opera, dance, and drama, as well as the **Fun Forest** amusement park (April–Oct Mon–Fri 11am–9pm, Sat noon–10pm, Sun noon–8pm; unlimited rides $20; ☏206/728-1585, ⓦwww .funforest.com), featuring mildly amusing, somewhat tacky carnival staples like a Ferris wheel, carousel and bumper cars, plus a sizable video-game arcade in an interior pavilion.

For sports fans, **Key Arena**, on the western edge of the Center, is the home of the city's pro basketball teams, the NBA Supersonics and the WNBA Storm, and a minor-league hockey franchise, the Thunderbirds (see Chapter 18, "Sports and outdoor activities"), and a regular concert venue for major rock and pop acts. The other large facilities, **Memorial Stadium** and **Mural Amphitheatre**, are venues for amateur sporting events and concerts of lesser-known performers. The amphitheatre often features some of the Northwest's largest festivals, notably the **Northwest Folklife Festival** (☎206/684-7300, ⊛www.nwfolklife.org), held around Memorial Day, with hundreds of multicultural theatrical, dance, and musical performances, and **Bumbershoot** (☎206/281-7788, ⊛www.bumbershoot .org), held around Labor Day, featuring thousands of artists and performers working in a wide variety of musical styles and art media.

For easy transportation from Downtown, the **Seattle Monorail** provides a quick link to the Westlake Center (Mon–Fri 7.30am–11pm, Sat & Sun 9am–11pm; one-way fare $3.50, kids $1.50; ⊛www.seattlemonorail.com) and terminates on the north side of the Fun Forest. Just before this, though, it curves around the east side of Center before passing dramatically through the center of the Experience Music Project.

The Space Needle

The most prominent relic of the World's Fair is the **Space Needle** (daily 9am– 11pm, Sat & Sun closes at midnight; ☎206/905-2100, ⊛www.spaceneedle.com), which the city balked at funding back in the 1960s; it's been privately owned and managed ever since. With a shaft rising 605 feet to support the familiar flying saucer at its summit, the tower was built to symbolize the unlimited future – though now it more resembles an oversized prop from a vintage sci-fi flick.

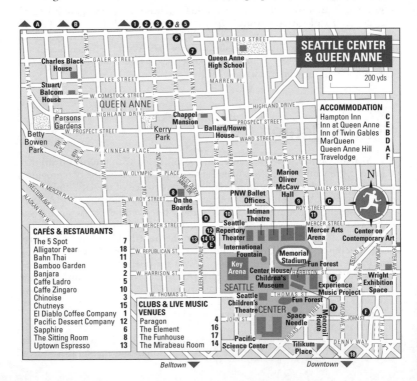

SEATTLE CENTER & QUEEN ANNE

0   200 yds

ACCOMMODATION

Hampton Inn	C
Inn at Queen Anne	E
Inn of Twin Gables	B
MarQueen	D
Queen Anne Hill	A
Travelodge	F

CAFÉS & RESTAURANTS

The 5 Spot	7
Alligator Pear	18
Bahn Thai	11
Bamboo Garden	9
Banjara	2
Caffe Ladro	5
Caffe Zingaro	10
Chinoise	3
Chutneys	15
El Diablo Coffee Company	1
Pacific Dessert Company	12
Sapphire	6
The Sitting Room	8
Uptown Espresso	13

CLUBS & LIVE MUSIC VENUES

Paragon	4
The Element	16
The Funhouse	17
The Mirabeau Room	14

△ The Space Needle

Whatever its architectural value, the Needle has become so inextricably linked to the skyline of Seattle that it's essentially the symbol of the city to the rest of the world – identifiable even in silhouette. Whether it's high on your agenda or not, you're bound to see it throughout your stay, as it's visible for miles around, serving as a useful orientation beacon – though it's only about three-fifths as tall as the city's largest structure, the Bank of America Tower.

The 43-second elevator ride to the **observation deck** ($13, kids $6, two trips in 24 hrs $17) is a pricey but obligatory experience for the first-time visitor to Seattle, and rightly so: any cynicism sparked by the mobs of tourists – more than four thousand visit daily in the summer – and overpriced admission tends to disappear upon arriving at the top. The panoramic view of the region is thoroughly impressive, encompassing urban lakes, the Downtown skyline, Puget Sound, Queen Anne, and distant peaks like Mount Rainier – provided the skies are clear, of course. If the day you plan to ascend the Needle turns out to be rainy and overcast, it's well worth changing your itinerary to visit whenever the sun eventually appears.

Below the observation deck, the elevator also stops at the **revolving restaurant** *SkyCity*, predictably better for the views than the food. If you feel like getting reasonably dressed up for a meal (no t-shirts and sneakers allowed), it offers with the price of a meal a free trip up the elevator and around the observation deck. On a final note, visitors might consider coming here in the evening to gaze from below at the Needle itself, dramatically lit up after dark.

Experience Music Project

Near the monorail, the impressive **Experience Music Project**, or **EMP** (Tues–Thurs 10am–5pm, Sat & Sun 10am–6pm; $20, kids $15; concert tickets at ☎206/770-2702, ⓦwww.emplive.com), is one of the two largest museums in the country devoted to popular music (the other being Cleveland's much more staid Rock and Roll Hall of Fame). Although some of the flashier wings are more suited to an amusement park than a cultural institution, the place does manage to please rock buffs and those in search of little more than a fun outing. Given the scale of the museum and its hefty entrance fee, it's a good idea to set aside the better chunk of a day to fully explore it, and avoid coming on a summer weekend, when the throngs of giddy adolescents can make the Experience's experience unbearable.

Largely funded by Microsoft co-founder and multibillionaire **Paul Allen**, the EMP was originally intended as a museum devoted to Seattle native **Jimi Hendrix** – until Allen and the Hendrix estate had a falling-out about unspecified matters. The final product still includes a fair amount of Hendrix memorabilia, but its focus is much broader than first intended, with interactive exhibits drawing from a collection of nearly 100,000 rock and pop artifacts. The controversial design by globe-trotting LA architect **Frank Gehry** – of Guggenheim Bilbao and Disney Hall fame – has not a single right angle in its swooping contortions of bright, spiny metal panels. Each of the facade's 21,000 shingles, in purple, silver, gold, red, and blue, has a different shape and size. This design was inspired by the many forms of electric guitars, according to Gehry, who wanted "to evoke the rock and roll experience without being too literal about it." Indeed, rock 'n' roll may be the last thing you think of when you see the finished structure, which resembles a shiny, metallic wad of Play-doh.

In addition to its chief exhibits, the EMP usually has special events of some sort going on daily. The **first floor** is mainly given over to the *Turntable* restaurant, but also features the **Digital Lab**, providing an electronic overview of the EMP's collections; workshops and demonstrations in the **Learning Lab**; and showings of old concert footage in the **JBL Theater**. In 2004, the **Science Fiction Museum** – also funded by Allen – opened at the site (see opposite), replacing the **Artist's Journey**, a memorable theme-park ride through the funky world of James Brown and other musical legends.

Level two

A visit to the EMP really begins on **level two**, where you'll be handed a bulky **Museum Exhibit Guide** (known as a "**MEG**"), a remote control unit with a built-in text screen, which, when pointed at displays in the museum, brings up content on whatever's being pointed at, with automated narration by rockers like Robbie Robertson. Although you might feel like a cyber-nerd strapped down with this contraption, it is truly essential if you hope to experience all the museum has to offer, especially since the actual artifacts assembled – mostly old records, posters, and magazines – aren't very striking without the commentary. That said, while the spread of genres examined in-depth is not comprehensive, many styles do have corners of their own, with **special exhibits** on topics from blues to bubblegum pop.

Of the exhibits on level two, standouts include the **Guitar Gallery**, with its dozens of acoustic and electric guitars and basses, such as the intriguing 1933 Dobro all-electric with built-in speakers, and the 1957 Gibson "Flying V," used by ace pickers Lonnie Mack and Albert King. **Northwest Passage** traces the local rock scene from instrumental pioneers The Ventures through the grunge era to modern rockers like Sleater Kinney and Modest Mouse, with an entire case devoted to the rock anthem *Louie Louie*, which highlights some of the nearly one thousand recordings made of the song. A new exhibit, running through summer 2007, is **Yes Yes Y'all**, tracing the rise of hip-hop, perhaps America's most globally influential genre since jazz, with a good number of samples and relics: track suits and jewelry worn by the early greats, turntables of the likes of Grandmaster Flash, and tags and graffiti emblematic of the rap scene as it was born in the Bronx in the early 1970s.

Elsewhere, the **Liquid Lounge** doles out potent libations, the **Sky Church** hosts the occasional concert, and a **costume gallery** displays the glitter boots, funky hats, and leather jackets worn by your favorite pop idols and punk screamers. The entire level is crowned by the EMP's signature image (at least for its interior spaces), the monumental **Roots and Branches** sculpture, no less than six hundred guitars tied together in a monster tree looming above the gallery floor.

Level three

On the EMP's **third level**, the large **Sound Lab** enables visitors to play guitar, bass, keyboards, drums, and DJ turntables, with a bit of help from the staff and interactive computer terminals; there are rooms for jamming, a chance to mix on a professional console, and an entire corner of effects pedals – all of it pure kid-in-a-candy-store stuff for music aficionados and, of course, for kids themselves, who bang, scratch and strum ceaselessly. More compelling, and a major reason why the EMP even exists, the **Hendrix Gallery** traces Jimi's career from his days as a sideman with the Isley Brothers to his short-lived psychedelic funk group Band of Gypsies – check out the handwritten draft of *Voodoo Chile*, which contains different lyrics than those that were eventually recorded.

Unfortunately, one of the EMP's key early attractions, the **Milestones** gallery – which covered the musical styles that influenced rock or have grown out from it, including jazz and R&B, country, punk, and rap – has disappeared in recent years to make way for new displays, though there are plans to re-install at least part of it. When this happens, standout items to watch for include Bo Diddley's trademark square guitar, the rainbow tunic worn by rap star Queen Latifah, and a recording of Bill Haley's 1952 single *Rock the Joint*, an early, pre-rock version of his much more famous *Rock Around the Clock*.

Science Fiction Museum and Hall of Fame

The **Science Fiction Museum and Hall of Fame** (same hours as EMP; $13, kids $9) is technically a separate institution, but the steep admission fee really requires that you purchase a combined ticket ($27, kids $20) to see both this and the EMP, which surrounds it. The collection is based on Paul Allen's own holdings of literary and cinematic antiques, and is therefore guided by his enthusiasms. Sci-fi fans will no doubt delight to the countless spaceship replicas, futuristic walk-through sets, and alien costumes on display, which are heavily weighted toward the film-and-TV fantasy elements of the genre – movie clips of the *Star Wars* spaceships, snippets from Orson Welles' "War of the Worlds" radio broadcast, the sleek costumes worn by the characters in *Blade Runner*, and all manner of weapons, from a simple phaser to a light saber to Jane Fonda's *Barbarella* crossbow. The Hall of Fame itself is a high-tech overview of the big names in the genre, mainly authors such as Asimov and Verne, for those with only a dim knowledge of science fiction beyond Hollywood.

The museum is grouped into different sections, which tend to run together – Spacesuits, Amazing Places and Brave New Worlds among several – and most of the prize items are reverentially shown under dramatic lighting in display cases – an odd sort of honor since some of the items, especially the movie props, are rather chintzy and hardly worth a second glance, except from the faithful. However, there are true gems from the golden years of science-fiction writing, including first editions of Ray Bradbury's *Fahrenheit 451* and the works of H.G. Wells, classic comics and posters from the mid-twentieth-century, and computer representations of literary utopias and dystopias. You can also find a few actual science-related items grouped in, such as a NASA spacesuit and a Martian rover replica. Ultimately, it's clear this is a first stab at the sci-fi museum concept (allegedly, no such institution had previously existed), and it will take time to separate the quality from the kitsch. Until then, the museum's core audience will most likely be drawn to the centerpiece of the collection: the captain's chair from *Star Trek*.

Pacific Science Center

Southwest of the EMP is a much more conventional science institution, the **Pacific Science Center** (June–Aug daily 10am–6pm; Sept–May 10am–5pm, Sat & Sun closes 6pm; $10, kids $7; ☎206/443-2001, ⊛www.pacsci.org), easily recognizable by its modernist white arches and shallow, stagnant "lake" below the exterior concrete walkways – one of the Seattle Center's most outdated buildings, but not without its charms. Curiously, the center began as a World's Fair exhibit – titled the Federal Science Pavilion – by Seattle-born architect Minoru Yamasaki, who went on to much greater fame as the builder of New York's World Trade Center, fourteen years later.

Comprising five interconnected buildings, the center's emphasis is firmly on interactive exhibits; some are computer-oriented, but most are simple enough for pre-adolescents to operate. As with many science museums, the displays are aimed mainly at children and present a basic, "kid's eye" view of the world of science and nature. Here, you can play tic-tac-toe against a ten-foot robot, ride a "High Rail bicycle" above the ground, or move a two-ton granite ball suspended on water. The **Tech Zone** offers various activities that, for example, allow you to create your own spooky music on a Theremin or make high-tech doodles. The **virtual reality** exhibits are more enticing, such as the pseudo-basketball court that has you playing one-on-one against a phantom opponent, or the impressive hang-gliding simulation – though you can expect long lines at either of these.

Younger children will be especially drawn to the colorful, oversized exhibits, like the 22-foot starship with a circular slide, and the robotic dinosaurs. You may also want a crack at the **Body Works** exhibit, which lets you measure your strength, peripheral vision, and sense of smell in a manner that's more akin to operating a pinball machine than getting tested at the doctor's office. Two good final stops are **Insect Village**, home to live and animatronic creepy crawlies, and the **Tropical Butterfly House**, in which exotic butterflies from around the globe roam freely, allowing close looks from a garden path.

Fans of giant-screen, nature-oriented **IMAX films** have a chance to see such oversized curiosities, for the price of a combination museum/film ticket ($15, kids $12, IMAX only $8–10). In the museum's **Smith Planetarium**, those who want to experience Pink Floyd's *Dark Side of the Moon* – or albums by the Beatles, Led Zeppelin or Nine Inch Nails – in fully synchronized, laser-beam glory, can take in a Laser Rock Show for less than the price of a regular movie (Thurs $5, Fri–Sun $7.50).

Seattle Children's Theatre and Children's Museum

Just north of the Science Center, a similarly engaging institution for kids is the **Seattle Children's Theatre** (kids $12–21, adults $20–27; tickets at ☎206/441-3322, ⊛www.sct.org). The cultural fare here is not necessarily dumbed-down, so adults can chaperone the younger set without feeling compelled to constantly check their watches. Presented in two different performing spaces (the sizeable Martin and cozier Alvord theaters), the performances are geared to different age levels, and involve local works created specifically for kids, as well as dramatic and musical adaptations of everything from Dr Seuss to *The Devil and Daniel Webster*. Shows run Fridays through Sundays, with matinees. Tickets tend to disappear quickly, so showing up an hour before showtime and expecting to get a seat is definitely not recommended.

Meanwhile, the **Children's Museum**, in the Center House complex (Mon–Fri 10am–5pm, Sat & Sun 10am–6pm; $7.50 for all ages; ℡206/441-1768, ℗www.thechildrensmuseum.org), offers tot-friendly attractions like the **artificial mountain forest**, which lets kids crawl through logs or simulate a rock climb. The **Discovery Bay** section has exhibits geared for those aged two-and-a-half or younger, and the **Global Village** is an earnest attempt to create multicultural awareness with international clothing, food, and toys. Those herding a group can try the "If I Had a Hammer" construction zone, where kids collaborate on building an eight-by-eleven-foot house.

The International Fountain

While there's a lot to do in the Seattle Center if you have a specific event or destination in mind, it's not a prime hangout spot. The lone exception to this is the **International Fountain**, east of Key Arena, a great place to splash around on hot days in the summer while world-beat tunes blare through the sound system. The fountain itself is something of a huge modernist toy – a hemispheric dome set in its own concrete crater that regularly pulses and blasts streams of water high in the air. The fun is watching the water spray up into the sky, then waiting as the torrent crashes down on you. On a much more sober occasion, it was around here in April 1994 that thousands of fans gathered to hold candlelight vigils for fallen icon Kurt Cobain (see box, p.128), shortly after the Nirvana leader committed suicide in his Seattle home.

Marion Oliver McCaw Hall

Just north of the International Fountain is the striking **Marion Oliver McCaw Hall** (℗www.seattleopera.org/hall), home of the Seattle Opera, as well as the Pacific Northwest Ballet; for more info on both, see p.191. The Hall does for opera what Benaroya Hall did for symphonic music in Seattle just a few years ago: act as an eye-popping architectural symbol of the creativity of the local high-culture scene, while replacing an outdated facility in the process. The hall opened to much fanfare in June of 2003, its sleek modernism enlivening its institutional surroundings. Although the glass curtain wall and steel beams of the lobby (open to the public) are appropriately bright and tasteful, the outside **Kreielsheimer Promenade** is the real highlight: a partially dry, partially water-glazed plaza topped with nine vertical, steel-mesh scrims for reducing and diffracting sunlight. The nighttime effect is even more dramatic, when more than 200 colored lights illuminate the scrims, and the strange glowing images seem to dance and swirl above the crowd in hypnotic fashion.

Queen Anne

While there's almost nothing in the way of museums or "official" sights in **Queen Anne**, immediately north of the Seattle Center, the neighborhood is one of Seattle's best places for strolling and looking out over the expansive Puget Sound land- and seascape. It's also one of the easiest as well, not more than a short drive or a vigorous jaunt from many of the city's top tourist draws.

Originally sited a fair distance from Seattle's nineteenth-century city center in Pioneer Square, the upscale citizens of "Queen Anne Town" lived in a different world than the rest of their neighbors, a rarefied place where historic-revival mansions towered above the city and the only neighborhood access, other than walking, was riding streetcars tugged by counterweights up a steep incline. Even after Seattle subsumed the elite village – whose name was soon shortened – near the turn of the last century, the grand homes continued to rise and the rest of the city's residents generally kept a respectful distance. This changed when the World's Fair was plunked down at Queen Anne's doorstep in the early 1960s: what was previously a snooty colony of bankers, lumber chiefs, and self-styled aristocrats became much more open to the outside world.

Lower Queen Anne

Because the traffic corridors bordering Queen Anne to the east and west – Aurora, Elliott, and 15th avenues – provide almost no access to the district, one of the few good routes into the neighborhood is via the steeply sloped **Queen Anne Avenue**, from the south. Beginning with a strip of affordable diners, clothing shops, and boutiques, the first part of the avenue, between Harrison and Roy streets, marks the area known as **Lower Queen Anne**, a commercially oriented stretch that has little in common with the more elegant estates above; its many decent **bars** and **nightspots** handle the crowds after sporting events and shows at Key Arena and Memorial Stadium. Two of the more notable establishments here are **Uptown Cinemas**, 511 Queen Anne Ave N (☎206/285-1022), a neighborhood theater offering a solid diet of mainstream and alternative fare, and **Easy Street Records**, 20 Mercer St (☎206/691-3279, ⓦwww.easystreetonline.com), one of the city's top independent businesses and, with its sprawling digs, a major local hangout – try to drop by on an evening when a local- or national-level band gives a free in-store concert.

Highland Drive and around

About midway up Queen Anne Hill, **Highland Drive** is Seattle's original home of the swells, featuring multimillion-dollar estates alongside smaller mansions, most with awe-inspiring views of the metropolis and Puget Sound. You won't find too many of the district's original Victorian houses here, however – they've mostly been replaced by other, grander creations – and this includes Queen Anne-style architecture, which was never prevalent here to begin with. The oldest structures, in fact, are the smaller-scale bungalows scattered throughout the neighborhood, which pale in comparison to the massive historic revival homes that generally date from the 1910s to the 1930s. Note that none of the mansions in the area are open to the public, but you can enjoy a more in-depth look at these grand estates (from the street) on an architectural walking trek provided by Discover Tours; see "Basics," p.36, for details.

Beginning on the eastern end of Highland Drive, a pair of huge period revival houses gives you a sense of the grandiose character of the area. The first, the 1906 **Chappel Mansion**, no. 21, is a half-timbered Tudor Revival hulk that looks nicely Shakespearean (even if it's far larger than most true Elizabethan residences), even though it was built by a fortune hunter who got rich in the Klondike Gold Rush. Just to the east, the **Ballard/Howe House**, no. 22, is a colossal 1901 Colonial Revival monument – named after a banker and hardware salesman who first came west on the Oregon Trail in 1852 – that towers over most other structures in the area, with its Neoclassical columns and high balconies.

On the western side of Queen Anne Avenue, West Highland continues with a solid row of big-ticket estates and chunky mansions, which become larger the further west you go. Amid the first collection of Neoclassical, Georgian, Italianate, and Colonial Revival dwellings is **Kerry Park**, West Highland at Second Avenue W, from where the entire city spreads out before your eyes, with Mount Rainier perfectly set in the distance. Indeed, the view presents an ideal phototaking perspective, and only the most bumbling shutterbug could go wrong.

Beyond this, a number of historic revival structures reward a look, including a giant **Mediterranean mansion** at no. 623, which features Spanish flourishes like a tiled roof and iron balconies, and the 1926 **Stuart/Balcom House**, one street north at 619 W Comstock, a neo-Georgian colossus that looms over the south slope of the hill, and a good candidate for the neighborhood's most imposing pile.

In the shadow of the Stuart/Balcom House are two small but worthwhile parks: **Parsons Gardens**, W Highland at Seventh Avenue, whose intimate pathways and charming foliage still make you feel like a trespasser among the elite, and tiny **Betty Bowen Park**, catercorner to the gardens, which complements the views of Kerry Park with a wider vista of Elliott Bay looking southwest.

Finally, two blocks north at 615 W Lee St, the quirky **Charles Black House** is a 1909 Arts and Crafts take on the Tudor Revival, with half-timbered walls, the quaint charm of an old English manor, and 33 spacious rooms, plus landscaping designed by the Olmsted brothers (sons of the more famous Frederick Law Olmsted), who were also responsible for some of the more appealing elements of Seattle's public park system (see Volunteer Park, p.94).

Upper Queen Anne

North of Roy Street, Queen Anne Avenue ascends dramatically along the south slope of the hill to arrive at **Upper Queen Anne**, which has a good number of high-end apartments, condos, and bungalows amongst its more elaborate structures. The main chunk of commercial activity here takes place between Galer and McGraw streets, a strip of fancy American and Asian eateries, gourmet groceries, yuppie-oriented coffeehouses, and the like.

As you reach the top of the hill, riddled with 500-foot radio and TV transmitters and disused old water towers, one building that stands out is the former **Queen Anne High School**, 201 Galer St, a monumental 1909 brick edifice that closed its doors to students in the early 1980s and now acts as apartment housing for the district's well-heeled renters. Check out the remodeled units – many still featuring their original chalkboards – at ⊛www.thequeenanneapts.com.

Capitol Hill

One of Seattle's best-loved neighborhoods, **Capitol Hill**, at the top of a steep but gradual rise east of Downtown, is known for both its easy-going, progressive vibe and its location within close reach of the city center. Much of Capitol Hill began in the early twentieth century, when a number of Seattle's most affluent citizens built mansions in the area, some of which still stand. Today, it is fairly mixed by class and, since the 1960s, has been a center for the city's left-leaning political and cultural forces. This influence is apparent in the area's alternative-minded shops and nightlife, its political canvassers who push petitions on the street corners, and its status as the undisputed center of Seattle's gay and lesbian community. This is never more in evidence than during the annual Gay Pride Parade (see p.202), which has become one of the city's most popular celebrations.

The neighborhood's boundaries – roughly, 23rd Avenue to the east, **Volunteer Park** to the north, Belmont Avenue to the west, and Madison Street to the south – contain some excellent green spaces, highlighted by Volunteer Park itself, a must for its **Asian Art Museum** and conservatory, and the **Washington Arboretum**, home to the Japanese Garden and some fine walking trails. Capitol Hill really starts to buzz along **Broadway**, a ten-block stretch of shops, cinemas, and eateries that, although more gentrified in recent years, is still Seattle's best bet for clubbing, offbeat shopping, and people watching. Around the edges of the area are quite a few points of interest: **Pike** and **Pine streets** are fun alternative commercial strips, while at the southwest corner of Capitol Hill there's First Hill, home to one of the city's more notable art collections, the **Frye Art Museum**. To the northwest, the southern shores of **Lake Union** are worth visiting both for the houseboat community in **Eastlake** and the Center for Wooden Boats; northeast is the moderately interesting Museum of History and Industry and the marshy paths of untamed Foster Island.

Broadway and around

Many who have lived in Seattle for decades will tell you that the creative spirit of **Broadway** is declining – a charge first leveled in the early 1980s when the ten-block drag between Roy and Pike streets began to gentrify. For all its recent commercialization, though, Broadway is still the place to hang out in Capitol Hill, whether you're browsing for trinkets, taking in the scene at a bar or club, popping into one of the many boutiques, or relaxing at one of the sidewalk cafés, watching the crowds.

Taking up an entire block between Republican and Harrison streets, **Broadway Market**, no. 401 (Mon–Sat 10am–9pm, Sun noon–6pm; ⓦwww .thebroadwaymarket.com), is the most visible example of the money that poured into Capitol Hill in the 1990s, though vacancies are more common than they used to be. A hodgepodge of trendy shops, fast-food joints, chain clothiers, coffeehouses, and fitness and beauty centers, the market also houses a day-of-show, half-price outlet called Ticket/Ticket (☎206/324-2744), selling tickets to concerts and theatrical events. The real activity, though, is out on the street, where you can sip a latte at a sidewalk stand like *Vivace Espresso* (see p.155), munch on tasty burgers and fries at *Dick's Drive In* (see p.170), listen to records at spots like Everyday Music (see p.225), or browse the racks of funky shirts and dresses set up on the sidewalk for regular sales.

On either side of Capitol Hill's north-south boundaries, the arthouses in the Landmark theater chain (ⓦwww.landmarktheatres.com) occupy appealingly converted buildings, allowing you to take in a flick in historic digs: **Harvard Exit**, 807 E Roy St, is a quaint 1925 charmer that originally housed the Women's Century Club, while the stately **Egyptian**, 805 E Pine St, is a former Masonic temple built in 1915.

The Harvard-Belmont Historic District

On the northern end of Broadway, between E Roy Street and E Highland Drive, the **Harvard–Belmont Historic District** has even more ostentatious properties than Millionaires' Row (see p.95), particularly the gated structures along Harvard between Highland and Aloha. The area is generally split between huge Neoclassical mansions and sprawling period-revival homes, whose designs borrow heavily from Tudor, Georgian, and Colonial Revival styles. If you'd like a guide to the area, the Seattle Architectural Foundation runs **tours** of this and other noteworthy Seattle neighborhoods ($10; info at ☎206/667-9186, ⓦwww .seattlearchitecture.org).

One long block south of the mansions, at the corner of Harvard and Roy streets, the Capitol Hill campus of the **Cornish College of the Arts** (☎1-800/726-ARTS, ⓦwww.cornish.edu) is a real anomaly, with its California Mission-style architecture at the east entrance, classically inspired frieze along the exterior corridor, and tombstone-shaped windows lining its south facade. It puts on a full schedule of **theater**, **dance**, and **music** productions, many of them free; see Chapter 15, "Performing arts and film," for more information.

Pike and Pine streets

A half-mile south of the historic district, running perpendicular to the southern section of Broadway, **Pike** and **Pine streets** are the alternative commercial strips in the area, and have a less gentrified feel, with funky clubs, oddball coffeehouses, independent record stores, and tattoo and piercing parlors. Spots worth visiting include Area 51, 401 E Pine St (daily noon–7pm, Sun closes at 6pm; ☎206/568-4782), loaded with ultra-modern furniture, sleek decor, and plastic doodads from the mid-twentieth century, and *Bauhaus Books and Coffee*, 301 E Pine St (daily 6am–1am, weekends opens 8am; ☎206/625-1600), the prototypical hipster-chic Seattle café, with an upper loft, goatee-clad clientele, and plenty of books on art, literature, philosophy, and the like. Also worth a stop, several blocks east, is **Northwest FilmForum**, 1515 12th Ave (schedule at ☎206/267-5380, ⓦwww.wigglyworld.org), the premier independent film organization in the region, which runs screenings of alternative, foreign,

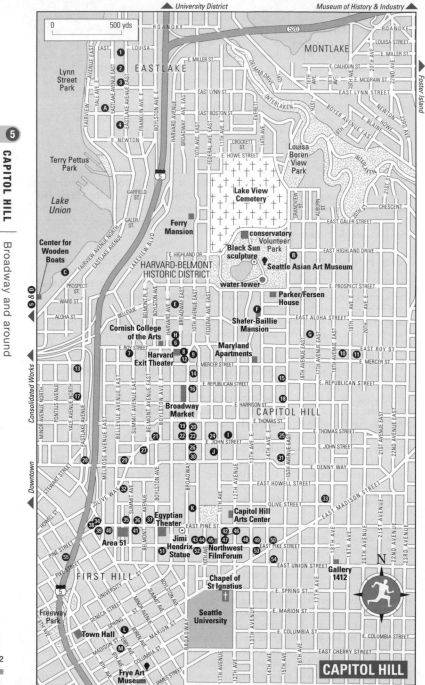

CAPITOL HILL | Broadway and around

experimental, and classic movies, and produces low-budget offerings through its own film collective. Check the website for the latest schedules, or drop in and expect to be surprised.

Somewhat incongruously, at the northeast corner of Pine Street and Broadway, there's a striking, life-sized statue of local rocker **Jimi Hendrix**, modeled on his famous pose from the 1967 Monterey Pop Festival, in which the guitar god kneeled down onstage to set his instrument ablaze.

The Chapel of Saint Ignatius

Three blocks south of the FilmForum, the campus of Seattle University merits a visit for the unusual **Chapel of Saint Ignatius**, next to the visitors parking lot at Marion and 12th (Mon–Thurs 7am–10pm, Fri 7am–7pm, Sat 9am–5pm, Sun 9am–10pm; ⊛www.seattleu.edu/chapel). Designed by maverick architect Steven Holl to represent "seven bottles of light in a stone box," the church's interior is notable for its hanging baffles and multi-hued windows – many of them thin rectangular slits – which combine to cast moving patterns of colored light throughout the church, with each hue representing a different sacrament or theme. Take a look at the **Blessed Sacrament Chapel** at the end of the processional corridor, where a candlelit sanctuary lamp hangs from a madrona tree, and gold-leaf prayers arc etched into the floor and embedded in the beeswax-coated walls. If you're truly inspired, the reflecting pool outside, and the nearby 52-foot chapel bell tower, provide a suitable setting for meditation.

Frye Art Museum

Immediately south of Pike Street and west of Broadway, the urban grid becomes canted at 45 degrees around the small district of **First Hill**, which was home to some of Seattle's most impressive mansions in the early twentieth century. Now dominated by bland modern housing complexes and three major medical centers (leading to the ubiquitous nickname, "Pill Hill"), it merits a visit mainly for the **Frye Art Museum**, 704 Terry Ave (Tues–Sat 10am–5pm, Sun noon–5pm, Thurs closes at 8pm; free; ☏206/622-9250, ⊛fryeart.org). For the most part, the Frye is devoted to the figurative painting of American and European artists from the last two centuries. The permanent collection is mostly ordinary, often outshone by the more daring temporary exhibits in its supplemental **Greathouse Galleries**. Recent exhibits have included a broad variety of work, including multimedia, performance, and installation pieces, along with such curiosities as the creepy childhood nightmares of Mark Ryden's paintings and the androgynous photographic self-portraits of Claude Cahun.

Nevertheless, the museum carries out the mission of **Charles** and **Emma Frye** – prosperous Seattleites who built their collection with proceeds from Charles's meat-packing business – with admirable style. Its spacious, dimly lit galleries display works by the likes of Winslow Homer, John Singer Sargent, Thomas Eakins, and a few (anti)modern artists like Andrew Wyeth. Look for Eakins' *Maybelle*, a stern portrait of a pudgy matron with pinched lips, and Homer's *The Wheat Gatherer*, a painting of a European farm laborer that's more in keeping with a French Realist like Courbet than an American known for his nautically inspired pieces.

The building also holds one of the most important concentrations of the **Munich school** of painting in the US, focusing on the belle époque years between 1870 and 1900, when Munich was second only to Paris as a center of European cultural activity. Heavily oriented around portraits and landscapes, it's somewhat less interesting overall than the handful of paintings from the more progressive Munich Secession movement of the *fin de siècle* – particularly Franz Stuck's *Sin*, which was regarded as scandalous for its lascivious portrait of a raven-haired temptress with half-exposed breasts wearing a snake. This striking image was reproduced by the artist no less than eight times; the version here is a later one, from 1906.

Volunteer Park and around

Up and a few blocks east from Broadway, Capitol Hill's quiet northern end features one of the city's most agreeable open spaces: **Volunteer Park**, 1247 15th Ave (daily 6am–11pm), named in honor of the Seattle soldiers of the 1898 Spanish-American War. On warm days, especially weekends, you'll find the park thick with frisbee players, hackysackers, and African drummers, plus the odd hot-dog vendor and rock band – the bandstand and front porch of the Seattle Asian Art Museum host occasional summer concerts.

Enter the park at Prospect and 14th Avenue to ascend the 106-step winding staircase of the **water tower**, which, with its imposing brick bulk and entry sign reading "Aqua Pura," looks more than a little medieval. At 75 feet, this is Capitol Hill's highest structure, and once you reach the top you'll find the budget alternative to the Space Needle's observation deck, offering a free panoramic view of Seattle – though the wire mesh covering the small windows may well remind you why it's free. At the top level, there's also an informative **exhibit** on the **Olmsted brothers**, designers of much of Seattle's park system, who laid out this park in 1909, and saw it completed three years later.

One of the Olmsteds' original park features, the **bandstand**, across a small reservoir to the north, is still functional, hosting summertime music and theater performances. On the southern side of the reservoir is Isamu Noguchi's stark, dark-granite **Black Sun** sculpture – looking like a giant, mangled donut – which also serves as a favorite target for camera-toting visitors, due in part to the Space Needle looming in the background. The sculpture is, reportedly, the inspiration for Soundgarden's grunge anthem "Black Hole Sun," even as the group itself was named for a different sculpture in Magnuson Park (see p.124).

Closer to the northern end of the park is an excellent **conservatory** (daily 10am–4pm, summer closes 7pm; free; ☎206/684-4743). Built in 1912 as something of a miniature version of London's Crystal Palace, it now cultivates a compact but often stunning array of botanical colors and fragrances. Divided into five greenhouses that simulate different climates, it's especially worthwhile for its orchid collection, just inside the entrance. There's also a wealth of ferns and cacti, olive trees and yuccas, and bromeliads (look for the silver, confetti-like tillandsias) that crawl over rocks, shrubs, and trees. The tallest of the plants is the fishtail palm, which nearly reaches the building's 35-foot-tall dome roof.

Seattle Asian Art Museum

Volunteer Park's top draw, the **Seattle Asian Art Museum**, 1400 E Prospect St (Wed–Sun 10am–5pm, Thurs closes 9pm; $7, kids under 12 free; ☎206/654-3100, ⊛www.seattleartmuseum.org), is across from the *Black Sun* in the center of the park and holds one of the most extensive collections of Asian art outside of Asia. As a branch of the larger Seattle Art Museum (see p.56), a ticket purchased here is good for admission to the Downtown location, and vice versa. The museum closed in 2005 for renovation, but reopened in January 2006 with its (ongoing) special presentation of Chinese art and calligraphy.

The single floor of **exhibits** comprise Japanese, Korean, Vietnamese, Chinese, and Southeast Asian art, spread across many centuries and dynasties. Among the more interesting pieces are the meticulously crafted Japanese **landscape scrolls** and the theatrically grim **statues** of tomb guardians, court attendants, and warriors in the early Chinese art wing. The uplifting yet humble sculpture of *Monk at the Moment of Enlightenment*, dating from the Yuan Dynasty (circa 1300s), can be seen in the Buddhist art room, which presents Chinese sculpture of a more spiritual nature. Best of all, though, is the wildly ornate array of Chinese jade and snuff bottles from the eighteenth through twentieth centuries, adorned with miniature portraits, animals, and rural landscapes.

Lake View Cemetery

Just north of Volunteer Park is the entrance to **Lake View Cemetery**, 1554 15th Ave E (daily 9am–8pm; ☎206/322-1582). While the graveyard is neither very atmospheric nor especially lovely, it does contain the resting places of some major figures in Seattle history, such as town co-founder Doc Maynard and Princess Angeline, daughter of Chief Sealth, the city's Native American namesake. The cemetery has also become a morbid sort of tourist attraction as the burial site of legendary kung fu film star **Bruce Lee**, the former Seattle resident who died mysteriously in 1973, and his son, actor **Brandon Lee**, who died in 1993, also under suspicious circumstances (see p.96). Their graves are somewhat out of the way, on the crest of the hill toward the rear of the cemetery: look for a small marble bench facing two large tombstones – Bruce's is red and rectangular, Brandon's is black and curved, and both are usually covered in flowers and fan letters.

After seeing the cemetery, a stroll to the northeast brings you to the small **Louisa Boren View Park**, 15th Ave E at E Olin Place (daily 4.30am–11.30pm; ☎206/684-4075), offering a quiet, nearly undiscovered setting that yields some of the best views of Lake Washington to be found in Seattle.

Millionaires' Row

Downhill from Volunteer Park and back toward Broadway is an area featuring some of Seattle's grandest mansions, though few are open to the public. **Millionaires' Row**, as it's known, holds the most celebrated cluster of these, with the highest concentration found along 14th Avenue E from the park

Bruce and Brandon Lee

More than thirty years after his death, **Bruce Lee** remains unsurpassed as the most famous martial arts film star of all time; his son **Brandon**, who followed him as an actor, has a devoted following as well. Unfortunately, neither gained international fame until after their respective deaths, which remain mysterious.

Born in San Francisco in 1940, the elder Lee grew up in Hong Kong, moving back to the US in the late 1950s and enrolling in the University of Washington in the early 1960s. A boxing champion famed for his **"one-inch punch"** – with his arm straight out, he could knock down his opponent with a lightning-quick shrug of his shoulder – he developed a style of martial arts that incorporated elements from karate, boxing, and many other types of hand-to-hand combat. Lee landed a supporting role in the *Green Hornet* TV series in the mid-1960s, but it was in Hong Kong that his career really took off with several action films. On the verge of a breakthrough in the US, he told his sister in early 1973 that he expected to die soon, a **prophecy** fulfilled that July – resting in bed while suffering from one of his recurring headaches, he died of a cerebral aneurysm. A month later, his film *Enter the Dragon* premiered in the US to great success.

Meanwhile, Brandon Lee, born in 1965, was determined to be known as an actor on his own accord (though his first role was in a TV movie playing the son of David Carradine's character from the *Kung Fu* series). He was on the brink of making it as an action star a few years later when, during filming of *The Crow* in 1993, Lee was shot to death in a **freak accident**. While filming a scene involving a gun (which was supposed to be empty), somehow a bullet tip had become lodged in the barrel; when the cameras rolled and the gun was fired at Lee, the tip struck his spine, and he died the same day. Perhaps inevitably, *The Crow*, like *Enter the Dragon* twenty years earlier, became a great posthumous success.

entrance to E Roy Street, though the homes are in actuality a bit scattered, not lined up in a tidy strip. Note especially the sprawling brickwork of the **Shafer–Baillie Mansion**, 907 14th Ave E, now remodeled into a bed and breakfast (see p.151 for a review), whose large, mostly hidden, yard often hosts weddings and receptions, and whose oak-paneled walls and Tudor Revival decor give the place a hint of the elegant character it had when built in 1914. Just north, facing the park near the water tower, the imposing white **Parker/Fersen House**, 1409 E Prospect Ave, is a Neoclassical mansion boasting four huge pillars and dragon statues guarding the entrance. Two blocks north of Prospect, a considerable Tudor Revival estate, the **Ferry Mansion**, 1531 10th Ave E – with a style that falls somewhere between Old English and Fairytale – sports half-timbered walls and a charming corner turret. Lastly, one of a handful of area multi-family structures built with a historic flair, the **Maryland Apartments**, 626 13th Ave E, draws attention for its huge columns, convex-walled facade, and covered balconies. For an in-depth look at the area, the Seattle Architectural Foundation runs periodic **tours** of the neighborhood, among many others of historical note ($10; info at ☎206/667-9186, ⊛www.seattlearchitecture.org).

Lake Union

The glistening gem of **Lake Union** is the closest lake to central Seattle, linked to much larger Lake Washington to the east and Elliott Bay to the west, via the Lake

Washington Ship Canal. Although the lake hosts naval ships as well as pleasure craft, and is a prime spot from which to view the city at a distance (especially from Gasworks Park; see p.121), it has also become known for its sizeable collection of **houseboats**, inhabited by locals who have a real zeal for living in these floating abodes. (The nearby, pleasant little Terry Pettus Park, Fairview Avenue E at Newton Street, is named after a 1970s activist for the now-formidable Floating Homes Association.) The lake is also a top draw for seaplanes – so don't be astonished to see a pontoon-sporting propeller craft diving down toward the middle of town. Although it was glacially carved tens of thousands of years ago, Lake Union is one of the more geometrical bodies of water in the area, and has been growing smaller in the last century or so, thanks to both the city's habit of dumping its earthen fill here from its various regrading projects, and because of the construction of I-5 to the east, which cleaved away part of its shore.

Eastlake and Lynn Street Park

Houseboats are particularly abundant on the shores of **Eastlake**, a small neighborhood northwest of Capitol Hill on the west side of I-5. Although these floating homes are private, you can get a closer look from a short distance away by strolling along Fairview Avenue E, taking an organized tour (see "Basics," p.36), or simply visiting **Lynn Street Park**, on the waterfront at Fairview Avenue E and E Lynn Street. This small green space features 160 hand-painted tiles on its concrete steps, as well as the **Stockley Bench**, artist Maggie Smith's whimsical creation of a basic concrete bench brought to life with colorful inlaid tiles featuring wine bottles, cheese, books, flowers, and so on – and, naturally, named after local houseboat owners. If you just can't get enough of these houses, and feel the need to get a much closer look, the Floating Homes Association offers biennial five-hour tours in September, giving you an up-close view of more than a dozen of them (next tour 2006; $25; ☎206/325-1132, ✆www.seattlefloatinghomes.org).

Just to the east of Lynn Street Park, Eastlake Avenue E is the neighborhood's **small commercial strip**, with a couple of decent cafés and the funky but popular *Eastlake Zoo* tavern; see p.176 for a review.

△ Houseboats on Lake Union

The Center for Wooden Boats and Northwest Seaport Maritime Heritage Center

If you're interested in watercraft other than houseboats, head a mile south along the lakeside to the **Center for Wooden Boats**, 1010 Valley St (daily 10am–6pm; free; ☎206/382-2628, ⊛www.cwb.org), where more than a hundred tree-hewn vessels are on display, ranging from a tiny hundred-year-old coracle, which looks barely big enough to fit one person, to the sixty-foot *Merry Maiden*, which has been used for round-the-world cruises. Sailboats and rowboats (from twelve to twenty feet) can be rented here for jaunts around Lake Union ($12.50–46/hr), and the center also hosts regular sailing classes, workshops, and seminars on maritime skills and nautical history. Don't miss the weekly **classic boat outings**, either (Sun 2–3pm; free), for an eye-opening trip around the lake on a craft such as the *Puffin*, a steam-powered vessel from 1906 that, with its little black boiler, looks like a fitting relic of the great Industrial Age.

An assortment of larger watercraft is on view at the adjacent **Northwest Seaport Maritime Heritage Center**, 1002 Valley St (daily 9am–5pm, Sun opens at noon; donation; ☎206/447-9800, ⊛www.nwseaport.org), including a tugboat, a lightship, and a salmon troller from the early twentieth century. The most striking ship, the 1897 *Wawona*, was North America's biggest three-mast (lumber) schooner when it was built. It certainly looks impressive from a distance, with its magisterial silhouette, but once you get a bit closer you notice the gamey wooden planks and sizable gouge taken out of the hull – it's unlikely to be out on the waves again any time soon.

Consolidated Works

For a marked change of pace from the maritime activity, head a few blocks south of Lake Union to **Consolidated Works**, 500 Boren Ave N (art gallery Thurs & Fri 4–8pm, Sat & Sun 1–8pm; $5; otherwise admission by advance ticket; ☎206/860-5245, ⊛www.conworks.org), an ultra-hip arts complex that features a wide range of contemporary pieces in several different media – and often in hybrid form – including theater, film, music, and the visual arts, with the emphasis strongly on quirky, conceptual, and alternative fare. Recent openings have included the touchable "kinesthetic sculptures" of Ergonomicon; experimental movies employing multiple projectors and screens; and walk-through installations with video monitors, mirrors, and other special effects. In late March, the Seattle Erotic Art Festival (⊛www.seattleerotic.org) is put on here, featuring plenty of painted nudes, oddball burlesque shows, and performers in strange – or no – costumes. Admission prices and performance times for anything at ConWorks can vary, so check the schedule online or by phone.

Washington Park and around

Boasting 230 acres and more than five thousand kinds of plants, **Washington Park**, just northeast of Capitol Hill, is a spectacular urban retreat. It marks the upper corner of central Seattle – around which curve Lake Washington to the east and its Ship Canal to the north – and is most familiar for its excellent **Arboretum** (daily 7am–dusk; free; ☎206/543-8800, ⊛depts.washington.edu/wpa), which occupies most of the park and is a lush showcase for the vegetation of the Puget Sound region. Despite its impressive statistics – plants from about 75 countries are represented – the Arboretum's wetlands have suffered damage from erosion, some of its most popular walking paths do not drain properly, and its trails are arranged somewhat haphazardly. Still, for most visitors, it remains a beautiful place to stroll (best on uncrowded weekdays) and observe the magnolias, camellias, witch hazels, and more exotic specimens. It's especially radiant in early spring, when Seattleites emerge from near-hibernation to turn the grassy, resplendent **Azalea Way** into a promenade, soaking up their first sunny rays in many months.

The **Graham Visitors Center**, at the north end of Arboretum Drive near Foster Island Road (daily 10am–4pm), has a free **trail map**, which is all you'll need to find your way about the ponds, glens, and rock gardens. The center also provides information about the numerous walks and activities held on the grounds, such as the free **tours** that leave from the center every Saturday and Sunday at 1pm.

The most popular destination in the Arboretum, the **Japanese Garden**, to the south near the Madison Street entrance (March–Nov daily 10am–dusk; $5; free tours Wed noon & Sat & Sun noon & 1pm; ☎206/684-4725), features the requisite stone lanterns, babbling brooks, and footpaths with picture-perfect views of the scenery. Constructed with more than five hundred granite boulders (from one to eleven tons each) taken from the Cascade Mountains, it's a lovely spot, particularly at the bridges near the Emperor's Gate, where exotically colored carp swim in the pond and terrapins sun themselves on Turtle Island. The **teahouse** here, originally created in Tokyo and shipped over in 1959, can only be viewed from the exterior most of the time, except during demonstrations of Chadõ tea rituals, which are offered free with admission at 1.30pm on the third Saturday of the month, from April to October.

The Museum of History and Industry

North of Washington Park, the **Museum of History and Industry**, 2700 24th Ave E (daily 10am–5pm, Thurs closes 8pm; $7, kids $5; ☎206/324-1126, ⊛www.seattlehistory.org), will content history buffs with its detailed overview of the Puget Sound region, from canneries and the timber industry to the Klondike gold rush, aviation pioneers, nautical life, and discarded neon signs. The highlight is the well-executed **Great Seattle Fire** exhibit, with an interactive terminal featuring graphics that show you how the fire began and eventually engulfed Downtown; nearby is the small glue pot believed to have started the blaze.

Other permanent displays, including a full-scale replica of a Seattle street from the 1880s and a section devoted to the salmon industry, are passing diversions; the wide-ranging temporary exhibits, which usually take up much of the building, are a bit more appealing in their scope. There's a daily **guided gallery tour** at 2pm, and the museum also gives historical walking tours throughout the city during the summer (see "City Tours," p.36). If you have a serious interest in Seattle history, you may wish to browse through the museum's immense **photo library**, which has more than half a million images of the Pacific Northwest from 1859 to the present (by appointment; ☎206/324-1126).

Arboretum Waterfront Trail and Foster Island

Near the Museum of History and Industry parking lot is an entry point for the fascinating **Arboretum Waterfront Trail**. The trail leads through the largest remaining wetland in Seattle, over a narrow floating walkway to Marsh Island,

and on to the much larger **Foster Island**, an appealing wildlife habitat whose marshes are crowded with birch, oak, and pine trees, as well as dragonflies, marsh wrens, and redwing blackbirds. In summer, occasional clusters of water lilies can also be seen from the bark-surfaced footpath. The path is also a good vantage point for watching the kayaks paddling along the Ship Canal under the elegant Montlake Bridge, and for taking a break at any of several strategically placed benches hiding among the reeds – just follow one of the trail's dead-end spurs to the marshy shoreline.

Numerous varieties of waterfowl, plants, and birds can be seen from the trail with a little patience; pick up a self-guided **trail pamphlet** for 50¢ (available at the Museum of History and Industry; see p.99) for assistance. If you take the route the full distance, you'll pass right under the 520 freeway, which seems to skim above the water's surface. After the path leaves Foster Island, take a right turn onto Foster Point Trail and continue for ten minutes to reach the edge of the Washington Park Arboretum.

The University District

L eaving Capitol Hill, and upon crossing the stately Montlake Bridge over the Lake Washington Ship Canal, you reach the **University District**. Centered on the **University of Washington**, the only state university north of San Francisco located in a major urban area, the U District, as it's called, is spread out over 639 acres and buzzes with around 35,000 students. The campus is home to the **Henry Art Gallery**, one of the finest art museums in Seattle, the **Burke Museum**, rich in its exhibits on Native Americans in the Pacific Northwest, and the **Medicinal Herb Garden**, an extensive collection of flora that's worth a visit. The U District's chief draw, however, is its main drag, **University Way**, with a dozen or so blocks of student-oriented establishments, such as pizza joints, book and record stores, and funky boutiques. While the U District lacks the hipster flair of Capitol Hill or the off-kilter artiness of Fremont, it still offers enough diversions to fill up half a day or so, with the school campus as the obvious starting point.

The University of Washington

The most prominent educational institution in the Northwest, the **University of Washington** (ⓦwww.washington.edu) – or UW (pronounced U-dub), as it's known – comprises sixteen schools and colleges. It's one of the top universities in the US, too, having received more federal research dollars than any other college in the last quarter of the twentieth century. Even if you're not a student, UW is worthwhile for its excellent museums, eclectic performances and public lectures, and spacious green lawns surrounded by striking twentieth-century brick architecture (as well as predictably grimmer modern versions).

Founded on a small Downtown hill in 1861, UW relocated to its present site north of town in 1895, expanding greatly with the **Alaska-Yukon-Pacific Exposition** of 1909. Held right on campus, the Exposition was a showcase for Seattle's industrial and commercial might, and is often characterized as the city's first World's Fair – predating the more famous one by a half century. With all the university's growth, the surrounding neighborhood benefited substantially, with an ensuing real-estate boom and, eventually, modernization. But at the outset, the area still lacked electricity, paved streets, and sewers; perhaps not surprisingly, when potential students were tested for admission in 1908, one of the early questions was to "name the great drainage systems of the United States."

At the northwest corner of the campus, near the Burke Museum (see p.105), you can get an initial glimpse of UW's heady, turn-of-the-century days at the

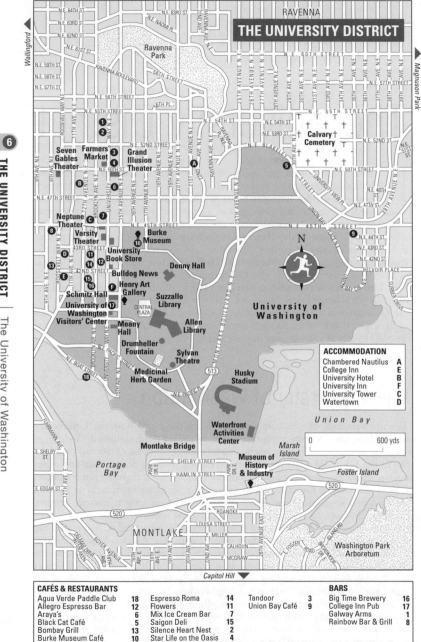

THE UNIVERSITY DISTRICT

ACCOMMODATION

Chambered Nautilus	A
College Inn	E
University Hotel	B
University Inn	F
University Tower	C
Watertown	D

CAFÉS & RESTAURANTS						**BARS**	
Agua Verde Paddle Club	18	Espresso Roma	14	Tandoor	3	Big Time Brewery	16
Allegro Espresso Bar	12	Flowers	11	Union Bay Café	9	College Inn Pub	17
Araya's	6	Mix Ice Cream Bar	7			Galway Arms	1
Black Cat Café	5	Saigon Deli	15			Rainbow Bar & Grill	8
Bombay Grill	13	Silence Heart Nest	2				
Burke Museum Café	10	Star Life on the Oasis	4				

1895 **Denny Hall**, the first and oldest building on campus, now undergoing renovation (due to be finished by late 2006). Named after Seattle co-founder Arthur Denny, the hall is styled like a French Renaissance mansion, with graceful towers, turrets, and a cupola, walls constructed of sandstone and brick, and sleek, classical arches at the entrance.

Practicalities

Laid out on an irregular, sloping plot, the university is not as easy to navigate as you might expect, so stop in first at the **Visitors' Information Center**, which, due to construction of a new center, is temporarily sited at Room 022 in the Odegaard Library, just east of the Henry Art Gallery (Mon–Fri 8am–5pm; ☎206/543-9198, ⊛depts.washington.edu/visitors); here you can pick up the free *Campus Walk* booklet, a self-guided tour of the university's highlights. Alternatively, free 90-minute **campus tours** run twice-daily during the week, starting at the third-floor lobby in Schmitz Hall, at the corner of NE 41st St and University Way NE (Mon & Fri 10.30am & 12.30pm), and once on weekends, starting one block east at the George Washington statue near the Henry Art Gallery (Sat 12.30pm).

The campus

Your likely starting point for exploration, just east of the Odegaard Library, is **Central Plaza** – dubbed "Red Square" for its red bricks – a major student socializing hotspot, though its bleak expanse doesn't invite you to linger for long. At the eastern edge of the plaza is the Gothic Revival monument of the **Suzzallo Library** (Mon–Fri 9am–5pm), whose reading room resembles the nave of a medieval church and whose pointy arches and forbidding statues recall the good old days of the thirteenth century. Attached to the Suzzallo, the **Allen Library** (same hours), one of several large Seattle projects funded by Microsoft co-founder Paul Allen, offers good temporary exhibits on cultural and historical topics; south from here is **Drumheller Fountain**, whose main aquajet – when it's running – spouts water one-hundred feet into the air. The fountain leads toward a sloping green belt that points south-southeast, around which you're likely to get lost without a map.

Bisecting the green belt, **Stevens Way** features some of the university's floral highlights. Scattered in plots along the curving course, the fetching **medicinal herb garden** showcases everything from the familiar poppies, goldenrod, and foxglove to the rarer and more bizarre monkeyflower, devil's tongue, panther lily, and Bible-leaf. Between some of these plots, to the west, are the elegant, newly restored Ionic columns of the outdoor **Sylvan Theater**, where student groups put on the odd production in leafy surrounds. Just west, the **botany greenhouse** of the herb garden (Mon–Fri 8am–5pm; free; tours May–Oct second Sun of month at noon; ⊛depts.washington.edu/biology/greenhouse) holds one of the largest collections of its kind in the US, with more than two thousand species. Particularly eye-catching are the long ghostly fingers, huge green leaves, and luridly erect stalk of the *Amorphophallus titanium* ("in the shape of a giant phallus"), also known as corpse flower – though it looks less like a cadaver than a creepy prop from the film *Invasion of the Body Snatchers*.

A ten-minute walk southeast from the herb garden takes you to the waterfront site of **Husky Stadium**, 3800 Montlake Blvd NE (tickets at ☎206/543-2200, ⊛gohuskies.com), the home of the school's football team, where it's claimed that "The Wave" – the fad in which spectators create a ripple effect by standing

△ Henry Art Gallery

and sitting in successive rows – originated in the early 1980s. Southeast from the stadium, the **Waterfront Activities Center** (Feb–Oct daily 10am–dusk; ☎206/543-9433, @depts.washington.edu/ima/IMA_wac.php) rents **rowboats** or **canoes** for $7.50 an hour, a great way to take in nearby Union Bay or go paddling around Foster Island.

Henry Art Gallery

One of Seattle's better museums, the university's **Henry Art Gallery**, west of Central Plaza at 15th Ave NE at NE 41st St (Tues–Sun 11am–5pm, Thurs closes 8pm; $8, free Thurs; ☎206/543-2280, @www.henryart.org), presents an imaginative scope of exhibits. Displays in each gallery change about three or four times a year, so what you see is likely to be completely different from one visit to the next. Adjacent to the old, brick-walled museum building, the more recent, and modernist, annex of the **Allen Center for the Visual Arts** was designed to triple the Henry's gallery space, and provides much greater room for multimedia exhibitions, huge conceptual installations, and the like. Selections from the Henry's **permanent collection** – which includes late nineteenth- and early twentieth-century landscapes by Winslow Homer and Ralph Blakelock, figurative paintings by Jacob Lawrence, prints by Rembrandt and Whistler, and photographs by Ansel Adams and Imogen Cunningham – may be on view in the small North Galleries on the **plaza level** of the old building, though they're usually incorporated into the type of conceptual shows the museum favors.

By contrast, the **lower level** is devoted to changing contemporary exhibits, with three galleries devoted to the avant-garde, sometimes incorporating multiscreen projections and high technology, as well as barn-sized installations combining sculpture, sound design, and architecture. It's quite a mixed bag – even presenting unexpected subjects like literature, biology, and urban planning – and you'll never know what you'll get; check the website if you don't like being surprised.

The small outdoor **sculpture court** on the middle level is not really much of a sculpture court anymore; instead, it's dominated by the huge, otherworldly shell of James Turrell's **Skyscape** installation – the unit's steel shape and spindly legs resembling an alien landing craft. The real value of *Skyscape* is its interior space (reached via catwalk on the upper level), an oval room with benches and a skylight hole in the roof, which allows sunlight to flit around the room at different angles depending on the hour and season. Here, you're invited to meditate, pray, or contemplate the nature of life and existence – as long as you can shut out the presence of other museum-goers also packed in to seek their own enlightenment.

The Burke Museum of Natural History and Culture

UW's other prime cultural attraction, the **Burke Museum of Natural History and Culture**, 17th Ave NE at NE 45th St (Tues–Sun 11am–5pm, Thurs closes 8pm; $8, free first Thurs of month; ☎206/543-5590, ⊛www.washington.edu /burkemuseum), lies a few blocks north of the Henry. Focusing mostly on the **natural** and **cultural history** of Washington, the Pacific Northwest, and the Pacific Rim, it holds the country's largest collection of Native American art and artifacts west of the Mississippi – mainly masks, totem poles, and baskets.

On the upper floor, the **Life and Times of Washington State** is a kid-oriented timeline of geological history with large text displays; highlights include volcanic crystals, a 140 million-year-old allosaurus skeleton, and a giant Ice Age-era sloth, found during construction of a Sea-Tac Airport runway. Elsewhere, you'll find specimens of and countless exhibits on birds, reptiles, fossils, and spiders – as well as a dramatic selection of **nature photography**, documenting such areas as the Arctic National Wildlife Refuge, before it is exploited by humans.

On the lower floor, **Pacific Voices** is a broad series of exhibits covering the cultures of Pacific island and coastal communities. Displays include videos of traditional ceremonies, such as a Lao fire-rocket festival and a Korean wedding, and a case of Hawaiian musical instruments, which you can hear as well as see. In the **Bill Holm Center**, insightful offerings focus on the art of Northwest coastal tribes, including masks used in the potlatch ceremonies of the Kwakwaka'wakw people. Particularly astounding are the transformation masks that change from one creature into another at the pull of a string. Make sure to look for the new "**grizzly bear house posts**" carved by Tlingit tribal artists Nathan and Stephen Jackson, which present modern carvings of the native legend of the hunter who married a bear – Nathan's is the more traditional, in wood, while Stephen's is more stylized and bizarre, in mixed-media.

Finally, beyond the view of the public, somewhere in the museum's recesses, are the remains of **Kennewick Man**, the ancient corpse of an early human found in 1996 near the Columbia River in Washington State. This *Homo sapiens* from the later Ice Age – his bones are almost ten thousand years old – soon became the subject of a heated court battle between national scientists who wanted to examine the body, and native tribes who fought to put him back in the ground; the latter lost the case in 2004.

University Way

Just off campus, the dozen or so blocks of **University Way** that stretch northwards from NE 41st Street form the heart of the U District. The area, known as "The Ave", is always jam-packed with students and shoppers, who frequent the strip's cheap restaurants, secondhand music stores, and funky vintage clothing boutiques. Once the center of Seattle's counterculture – the underground newspaper, *The Helix*, set up shop a few blocks away on Roosevelt in 1967 – it's not quite so bohemian today, with the usual fast-food joints and chain stores littered throughout.

There are a number of notable new and used **bookstores** along the strip: the latest alternative journals and in-your-face zines are available at the excellent Bulldog News, no. 4208 (☎206/632-6397, ⓦwww.bulldognews.com), which also has Internet access for $3 per hour, and the huge University Book Store, no. 4326 (☎206/634-3400, ⓦwww.bookstore.washington.edu), holds an impressive inventory of wide-ranging titles and offers engaging author readings. The main stretch of University Way is also home to some excellent **cinemas**, particularly in the Landmark chain, whose Neptune, Varsity, and Seven Gables theaters are historic treasures (see Chapter 15, "Performing arts and film"). The district's best-programmed moviehouse, though, is the venerable **Grand Illusion**, 1403 50th St at University Ave ($7.50; ☎206/523-3935, ⓦwww.grandillusioncinema.org), one of the last true arthouse cinemas in the Pacific Northwest. Dating back nearly a hundred years, it presents an eye-opening schedule of enigmatic foreign films, obscure cult movies, leftist documentaries, and forgotten classics – though the screening room is a bit on the small side, with just a few dozen seats.

Ravenna Park

At the northern end of the U District, accessible along University Way, **Ravenna Park**, 5520 Ravenna Ave NE (daily 4am–11.30pm; ☎206/684-4075), is one of Seattle's best neighborhood parks, its fifty acres of deep channels and ravines – carved by Ice Age glaciers – offering ideal scenery for solitary strolls. A new renovation, due to be complete in 2006, promises to remove some of the earlier asphalt and redevelop the park's creek into a more inviting habitat. On Saturdays, you can catch the **farmers' market** on your way there; it's held on the lot at the northwest corner of 50th and University (late May to early Nov 9am–2pm), with vendors offering a nice array of meats, pastries, cheeses, flowers, and trinkets, along with locally grown fruits, nuts, and vegetables.

Magnolia and Ballard

The largely residential areas northwest of Downtown Seattle – **Magnolia** and **Ballard** – are predictably limited in their offerings, but alongside the Lake Washington Ship Canal there are a handful of interesting sights at the water's edge. As for local color, Magnolia is the more affluent and sedate of the two, providing some excellent views of Elliott Bay, while Ballard was historically a working-class industrial district, though its social character has shifted over the decades to become something of a nightlife zone in recent years.

There are three major sights that draw outsiders to these neighborhoods: Magnolia's sprawling, majestic **Discovery Park**, home to the historic confines of Fort Lawton and a picturesque lighthouse; the **Hiram M. Chittenden Locks**, also known as the **Ballard Locks**, where salmon and boat traffic offer plenty of quiet fascination in their aquatic course through the Ship Canal; and **Fishermen's Terminal**, just east, the commercial centerpiece of the local fishing industry and a decent place to snack on fish-and-chips or take a harbor cruise.

Magnolia

Even though it's only a few miles along the curve of Elliott Bay from Downtown, **Magnolia** feels much further away, with its pleasant tree-lined slopes and aura of suburban isolation. The area was actually native terrain for **madronas**, not magnolias, when it was first sighted by explorers; legend has it that a seaman misidentified the foliage in a ship's log around the turn of the last century, leading to the name that has stuck. Mockingly nicknamed "Mongolia" by some locals because of its insularity, the district's most exclusive homes cluster around the bluffs at its southwestern edge – though architecture buffs will find little here to excite them.

There's little commercial activity here, too, save for the three blocks or so around W McGraw Street and 32nd Avenue W, known as **Magnolia Village**, an assortment of smart boutiques and restaurants that mainly cater to the residents. For a much more interesting trip, head instead for **Magnolia Boulevard**, which hugs the bluffs overlooking Puget Sound as it rises toward Discovery Park, and is lined on its seaward side with the linear, twelve-acre **Magnolia Park**, a good place to stop and enjoy the views. On this street and those adjacent to it, Seattle's elite has carved out some rather impressive lots with expansive vistas – too impressive, perhaps, as occasional mudslides here have caused severe damage to some of the residences.

Not surprisingly, given the presence of a massive railyard, there are few easy **entry routes** into Magnolia, and this lack of accessibility gives the district its

CAFÉS &
RESTAURANTS

Carnegie's	6
Chinook's	3
Hattie's Hat	13
The Hi-Life	8
Kinnaree	19
Madame K's	12
Mr. Spot's Chai House	10
Palisade	18
Q Café	4
Ray's Cafe	1
Szmania's	20
Vera	7
Verite Coffee	5

BARS, CLUBS &
LIVE MUSIC VENUES

Conor Byrne Pub	16
Hale's Ales	2
Lock & Keel Tavern	15
The Paradox	17
People's Pub	11
Sunset Tavern	9
Tractor Tavern	14

ACCOMMODATION

Canal Cottages	B
Dibble House	A

BALLARD & MAGNOLIA

DOWNTOWN BALLARD

walled-off feel. If you're not coming south over the Ballard Bridge around 15th Avenue W, you can get here from W Nickerson Street from Lake Union and Queen Anne (the best course for the major sights), or from Elliott Avenue north of Belltown leading to Magnolia Boulevard West, which is mainly worthwhile for its views of Elliott Bay.

Discovery Park

With five hundred acres of rustic fields, woods, and trails, as well as dramatic waterside vistas, brisk air, and abundant wildlife, **Discovery Park** (daily 4am–11.30pm) is a rugged swath of wilderness sitting on the edge of the city. Even on the most beautiful spring days it remains uncrowded, and on weekdays and weekend mornings it can resemble an urban arcadia with its lush topography, idyllic landscapes, and occasional glimpses of endangered animals – one of the few spots in the lower 48 where you'll have a chance to see bald eagles.

As pleasant as the park is now, it's occupied in several places by the military (as signs will attest), a presence that has been longstanding since the early 1900s. During this era **Fort Lawton** stood guard over Magnolia Bluff, but by the mid-1930s the Army found it outmoded and offered it to Seattle for a mere dollar – which the city declined, fearing the cost of Depression-era maintenance would be too great. World War II subsequently transformed the fort into a major processor of enlisted personnel, and in the mid-1960s the Department of Defense announced plans to turn the fort into an anti-ballistic missile site, which led to public outcry for the grounds to be converted into a park. It was only through the personal intervention of Washington senator Henry "Scoop" Jackson (normally a rabid hawk) that plans for the base were abandoned and those for a park went forward.

The **visitors' center** (Tues–Sun 8.30am–5pm; ☎206/386-4236), also known as the Environmental Learning Center, is just inside the east entrance, at 36th Avenue W and W Government Way, and sells **maps** of the park for a dollar and has a small exhibit on the park's history and vegetation. It also organizes weekend walks showcasing the local flora and fauna, including a fine look at the park's bird species (April–Nov Sat 8–10am; free; by reservation through the visitors' center), highlighted by **Birder's Paradise**, offering taped birdcalls of the winter wren and Rufus hummingbird, among others.

Park trails and Fort Lawton

The park's best paths include a 2.8-mile **Loop Trail**, beginning at the visitors' center and winding through some rather dense forests as it makes its way around the periphery of the park; and the trail from the south entrance on W Emerson Street near Magnolia Boulevard, which begins with the Loop Trail and then branches off across windswept meadows between the parking lot and the nearby bluffs. From this vantage point, the view is one of the area's best, taking in Puget Sound ships, Bainbridge Island, and, on a clear day, the snow-capped Mount Rainier. Follow the path at the edge of the bluff north until you reach the **South Beach Trail**, from which a long set of wooden stairs winds down to the narrow, rocky, unswimmable beach to the south, and the **West Point Lighthouse** to the north – a squat 1881 structure that's the city's oldest, with a vaguely New England feel. From South Beach itself, the mile-long waterside trail leads to the more deserted North Beach, with a sewage-treatment plant mercifully hidden from your eyes, if not your nose.

There are still vestiges of the military's presence in the old **fort buildings** in the park's southwestern corner, along with a few bland modern homes used by defense personnel. The visitors' center has occasional **Fort Lawton history tours** (on periodic Sat 2–4pm; free; call for details) that provide details on the park's namesake, Henry Lawton – once famous for capturing Geronimo – and take you inside the **guard house**, where drunk or misbehaving soldiers were jailed in three solitary confinement cells, each measuring just four feet by eight feet. Near the park's east entrance, the **military cemetery** holds the gravesites

Riot in Discovery Park

On August 14, 1944, 32-year-old Italian prisoner of war **Guglielmo Olivotto** was lynched by American servicemen in Discovery Park, a death that was instigated by tension in Fort Lawton between Italian POWs and black American soldiers. At the time – although Italy had ended its involvement in World War II in September 1943 – some three thousand Italians were still being held at Fort Lawton and other locations in the Seattle region, doing war-related work for the US. Perversely, the Italian POWs had far looser restrictions than black American soldiers at Fort Lawton, even being allowed to roam freely off the base.

Angered by this unjust treatment, the soldiers **rioted** and stormed the Italian barracks that August night with axes, stones, bottles, and shovels, injuring dozens; Olivotto's body was later found hanging from his neck by a steel support cable, more than ten feet off the ground. Forty-two black servicemen were charged in the lynching, three of whom were accused of manslaughter; twenty-six of these men were convicted, resulting in dishonorable discharges from the army and sentences totaling more than two hundred years. The trial judge advocate in the courts-martial was none other than Lieutenant Colonel **Leon Jaworski** – the same Leon Jaworski who, three decades later, would become famous as the government's special prosecutor in the Watergate scandal.

(they're at the rear near the green sheds) of two notable prisoners of war, one a German pharmacist who killed himself by drinking lacquer thinner rather than return to Deutschland, and the other Guglielmo Olivotto, murdered by a racially motivated mob (see box).

Daybreak Star Indian Cultural Center

Apart from the old military fragments, the majority of the parkland is for public use, with a tiny parcel granted to the United Indians of All Tribes for the **Daybreak Star Indian Cultural Center** (follow signs from the north parking lot; ☎206/285-4425, ☜www.unitedindians.com). The center has small exhibits featuring native artists at the **Sacred Circle Gallery of American Indian Art** (daily 10am–5pm, Sun opens at noon; free), and an **art market** (Oct–March second Sat of the month, Dec every Sat, 11am–4pm; free) with local artists and craftspeople selling their work. Traditional Native American lunches such as baked salmon, Indian tacos, and fry bread are available throughout the day, and native performances are also part of the event. Keep in mind that the information for the gallery and market may be subject to change in coming years with the construction of the **People's Lodge**, a new complex designed to handle the various vendors and activities in three buildings. Finally, as part of citywide Seafair celebrations in July (see p.204), the center hosts a giant **powwow** (information at ☎206/285-4425) featuring some five hundred dancers, drummers and ceremonial figures, along with traditional food, art, and jewelry for sale.

Fishermen's Terminal

About a mile east of Discovery Park, **Fishermen's Terminal**, 3919 18th Ave W (daily 7am–4.30pm; ☎206/728-3395, ☜www.portseattle.org/seaport), between Salmon Bay and the Lake Washington Ship Canal, is a leading homeport for West Coast commercial fishing, providing moorage for about seven hundred vessels. Ranging in length from a few dozen feet to a few hundred, many of these trollers are on view at the dock by the parking lot; during weekdays, you may catch their operators unloading their crab and salmon hauls. Near the dock is the striking **Fishermen's Memorial**, unmissable in the center of the complex, a towering granite pillar topped by a fisherman hauling in his catch, featuring a copper frieze of swarms of fish around the base. The Memorial honors the five hundred local fishermen who have lost their lives at sea in the last hundred years.

After you've poked around the fleet for a few minutes, you can indulge in some freshly caught fish at the terminal's small daytime indoor **markets** or have a proper sit-down meal at *Chinook's*, rightly one of the city's most celebrated seafood restaurants, both for its menu and its dockside view (see review p.169).

If your next stop from here is the Ballard Locks, park at the small lot about a mile northwest of the Terminal in minuscule **Commodore Park**, from which footbridges lead you over Salmon Bay to the locks.

Ballard

Positioned on Salmon Bay at the edge of the Lake Washington Ship Canal, the once strictly blue-collar neighborhood of **Ballard** was always well sited for fishing and other nautical commerce in the earlier twentieth century, though in recent decades gentrification has altered its low-key working-class atmosphere. Its demographics, once strongly Scandinavian, have also begun to fall in line with the city's mainstream, due to an influx of middle-class families, artists, and young people attracted by low rents – at least compared to the rest of town. As a result, Ballard's become a surprisingly hip scene in places, loaded with rugged

△ Fishermen's Terminal

old buildings housing grass-roots galleries, alternative clubs, old-style dive bars, and scruffy diners. Despite its mildly bohemian appeal, the district has nowhere near the arty pull of nearby Fremont, nor has it experienced the same tidal wave of development as in Belltown. Most visitors, in any case, just come to see the Locks.

The Hiram M. Chittenden Locks

On the north side of Salmon Bay and just west of Fishermen's Terminal, near NW 54th and Market streets, the **Ballard Locks** are officially known as the **Hiram M. Chittenden Locks** (daily 7.30am–9pm; ☎206/783-7059, ⓦwww .nws.usace.army.mil), named after the US Army Corps engineer who designed them, and built in the early twentieth century to help keep the freshwater lakes uncontaminated by salt. At the time the locks were constructed, only those of the Panama Canal exceeded them in size, and they remain the busiest in the nation, their gateways herding commercial vessels and pleasure craft around the clock every day of the year. Rising and sinking in slow motion as the locks are drained and filled, the ships can be seen from overlooking platforms and catwalks; these crisscross the complex and connect the Magnolia and Ballard sides of the bay, at least until the boats are ready to cruise through – so try to avoid finding yourself on the wrong side of the water if you have a deadline to meet. The simple spectacle amounts to an interesting free show that draws over a million viewers a year – though many locals wonder what all the fuss is about.

Visiting the locks

The stately old **visitors' center**, between the Ballard-side parking lot and the platforms (Oct–April Thurs–Mon 10am–4pm, summer daily 10am–6pm; free), shows a twelve-minute slide and video show every half-hour, while upstairs are interesting exhibits about the history of the Ship Canal and the locks' extensive construction. Interactive displays allow you to operate a model-sized replica of the locks via remote control, or try to navigate a near-impossible maze that simulates the journey of salmon through their life cycle, in which fewer than one egg in a thousand may survive to spawn as an adult. Free **guided tours** of the locks are also offered (information and reservations at ☎206/783-7059), with explanations and anecdotes in common English, rather than engineer-speak.

Simply put, the two concrete locks – one designed for vessels up to 80 feet wide and 825 feet long, the other measuring 30 by 150 feet for much smaller craft – allow boats to pass from the freshwater lakes to saltwater Puget Sound and vice versa, gating them into chambers that drain one type of water before allowing them to proceed to the next. The process takes about five minutes for the small lock, and about fifteen for the bigger one, which can fit dozens of the smaller ships at once. The parade of **vessels** varies from tiny private cruisers to pleasure-seeking tourist boats to massive ships hauling tons of cargo into the Pacific. It's impossible to predict what might be going on at any given hour, and you might find yourself lingering a half hour or more before anything happens. It's best to come on the weekends, when many amateur sailors take to the water and chat with spectators as their boats are guided through the portals at agonizingly slow speeds – captains who don't obey the glacial speed limit get a stern yell from the lock-workers. Better still are holidays such as Labor Day, when the heavy traffic can cause backups of more than a hundred boats, which have no alternative but to wait their turn.

Coffee culture

In Seattle, a steamy cup o' joe is as intrinsic a city icon as the Space Needle itself. Whether you're looking for a basic black brew at an old-fashioned diner or a complex concoction gussied up with fancy spices, syrups, and sprinkles, the local coffee culture has everything to suit your mood. Moreover, the range of java joints is staggering – with everything from the ubiquitous Starbucks outposts to café/art spaces, where the visual design and live performances attract at least as much attention as the coffee.

PUBLIC MARKET

A rich and savory history

By the 1950s, the US had already seen its cafés become hubs of political, artistic, and intellectual endeavors – most famously with the emerging Beat culture, but also long before that with Italian-run shops in places like New York's Greenwich Village and San Francisco's North Beach, where you could get a genuine slug of espresso while enjoying a bite of a panino. Seattle's **coffeehouses**, like those of other West Coast cities, embraced the counterculture in its more youth-oriented neighborhoods, and doled out strong coffee while hosting folk musicians and Leftist political activity. Even after the scene declined, the city's java joints remained quirky bastions for art and music, though the national hype surrounding them would have to wait a few more decades.

Seattle's mainstream coffeehouse culture and taste for **gourmet blends** is said – at least according to popular opinion – to date to Howard Schultz's momentous 1985 visit to Europe to sample Italian espresso bars. Hoping to displace bland American commercial varieties with something more authentic, he subsequently oversaw what would become a globe-trotting colossus: Starbucks, whose first store had opened in humble Pike Place Market digs some fourteen years earlier. From this, a slew of imitators was able to pick up on the public desire for rich, savory espresso and cappuccino while removing the edgier aspects of the coffee scene left over from the hippie era, making it palatable for Middle America. Even the firm's original bare-chested mermaid logo got a new, anodyne look.

Survival of the alternative brew

While Starbucks was busy dominating the rest of the world, Seattle's alternative coffee culture did not fade away quietly. Although there were some lean times in the 1970s, a decade later the arty coffeehouse scene had begun to form its own zeitgeist (also the name of an excellent local joint). Cafés nearly became synonymous with **art galleries** and **performance spaces** in neighborhoods such as Capitol Hill, while other, more conventional cafés developed a nearly fanatical attention to top-notch beans and proper brewing. Such vendors began to emphasize their links to organic farming and fair trade practices, while creating a meticulous process for getting the most out of every cup, which meant abandoning the conventional percolators and drip machines for expensive Italian contraptions.

To a large degree, though, Seattle's caffeinated fame is prominently linked to its emergence as a center for modern-rock music and the high-tech industry. Indeed, Seattle led the way with the development of **cybercafés**, catering to discriminating computer geeks with in-store dial-up connections and, later, broadband and Wi-Fi access; it also blazed a trail for musicians by giving over its coffeehouse stages to alternative rockers – not just folk singer-songwriters. (Popular legend even has it that the grunge revolution began in 1986 at the now defunct coffeehouse Java'Tude, when two future members of the band Mother Love Bone demanded that Huey Lewis be removed from the jukebox in favor of darker rock tunes.)

Café counterculture

Although many of Seattle's central neighborhoods have long had their bohemian-flavored coffeehouses, it was the University District that provided the nexus of the genre's **countercultural** social and political activity. In the 1960s the area was home to such notable establishments as the Edge, Eigerwand, Pamir House, and the Coffee Corral, whose building was also headquarters for a "free university" and underground newspaper. Apart from being places to get filled in on the latest events – protests, jam sessions, "be-ins," and the like – the shops were ideal places to hang out for those without a lot of money but plenty of time on their hands (ie, students). Indeed, enjoying an espresso and a bran muffin while listening to earnest folk singer-songwriters was a cheap way to wile away an afternoon and debate the failings of modern society, sometimes with the aid of a marijuana brownie – strictly off the menu, of course. Although the modern coffee (counter) culture looks a bit different than it did in the 60s, you can still find a steady boho or neo-hippie vibe in places from Ballard to Fremont to Capitol Hill – though not as much in the more business- (and less hippie-) oriented U District. If it's studious leftist attitudes you're after, *Bauhaus* is an obvious choice; if it's irreverent art and kitsch, *Coffee Messiah*; for underground theater and spoken-word events, head to *Victrola Coffee*; and if you're searching for oddball performance art and music, as well as Tarot-card and palm readings, check out *Aurafice*.

The modern method

The process of **ordering an espresso** beverage serves as an antidote for the fast-food industry, and each cup of anything beyond the house coffee (often served in pump thermoses) takes at least five minutes to prepare. As such, the specialized position of **barista** has become as vaunted a service-industry job as can be, often involving overseeing the grinding of the beans, the processing through a French press or (preferably Italian-made) espresso machine, and the creation of a nice dollop of foam to round out the perfect cup – ideally, a demitasse, rather than the hulking Big Gulp-sized containers found at Starbucks.

Because the process can take some time, cafés are most identifiable not by their visual design, menu, or atmosphere, but simply by the presence of a handful of patrons milling about, waiting for their steaming java to arrive. But when you hear the barista's crisp shout of "Double skinny latte!" then you can finally sit down and nestle in for a few hours behind a book, newspaper, or laptop – content to escape the rain outside.

Coffee glossary

While each café may have its own lexicon for different kinds of beverages, it's still helpful to have some kind of starting point for exploring the world of Seattle java. The botany and agriculture of coffee has its own nomenclature (arabica, robusta, etc) that will appeal to true enthusiasts, but what follows focuses on the way beverages are created and presented in cafés.

americano one or more shots of espresso diluted with hot water

barista the employee in charge of making espresso beverages

breve espresso with half-and-half

cappuccino equal parts espresso, steamed milk, and frothed (foamed) milk, though Italian recipes call for more foam

con panna espresso topped with whipped cream

crema the thin layer of amber (non-milk) foam atop an espresso, whose presence is said to be the defining mark of an expert barista

demitasse a 3-ounce cup, often ceramic

doppio two espresso shots in a cup

double or "**double shot**," two espresso shots in any beverage

dry cappuccino served with little (or without) steamed milk, but with foam; also known as a "scuro"

espresso or "pressed" coffee, which occurs when highly pressurized boiling water is forced through finely ground coffee

foam usually refers to frothed milk, though sometimes to the crema, which has no milk

frappuccino a latte or mocha mixed with crushed ice, often with other flavors such as caramel, vanilla, etc

freddo iced espresso

French press a glass cylinder used to make regular coffee (not espresso) by steeping, then forcing, fine grounds through hot water

grande a 16-ounce cup

granita a latte mixed with crushed ice and sugar

latte one part espresso to two parts steamed milk; known as *café au lait* when regular coffee is used instead of espresso

macchiato an espresso topped with a thin layer of milk foam

mocha a latte with a variant blend of cocoa or chocolate

mochaccino a cappuccino with chocolate syrup, and sometimes whipped cream on top

quad four espresso shots in any beverage

ristretto concentrated espresso, using less water in the press

short an 8-ounce cup

skinny a latte with skim milk

soy a latte with soy milk

tall a 12-ounce cup

triple or "**triple shot**," three espresso shots in any beverage

venti a 20-ounce cup

wet cappuccino served with little or no foam, but with steamed milk; also known as a "chiaro"

whip whipped cream

The fish ladder and Carl S. English Botanical Garden

Somewhat more fascinating than the locks – if you're here in the right season – is the **fish ladder**, which is on the Magnolia side of the water, but is easily accessible via a footbridge along the canal's dam (provided the locks aren't open). Built to allow salmon to pass around the locks and dam, the ladder is one of the few in the world located where salty and fresh waters meet; it enables the fish to lay and fertilize their eggs, tasks that must be completed in fresh water. The ladder's 21 "**steps**," or weirs, are best viewed between July and September, when chinook, sockeye, and coho salmon jump around the ladder at the peak of their upstream migration. Midwinter is when steelhead salmon appear, but during April and May, little but green muck is visible through the observation windows, with migration at such a low point that it's almost nonexistent.

Lastly, across from the visitors' center, the tiny **Carl S. English Botanical Garden** (daily 7.30am–9pm; free) has sloping hillsides that are good vantage points for watching the ships, along with some five hundred types of plants and flowers, including camellias, snowberries, and oaks, on garden turf built over earthen fill that was put here during the construction of the locks.

Ballard Avenue and around

Just north of the locks is Ballard's small but appealing cultural zone, on and around **Ballard Avenue** between 17th and 22nd avenues NW. Much of this stretch is an official Historic Landmark District, so designated by the city for its wealth of early twentieth-century architecture and many preserved buildings, mainly former commercial and industrial sites. The visual highlight is the old **Firehouse no. 18**, 5429 Russell Ave NW, an eye-catching brick structure from 1911 with wooden roof brackets, looming tower, and quaint red gates that once opened for the station's horse-drawn fire engines. Decommissioned in 1974, it's since become home to a restaurant (the *Hi-Life*; see p.169 for review), as has the classic **Carnegie Library** right across Market Street, predictably known as

---

Salmon troubles

Salmon fishing is a major industry in the Pacific Northwest, with a $300 million annual harvest. Salmon are born and reared in fresh water before migrating to the ocean for a few years, after which they return to fresh water to spawn. The fish travel so widely that both the US and Canada cannot help but catch a good deal of fish that spawn within each other's borders. Consequently, a 1985 Canada–US **Pacific Salmon Treaty**, established to ensure equity between Canadian and American harvests and prevent overfishing, was updated in 2000 with new quotas geared toward the best interest of salmon, rather than industry. Toward that end, $140 million was provided by the US government for **habitat restoration**, designed to rebuild the salmon runs in both countries, and to support native tribes in managing their own stocks of salmon. As fishing quotas can be difficult to measure and enforce, the amended treaty also spelled out the researchers' role in tracking the salmon population's development.

Since then, administered by federal and state regulators, as well as entities like the **Pacific Salmon Commission**, the new agreement has helped to lessen previous conflicts to some degree. However, the continuing decline of salmon populations throughout the West continues largely unabated, and unless major changes are made to improve the inland conditions for the fish (such as dam removal, for one), all the complex rules may end up regulating a fish that no longer exists.

Carnegie's (see p.169). Even more appealing for its striking design is the facility, opened in 2005, for the local **Ballard Library**, just a block north at 5614 22nd Ave NW (call for hours at ☎206/684-4089, ⊛www.spl.org), which like its Downtown counterpart (see p.59) offers an inviting modern look – a curving, steel-shingled facade under sweeping, cantilevered wooden beams. It's most notable, though, for its "**green roof**" equipped with solar panels and 18,000 hardy plants to soak up what would otherwise be wastewater, along with small, mysterious-looking domes that, according to the library, "measure wind speed and direction, sunlight and the sound of rain."

Beyond eateries and architecture, there are plenty of fine bars and clubs in the vicinity, and the neighborhood pulses with activity on weekend nights, when crowds come to the **Tractor Tavern**, 5213 Ballard Ave NW, and other venues for a helping of the latest Seattle rock. If the tunes don't grab you, visit on the second Saturday night of the month for one of the district's groovy **Art Walks** (6–9pm), where you can immerse yourself in the trendy local art scene at the late-closing galleries, and drop in on the neighborhood's secondhand clothing boutiques or all-American eateries while you're at it. To take the official stroll, start along Ballard Avenue at 22nd Avenue and continue to 17th, then turn west on Market Street for five blocks. Once you finish, you're within sight of the apotheosis of Seattle quirkiness, **Archie McPhee**, 2428 NW Market St (Mon–Sat 9am–7pm, Sun 10am–6pm; ☎206/297-0240, ⊛www.mcphee .com), a legendary clearinghouse for all kinds of antique junk, novelty trinkets, and cultural detritus, with a heavy emphasis on lounge-lizard and Tiki decor. Step inside for a look at such must-see items as replica otter and baboon skulls, Frankenstein and Dracula coffee mugs, Day-Glo wigs and Viking helmets, voodoo dolls, garden gnomes, and even an ancient cast-iron monkey bank.

The Nordic Heritage Museum

When Ballard was settled in the late nineteenth century, Scandinavians dominated the population. Today, their cultural presence remains strong, with more than half a million Washingtonians claiming Scandinavian ancestry. As such, there's an annual May 17 parade held in honor of Norwegian Constitution Day, as well as the **Nordic Heritage Museum**, about two-thirds of a mile north of the locks at 3014 NW 67th St (daily 10am–4pm, Sun opens at noon; $6; ⊛www.nordicmuseum.org), which celebrates this history with three floors of earnest exhibits.

The ground floor is the most informative, with a sizable **Dream of America** exhibit that takes you through the Scandinavian-American immigrant experience from 1840 to 1920, telling how many of them escaped from rural poverty in their native lands to be processed at Ellis Island, only later to struggle against the elements in the rugged West. The **Ballard Story** display recreates these early days of the local community in old photographs, relics, and historical narratives.

The second floor hosts the **Heritage Rooms**, devoted to fishing and logging, along with artifacts from five Nordic groups, including traditional clothing, tapestries, and household items decorated with folk art, such as a Danish flax beater and a Finnish birdhouse designed to look like a church.

The top floor, with separate wings given over to folk art and the Northwest immigrant communities of Norway, Iceland, Denmark, Finland, and Sweden, has yet more common household items and furnishings – such as farm tools used by Icelandic-American farmers – and pictures of Scandinavian-American organizations from the early 1900s. The highlight is the **Iceland Room**, a replica of the interior of a rural farmhouse from the early twentieth century, featuring the woolen garments and simple wooden architecture and furniture you'd expect – but without the bone-chilling cold of the Arctic Circle. Finally, the museum's temporary exhibitions showcase the wide-ranging achievements and art of Scandinavians – everything from rough-hewn carvings to modern landscape photography – while a spring **film festival** gives a glimpse of the current state of cinema from the northern latitudes.

Golden Gardens Park

Continuing north along Shilshole Bay, above the Salmon Bay inlet, once you reach the end of Seaview Avenue, **Golden Gardens Park**, 8498 Seaview Ave (daily 6am–11.30pm; ☎206/684-4075), offers a small slice of local beach culture, its small sandy shoreline far less known than West Seattle's Alki Beach (see p.137). Its relative lack of popularity makes for peaceful beachcombing during most of the year, though it can get more crowded in warm weather. You won't want to swim here, as the water is usually too cold for comfort, but there are some dunes and wetlands in the northern part that make for good, if limited, wandering – most of the trails are one-fourth to one-half of a mile long. The park also offers some amusement for teens with its **Brick House** social center, 8498 Seaview Ave NW (information at ☎206/684-4031), with the usual sports facilities as well as a concert stage on Saturday nights for visiting rock and rap groups.

Fremont, Wallingford, and the far north

The northern Seattle neighborhoods of **Fremont** and **Wallingford** are vigorous, spirited communities that, thanks to their quirky appeal and unpretentious bohemian vibe, are being forced to cope with an influx of newcomers and significant new development. What makes these places so engaging has little to do with their location (isolated by Lake Union and the Ship Canal from much of the city) or their conventional attractions (few in number), but rather their laid-back attitude and preservation of a certain old-fashioned Seattle style, before the city exploded with the high-tech boom and changed its character from a mellow, oddball place to one obsessed with its international image and the bottom line. Today, even with new condos sprouting here and there, Fremont and Wallingford retain their eccentric charm, as do districts further north like **Greenwood** and **Green Lake**, which make for an appealing diversion if you're already in the area. **Further north** the attractions are fewer and more spread out, as Seattle moves from its dense urban core to endless miles of bedroom communities.

Fremont

As you cross into **Fremont** from Ballard (via Leary Way NW) or from Queen Anne (via the Fremont Bridge), signs proclaim, "Welcome to Fremont, Center of the Universe." This offers fair warning that the self-described **Artists' Republic of Fremont** is not for those who take themselves too seriously: this mostly white, middle-class area is far more fun than most districts, with a friendly, offbeat charm that makes it a great place to while away a few hours.

In the shadow of the towering Aurora Bridge (by no means a good access route into the district), the neighborhood's triangular core is the stretch of **Fremont Avenue** that runs from the tiny, ramshackle Fremont Bridge at N 34th Street to N 37th Street. Here you'll find an engaging array of coffeehouses, restaurants, used bookstores, and secondhand boutiques, more or less evenly divided between countercultural shops and the standard chains. A few establishments with even more commercial clout have also set up digs in Fremont, notably the software giant Adobe Systems, located right by the Fremont Bridge.

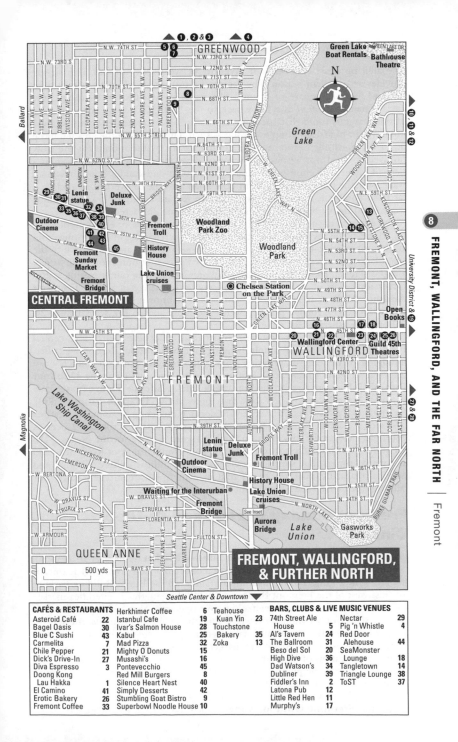

Fremont Avenue

The alluring heart of **Fremont Avenue**, between N 34th and 37th streets, provides an excellent reason why thoughtful tourists should depart from their standard Pioneer Square-to-Capitol Hill itinerary and take in a groovy little enclave that styles itself as a throwback to the 1960s. Of course, the marketing of this image is somewhat specious, as you'll find fewer actual hemp-wearing hippies than high-tech yuppies posing as such. The homes in the area fetch top dollar for northside Seattle, and it's getting harder by the month for the truly tie-dyed to hold out against the wave of development, which has brought a slew of chain coffeehouses and high-priced soap-and-candle boutiques in its wake. Still, the transformation from bohemian art-ville to overpriced enclave is far from complete, as Fremont continues to feature enough off-kilter antique dealers and freaky boutiques to maintain its unique character.

The epitome of these quirky merchants is **Deluxe Junk**, 3518 Fremont Place N, whose name says it all. True to its bizarre merchandise – everything from antique silver stick-pins, to posters of geishas selling soap and bug-spray, to the finest leisure suits – the store is identifiable by its six-foot humanoid sculpture of a cup of French fries with a demented expression, glaring out at passing traffic. Other top sellers of objects from the recent and distant past are the **Fremont Antique Mall** at No. 3419, the district's best-known dealer, and **Antique Alley**, No. 3519, for art prints, jewelry, clothing, and so on; see Chapter 20, "Shops and galleries," for reviews.

Along with hunting for vintage or worn-out collectibles, a trip into central Fremont is also good for simply hanging out with the locals, sipping coffee, indulging in desserts, or drinking your troubles away. You can munch on a spicy pie at **Mad Pizza**, 3601 Fremont Ave N; get bombed at the **Dubliner Pub**, 3517 Fremont Ave N; dine on veggie fare at **Silence Heart Nest**, 3508 Fremont Place N; or knock back a tasty brew at the **Triangle Lounge**, 3507 Fremont Place N, where the eccentric decor is matched by some of Seattle's best ales – indeed, Fremont has several fine bars with microbrewed beer. A good place to get the lowdown on the local scene is at **Fremont News**, 3416 Fremont Ave N, which not only offers a nice complement of local zines and alternative papers, but supplies a wide stock of offbeat culture, fashion, and political magazines that you won't find in many mainstream chain stores; for late-night readers, it stays open until 11pm on weekends.

Fremont Sunday Market and Outdoor Cinema

Just off Fremont Avenue, the **Fremont Sunday Market** (Apil–Oct 10am–5pm, Nov–March 10am–4pm; free; www.fremontmarket.com/fremont) is one of the area's most longstanding institutions. Filling up the Burke Building parking lot (just west of the Fremont Bridge on N 34th Street), this spirited flea market has, for nearly fifteen years, been a low-cost operation that highlights the city's bargain sellers of secondhand jewelry, furniture, clothing, trinkets, music, and other curiosities, the merchants' stalls teeming with regional buyers as well as wide-eyed browsers. Although the market has had its share of difficulties – first with the relocation of its produce market to Ballard, and second with lawsuits from its corporate neighbors – it's still one of Seattle's best agoras, and should not be missed on any trip to Fremont.

One long block west of the market site, Seattle's most unusual summer movie venue, the **Fremont Outdoor Cinema** (late June–Aug; $5; ☎206/781 4230,

ⓦfremontoutdoormovies.com), runs a colorful variety of Hollywood block-busters, cult films, and sing-a-long musicals every Saturday night at dusk during the summer. This particular "cinema" isn't much more than the sparsely decorated side of a pet-products warehouse at 35th and N Phinney Avenue, but is nonetheless quite enjoyable, as much for its energetic viewers as for the familiar flicks. There's improv comedy and assorted hijinks before many of the screenings, and audience members are encouraged to bring their own imaginative seating and movie-themed costumes, with prizes offered for the best in each category.

History House

For a more far-reaching perspective on life in Fremont, venture a block east of Fremont Avenue to the **History House**, 790 N 34th St (Wed–Sun noon–5pm; $1 suggested donation; ☎206/675-1875, ⓦwww.historyhouse.org), which details the late nineteenth- and early twentieth-century history of the area (and other Seattle districts), when it was mainly a working-class town full of mill- and dock-workers. For the most part, the historic photos are rather dull, though there are exceptions, like the images of hydroplanes racing on Green Lake, and those of actual commuters – not just statues of commuters – waiting at the site where the *Waiting for the Interurban* sculpture now stands (see box, p.120). There are also a few worthwhile videos, such as one on the construction of the Seattle–Tacoma railroad – of greatest interest when a sudden Seattle downpour makes it imperative to kill an hour or so indoors.

Lake Union cruises

When you've had your fill of Fremont's quirkiness, you can get some fresh air by seeing **Lake Union** via hourly **Sunday cruises** on the *Fremont Avenue* ferry, which departs from under the Aurora Bridge, 801 N Northlake Way (daily on the

△ Fremont Troll

Fremont's vivid display of **public art** is testament to the community's playful sense of surrealism, and, prodded on by descriptive signs at each attraction, tourists are encouraged to wander around visiting one sculpted or painted curiosity after another. Start your tour by picking up the free *Walking Guide to Fremont* at the kiosk of the **Rocket at the Center of the Universe**, a 53-foot monument at the corner of N 35th Street and Evanston Avenue that looks more like a giant toy model than a space-traveling vessel, even though it's alleged to be an actual rocket fuselage taken from the facade of an Army surplus store. Whatever its origin, as the "Story of the Rocket" placard at the bottom deadpans, it was intended as a monument to commemorate the discovery of the center of the universe in Fremont in 1991.

A block north, at the triangular corner of 36th and Fremont Place, another oddity is almost as eye-catching, or at least jaw-dropping: a colossal, somewhat ominous statue of **Vladimir Lenin** stands thrusting forth toward passing motorists, surrounded by blocky flames. This sculpture, by Slavic artist Emil Venkov, is said to be the only representation of Lenin "surrounded by guns and flames instead of holding a book or waving a hat." One Lewis Carpenter found it in Slovakia after it was toppled in the 1989 Velvet Revolution, and mortgaged his home to bring it back to Issaquah, a small town near Seattle.

Down the road at N 34th Street, a much less aggressive piece can be seen just east of Fremont Bridge: Richard Beyer's brilliant late-1970s **Waiting for the Inter-urban**. The sculpture – lifelike aluminum statues of five dour commuters waiting for the bus with a small child and a dog – is regularly adorned by locals with football helmets, Hawaiian leis, and other offbeat additions. The title refers to a long-disap-peared transit line that ran through here until the 1930s, and the visual motifs borrow heavily from the work of sculptor George Segal, though with a facetious bent. Less interesting is the pair of metal-frame **dinosaurs** two long blocks to the west, at 34th and Phinney Avenue N, only worth a glance if you're intent on seeing all the major artworks in Fremont.

The undeniable highlight of the district, though, is the eighteen-foot ferroconcrete **Fremont Troll** that lurks underneath Aurora Bridge, a five-minute walk from the

hour 11am–5pm; $8, kids $5; ☎206/713-8446, ⓦwww.seattleferryservice.com). The cruise includes close-up perspectives on Seattle's canals and lakes, views of noteworthy houseboats, and a glimpse at big-name glass blower Dale Chihuly's waterside studio. If you'd rather enjoy the lake from dry land, a **shoreline path** begins at the Fremont Bridge and continues east to to the lake at Gasworks Park (see p.122), where it merges with the famed Burke-Gilman Trail, extending another twelve miles through the U District and Lake Washington areas.

Wallingford

Between Fremont and the University District lies **Wallingford**, a mildly alterna-tive district with a liberal, middle-class air and some good restaurants and cinemas along its axis of **North 45th Street**. Often tagged by Seattlites as "the next Fremont" – with all the implications of higher rents and new development that label carries with it – Wallingford is in fact different in several ways from its neigh-bor to the west. For one, an assertively bohemian atmosphere is lacking here; in its place is a friendlier, more relaxed vibe, though still with an excellent assortment of

Interurban at N 36th Street and Aurora Avenue N. Like several of the public artworks in the district, the Troll was commissioned by the Fremont Arts Council (@www. fremontartscouncil.org), a volunteer community organization that promotes visual spectacles and festivities to make the community a cheerier place. Under the steel lid of Aurora Avenue and between the concrete bridge pilings, the beast really does seem to preside over his gloomy lair; the left hand of the creature is even eternally crushing a real Volkswagen Bug. The sculpture also serves as an inspiration for Fremont's Luminary Procession on October 31, dubbed "**Trolloween**." Starting here, this parade of costumed masqueraders – some wearing jester outfits and wielding torches – moves through Fremont, with lively street performances and cacophonous music throughout.

If you're in the area on the official beginning of summer (mid-June), you can get another good taste of Fremont's artistic leanings at the colorful **Fremont Fair** and **Solstice Parade**, founded in 1974 by the Fremont Public Association to raise money for low-income residents (information at ☎206/633-4409 or @www.fremontfair.com). The fair offers hundreds of multiethnic food stalls and arts-and-crafts vendors, while the parade allows only human-powered floats and costumes, ranging from giant puppets and two-man dragons to robots on stilts, and even nude bicyclists – who begin the parade in the buff painted like giant bees, peacocks and cows, among other incarnations (for more information, see "Festivals and events," p.202). The parade is often followed by a similar nature-oriented **pageant** that takes place at the end of the route in Gasworks Park (see p.122), with all donations supporting the festivities collected by – what else? – a giant, roving green hat.

If this sounds a little too bizarre, or you prefer a spectacle of the intoxicating variety, don't miss Fremont's own **Oktobertfest** (late Sept; family events free, beer tastings $20; www.fremontoktoberfest.com), when dozens of vendors from local brewpubs come together to offer their latest suds, all in an atmosphere of plentiful music, food, and (of course) quirky displays of art. To catch up on what else Fremont offers throughout the year, see wwww.fremontseattle.com.

restaurants, bars, antique stores, and vintage clothing dealers. Secondly, the district's big draws – the attractive and spacious **Woodland Park Zoo**, and the curious industrial playground of **Gasworks Park** – are, unlike the top sights in Fremont, rather far-flung, and make for a lengthy hike if you want to visit them on foot.

Forty-fifth Street

One strip that *is* easily walkable is the stretch from Woodlawn to Bagley avenues along **North 45th Street**, the neighborhood's five-block main drag. It's a fine place to dine on Asian or Mexican cuisine, shop for books or secondhand clothing, sip on coffee, or knock back a beer. Notable merchants along the street include the **Erotic Bakery**, no. 2323, selling cakes and pastries decorated with risqué messages and scandalous designs; **Open Books**, below a wine bar at no. 2414, a self-described "poem emporium," flush with mainstream and alternative poetry, and hosting readings by notable authors; and the **Seamonster Lounge**, no. 2202, chock full of art on the walls, inventive cocktails like the "Oatmeal Nipple," and widely eclectic live music – anything from electro-funk to avant-garde jazz to multimedia noodling. The excellent pair of movie theaters known collectively as the **Guild 45th**, no. 2115 (☎206/633-3353, @www.landmarktheatres.com), is a draw for its mainstream and independent fare presented in two distinct cinemas, one of them dating from 1919; while the **Wallingford Center**, no. 1815, has variable boutiques and restaurants in a three-story former school building. Across the street, the very center of the strip is marked with giant capital letters atop a supermarket at no. 1801, spelling out "WALLINGFORD" in blue-and-white neon.

Gasworks Park

At the southern tip of Wallingford, along the shores of Lake Union, is one of the best and most bizarre places to get an expansive view of the city: the twenty-acre **Gasworks Park**, 2101 N Northlake Way (daily 6am–11.30pm, parking lot open 6am–9pm; ☎206/684-4075). Unlike most parks in Seattle, which either originated from the Olmsted brothers' masterplan or simply protected the existing natural turf from development, the grounds of this park were, from 1906 until the mid-1950s, occupied by the **Seattle Gas Company**, whose massive industrial plant converted coal and oil into gas. Several gigantic, brown oxygen gas-generator towers still remain, the clash between the dark, fenced-off structures and the surrounding green hills lending the site a strangely artistic vibe – a feeling enhanced by the imaginative graffiti that's been splattered by locals over the years onto the monoliths. Its small hills and windy location on the banks of the lake make it a favorite spot for kite flyers, and its location makes it Seattle's prime vantage point for Fourth of July fireworks, with Downtown and the Space Needle gleaming to the south.

Be advised that there's still some contamination in the soil and ground water, so children should be supervised or herded into the picnic area and **playbarn** – its large, brightly painted industrial pipes, engines, and wheels making for a surreal experience for the tots – located alongside a more conventional playground. Gasworks Park is also a good spot for a stroll, either west toward the core of Fremont or east to a small collection of houseboats on Lake Union. From the park, you can hop onto the sixteen-mile **Burke-Gilman Trail**, Seattle's most popular biking route (also open to walkers and joggers), which starts in Fremont and runs along the lake before swinging north to the University of Washington and beyond. (For information on renting bikes in Seattle, see p.209.)

Woodland Park Zoo

Centrally located near the boundaries of Fremont, Wallingford, and Green Lake, more than 250 species reside in the **Woodland Park Zoo**, a mile northwest of central Wallingford (daily 9.30am–4pm, summer closes at 6pm; $10, kids $7; ☎206/684-4026, ⊛www.zoo.org); it's a sleek facility whose spacious layout, humane exhibits, and botanical garden-quality trees and plants make it attractive to anyone with a love of nature. The large plots of open space might cause some to yearn for more creatures and less park, but it's far less cramped than the typical zoo, with natural habitats constructed for maximal space and geographical accuracy. Most of the exhibits are thematically arranged to reflect different climates and terrains – Northern Trail, Tropical Asia, Tropical Forest, Temperate Forest, and so on – and this verisimilitude gives Woodland Park an engaging, bucolic feel, unlike the hemmed-in concrete bunkers of some big-city zoos.

The zoo is surrounded by the nearly two hundred acres of **Woodland Park** proper (daily 4am–11.30pm; ☎206/684-4075), a nice refuge from the city and a natural preserve that's home to hiking trails, picnic tables, athletic facilities for tennis and lawn bowling, and a worthwhile **rose garden** (daily 7am–dusk;

free), where you can sniff and gaze at nearly three hundred varieties of flowers in five-thousand plantings – both old-fashioned red and pink roses as well as modern, multi-hued varieties.

Animal exhibits

The diversity of **animal exhibits** at the zoo is impressive, including such exotic species as lion-tailed macaques, kookaburras and wallabies, black-and-white colobus monkeys with lustrous white tails, porcupines, Sumatran tigers, pygmy marmosets (the smallest primate in the world), and a Malayan sun bear (the smallest bear in the world). Make sure to check out the indoor **Day and Night** section, where you creep along in near-darkness so as not to disturb an assortment of nocturnal birds and reptiles that slither in and out of sight. Nearby are gorillas almost close enough to touch, and more than close enough to examine their facial expressions, albeit behind protective glass. This area of the park, the **Tropical Rain Forest**, also features the recently built **Jaguar Cove**, a sprawling enclosure with a waterfall, Central American trees, fish pool, and babbling streams – all devoted to just one big cat, who roams around at will and occasionally makes appearances for the public.

You can get within a few feet of the elephants in the **Tropical Asia** section; the mighty pachyderms are bathed daily at 10am, and the herd is a tightly knit group of three females, with the youngest, Hansa, just four years old. However, you'll have to be content to see the zebras and giraffes from a much greater distance: they're allowed to roam uncaged through the large field of the **African Savanna** – not quite the Serengeti plain, but about as accurate as a Pacific Northwest version can get. Don't leave before taking a peek at the tiny, burrowing prairie dog, tucked into an easily missed corner behind the Pony Ring; it's one of several species on display like snow leopards, Komodo dragons, and penguins that don't lend themselves to quick categorization.

Finally, climbing the low rocks that provide a viewing platform for the African Savanna, classic rock fans should be on the lookout for a tiny gold, sunburst-shaped memorial to **Jimi Hendrix**, perhaps the city's most inconspicuous memorial to its native son, though the space covered by the design is small enough to be obscured by a few birds.

The far north

North of Fremont and Wallingford are several destinations more frequented by locals than tourists, making for a relaxed outing if you're not in the mood for a vigorous sightseeing agenda. Immediately north of Woodland Park, **Green Lake** is one of Seattle's favorite natural preserves within the city limits. Meanwhile, just to the north and west, **Greenwood** is a hot spot for alternative clothes-shopping and "antiquing." A long trek to the east takes you to the breezy promontory of **Magnuson Park**, while a journey to the northwest leads to **Carkeek Park**, offering a nice set of beaches, forest walks, and spawning grounds for salmon.

Green Lake

Several blocks northeast of Woodland Park, landlocked **Green Lake** is a popular recreational retreat encircled by a lakeside park and three-mile **athletic path** that's so heavily used by joggers, rollerbladers, walkers, and bikers that signs give directions for what side of the strip you should occupy, depending on your sport. The lake beyond certainly makes for an inviting backdrop to such healthy pursuits, but it was not always so.

Though it might not look it today, the lake was well on its way toward becoming a **swamp** at the turn of the century, when its water level was lowered to create additional shoreline, and the creeks that fed and drained it were mistakenly cut off. Stagnation, foul odors, and algae blooms quickly followed, along with public indifference and subsequent pollution by heavy industry bordering the lake; only in the last few decades have a local environmental push and government action turned the ecology around, to the point where the lake now looks tantalizingly clean – even though it's still contaminated in places – and acts as a home to more than 150 species of birds.

Appropriately, some of the attractions here include tiny **Duck Island**, designated as a wildlife reserve for the lake's remaining quackers; the **Bathhouse Theatre**, 7312 W Green Lake Drive N, a former bathing facility that's now home to the Seattle Public Theatre (☏206/524-1300, ⊛www.seattlepub-lictheater.org); and **Green Lake Boat Rentals**, at the lake's northeastern corner, 7351 Greenlake Drive N (April–Sept daily 10am–6pm; ☏206/527-0171), which rents rowboats, paddleboats, canoes, and one-person kayaks for $10/hr, two-person kayaks for $12/hr, and sailboats and windsurfers for $14/hr. The perimeter boulevards beyond the lake and park, **Green Lake Way** and **Green Lake Drive**, also have a scattered selection of diners, bars, and boutiques, mainly of interest to locals.

Greenwood

With the businesses bordering Green Lake all fairly unexceptional, it's worth traveling a few blocks north and west to the quaint pocket of **Greenwood** to get a taste of an up-and-coming neighborhood that's increasingly popular with lower-income artists, families, and young people who've been priced out of Fremont and Wallingford. The hub of the area lies along **Greenwood Avenue N** between N 70th and N 75th streets, where you can find an array of boutiques, restaurants, thrift stores, junk merchants, and coffeehouses.

Another decent selection of shops can be found less than a mile further north where Greenwood Avenue meets **85th Street**. Here, the fare is a bit on the grungy side, but you're also more apt to find better deals than elsewhere. The main draw for anyone interested in hunting down cut-rate collectibles is **Thriftko**, no. 124 (☏206/789-5357), a junk emporium where you can snap up trash for treasures for a couple of bucks, while across the street, **Squirrel's Accumulate**, no. 119 (☏206/789-8486), offers a nice clutter of antique goods and trinkets. One of Seattle's best spots for acquiring creative playthings is **Top Ten Toys**, no. 104 (☏206/782-0098), among them model trains, dolls and puppets, musical instruments, and inventive board games.

Magnuson and Carkeek parks

Lying at opposite sides of north Seattle, Magnuson and Carkeek parks are the northernmost attractions in the city that reward a visit. Located at the terminus of the sixteen-mile Burke-Gilman Trail, the 350 acres of **Magnuson Park**, 7400 Sand Point Way NE (daily 4am–10pm, summer closes 11.30pm), sit on the wind-scoured promontory of Sand Point, looking out at Lake Washington and offering decent athletic facilities and a pleasant set of trails. At the northeastern section, an **Art Walk** is centered around John Young's installation, *From Swords to Ploughshares*, a strange array of black submarine fins that have been sliced off their military vessels and wedged into the earth at seemingly random angles – calling to mind a school of ominous subterranean fish.

Unfortunately, one of Seattle's best public artworks is now much more inconvenient to view. The adjacent campus of the **National Oceanic and Atmospheric Administration** (NOAA), also on Sand Point, holds Douglas Hollis's kinetic **Sound Garden** sculpture, which became the namesake of the now-defunct grunge band. If you don't mind being searched by agents of the increasingly paranoid federal government, you can gain access to the facility through its front gate off Sand Point Way NE (foot traffic only; Mon–Fri 9am–5pm; ☎206/526-6163) or show up in time for the brief openings of the back gate, which connects to Magnuson Park (Mon–Fri 11.30am–1.30pm). Once you get in, you'll come to a curving path that leads to eleven spindly metal towers. Hollow pipes dangle to the side of the towers, helping to produce low hums that can be mistaken for horns from distant ships in the water. A windy environment is needed for maximum effect (which usually isn't a problem); if you're here on a calm day, you'll find the Sound Garden eerily soundless.

On the Puget Sound side of north Seattle, **Carkeek Park**, 950 NW Carkeek Park Rd (daily 6am–10pm; ☎206/684-0877), is marked by its abundance of plant life, including Douglas firs, pine trees, cattails, and impressive lady ferns, as well as its rugged hiking trails and 22 acres of beaches – about a tenth the total area of the park, which also encompasses striking canyons, ravines, and forests. The park's **Pipers Creek** is home to spawning native salmon, which, despite their decline throughout the Pacific Northwest, have returned to this area through the intrepid work of volunteers.

Lake Washington and the suburbs

Away from the city center, Seattle's bedroom communities lie mostly around huge **Lake Washington**, a strikingly scenic body of water that cuts off Seattle proper from the rest of the region to the east. The suburbs along and near the lake's western shore – Madison Park, Madrona, Mount Baker, and Columbia City – may merit a visit if you're here for more than a week or so (or are racing in the popular Seattle Marathon, whose route mostly runs through here). Keep in mind, though, that the attractions on the lake's western edge are spread out more widely than in other parts of town, so you may need a vehicle of your own to navigate them – or plenty of time and patience to go by bus.

On the eastern side of Lake Washington – an area collectively known as the **Eastside** – you'll find the headquarters for Microsoft and other major technology companies. Bellevue is the largest of the suburbs here, with a handful of worthwhile stops, including a good art museum and pair of terrific parks, while the only reason to visit Renton, further south, is to pay your respects at **Jimi Hendrix's grave** in Greenwood Cemetery. To the south and west of Downtown, Seattle becomes more industrial, though West Seattle does have **Alki Beach**, the most popular of the city's few beaches. In the heart of Seattle's southern manufacturing area, the cavernous **Museum of Flight** is one of the better museums in the Northwest.

Lake Washington and around

Eighteen miles long and about three-and-a-half miles wide, **Lake Washington** is a formidable buffer between Seattle and the Eastside. Though the lakeshore is partially occupied by plush, exclusive estates, much of it remains dedicated for public use by bicyclists, joggers, and rollerbladers, ever since a 1960s cleanup mostly rid the lake of pollution (though the water is too cold for swimming). If you want to get out on the lake without getting in, **boat rentals** are available at the University of Washington's Waterfront Activities Center (see p.104) and from **Stan Sayres Park** (see p.129).

A bike ride or car trip along **Lake Washington Boulevard** – which runs the length of the lake, and is the eastern boundary for the central city – takes you by some of Seattle's best domestic architecture and prettiest locales, with attractive, isolated walks by the water's edge and a few pockets of dense city-park greenery to get lost in.

Madison Park

From the south end of the Washington Park Arboretum (see p.98), Lake Washington Boulevard meanders through wealthy **Madison Park**, whose central district lies near the terminus of E Madison Street at the lake's edge. Once a turn-of-the-century amusement center with a shoreline bathhouse, dramatic stage, and aquatic park, nowadays the "downtown" area has few attractions and only a handful of restaurants worth seeking out. Still, the neighborhood overall is one of Seattle's more interesting upscale preserves, with an easygoing mix of upper-middle-class families and older gay couples, and a compelling blend of historic bungalows and modest mansions. To really get a sense of the district, it's worth wandering along the pleasant lakeside **Madison Park** (daily 4am–11.30pm), with its own beach, or exploring the architecturally rich areas off McGilvra and Lake Washington boulevards.

Denny Blaine

A good place to start is on the twisting streets south of Madison Street, around the sub-district of **Denny Blaine** (named after two different Seattle founders), where a number of classic early twentieth-century structures offer a vivid look at Seattle's past. One of the best examples is the 1910 **Samuel Hyde House**, 3726 E Madison St, an imposing Colonial Revival affair – said to have been landscaped by the Olmsted brothers

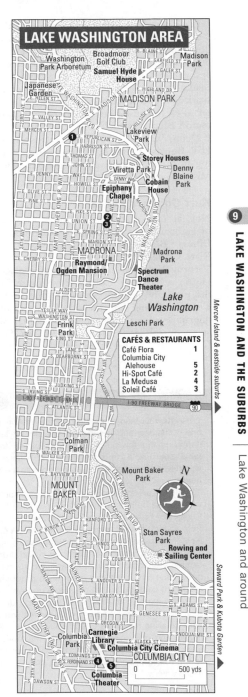

LAKE WASHINGTON AREA

Washington Park Arboretum
Broadmoor Golf Club
Samuel Hyde House
Japanese Garden
MADISON PARK
Madison Park
Lakeview Park
Storey Houses
Viretta Park
Denny Blaine Park
Epiphany Chapel
Cobain House
MADRONA
Raymond/Ogden Mansion
Madrona Park
Spectrum Dance Theater
Lake Washington
Frink Park
Leschi Park
Colman Park
Mount Baker Park
MOUNT BAKER
Stan Sayres Park
Rowing and Sailing Center
Carnegie Library
Columbia Park
Columbia City Cinema
COLUMBIA CITY
Columbia Theater

CAFÉS & RESTAURANTS

Café Flora	1
Columbia City Alehouse	5
Hi-Spot Café	2
La Medusa	4
Soleil Café	3

0   500 yds

Mercer Island & eastside suburbs

Seward Park & Kubota Garden

– that's now home to the Russian consulate. Much less ostentatious are the 1903 **Storey Houses**, ten blocks south, off Lake Washington Boulevard at 260 and 270 Dorffel Drive E, once home to the noted architect Ellsworth Storey and his parents, respectively. Both use regional materials like river rock and native wood to create a local version of the Craftsman style, with more than a touch of Swiss chalet thrown in for good measure. Storey's inspired work is found throughout this and other neighboring districts, including a set of eleven rustic but charming **cottages**, around 1700–1800 Lake Washington Blvd, and such minor masterpieces as the **Epiphany Chapel**, 3719 E Denny Way, a 1911 mix of Craftsman and Tudor Revival, and the **Beacon Hill Baptist Church**, two miles south at 1607 S Forest Ave, an eye-opening hodgepodge of everything from Gothic window tracery to a Spanish Mission bell tower.

Kurt Cobain's house

Not far from the Storey Houses, you can find an entirely different sort of landmark: the handsome stone-walled residence of district co-founder **Elbert Blaine**, which later became the home of Nirvana frontman **Kurt Cobain**, at 171 Lake Washington Blvd E. Best viewed from adjacent **Viretta Park**, a small, two-acre green space (daily 4am–11.30pm), the Blaine House was where Cobain shot himself to death in an apartment above the property's garage. Although that unit has since been torn down (and Cobain's widow, Courtney Love, moved out in 1997), diehard fans still make pilgrimages here, sometimes leaving makeshift memorials to their fallen idol at various places in the park (see box). For a fictionalized glimpse of what Cobain's end might have been like, check out Gus Van Sant's glacially paced film *Last Days*.

The death of Kurt Cobain

When **Kurt Cobain** committed suicide on April 5, 1994, Seattle's own **Nirvana** was one of the best-selling and most critically acclaimed rock bands in the world. They had gone, in a few quick years, from just another unknown group on the **Sub Pop label** (see box, p.78) to the leaders of a perceived "movement" – though Cobain was never comfortable in the rock idol role, or with the limited concept of "grunge" music.

While the group's sudden success was a surprise, Cobain's death, unfortunately, was not, as he had spent his last few years battling drug and medical problems. Rumors of his instability had multiplied just a month before, when he nearly died from an overdose of tranquilizers in Rome. A couple of weeks later, Cobain's wife, Hole frontwoman Courtney Love, reported a suicide threat by her husband to the Seattle police, who confiscated a gun and drugs when they arrived. A week later, Cobain's bandmates, friends, and record-company representatives intervened, convincing him to enter a drug rehab program in California – though he fled the treatment center after only a couple of days, disappearing without a trace.

On the morning of April 8, an electrician doing work on Cobain's Seattle property found his dead body. The singer had left behind a lengthy, rambling suicide note detailing his failure to enjoy success, increasing lack of excitement regarding music, and guilt over going through the motions of being a superstar. The note, however, is most infamous for a chilling sentence inspired by a Neil Young lyric: "I don't have the passion any more, and so remember, it's better to burn out than to fade away."

Madrona

Further south, as Lake Washington Boulevard reaches the shores of the lake itself, it hugs the water's edge for about five miles, making it one of Seattle's most scenic drives and a good spot to watch runners going about their business in the Seattle Marathon (see p.210). Just south of Denny Blaine at Howell Street, the cozy district of **MADRONA** – named after the native tree – merges almost seamlessly with Madison Park, as do its swank bungalows and upscale estates, one of which is the striking neo-Georgian **Raymond/Ogden Mansion**, 702 35th Ave, featuring 33 luxurious rooms on a bluff overlooking the lake. It may be worth grabbing an architecture guide (see p.219, "Books," for recommendations) and hunting down more of the area's appealing houses, or simply taking in the excellent vistas along Lake Washington Boulevard and stopping in any number of worthwhile roadside parks.

The first of these, linear, lakeside **Madrona Park**, 853 Lake Washington Blvd (all parks below daily 4am–11.30pm) is good for jogging and hiking, and offers free swimming lessons during the summer. A few blocks south, **Leschi Park**, 201 Lakeside Ave S, is a one-time amusement park that now features pleasant nature walks amid trees and flower gardens; in adjacent **Frink Park**, 398 Lake Washington Blvd S, wooded hiking terrain has been built around a steep ravine and the curve of Lake Washington Boulevard. As you wander about, keep in mind that the park's forest and wetlands are slowly being restored (information at ⓦwww.frinkpark.org) to fit more closely into the park plan devised by the Olmsted brothers early in the twentieth century.

Colman Park to Mount Baker

After another ten blocks southward, Lake Washington Boulevard passes over the tunnel section of I-90, soon reaching the fetching trails and woods of **Colman Park** (all parks below daily 6am–10pm), where it continues on its winding, lakeside route through **Mount Baker Park** and down to **Seward Park**. The entire three-mile stretch is set up as a linear parkway, and it's best on the occasional weekend days (May–Sept second Sat & third Sun 10am–6pm) when it's closed to traffic and the tree-lined concourse fills with cyclists and joggers. The most scenic bike route along the lake follows the same route, though if you prefer to leave the road once you've reached the water, there are paved bike/pedestrian paths on the lake side of the boulevard for much of its shoreline route. (See p.208 for details on Seattle's best bike routes and bike rental options.) In the middle of this stretch, the small, peninsular **Stan Sayres Park**, 3808 Lake Washington Blvd S, is known mainly for its **Mount Baker Rowing and Sailing Center** (Mon & Wed & Fri 9am–6.30pm, Tues & Thurs 5.30am–6.30pm, Sat 7am–4pm, Sun 12.30–5pm; prices vary; information at ☎206/386-1913), from which you can launch anything from a dinghy to a sailboat and take classes on kayaking, canoeing, or general sailing.

A half-mile west of Colman and Sayres parks, **Mount Baker** is of interest mainly to aficionados of early twentieth-century Arts and Crafts and period revival architecture. There are no must-see items, but the route from S Mount Baker Boulevard to S Court Street around Cascadia Avenue S offers more than a few eye-catchers, among them exemplars of Colonial Revival (no. 3311), Craftsman (no. 3105), and Tudor Revival (2812 Mt St Helens Place). Surprisingly enough, until the 1970s this area was considered an urban blight, its structures redlined by bank lenders and ignored by city planners.

Seward Park and Kubota Garden

At the southern end of Lake Washington Boulevard, peninsular **Seward Park** (daily 4am–11.30pm), named after the "Radical Republican" Secretary of State under Lincoln, is a serene turnaround point for cyclists, pedestrians, and roller bladers, spread over 277 acres. Encircled by a two-and-a-half-mile loop path alongside Lake Washington, the park has its own **beach** and a secluded **old-growth forest** preserve at its hilly center, full of Douglas firs, cedars, and maples – which you can see on the rugged inner trails. Designed as part of the Olmsted brothers' masterplan, the park features many of its original historic structures, including a fish hatchery, Greek amphitheater, and bathhouse, all of which were constructed between 1927 and 1953. The park's rich wildlife is highlighted by several bald eagles, and Friends of Seward Park offers regular walking tours (first Sat of month 10am; information at ⊛www.sewardpark.net) on changing themes, from the park's flora and fauna to its geology, history, and restoration. Also on the grounds is the **Seward Park Clay Studio**, 5900 Lake Washington Blvd S (Mon–Fri noon–5pm; free; ☎206-722-6342, ⊛www.sewardparkart.org), which has a ceramics gallery and introductory classes for prospective potters and sculptors.

For an even more secluded natural experience, venture a couple miles south of Seward Park to **Kubota Garden**, at Renton Ave and 55th Ave S (daily dawn–dusk; free; ☎206/684-4584, ⊛www.kubota.org). Established in 1927 by landscaper Fukitaro Kubota, this Japanese garden – traversed by paths made to simulate a miniature mountain walk on a 65-foot hillside – has twenty acres of tranquil ponds, pines, cypresses, bamboos, carved stones, open lawn space, and a waterfall. Not surprisingly, the place is a popular location for weddings, garden shows, and plant sales. Free hour-long guided **tours** are given from the parking lot (April–Oct, fourth Sat & Sun of each month, at 10am).

Columbia City

Laid out as a mill town in the 1890s, then swallowed up by Seattle fourteen years after its inception, **COLUMBIA CITY** still retains the atmosphere of a small town in the Pacific Northwest. Despite an arty, multicultural vibe and the grand old buildings along the main drag, Rainier Avenue S, the district has yet to be gentrified, likely thanks to its distance from the central part of the city, as well as its reputation up until the 1990s as a decrepit no-man's-land.

The focus of the neighborhood, **Columbia Park**, Rainier Avenue S between Alaska and Edmunds streets, hosts community festivals and events like the **Columbia City Farmers Market** (May–Oct Wed 3–7pm), where up to forty vendors hawk their wares – fruits and vegetables, cheeses and breads, and so on – in a festive setting with live music and cooking demonstrations. In the same spot, the **Columbia City Bazaar** (summer Sun 10am–5pm) is another of Seattle's top-notch flea markets, where you can pick up anything from a collectible LP to an old light fixture for not more than a couple bucks. Another prime event, the **Columbia City BeatWalk** (April–Sept first Fri of month 8–11pm; $5; ⊛www.columbiacitybeatwalk.org), offers a cheap opportunity to see a half-dozen local bands performing at area venues, many of them in converted old structures from the turn of the last century.

Next to Columbia Park you'll find **Carnegie Library**, 4721 Rainier Ave S (Mon & Tues 1–8pm, Wed 10am–8pm, Thurs–Sat 10am–6pm, Sun 1–5pm; ☎206/386-1908, ⊛www.spl.org), an elegant 1915 neo-Georgian gem on a sloping site and also the district's most prominent architectural survivor. Other preserved buildings in the area, such as the former **Masonic Temple**, 4816

Rainier Ave S, are likewise now used for contemporary businesses, in this case for the **Columbia City Cinema** ($8 tickets; info at ☎206/721-3156, ⓦwww .columbiacitycinema.com), a stylishly renovated space that offers first-run movies amid a dash of stately old architecture.

The Seattle suburbs

Predictably, most parts of the **Seattle suburbs** offer little more than highway gridlock, anonymous malls and chain stores, mass-housing tracts, and geographic isolation – typically cut off from the central city by sizable lakes, bays, and islands. That said, there are several exceptions: upstart **Bellevue** has a handful of interesting and unique sights, from quirky museums to idyllic parks; **Kirkland** features a small pocket of historic architecture; and **Renton** is home to Jimi Hendrix's gravesite. Well south of Downtown Seattle, the compelling **Museum of Flight** is stuffed with antique fighters and military craft, while, further seaward, **West Seattle** boasts the popular **Alki Beach**. Thirty miles north of the city is **Everett**, home to airplane manufacturer Boeing, as well as a smattering of historic buildings.

Bellevue

Directly across Lake Washington from Seattle proper, the biggest of the region's suburbs, **BELLEVUE**, is actually the fourth-largest city in Washington,

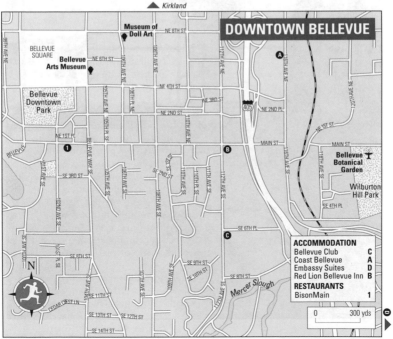

Kirkland

DOWNTOWN BELLEVUE

Museum of Doll Art

BELLEVUE SQUARE

Bellevue Arts Museum

Bellevue Downtown Park

Bellevue Botanical Garden

Wilburton Hill Park

N

Mercer Slough

ACCOMMODATION
Bellevue Club   C
Coast Bellevue   A
Embassy Suites   D
Red Lion Bellevue Inn   B
RESTAURANTS
BisonMain   1

0   300 yds

Mercer Slough Nature Park

complete with squat skyscrapers and thriving local businesses. Indeed, behind urbanites' oft-repeated slurs against "Blahville" and "Hellvue" is a feeling not just of anti-suburban animus, but growing civic rivalry: downtown Bellevue has become one of the hottest office real-estate markets in the US. While you're not likely to spend more than half a day here, it does merit a stop if you find yourself on the east side of Lake Washington. The city is accessible via the 1.4-mile **Hwy-520/Evergreen Point Floating Bridge**, the longest floating bridge in the world, which traverses the lake from the northern edge of Capitol Hill.

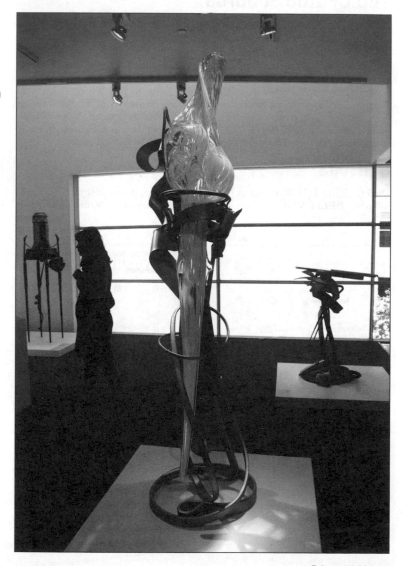

△ Bellevue Arts Museum

Bellevue Square and the Bellevue Arts Museum

Bellevue's city center is dominated by **Bellevue Square** (Mon–Sat 9.30am–9.30pm, Sun 11am–7pm; ⊛www.bellevuesquare.com), a shopping plaza that holds a number of stores and restaurants, but across the street you'll find the much more enticing **Bellevue Arts Museum** (BAM for short), 510 Bellevue Way NE (Tues–Sat 10am–5.30pm, Fri closes 9pm, Sun 11am–5.30pm; $7; ☎425/519-0770, ⊛www.bellevueart.org), housed in a modern complex designed by Steven Holl (known for his Chapel of Saint Ignatius; see p.93). The museum is devoted exclusively to rotating exhibits of contemporary work, frequently by Pacific Northwestern artists, and has far more cutting-edge stuff than you'd expect, given its suburban location: there's conceptual art, comicbook and pop-art designs, postmodern puppetry, and so on. Another emphasis is on industrial and commercial design – sleek exhibits on subjects from teapots to typewriters – and on **glass art**. Indeed, there are regular showings of work from the **Pilchuck School**, as well as **Dale Chihuly**, that feature its signature style of glossy, curvaceous bursts of color, functional vases and household objects in human and animal shapes, and glittering baubles awash in metallic sparkle.

The Museum of Doll Art

A few blocks northeast of BAM, the unusual and slightly eerie **Museum of Doll Art**, 1116 108th Ave NE (Mon–Sat 10am–5pm, Sun 1–5pm; $7; ☎425/455-1116, ⊛www.dollart.com), is surprisingly fascinating, with appeal for both adults and children. The large facility's two floors contain more than 1200 dolls of all sizes and nationalities from the last few centuries; among the most intriguing are Peruvian burial dolls, African fertility dolls, and Day of the Dead ceremonial figures. There are also exquisitely crafted miniatures – look for the Japanese boy made from ground oyster shells – and unexpected tableaux in the dollhouse wing such as a seventeenth-century Russian Orthodox wedding and a 1930s simulation of an "Oriental Shop." More conventional dolls are represented on the first floor's twentieth-century doll gallery, with vintage Barbies – including the first, from 1959 – and celebrities from Elvis and the Beatles to Lucille Ball and Bart Simpson. A good antidote to the quaintness is the gruesome monkey violinist in the mechanical doll case on the second floor, and the birdlike "Jacqueline de la Colombiere and Her Beau" figure, made partially from animal skull, opposite the pop-culture icons on the first floor.

Bellevue Botanical Garden

Though not well known to urbanites, the **Bellevue Botanical Garden**, 12001 Main St (daily dawn–dusk; free; ☎425/451-3755, ⊛www.bellevuebotanical.org), about a mile east of the Museum of Doll Art, is an excellent destination if you're anywhere around Bellevue. Located in Wilburton Hill Park, the garden features a nice range of variously themed sections on almost forty acres, including plots devoted to the **Yao Japanese Garden**, with its mix of Asian and Pacific Northwestern plants; the colorful array of blooms found in the Perennial Border Garden; a water-conservation zone filled with hardy specimens; and an Alpine Rock Garden that features imported plants from northern elevations growing in soil usually found at high elevations. The botanical garden also has trails that lead through the surrounding woods and wetlands, the longest being the **Lost Meadow Trail**, which loops around through groves of maple, fir and cedar. During December, many of the plants throughout the garden are illuminated in seasonal colors by up to a half-million lights – an odd but enchanting spectacle that really draws the crowds.

Mercer Slough Nature Park

The largest remaining wetland on Lake Washington, **Mercer Slough Nature Park**, at 2102 Bellevue Way SE, a couple of miles south of Bellevue Square, encompasses some three hundred acres, with more than seven miles of trails and boardwalks through marshes and meadows, plus solo or guided canoeing and kayaking trips (information at ☏425/452-2752) on the park's own canoe trail; there's even a blueberry farm, from which you can purchase the fruit when it's in season. The park is a favorite haunt for birdwatchers – more than one hundred species of birds inhabit the premises – though the loud hum of nearby I-405 makes it a less than idyllic retreat. Trail maps are available at the **visitors' center** in the Mediterranean-styled **Winters House**, 2102 Bellevue Way SE (daily 10am–4pm, Sun opens at noon), which also serves as the home of the Bellevue Historical Society, and park rangers lead free hour-long nature walks that meet outside the building on Sundays at 11am.

To get a vessel and paddle around the nature park at your own pace, drop by **Cascade Canoe & Kayak Center**, in Enatai Beach Park just southwest of Mercer Slough, 3519 108th Avenue SE (April to mid-June & Sept, Sat & Sun 11am–6pm; mid-June to Aug daily 11am–7pm; ☏425/430-0111, ⊛www .canoe-kayak.com), which offers classes and training, as well as rentals for an affordable daily rate (kayaks $11–22/hr, $46-92/day; canoes $15/hr, $57/day).

Marymoor Park

Elsewhere around Bellevue, **Marymoor Park** (daily 8am–dusk), located between the 520 and 202 highways on the north end of Lake Sammamish, at 6046 West Lake Sammamish Parkway NE, is the main attraction. It's an expansive park with jogging trails and tennis courts, and occupies the former estate of local businessman James Clise, who built a 1904 mansion, plus nearly thirty other buildings, on 350 acres; a quaint windmill serves as the park's icon. There used to be a regional history center in the now-closed mansion, but that has moved to the Winters House (see p.134); what remains at the site, however, is still compelling. Marymoor is allegedly the most popular park in King County, hosting summer concerts by big names in the grassy, open-air **amphitheatre** (see ⊛www.concertsatmarymoor.com for details), and regular bike-racing events at the onsite **velodrome** (May–Sept Wed & Fri 6–10pm), which is otherwise open for public cycling; elsewhere, climbers can scramble up a 45-foot high **Climbing Rock**. There are also trails that lead through woods and wetlands, facilities for rowing, baseball, and soccer, and even a cricket pitch.

The hardiest urban hikers may want to try out the **Sammamish River Trail**, which begins in the park and leads north ten miles to the suburb of Bothell. From there it links up with the better-known Burke-Gilman Trail, which runs along the west side of Lake Washington, over Lake Union, and all the way to the Fremont district. The total journey is 27 miles, slightly more than walking a marathon course, and it's a very scenic trek if you have the stamina.

Jimi Hendrix gravesite and home

Beyond the southeastern edge of Lake Washington lies the charmless burg of **Renton**, notable only for **Greenwood Cemetery** (Mon–Sat 8am–5pm, Sun by appointment), 350 Monroe Ave NE at NE 4th St, where **Jimi Hendrix**, the most inventive, and perhaps the greatest, guitarist in rock history, was buried in 1970 at the age of 27, shortly after dying of asphyxiation a continent and an ocean away, in London.

Although born and raised in Seattle, **Jimi Hendrix** spent barely a day in his hometown over the last ten years of his life. Still, before he left at age eighteen, he had just enough time to attend rock 'n' roll shows at the long-demolished Spanish Castle Ballroom (halfway between Seattle and Tacoma), the inspiration for his "Spanish Castle Magic" song on the *Axis: Bold as Love* album. In 1961, he was sentenced to two years in prison for riding in a stolen car, but because he'd decided to enlist in the army, his sentence was suspended, and he left Seattle to serve Uncle Sam as a paratrooper for the 101st Airborne (though this period has recently come under suspicion, with author Charles Cross claiming, in his recent book *Room Full of Mirrors*, that Hendrix got out of military service by claiming he was gay). Afterwards, he went on to New York and London to develop his craft; consequently, the man's work owes virtually nothing to the local music scene of his day. Indeed, during one notoriously disastrous 1968 concert at Seattle Center Arena, Hendrix was reduced to repeatedly yelling "I hate you, Seattle!" to an antagonistic crowd. Perhaps fittingly, then, when local Eastside billionaire Paul Allen decided to develop the Seattle Center's Experience Music Project (see p.85) around Hendrix's music and memorabilia thirty years later, he ran into trouble from the musician's estate and had to re-orient the museum with a broader focus.

Aside from the EMP, a handful of sites around the region have Hendrix-related memorials, which include a statue in Capitol Hill (see p.93), his gravesite and childhood home in Renton (see p.134), and a plaque in Woodland Park Zoo (see p.123).

The cemetery, just off I-405, is quite a trek from Seattle (it's accessible by bus on the #101 or #106 from Downtown, transferring to the #105 in Renton), and isn't as visited by the faithful as you might expect, with none of the nonstop crowds found at, say, Jim Morrison's grave at Père Lachaise Cemetery in Paris. Formerly, there wasn't much to see here – basically a simple, faded headstone engraved with a guitar – but in 2004 Hendrix's surviving relatives re-interred the body of the rock god (along with other family members) in a much larger **memorial** (www.jimihendrixmemorial.com) in the southwest part of the cemetery. Now featuring a thirty-foot-high dome, shimmering granite columns, and a scale bronze sculpture of Hendrix, this new, more garish memorial is obviously designed to draw the crowds. Whether it does justice to Hendrix's memory is another matter.

Note that in August 2005, Hendrix's **boyhood home** in the hardscrabble Central District of Seattle was due to be razed and replaced with a housing development. At the last minute, Hendrix's family foundation and the city of Renton helped to move the structure across the street from Greenwood Cemetery. In coming years it will be developed into a museum for Hendrix-related memorabilia – an honor that is long overdue.

Museum of Flight

West of Renton and well inland from the western side of Lake Washington, Seattle's unappealing industrial zone is of sole interest to visitors for the **Museum of Flight**, 9404 E Marginal Way S (daily 10am–5pm; $14, kids $7.50; 206/764-5720, www.museumofflight.org), the largest air and space museum on the West Coast, located in colorless Tukwila, a thirty-minute drive or bus ride south from Downtown. One of Seattle's best museums, its collection includes more than 130 military and civilian aircraft, as well as several large complementary exhibits – although only those with an abiding fascination for aviation history will need the entire day to see it.

Kirkland: the steel town that failed

Unlike many Eastside suburbs, **Kirkland** actually has an interesting history – one consisting mostly of failure. While Pioneer Square was rebuilding in the early 1890s from the devastating fire that consumed Downtown Seattle, the Eastside's own upstart community was developing in Kirkland. Named after **Peter Kirk**, an English businessman who fancied himself as an American industrial baron, the town grew in a sudden fit when Kirk outlined plans for a steel operation to be placed at the edge of Lake Washington. As soon as his investors put up the money, Kirk started work on his steel mill, and, in the meantime, attractive brick buildings took root at the corner of what is now Seventh Avenue and Market Street. The three architectural survivors of those heady days include the **Campbell Building**, once a grocery; the **Sears Building**, a stately Georgian that was built (though never opened) as a bank, and is now a religious bookstore; and the **Peter Kirk Building**, an elegantly turreted Romanesque Revival creation that reflected its owner's proud faith in himself – it's now home to the **Kirkland Arts Center** (Mon–Fri 11am–6pm, Sat 11am–5pm; donation; ⓦwww.kirklandartscenter.org), with a gallery of traditional and irreverent works by local artists.

Ultimately, Kirk never got the chance to be the next Andrew Carnegie, thanks largely to the national **Panic of 1893**, a near-depression that sent financial markets tumbling and dried up sources of investment capital. The Panic also halted new construction in Pioneer Square, though many of its chief structures had already been built, and the bad times were soon replaced by the frenzy of the Klondike Gold Rush a few years later. No such renaissance happened in Kirkland, and all that remains from those times is this cluster of stylish Victorians on a hill. There are decent restaurants and antique shops further south, though none of any particular note. After you soak in the history, it's a short walk downhill to **Marina Park**, 25 Lake Shore Plaza, excellent for its vistas of Lake Washington and recreational opportunities – the park is at the northern end of an appealing mile-long jogging and biking route that leads down to Carillon Point, offering some of the area's best views of the lakeside.

The main collection

The museum's centerpiece is the huge, hangarlike **Great Gallery**, which displays more than fifty full-sized vintage aircraft, many of which are suspended from the steel-and-glass roof. The first presidential jet, Air Force One (used by Eisenhower in 1959), is parked just outside, and there are early commercial planes and bizarre manifestations of aviation design such as the *Aerocar III*, a flying automobile that converted from car to aircraft in ten minutes. More interesting than the conventional bombers are the early airmail planes and wacky homebuilt designs, including transcontinental gliders such as the *Aerosonde*, a robotic flier that took more than one day and less than two gallons of gas to cross the Atlantic, and the *Gossamer Albatross II*, whose propellers were connected through a series of gears to a constantly pedaling pilot.

The best of the exhibits on the floors overlooking the main gallery include a display on the US space program, a somewhat convincing F-18 flight simulator, and a mock-up of the inside of an air-control tower, where you – or, more likely, your kids – guide mock takeoffs and landings with prompts from electronic screens and headsets. Aerospace films run throughout the day, but better are the free **tours** sometimes given by ex-Boeing employees that run through the highlights of the main galleries and add an insider's perspective; check at the tour desk between the entrance and the Great Gallery for details.

On June 6, 2004, the sixtieth anniversary of D-Day, the museum opened the **Personal Courage Wing** in a three-story expansion building, highlighted by the **Champlin Collection**, with around thirty classic fighters from both world wars, among them numerous German planes like the Messerschmidt and the Fokker, as well as the legendary Sopwith Camel from World War I. Also featured are personal narratives of those who flew during the conflicts, and replicas and dioramas of the fields of battle, which include trenches, landing strips, Quonset huts, and aircraft carriers – not to mention the ever-perilous French hedgerows, unexpected landscape features that made landing a powerless glider in the dawn of D–Day a hair-raising nightmare.

The Red Barn and Airpark

In another wing, Boeing's original manufacturing plant, the 1909 **Red Barn** (moved here in 1975), offers a serious-minded, text-heavy spread of relics from the early days of flight. The achievements of the Wright Brothers get their due – there is a working replica of the wind tunnel they used – but the displays also include the ambitious designs of dreamers without the technology to enact their fantasies, and showcase European pioneers like the French who helped develop manned flight in the early 1900s (such as the crossing of the English Channel in Louis Bleriot's *Model XI* in 1909). The impact of World War I and the early years of commercial flight are also traced: check out the nearly decrepit 1914 *Caproni Ca 20*, the world's first fighter plane. The birth of Boeing itself – still a powerful company in the Pacific Northwest, though its corporate headquarters have moved to Chicago – is also chronicled, but you'll have to venture to the other side of the metropolis to catch a glimpse of the company's present-day factory (see p.140).

More Boeing icons are on display outside in the museum's expansive **Airpark** (daily 11am–3.30pm, summer closes 4.30pm; free with museum admission), which has a walk-in collection of models that include the 727, 737, and jumbo-jet 747. The undisputed centerpiece, however, is another plane entirely – the supersonic **Concorde**, which, now that British Airways has discontinued its flights, is one of only four remaining in the United States. Those who have never flown on the needle-nosed jet can get a vague sense of it by wandering around inside, though the thick summer crowds waiting to board can quickly dull your sense of adventure.

West Seattle and Alki Beach

The isolated neighborhood of **WEST SEATTLE**, separated from Down-town by the industrial piers and waterways of Harbor Island, is technically within the city limits, though it feels as much like a suburb as Bellevue does. It holds few attractions other than **Alki Beach** (daily 6am–11pm), located on the peninsula's northwestern edge and around its northern tip of Duwamish Head. The city's most popular beach is crowded on warm days with bathers, volleyball players, and other recreants, and the northward view across the bay is impressive, taking in the Space Needle, Magnolia, and Queen Anne Hill. A **pedestrian/bike path** leading east from the beach curves along the water-front for two miles and offers some of Seattle's best panoramas (bus #37 from Downtown travels along this route), though the water here is usually much too cold for swimming. You can also get to the beach by water taxi from the Downtown waterfront (see p.54), though you'll be dropped off on the opposite side of the peninsula and likely have to catch a bus (#53 or #773) to make the lengthy journey.

Two blocks inland from the beach, the history of West Seattle and Alki is recounted in depth at the **Log House Museum**, 3003 61st Ave SW (Thurs noon–6pm, Sat

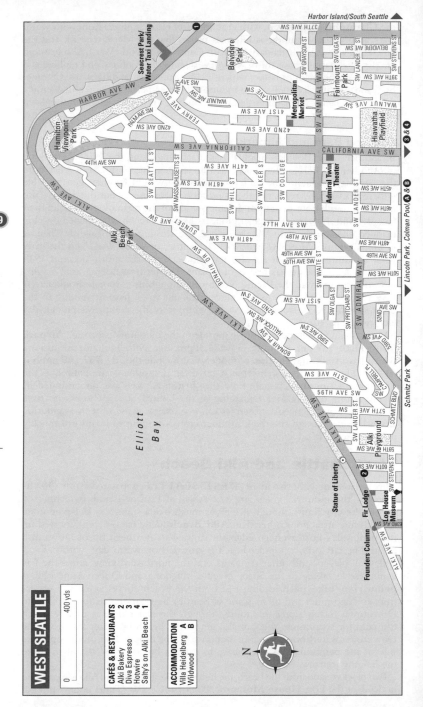

Harbor Island/South Seattle

WEST SEATTLE

0 — 400 yds

CAFÉS & RESTAURANTS
Alki Bakery 2
Diva Espresso 3
Hotwire 4
Salty's on Alki Beach 1

ACCOMMODATION
Villa Heidelberg A
Wildwood B

Elliott Bay

N

Seacrest Park/
Water Taxi Landing

Belvidere Park

37TH AVE SW
SW GRAYSON ST
SW OLGA ST
BELVIDERE ST
SW STEVENS ST

HARBOR AVE AW
SW ADMIRAL WAY

Fairmount
Park

WALNUT AVE SW
39TH AVE SW
WALNUT AVE SW

Metropolitan
Market

Hamilton
Viewpoint
Park

FERRY AVE SW
PALM AVE SW
ARCH
WALNUT AVE SW
41ST AVE SW
42ND AVE SW

Hiawatha
Playfield

3 & 4

CALIFORNIA AVE SW

44TH AVE SW
SW SEATTLE ST
SW MASSACHUSETTS ST
SW HILL ST
SW WALKER ST
SW COLLEGE
44TH AVE SW
46TH AVE SW
Admiral Twin
Theater

CALIFORNIA AVE SW

45TH AVE SW
46TH AVE SW
SW LANDER ST

Lincoln Park, Colman Pool A & B

Alki
Beach
Park

SUNSET AVE SW
47TH AVE SW
48TH AVE SW
48TH AVE S
49TH AVE SW
50TH AVE SW
SW WAITE ST

48TH AVE SW
49TH AVE SW
50TH AVE SW
SW ADMIRAL WAY

BONAIR DR SW
BONAIR PL SW
51ST AVE SW
52ND AVE SW
HALLOCK AVE SW
SW OLGA ST
SW PRITCHARD ST
52ND AVE SW

Schmitz Park

ALKI AVE SW
53RD AVE SW
55TH AVE SW
56TH AVE SW
57TH AVE
SW
SW LANDER ST
SW CAMPBELL PL
SCHMITZ BLVD

Statue of Liberty

ALKI AVE SW
59TH AVE SW
60TH AVE SW
SW STEVENS ST

Alki
Playground

Fir Lodge
Log House
Museum

Founders Column

63RD AVE SW
ALKI AVE SW

& Sun noon–3pm; $2; ☎206/938-5293, ⊛www.loghousemuseum.org), which also serves as headquarters for the Southwest Seattle Historical Society. The museum has plenty of exhibits about the settlement of the city, the less interesting development of West Seattle, and history of Native Americans in the region. As for the building itself, it's the renovated carriage house of a local soap magnate, built around 1903 in an agreeable Arts and Crafts style. More visually interesting, perhaps, is the nearby **Fir Lodge** manor, 2717 61st Ave SW, to which the log house was once attached; it was constructed from deadwood taken from the sea, and is now a run-of-the-mill restaurant, though one with a handsome stone fireplace.

Other West Seattle attractions

As Alki Avenue curves south around Alki Point it turns into **Beach Drive**, a scenic coastal route with good views of Puget Sound and the Olympic Mountains. A few miles down the road, **Lincoln Park** (daily 4am–11.30pm) has a narrow beach with a paved promenade, picnic tables, fourteen trails (almost all under a mile long), and the onsite **Colman Pool**, 8603 Fauntleroy Way SW (daily mid-June through Aug; ☎206/684-7494), a heated outdoor saltwater swimming pool with diving boards and an aqua-slide. Avid hikers might also want to wander through the rugged, 53-acre **Schmitz Park** (daily 4am– 11.30pm; ⊛www.schmitzpark.org), about ten blocks from Alki Point (enter at SW Admiral Way and SW Stevens Street), based around an old-growth forest with Douglas fir, Western red cedar, and Western hemlock. Banker and realtor Ferdinand Schmitz, a member of Seattle's park commission, donated the land to the city for park use in the early twentieth century, with the provision that no improvements ever be made – and Seattle has kept its end of the deal, making the park one of the city's most pristine tracts of land.

Away from the historical sites and beaches, there are few notable attractions in West Seattle, although the business district, centered on Admiral Way and California Avenue, has a few quirky boutiques, good restaurants, and decent bars scattered here and there. The main point of interest is the delightful **Admiral**

Alki Beach: New York by and by

The beckoning white strip of Alki Beach is the place where the first party of Seattle's white settlers landed in November 1851. Ten adults and twelve children were met by advance scout and fellow pioneer **David Denny**, who helped them ashore in the midst of heavy rain. The settlement – comprising a mere four cabins – was optimistically named New York in honor of settler Charles Terry's home state. This was quickly amended with the addition of the Chinook slang word "alki", producing the sardonic New York-Alki, which roughly translates to "New York eventually" or "New York by and by." Although Seattle never quite got that big, the one icon of Gotham that did get replicated was the **Statue of Liberty**, a miniature rendition of which now occupies the beachfront across from 60th Avenue SW, holding its (unlit) bronze torch out to surfers and boaters on Elliott Bay.

Ultimately, Alki never developed into much of anything beyond a weekend pleasure zone. The settlers determined that the deep-water harbor further north on the bay would be far more suitable for populating, especially as ships could not dock at Alki, and the pioneers began staking claims around the area where Pioneer Square is now located. Near 63rd and Alki avenues, a small **commemorative column** in Alki Beach Park, inscribed with the names of the settlers, identifies the spot of the 1851 landing, and its base also features a stone from an even more famous landing site – Plymouth Rock in Massachusetts.

Twin Theater, 2347 California Ave (☎206/938-3456), a 1938 Streamline Moderne charmer with a nautical theme: boatlike motifs on the facade, interior designs of whales and etched-in-glass seahorses, and two auditoriums called Port 1 and Port 2. Cult movie fans might also want to stop by on the first Saturday of the month, when midnight presentations of the *Rocky Horror Picture Show* ($5) feature all manner of inspired craziness, from elaborately costumed viewer-participants to spirited sing-a-longs.

Finally, beyond the downtown waterfront, West Seattle holds the other urban port for **Washington State Ferries**, just south of Lincoln Park at 4829 SW Barton St (see "Basics," p.34, for details), which regularly leave from this Fauntleroy terminal for Vashon Island. It's the only way you can get a car out there from Seattle proper, since the waterfront terminal is solely for passenger travel to the island.

Everett and the Boeing Tour Center

Thirty miles north of Seattle, the last major suburb along I-5, **EVERETT**, is home to the manufacturing plant for **Boeing**, a huge corporation with about 135,000 employees worldwide. If you find yourself up here, don't miss the hour-long tours at the **Boeing Tour Center**, which has its entrance on Hwy-526, a few miles west of exit 189 off I-5 (tours Mon–Fri 9am–3pm on the hour, except noon; $5 for same-day tickets, $10 in advance; tickets and info at ☎1-800/464-1476, ⊛www.boeing.com/companyoffices/aboutus/tours). It's a good idea to arrive early, as the first-come, first-served tickets, available from

The Boeing story

Of all the signature corporations based out of the Seattle area, by far the most long-standing is Boeing. The company's history dates back to when Seattle timberman **William Boeing** started the Pacific Aero Products Company in 1916, changing the name to the **Boeing Airplane Company** in 1917. Boeing supplied the Navy with planes during World War I, but after the war the engineering staff was reduced to two, and Boeing resorted to making boats and furniture to survive. It bounced back in the early 1920s by modernizing war planes and, with the vision of engineer **Claire Egtvedt**, designing original aircraft. In 1928, the company debuted the first American airliner, though it wouldn't truly reap the rewards for years to come. Boeing's fortunes fluctuated again with World War II, but hit a stride in the 1950s and 1960s, especially after diversifying into space technology. The boom slacked off in the 1970s with the end of the Apollo space project, a 747 program plagued by problems, and a severe recession. Its workforce was cut by half between 1970 and 1971, a ripple that created bad times for all of Seattle (at the time, a billboard was even erected near the city limits reading, "Will the last person leaving Seattle turn out the lights?").

Yet Boeing came back again: by the late 1990s it was cranking out more than forty commercial jets a month, and, with Lockheed Martin, the company developed the F-22, considered the most advanced tactical fighter in the world. Though the European Commission feared Boeing's merger with McDonnell Douglas would threaten the European Airbus, the EC eventually approved the alliance when Boeing dropped plans to become the exclusive manufacturer for three US airlines. Since then, slowdowns in airplane production have forced the company to cut tens of thousand of jobs, and Seattle's economic reputation took a big hit when Boeing decided to move its corporate headquarters to Chicago. Through all this, though, the company has still kept its biggest factory in Everett, which has justifiably become one of the region's top tourist draws.

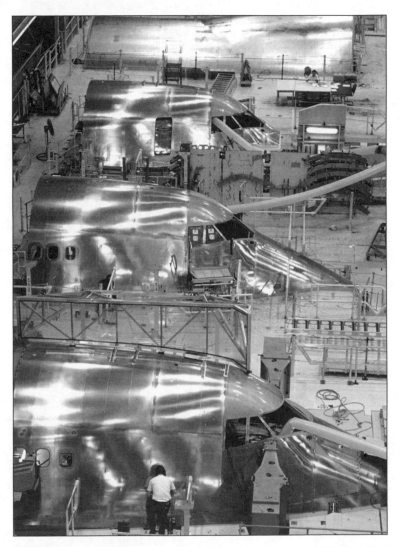

△ Boeing Tour Center

the counter just inside the center, often run out quickly, with waits of an hour or more not uncommon once you've gotten your time slot – an ordeal avoided by purchasing the higher-priced advance tickets.

On the tour, don't expect to learn about the company's military contracts or Washington lobbying on behalf of the defense industry; instead, it's a smoothly executed PR exercise, focusing on Boeing's impressive technological accomplishments, including the 98-acre factory that's listed in the *Guinness Book of World Records* as the largest building in the world by volume (472 million cubic feet). Overhead platforms afford views of much of the floor space, cluttered by new planes in various phases of construction; if it's break-time, you may even see workers relieving stress by shooting hoops among the planes-in-progress. The tour concludes with a bus ride along the "flight line," where finished 747, 767, and 777 models are tested, and eventually the 787, the newest jumbo & jet, planned to hit the skies in 2008.

The rest of the city

Although Everett has a fetching stretch of shoreline along Puget Sound, with good views across to Whidbey Island, the city center is only worth exploring if you have an interest in classic urban design. The local history society, the **Snohomish County Museum**, 913 Hewitt Ave (Wed–Sat 1–4pm; donation; ⓦwww.whidbey.com/snocomuseum), will get you started on your explorations with a free **walking guide** and suggestions.

Some of the more compelling structures include the **Everett Public Library**, 2702 Hoyt Ave (Mon–Thurs 10am–9pm, Fri & Sat 10am–6pm, Sun 1–5pm; ⓦwww.epls.org), one of the rare surviving examples of 1930s Streamline Moderne design in the Pacific Northwest, with wraparound windows and a sleek horizontal layout; the **Snohomish County Courthouse**, 3000 Rockefeller Ave (daily 8am–5pm), a striking mock-Spanish Mission from 1910 that would look more at home near the Mexican rather than the Canadian border; the elegant Renaissance Revival **Carnegie Library**, 3101 Oakes Ave, one of a handful of extant Carnegie institutions around Seattle, now housing government offices; and the landmark 1905 **Rucker Mansion**, 412 Laurel Drive, a private enclave perched atop a hill that's an imposing blend of Queen Anne and Georgian designs.

Listings

Listings

Accommodation

I n most of its neighborhoods, Seattle has plenty of choices for **accommo-dation**; the problem is not so much getting a room as finding good mid-range deals, achieving a balance between decent amenities, affordable rates, and a central location. In Downtown in particular, there's not much middle ground between the swank luxury **hotels** and bottom-end dives. If you want something at least minimally clean and attractive with modern conveniences, your options start at $90 a night. Good alternatives include **bed-and-break-fasts**, many of them in Capitol Hill, which have more character and are usually a better value, though you might have to share a bathroom to get a rate around $80. **Hostels** offer the best deals for the budget traveler, with dorm beds going for around $17–21 a night, along with inexpensive private rooms ($50–60) for which you should always call ahead. There are no state **campgrounds** in the metropolitan area, but they are in abundance in outlying areas; see "Out of the City" (pp.233–284) for the various choices.

As in any large city, it's best to make **reservations** for a place to stay, espe-cially during summer, when popular festivals can make rooms scarce and you might be forced to settle for an out-of-the-way motel or grim roadside dive if you don't book well in advance. Rates sometimes dip in the **off-season** (Oct–April), and there are often discounts for multi-day visits or weekday stays at corporate- and convention-oriented hotels. Bear in mind that Seattle imposes a steep **hotel room tax** of 15.6 percent, a figure that isn't quite so high outside the city – notably on the islands, where it's at or below 10 percent. Overall, rates across the board have been kept in check for the last five years by the state's weak economy, and many establishments now offer special bargains and entice-ments in an effort to maintain a reasonable occupancy rate – so make sure to shop around for the best deals, and don't be afraid to ask about inexpensive or even complimentary upgrades if the place looks like it needs the business.

Hotels

Seattle's **hotels** are mostly geared toward the business traveler, with many four-star accommodations Downtown that easily run $200 or more a night – plus $25–30 a night for parking. There aren't many good mid-level options here, though, and if you want a room for under $80 a night, the level of service and cleanliness tends to drop dramatically. There are also few quality, upper-end hotels outside Downtown and the Seattle Center, and the smattering of mid-level choices in the city's neighborhoods tend to be limited in comfort and amenities. Further out, the conspicuous chain motels on Aurora Avenue (Highway 99) and around Sea-Tac Airport are rather inhospitable options, and best avoided.

The Convention and Visitors' Bureau's **Seattle Super Saver** program can make reservations for you at local hotels from April to October, Monday through Friday 8.30am to 5pm (☎206/461-5882 or 1-800/535-7071, ⒲www .seattlesupersaver.com). During the winter (Nov–March), the hotline features low season discount deals of up to fifty percent off normal rates at nearly eighty hotels in and around town. Still, it's often easier to get information about special deals and amenities by calling the various hotels and motels directly.

Pike Place Market and around

🏃 **Alexis** 1007 First Ave ☎206/624-4844 or 1-800/426-7033, ⒲www.alexishotel.com. Plush decor at this top-notch hotel, as well as a spa, a steam room, the *Library Bistro* restaurant (see p.163), and the refined *Bookstore Bar & Café* (see p.153) in the lobby – which is also graced by the bright, lurid tentacles of a Dale Chihuly sculpture. Nearly half the rooms are suites that, at their largest, have luxurious touches like fireplaces and dining rooms. $289.

Inn at Harbor Steps 1221 First Ave ☎206/748-0973 or 1-888/728-8910, ⒲www.foursisters .com. Intimate rooms in an upscale hotel near the market and the Seattle Art Museum. Each room has a fireplace, fridge, complimentary breakfast, Wi-Fi Internet access, and a balcony overlooking an interior garden courtyard; some have spa tubs. $165.

Inn at the Market 86 Pine St ☎206/443-3600 or 1-800/446-4484, ⒲www.innatthemarket.com. As the name suggests, perfect for visiting the market, and good also for its sweeping views of Elliott Bay; seventy boutique-styled units offer chic modern furnishings, in-room fridges, and larger suite accommodations (up to $400). Great location means higher prices. $165.

Moore 1926 Second Ave ☎206/448-4851 or 1-800/421-5508, ⒲www.moorehotel.com. Ancient-feeling 1908 structure with rooms that offer little in the way of charm or amenities, though it's well-placed to take advantage of Downtown sightseeing, Belltown nightlife, and the market itself. Excellent

rates, too: from $45 for single room with shared bath up to $95–130 for a suite.

The Business District

Crowne Plaza 1113 6th Ave ☎206/464-1980, ⒲www.crowneplazaseattle.com. One of the better of the chain options, a sleek modern pile with a prime location and onsite gym, high-speed Net access, and in-room CD players. Recently remodeled units are nicely decorated, if a bit cozy. $119; add $50 for high season.

Elliott Grand Hyatt 727 Pine St ☎206/219-6916, ⒲grandseattle.hyatt.com. Ultra-swanky accommodations in the Business District near I-5, frequented by a mostly suit-clad clientele. Great views from rooms stuffed with pricey furnishings; there's also plenty of onsite dining and a health club. $239 weekends; $315 weekdays.

Executive Pacific Plaza 400 Spring St ☎206/623-3900 or 1-800/426-1165, ⒲www .pacificplazahotel.com. Newly remodeled version of a stately 1928 building near the center of the Business District. As the name suggests, the place is aimed at the (budget-conscious) tie-and-jacket crowd, but the rooms are clean and comfortable, and the price – especially the Spartan "Executive Escape" rooms – can't be beat for value, at $94.

Fairmont Olympic 411 University St ☎206/621-1700 or 1-800/223-8772, ⒲www.fairmont .com. Proclaims itself the height of luxury accommodation in Seattle, though this Renaissance Revival jewel has been through a few name changes since it was built in

1924. Located on a hill in the Business District, half of the 450 rooms are suites – with marble bathrooms, fireplaces, and antique decor – and frequented by visiting celebrities and politicians, with prices to match: the top suites fetch up to $3000 per night. $299.

Hotel Max 620 Stewart St ☎ 206/441-4200 or 1-800/426-0670, ⓦ www.hotelmaxseattle.com. Located in a renovated 1920s building a block from the monorail, with 165 stylish rooms kitted out with vaguely "artistic" themes – with different photographers showcased on each floor and original art in each room – though few amenities other than nice decor, Wi-Fi Internet access and a gym. Try to get a room with a Space Needle view. Price is good for the area, starting at $129.

Hotel Seattle 315 Seneca St ☎ 206/623-5110 or 1-800/623-5110. Basic, clean rooms in a central location, a refurbished old pile with a modern – but not antiseptic – ambiance, all in an affordable price range. One of the few deals in this area. $95.

Hotel Vintage Park 1100 Fifth Ave ☎ 206/624-8000, ⓦ www.hotelvintagepark .com. Offering splashy upscale decor without any accompanying attitude, a stylish boutique hotel with rooms themed around wine-drinking and vineyards; amenities at "the Vintage" include fireplaces, Jacuzzis, stereos, and of course, nightly tastings of vino. $139.

Monaco 1101 Fourth Ave ☎ 206/621-1770 or 1-800/715-6513, ⓦ www .monaco-seattle.com. One-time Pacific Northwest Bell telephone switching office, since converted into a boutique hotel, part of the upscale Monaco chain. Inside, it's all luxurious guestrooms (some of which have Jacuzzis), with CD players, high-speed Net access, and an onsite fitness center. $175.

Paramount 724 Pine St ☎ 206/292-9500 or 1-800/426-0670, ⓦ www.coasthotels.com. Luxury chain hotel with impressive European-styled exterior, though the somewhat unexciting rooms don't live up to the mid-to-high rates. Still, some suites have hot tubs, and there's a popular pan-Asian restaurant, *Dragonfish* (see review, p.163), on the ground floor. $139.

Roosevelt 1531 7th Ave ☎ 206/621-1200, ⓦ www.roosevelthotel.com. Renovated high-rise dating from 1929, with basic but comfortable rooms and fancier suites with whirlpool tubs; centrally located near Westlake Center. $135.

Sorrento 900 Madison St ☎ 206/622-4400 or 1-800/426-1265, ⓦ www.hotelsorrento.com. Just east of the I-5 freeway, a modernized, 76-room edifice with a European flair (more than half suites), stylish decor, and posh onsite restaurant *The Hunt Club*. The regal 1908 exterior surrounds a circular courtyard with palm trees; some rooms have views of Puget Sound. $229.

▽ W Seattle

W Seattle 1112 Fourth Ave ☎ 206/264-6000, ⓦ www.whotels.com. Stylish modern tower in the Business District, with a staff of beautiful people and smart, cozy rooms with high style, if rather basic amenities. There's a chic lobby bar with often-packed "cocktail couches" downstairs, and an adjoining Northwest Cuisine restaurant, *Earth & Ocean* (see review, p.163), that's one of the city's best. $299.

Pioneer Square

Pioneer Square Hotel 77 Yesler Way ☎ 206/340-1234 or 1-800/800-5514, ⓦ www.pioneersquare .com. Restored 1914 brick hotel, originally built by Seattle pioneer Henry Yesler; one of the few good Pioneer Square choices for accommodations (now a Best Western) with adequate comfort. There's a juice bar on the lobby floor, as well as a saloon with microbrews on tap. $139.

Belltown

Ace 2423 First Ave ☎ 206/448-4721, ⓦ www.theacehotel.com. A Seattle favorite with modern, if somewhat austere, rooms and a chic white lobby in the heart of Belltown, above the fun *Cyclops* restaurant (see review, p.165). Hardwood floors, lofty ceilings, and shared bathrooms for $75; more comfortable and well-appointed suites start at around twice as much.

1

Edgewater Pier 67, 2411 Alaskan Way
☏206/728-7000 or 1-800/624-0670, ⓦwww
.edgewaterhotel.com. Seattle's top waterfront
hotel has a central location and nice rooms,
the best of which have windows right on the
bay – though for those you'll need to both
pay about $50 more and reserve well in
advance. $229.

Hotel Andra 2000 Fourth Ave ☏206/448-8600
or 1-877/448-8601, ⓦwww.hotelandra.com.
The former Claremont hotel now remodeled
into an intimate, boutique hotel with 120
chic, modern units – more than half of them
suites. Onsite gym and restaurant, and
high-speed Internet access. An abundance
of style for steep rates. $199.

Inn at El Gaucho 2505 First Ave ☏206/728-
1133, ⓦinn.elgaucho.com. Located above a
chain steakhouse in the heart of Belltown's
gentrified First Avenue, this former merchant
marine quarters has been converted into an
18-suite boutique hotel. Units have smart,
stylish furnishings, if a bit cramped for the
price, and there's a free continental breakfast. $165.

Sixth Avenue Inn 2000 Sixth Ave ☏206/441-
8300, ⓦwww.sixthavenueinn.com. Although a
bit east of the main attractions, a practical
choice if you really need to save money,
with gym and Internet access, and Spartan
but clean rooms. $79.

Warwick 401 Lenora St ☏206/443-4300,
ⓦwww.warwickwa.com. Guestrooms with
balconies and prime views overlooking
the Seattle Center, pool, sauna, gym, and
Jacuzzi make this one of the more desirable
choices in the area. Also good for accessing
Pike Place Market, about five blocks south.
$139.

Westin 1900 Fifth Ave ☏206/728-1000 or 1-
800/WESTIN-1, ⓦwww.westin.com. The rates
are as high as the views from the highest of
the 865 rooms in these twin cylinder towers
– one from 1969, the other from the 1980s
– with spacious, but not stunning, rooms
and good amenities including indoor swimming pool, health club, and spa. $189.

Seattle Center and Queen Anne

Hampton Inn 700 Fifth Ave N ☏206/282-7700
or 1-800/HAMPTON, ⓦwww.hamptoninnseattle
.com. A reasonable choice for the Seattle Center area, this modern chain hotel
has around 200 rooms and suites offering
fridges, microwaves, kitchenettes, and fire-

places; onsite amenities include an exercise
room with Jacuzzi. $119.

Inn at Queen Anne 505 First Ave N ☏206/
282-7357 or 1-800/952-5043, ⓦwww
.innatqueenanne.com. Small but comfortable
studio apartment-style lodgings on the edge
of Seattle Center; rooms come with queen-
sized beds, kitchenettes, and microwaves,
plus complimentary breakfast and Downtown shuttle service thrown in for good
measure, and – on selected evenings –
wine tastings. $79.

MarQueen 600 Queen Ave N ☏206/282-7407
or 1-800/445-3076, ⓦwww.marqueen.com. A
refurbished, classically styled 1918 building
with 56 rooms and suites, featuring period
antiques and pluses like hardwood floors,
kitchenettes, microwaves, and fridges, as
well as an onsite spa. $130.

Travelodge 200 Sixth Ave N ☏206/441-7878,
ⓦwww.travelodge.com. A good overflow
space if you come during a busy period,
this reliable chain two blocks from Seattle
Center, offers the usual basics – complimentary breakfast, fridges, swimming pool
– for a decent rate. $79.

Capitol Hill and Lake Union

Eastlake Inn 2215 Eastlake Ave E ☏206/322-
7726. Average motor lodge, but more conveniently situated than most – it's a few blocks
from Lake Union's houseboats – and cheaper
than the ones around Seattle Center; some
units are mini-suites with kitchens. $65.

Inn at Virginia Mason 1006 Spring St
☏206/583-6453 or 1-800/283-6453, ⓦwww
.vmmc.org/dbAccommodations. A remodeled hotel on First Hill – part of a hospital
complex – whose rooftop patio affords
an excellent view of Downtown. Entry-
level rooms are clean and basic (some
with decent views) for $119, while fifteen
spacious suites offer added touches like
fridges and microwaves, for $179.

Marriott Residence Inn 800 Fairview Ave N
☏206/624-6000, ⓦwww.marriott.com. A serviceable choice for staying near Lake Union,
offering suites with balconies, kitchens and
fine waterside views, and onsite gym, spa,
sauna and Jacuzzi. $159.

Silver Cloud Inn 1150 Fairview Ave N ☏206/447-
9500, ⓦwww.scinns.com. A few blocks west
of I-5 near Lake Union, with clean, modern
rooms and gym and pool; amenities include
fridges and microwaves, and most rooms

have a view of the lake as well. There's another location near the University of Washington at 5036 25th Ave NE (T 206/526-5200 or 1-800/205-6940). Both $149.

University District

University Hotel 4731 12th Ave NE T 206/522-4724, W university-hotel.com. Clean, simple suites, each with separate bedroom, living room, and full kitchen, suitable for extended stays, with onsite laundry facility. Bottom-end rates are a little lower than the other university hotels. $69.

University Inn 4140 Roosevelt Way NE T 206/632-5055 or 1-800/733-3855, W www.universityinnseattle.com. Plain-looking business-oriented hotel off University Way. Some rooms have kitchens, and your stay comes with complimentary continental breakfast; there's also an onsite pool and spa, and high-speed Internet access. $95.

University Tower 4507 Brooklyn Ave NE T 206/634-2000 or 1-800/899-0251, W www.meany.com. Previously the *Edmond Meany Hotel*, located near the main action on University Way; now a Best Western, and a little more attractive than some of the other big hotels in the U District, with onsite gym, rooms in bright retro-Art Deco motifs, and fine views of the city and campus. $119; tack on $30 for the high season.

Watertown 4242 Roosevelt Way NE T 206/826-4242, W www.watertownseattle.com. The latest stab at making a nice, semi-upscale hotel in the U District - this one with gym and boutique-flavored rooms with microwaves and refrigerators, plus rentable bikes and a central location just north of the main action. $135; add $40 for suites.

Lake Washington and the suburbs

Bellevue Club 11200 SE Sixth Ave, Bellevue T 425/454-4424, W www.bellevueclubhotel.com. Maximum-chic spa hotel in the suburbs with in-room soaking tubs, elegant decor, fitness complex, swimming pool, basketball and tennis courts, and a guest list of well-tanned yuppies with perfect teeth. $189.

Coast Bellevue 625 116th Ave NE T 425/455-9444, W www.coasthotels.com. A good alternative for Bellevue, with gym, pool, and rooms with fridges and high-speed Internet access. Local shuttle for suburban travel within five miles. $89; add $15 for weekdays.

Embassy Suites 3225 158th Ave SE, Bellevue T 425/644-2500, W www.embassysuites.com. Ten miles from downtown Seattle on the Eastside, this all-suite hotel is one of the area's best choices for business and disabled travelers. The shiny, modern complex has elegant, spacious rooms, fitness center, pool, and sauna. $109.

Red Lion Bellevue Inn 11211 Main St, Bellevue T 425/455-5240 or 1-800/RED-LION, W www.redlion.com. One of the better branches of this chain, located in downtown Bellevue. Features tasteful gardens, courtyards, and patios, as well as in-room fridges and an onsite fitness center. $179.

Travelodge Mercer Island 7645 Sunset Hwy, Mercer Island T 206/232-8000, W www.travelodge.com. Budget chain hotel with the standard clean rooms, some with microwaves and fridges, and even a few with Jacuzzis. You won't even come close to finding rates this cheap on the otherwise uber-upscale island. $74.

Woodmark 1200 Carillon Point, Kirkland T 425/822-3700 or 1-800/822-3700, W www.thewoodmark.com. High-priced luxury hotel on the edge of Lake Washington, with some of the best waterside views around; not every room overlooks the lake, though – those that do cost about $50 extra. Also houses a popular (and expensive) lakeside seafood restaurant, *Waters, a Lakeside Bistro* (see review, p.172). $249.

Bed-and-breakfasts

Seattle's **bed-and-breakfasts** typically offer a good balance of comfort and value: the comfortable rooms are almost always bigger and nicer than hotel units that go for the same rates, and many are in converted early twentieth-century mansions – mostly grand old Capitol Hill homes – with period decor and antique furnishings. As there are often fewer than ten rooms in each (sometimes just three or four), reservations are a necessity during the high season; there may be a two-night minimum stay as well. Proprietors can usually fill you in on the historic background of each property, and are frequently a good source of information about the surrounding area and its history.

For **booking assistance**, call A Pacific Reservation Service (T 206/439-7677 or 1–800/684–2932, W www.seattlebedandbreakfast.com), which makes reservations across Washington and the rest of the West Coast and has a list of guest homes, apartments, and even houseboats available; or the Seattle Bed and Breakfast Association (T 206/547-1020 or 1–800/348–5630, W www.lodginginseattle.com), which sticks more to mainstream B&Bs in the Seattle area.

International District

Amaranth Inn 1451 S Main St T 206/720-7161 or 1–800/720-7161, W www.amaranthinn .com. Overflowing with antiques and fancy rugs, this 1906 Craftsman re-imagined as a B&B has quaint late-Victorian furnishings and eight flowery-decor rooms, some with hot tubs and fireplaces. Located east of I-5, roughly between the International District, First Hill, and the Central District. $75–100, depending on season.

Belltown

Pensione Nichols 1923 First Ave T 206/441-7125, W www.seattle-bed-breakfast.com. Considering the pricey area it's in, this classy little B&B is a great deal, with small but clean rooms, shared baths, and simple, tasteful decor – easy on the retro-kitsch – in a classic 1904 building. Suites with kitchenettes add about $75 per night to the price, but can be shared by four people. Basic units with shared bath $110.

Queen Anne

Inn of Twin Gables 3258 14th Ave W T 206/284-3979, W www.innoftwingables .com. One of the few options in the area for accommodations, with a trio of simple rooms in a stately Craftsman manor. Good rates in the low season ($80), not so good in the high ($145).

Queen Anne Hill 1835 Seventh Ave W T 206/284-9779. Just a few blocks north of Highland Drive, the smallish *Queen Anne Hill* has four cozy rooms, old-fashioned furniture, and Victorian decor, with free continental breakfast and good views of the metropolis and Elliott Bay. $125.

Capitol Hill and Lake Union

11th Avenue Inn 121 11th Ave E T 206/669-4373, W www.11thavenueinn.com. Eight units named after gems, with mild chintz and retro decor, and Wi-Fi Internet access. Shared bathrooms bring down the cost to $75 in low season; otherwise add $40 for high season.

Bacon Mansion 959 Broadway E T 206/329-1864 or 1–800/240-1864, W www.baconmansion .com. Eleven elegant rooms and spacious suites in a grand 1909 Tudor Revival structure, just north of Broadway's main drag. Well-decorated, if a bit small, the least expensive rooms are fairly cheap for Capitol Hill, at $82, although the price is more than double at the high end. Two-night minimum stay on weekends.

Bed & Breakfast on Broadway 722 Broadway Ave E T 206/329-8933, W www.bbonbroadway .com. Located where the main part of Broadway ends, but close enough to the main action on Capitol Hill, this early twentieth-century dwelling features various period antiques, hardwood floors, oriental rugs, and four pleasant rooms. $125.

Gaslight Inn 1727 15th Ave T 206/325-3654, W www.gaslight-inn.com. Fifteen rooms with large common areas, some units with fireplaces, small gardens and decks, and more expensive suites for longer-term stays. Homemade scones, swimming pool, hot tub, and a prime Capitol Hill location – not to mention the contemporary decor and colorful modern art on view – make this a unique, compelling option. $78 shared bath; add $50 for private bath.

Hill House 1113 E John St T 206/720-7161 or 1–800/720-7161, W www.seattlehillhouse.com. Elegant accommodation with seven rooms and suites decorated with controlled Victorian frilliness; there's a garden and covered patio, and some units have VCRs, fridges, and clawfoot tubs. Children welcome. $75 low season, $115 high.

Mildred's 1202 15th Ave E ☎206/325-6072, ⓦwww.mildredsbnb.com. Four rooms – the Green, with southern and eastern views, the Blue, with a sitting alcove, the Lace, with a skylight in the bath, and the Rose, with a private deck – in a vaguely Dutch Colonial 1890 Victorian with a wraparound veranda, near Volunteer Park. All units have TVs and VCRs. $90.

Salisbury House 750 16th Ave E ☎206/328-8682, ⓦwww.salisburyhouse.com. Four smart doubles and an attractive suite (with hot tub and fireplace) in a Capitol Hill mansion with maple floors, high ceilings, and a quiet yet convenient location. Ask for the Blue Room if you want morning sun, or the Lavender Room if you want the biggest space. $89 in off-season, add $25–40 more in spring and summer.

🏃 **Shafer-Baillie Mansion 907 14th Ave E** ☎206/322-4654, ⓦshaferbaillie.tripod .com. Always a popular site for weddings and receptions, this mansion's oak-paneled walls and late-Victorian decor echo its 1914 construction. It offers a range of eleven period-furnished rooms, from three cramped "servants' quarters" ($95) to more spacious suites with antique tubs and refrigerators ($140–195).

University District

Chambered Nautilus 5005 22nd Ave NE ☎206/522-2536 or 1-800/545-8459, ⓦwww .chamberednautilus.com. Five blocks north of UW, this quaint B&B offers six taste-ful rooms bearing names like "Crow's Nest" and "Scallop Chamber." Four rooms have porches, and four adjoining suites are furnished with more recent, if more drab, decor; apple quiche is the breakfast specialty. Reservations a month or two ahead of time are advisable in the summer months. Rooms start at $89; add $15 for basic suites, and $25 to both for high-season rates.

College Inn 4000 University Ave NE ☎206/633-4441, ⓦwww.collegeinnseattle.com. The city's most budget-friendly B&B, with 27 basic but comfortable rooms in a Tudor-styled complex on the edge of UW's campus. Reservations are advisable, especially around university graduation (early summer)

and orientation (late summer). Bargain rates: $55 for a basic unit, and $80 for a larger room.

Ballard and Fremont

Canal Cottages on Lake Washington Ship Canal near NW Market St ☎206/498-4647, ⓦcanalcottages.com. A pair of charming, rentable cottages near the Ballard Locks: the best is the Caretaker's Cottage, a two-bedroom item with spacious, homey environs and basic, clean decor; the Boat-house is a simpler, if cheaper, unit with a kitchen. $105.

Chelsea Station on the Park 4915 Linden Ave N, Fremont ☎206/547-6077, ⓦwww.bandbseattle .com. An appealing old-fashioned dwelling offering six rooms and suites, some with antique tubs and good views. Located on a quiet block across from the Woodland Park Zoo. Basic units go for $110, suites only $20–30 more.

Dibble House 7301 Dibble Ave NW, north of Ballard ☎206/783-0320. Found just a short drive from the zoo and the Chittenden Locks, this B&B has cheaper rates than other comparable lodgings, though the rooms are smaller. Three of the five bedrooms have queen-sized beds, the other two have twins; all but one have shared bath. $55.

West Seattle

Villa Heidelberg 4845 45th Ave SW ☎206/938-3658 or 1-800/671-2942, ⓦwww .villaheidelberg.com. Sizable German-themed B&B featuring five elegant rooms, basic amenities, and period decor, plus private decks and fireplaces in some units. Located south of the main sights in West Seattle. Rates start at $90 (up to $150 for suites) and leap by $40–100 in high season.

Wildwood 4518 SW Wildwood Place ☎206/819-9075 or 1-800/840-8410, ⓦwww .wildwoodseattle.com. Located near Lincoln Park, right on the bus line going into Downtown Seattle, and worth looking into if you're in search of a bargain. Converted stucco home has covered porches, gardens, and five Victorian-furnished rooms. Only one unit has a private bath, for $115; other rooms are much cheaper, at $70–90.

Hostels

Seattle's **hostels** are generally close to the center of Downtown. Memberships in IYHF or AYH (@www.hihostels.com, @www.hiayh.org) are useful for procuring space or getting reduced rates, but are not necessary to qualify for a bed in most cases. There's usually a limit to the number of consecutive days you can stay, though at the private hostels these rules are sometimes relaxed during the off-season. Most of the hostels offer private rooms for couples and single travelers, although per night they cost about two or three times the dorm rate. Don't take vacancy for granted, either: though you may be able to get a space just by showing up, you'd do well to call ahead.

Bigfoot Backpackers 126 Broadway Ave E, Capitol Hill ☎206/720-2965 or 1-800/600-2965. Reached via an alley near the busiest corner in Capitol Hill, with 45 beds, including dorms ($18) and a few private rooms ($38 single, $48 double). No curfew and lots of extras: free breakfast, Downtown pickup, Internet access, and parking. It also runs tours to the graves of Jimi Hendrix and Bruce Lee, with a stop at Kurt Cobain's former home in Madrona.

Green Tortoise 1525 Second Ave, Downtown ☎206/340-1222 or 1-888/424-6783, @www.greentortoise.net. In a somewhat grim location a block away from Pike Place Market, these old-style digs – operated by the Green Tortoise alternative tour-bus company – have four-to-a-room dorm beds for $23, or private doubles for $48. Free Downtown pickup and Internet access; they also do summer walking tours of the city.

Hosteling International Seattle 84 Union St, Downtown ☎206/622-5443 or 1-888/622-5443, @www.hiseattle.org. For location, *HI*'s hard to beat: just a block from Pike Place Market, with Pioneer Square minutes away. Modern, comfortable dorms, with 130 beds ($23; add $3 for non-members), though reservations are still advisable June–Sept, when the price increases to $35. Private rooms with shared baths cost $55, while hotel-type units with private bathrooms and kitchens cost around $100. Free pickup from bus and train stations.

YWCA 1118 Fifth Ave, Downtown ☎206/461-4888, @www.ywcaworks.org. Open to women only, the ambiance here is more functional than colorful, but it's safe and clean, a reasonable choice for women visitors on a budget; $46–75 (the higher-priced rooms include a private bath). Twenty-one rooms in all.

Cafés

M ore than simply places to knock back a java, **cafés** in Seattle are centers of urban social activity, attracting a wide range of regulars and curious visitors, and sometimes exhibiting art or staging live music. Indeed, one of the great pleasures of Seattle cafés is their multipurpose character, verve and irreverent attitude, which also shows up in the off-kilter decor – at its most extreme, you may be unsure of whether the voodoo-doll lamp on your table is a featured artwork or a garage-sale relic.

Seattle being a center for computer technology, there are a number of **cyber-cafés** around town, particularly on Capitol Hill. Even "regular" cafés often have a few stray computers tucked into their corners; fees usually start at $6/hour. You'll also find countless **espresso carts** throughout the city – some with small seating areas, some wedged into alleys or parked on narrow curbs, and some offering drive-in service in parking lots.

Coffeehouses

Ordering a single beverage at a Seattle **coffeehouse** pretty much gives you carte blanche to park yourself in a seat all day; you can blend in with the locals by doodling in a notebook, watching the endless parade of street characters, or typing away on the Great American Novel. The *Starbucks* chain is as ubiquitous here as it is elsewhere, but offers little charm or personality – it's best mainly for picking up a cup o' joe when you're in desperate need of one.

If you want a taste of the bohemian scene, check out the cafés in Fremont; for an odd assortment of alternative-chic and yuppie smugness, Belltown; for boisterous socializing, Capitol Hill or the University District; or for a wider mix of hipsters and the working-class, Pioneer Square. Whatever your preference, there's bound to be a café to suit every taste and mood.

Downtown and Pioneer Square

All City Coffee 125 Prefontaine Place S
☏ 206/652-8331. Something of an institution in far-south Seattle (1205 S Vale St, ☏ 206/767-7146), this more central, Pioneer Square branch has the same hip attitude. Serves tasty cupcakes, soups, and sandwiches, and particularly good coffee – the Luna and Del Sol varieties are well worth a gulp. Local artworks are displayed throughout. Mon–Fri 6am–11pm, Sat 7am–11pm, Sun 8am–9pm.

Bookstore Bar & Cafe 1007 First Ave
☏ 206/382-1506. This cozy, upscale spot for light lunches and dinners, off the lobby of the *Alexis* hotel (see p.146), is most notable for its collection of browsable books, international magazines, and newspapers. Also known for its bourbons, ports, cognacs,

Coffee-bar culture in Seattle

There's no simple explanation for the astonishing proliferation of **coffee bars** in Seattle, with hundreds of java-oriented establishments displaying all manner of fascinating idiosyncrasies and gimmicks. Capitol Hill's *Coffee Messiah*, for example, is crammed with Christian icons and crucifixes, and sports a sign declaring "Caffeine Saves," while the Espresso Dental Clinic in Greenwood (6725 Greenwood Ave, ☎206/284-2483) serves lattes to waiting patients.

The caffeine subculturists of Seattle long ago evolved their own method of ordering the brew, which has now spread to most of the country, if not the world. Locals are obsessive about coffee preparation, specifying type of milk, number of shots of espresso, accompanying syrup (amaretto, hazelnut, etc) and other embellishments – not to mention the Starbucks-induced welter of frozen concoctions such as frappuccinos and the like. If you're determined to start off by passing for a local, just ask for a "double skinny latte," which, in layman's terms, is a latte made with skim milk and a double shot of espresso.

For more on the culture and terminology of Seattle's coffee scene, see the color insert entitled "Coffee culture."

and malt scotches (along with its rash of cigar-smokers). A small sidewalk patio is set up in warmer months. Daily noon–midnight.

Pegasus Coffee Bar 711 Third Ave ☎206/682-3113. A bit less pretentious than some Seattle coffee bars, with brews of Pegasus beans, whose roasting facilities are on Bainbridge Island (on which there's another branch at 125 Parfitt Way SW ☎206/842-3113). Located in the lobby of the Dexter Horton Building. Mon–Fri 6.30am–4.30pm.

Torrefazione Italia 320 Occidental Ave S ☎206/624-5847. This Pioneer Square espresso bar serves top-notch coffee in an Old World–styled setting, heightened by the outdoor seating area on the pedestrianized part of Occidental Avenue. Part of a chain with several other city branches. Mon–Fri 6am–6pm, Sat 7am–6pm, Sun 7am–5pm.

Zeitgeist Coffee 171 S Jackson St ☎206/583-0497, ⓦzeitgeistcoffee.com. Mostly coffee, a few sandwiches, some pastries, and modern art are found at this haunt in the heart of Pioneer Square's gallery scene. Hosts periodic showings of local and independent films. Mon–Fri 6am–7pm, Sat & Sun 8am–7pm.

Belltown

Bellino 2421 2nd Ave ☎206/956-4237. In a stretch awash in chain coffeehouses (especially on neighboring 1st Ave), this independent is worth seeking out for its carefully crafted organic brews and savory espresso drinks (with beans from Vivace) – along with pastries and desserts and a splash of arty color on the walls. Daily 7am–6pm.

Motore Coffee 1904 9th Ave, a few blocks east of Belltown ☎206/388-2803. Fairly new coffeehouse with style to spare, with Vespa-inspired decor and new iMacs for Web-browsing. The coffee (Caffé Vita) is supreme, as are the delicious sandwiches and the entire coffee-tea-chocolate drink menu. Local artwork hangs on the walls. Mon-Sat 7am-4pm.

Top Pot Coffee & Doughnuts 2124 5th Ave ☎206/728-1966. Fifth, instead of Second, Avenue is really the place is do your caffeinating in Belltown, and this primo java-and-donut haunt is an excellent choice, with hip decor, Wi-Fi Internet access, and coffee-bean connection to Pioneer Square's Zeitgeist. Commence to guzzling. Daily 6am-7pm.

Seattle Center and Queen Anne

Caffe Ladro 2205 Queen Anne Ave N ☎206/282-5313, ⓦwww.caffeladro.com. A groovy mix of industrial and organic designs at this enjoyable neighborhood coffeehouse – the name translates to "coffee thief" – with an arty flair, hearty coffees, and a range of light meals (some veggie options). There are eight other branches in the city, including another one in Upper Queen Anne, at 600 Queen Anne Ave N (☎206/282-1549). All branches daily 5.30am–11pm.

Caffè Zingaro 127 Mercer St ☎206/352-2861. One of the better choices in the vicinity of the Opera House and Seattle Center, where you can munch on bagels or pastries and sip the organic espressos on offer. Wi-Fi Internet access is available. Mon–Wed 7am–9pm, Thurs–Sat 7am–11pm, Sun 8am–9pm.

Uptown Espresso 525 Queen Anne Ave N ☎206/285-3757, ⓦwww.uptownespresso.net. Despite the name, the *Uptown* is located in *Lower* Queen Anne. Caters to bleary-eyed morning regulars and late-night revelers – come here to sip quality coffee and munch on succulent pastries. Mon–Thurs 5am–10pm, Fri 5am–11pm, Sat 6am–11pm, Sun 6am–10pm. Also in Belltown at 2504 4th Ave (Mon–Fri 5am–7pm, Sat & Sun 6am–7pm; ☎206/441-1084).

Capitol Hill

Aurafice 616 E Pine St ☎206/860-9977, ⓦwww.aurafice.com. Internet coffee bar with an arty ambiance, featuring occasional performance art, music, and goth-industrial DJs, as well as Tarot card and palm readings. Sun–Thurs 8am–11pm, Fri & Sat 8am–midnight.

B&O Espresso 204 Belmont Ave E ☎206/322-5028. For those who desire elegance without sacrificing a casual atmosphere, this is the place – with a cool, dark interior, outdoor seating, and a fine assortment of drinks and desserts (the brownies are especially good). Mon–Thurs 7am–midnight, Fri 8am–1am, Sat 7am–1am, Sun 8am–midnight.

Bauhaus Books & Coffee 301 E Pine St ☎206/625-1600. Busy hangout on the south end of Capitol Hill, edging toward Downtown. Dispenses coffee and tea in a self-consciously somber atmosphere, with tall chairs at the windowside counter, and a decent selection of used books in the arts and humanities. Mon–Fri 6am–1am, Sat & Sun 8am–1am.

Café Dilettante 416 Broadway E ☎206/329-6463. Though they serve very good coffee and cocoa, people come here more for the delicious desserts and chocolate treats, some of the best in town. Sun–Thurs 11am–midnight, Fri & Sat 11am–1am.

Caffé Vita 1005 E Pike St ☎206/709-4440. *The* place on Capitol Hill for folks into both serious coffee – this brand is one of the city's best – and hanging out with a predominantly bohemian-styled crowd. Mon–Fri 6am–11pm, Sat & Sun 7am–11pm. Also in

Queen Anne at 813 5th Ave N (☎206/285-9662). Mon–Fri 6am–8pm, Sat & Sun 7am–8pm.

Capitol Hill Café 216 Broadway E ☎206/860-6858. Low-key, lofty space offering muffins and espresso, but the chief attractions are Web-browsing, graphic design, computer games, CD-burning, and other high-tech activities available on ten computers for ten cents a minute. Daily 8am–midnight.

Coffee Messiah 1554 E Olive Way ☎206/861-8233, ⓦwww.coffeemessiah.com. With its kitschy religious decor, this is not the place for those without a sense of irreverence. If it's just coffee you're after, they have that, too (featuring a "Blood of Christ" blend), as well as chai, herbal tea, and juices, plus occasional free live music and spoken-word shows. Daily 7am–7pm.

Online Coffee Company 1720 E Olive Way ☎206/328-3731, ⓦwww.onlinecoffeeco.com. Spacious and relaxed Internet café with coffee, beer, wine, and baked goods; the outside patio has a view of Puget Sound. Mon–Fri 8am–1am, Sat & Sun 9am–1am. Also Downtown at 1111 First Ave (☎206/381-1911). Mon–Fri 7am–10pm, Sat 9am–10pm, Sun 9am–8pm.

Perkatory Cafe 1400 14th Ave ☎206/568-2345. A local favorite for its pastries and baked goods, free Wi-Fi Internet access, and cozy decor with art abounding – not to mention a nice selection of organic java and teas. Mon–Thurs 7am–8pm, Fri 7am–7pm, Sat 8am–7pm, Sun 1–5pm.

Top Pot Coffee & Doughnuts 609 Summit Ave E ☎206/323-7841. Chic and modern spot for knocking back a cup o' mud and eating sugary treats 'til late in the evening. The donuts - in traditional glazed, chocolate, maple, and sprinkled varieties – are scrumptious gut-busters, and the java is made by the talented folks at Downtown's *Zeitgeist Coffee* (see p.154). Daily 6am–11pm, weekends opens 8am.

Victrola Coffee and Art 411 15th Ave E ☎206/325-6520, ⓦwww.victrolacoffee.com. A good place for browsing some local modern art, taking in a spoken-word or musical performance, savoring rich brews – single-origin beans from Rwanda and other countries – and devouring a range of healthy snacks and light fare, some of it vegan-friendly. Daily 5.30am–11pm.

Vivace Espresso 901 E Denny Way ☎206/860-5869. This large haunt of Capitol Hill's serious coffee-drinkers is run by self-proclaimed "espresso roasting and preparation specialists". More chic is their sidewalk café at 321 Broadway E (same phone), the prime people-watching perch in the area, with a few outdoor tables and perennial takeout lines. Daily 6.30am–11pm.

University District

Allegro Espresso Bar 4214 University Way NE, in an alley between University and 15th Ave NE ☎206/633-3030. One of the favorite spots of committed caffeine-addicts, and also a popular student hangout with an adjoining room of computer terminals with Internet access. Mon–Fri 6.30am–11pm, Sat 7am–11pm, Sun 8am–11pm.

Espresso Roma 4201 University Way NE ☎206/632-6001. Worth patronizing mostly for its outdoor porch, a good viewpoint to watch the passing foot traffic on University Way; occasional art displays are an interesting sidelight. Mon–Fri 7am–11pm, Sat & Sun 8am–11pm.

Star Life on the Oasis 1405 NE 50th St ☎206/729-3542. The homeliest of the popular U District cafés, this spot – connected to the Grand Illusion cinema – has a living-room feel and good snacks, as well as basic light meals and some outdoor seating. A great place to peruse a newspaper or book for a couple of hours. Daily 10am–midnight.

Magnolia and Ballard

Mr Spot's Chai House 5463 Leary Ave ☎206/297-CHAI. The self-proclaimed leader of Seattle's chai scene. Doles out the spicy Indian beverage, as well as a full selection of coffee drinks, plus incense, candles, soap, and the like. Live music is another draw, with regular open-mike nights and hippie jam sessions (Thurs–Sat). Mon–Wed 7am–10pm, Thurs–Fri 7am–2am, Sat 8am–2am, Sun 8am–8pm.

Q Cafe 3223 15th Ave W ☎206/352-2525. The quintessential Seattle café: underground art on the walls, open mike (Tues 8–10pm) and live-music shows (Fri 7–10pm; $5–12), excellent coffee and snacks, and a non-profit mission to help out the homeless and support progressive causes. The only challenge is finding it, in the community of Interbay, east of Magnolia. Mon–Thurs 8am–10pm, Fri 8am–11pm, Sat 9am–4pm.

Vérité Coffee 2052 NW Market St ☎206/709-4497. Fun and prominent coffee shop along the main drag of downtown Ballard, with excellent coffee and – notably – flavorful cupcakes with offbeat toppings like gummy fish and candy flowers. Mon–Thurs 6.30am–10pm, Sat 6.30am–midnight, Sun 6.30am–9pm.

▽ Vérité Coffee

Fremont, Wallingford, and further north

Diva Espresso 7916 Greenwood Ave N ☎206/781-1213. Located north of Fremont in Greenwood's increasingly hip boutique zone, *Diva* is a favorite for its antique decor and rich, flavorful coffee and tea drinks. Also a branch in West Seattle (see p.157). Mon–Sat 5.30am–10pm, Sun 7am–8pm.

Fremont Coffee 459 N 36th St ☎206/632-3633. Now that the beloved *Still Life* has gone under, this is the most prominent coffeehouse in the district – an actual house with artwork and cozy furniture, plus excellent coffee (Lighthouse and Vivace brands), handcrafted sodas, and free wireless Internet. Daily 7am–8pm.

Herkimer Coffee 7320 Greenwood Ave N ☎206/784-0202. Gimmicks are kept to a minimum at this straightforward Greenwood café, where the art of the brew is the draw. Meticulous preparation and primo ingredients (plus Caffé Vita beans). Mon–Fri 6am–6pm, Sat & Sun 7am–6pm.

Teahouse Kuan Yin 1911 N 45th St, Wallingford ☎206/632-2055. A necessary antidote in coffee-happy Seattle, serving several dozen varieties of black, oolong, green, and herbal teas, as well as light snacks, in a comfortable, very subdued setting. Occasional live music shows (traditional koto and guitar). Daily 10am–11pm.

Zoka Coffee 2200 N 56th St, Green Lake ☎206/545-4277. Proud of its international and artisan coffees, with especially good blends, such as the piquant Colonel Fitzroy's and the rich, succulent Baltoro.

CAFÉS | Coffeehouses

Serves up fine tea and snacks too. Also in the U District, at 2901 Blakely St (☎206/527-0990). Both daily 6am–11pm.

West Seattle

Diva Espresso 4480 Fauntleroy Way SW ☎206/937-5225. Just off the highway, the second branch of a local favorite on the java scene (see p.156 for another in Greenwood), stuffed with antique bric a-brac and

fancy chandeliers, and doling out piping-hot brews of all your favorite espresso concoctions. Mon–Fri 6am–9pm, Sat 7am–9pm, Sun 7am–6pm.

Hotwire 4410 California Ave SW ☎206/935-1510, ⓦwww.hotwirecoffee.com. West Seattle choice for java and Internet access, with a comfortable atmosphere, quirky art installations, and a location within easy reach of Alki Beach, to the north. Daily 6am–10pm.

Light meals, bakeries, and desserts

While most cafés in Seattle serve at least some snack–type edibles, such as biscotti or muffins, the places we've listed below offer something a bit more substantial, be it creative sandwiches and salads or quiches and piroshkis (Russian bread pastries with tasty fillings). In addition to these good choices for a **light meal**, Seattle has a substantial number of quality **bakeries**, as well as numerous spots to satisfy your sweet tooth with a rich **dessert**.

Downtown

Cinnamon Works 1530 Pike Place ☎206/583-0085. Delicious oat-fruit bars, sticky buns, and aptly named "Monster" cookies at this bakery counter in the heart of Pike Place Market. Mon–Fri 7.30am–5pm, Sat & Sun 8am–5pm; closing times vary according to level of business.

Le Panier 1902 Pike Place ☎206/441-3669. French bakery serving up a wide variety of breads, croissants, and both savory and sweet pastries. Also one of the more popular hangouts in Pike Place Market. Mon–Sat 7am–6pm, Sun 8am–5pm.

Piroshky-Piroshky 1908 Pike Place ☎206/441-6068. Russian bakery with pastries and piroshkis that satisfy those urges for something between a snack and a full meal. Get something with potato inside and you can't go wrong; good apple, cinnamon, and cheese rolls, too. Daily 8.30am–5pm.

Taste SAM 100 University St ☎206/254-1273. The esteemed café of the Seattle Art Museum, doling out good nouveau Northwest cuisine, including savory sandwiches, pasta, and frittatas, plus burgers and pizzas and, of course, good coffee. Tues–Sun 10am–4pm.

Three Girls Bakery lower floor of Sanitary Market, Pike Place Market ☎206/622-1045. Endure the long lines at this well-loved haunt for large, tasty sandwiches – such as

herb focaccia with hummus – available at the takeout counter or the adjoining café. Daily 7am–6pm.

Pioneer Square

Elliott Bay Café First Ave S and S Main St ☎206/682-6664. A good assortment of mid-priced, wholefood-oriented soups, salads, quiches, and the like. Located in the basement of Elliott Bay Book Company. Mon–Fri 8am–9pm, Sat 9am–9pm, Sun 11am–7pm.

Grand Central Bakery 214 First Ave S ☎206/622-3644. A favorite breakfast and lunch spot for its handcrafted, nicely seasoned salads, desserts, and light meals, including tasty roast-beef sandwiches and hearty chicken rolls and hoagies. Mon–Fri 7am–5pm, Sat 8am–4pm. Also at 1616 Eastlake Ave E (☎206/957-9505); Mon–Fri 6.30am–6.30pm, Sat & Sun 8am–4.30pm.

Salumi 309 Third Ave S ☎206/621-8772. Sausages made the old-fashioned way, served in delicious sandwiches with homemade bread, and issued piping hot. Succulent, heavy ingredients at this Pioneer Square institution – run by TV superchef Mario Batali's dad – include oxtail, prosciutto, lamb, and numerous kinds of hog parts. If you come around lunchtime, expect to wait in a long line. Tues–Fri 11am–4pm.

Belltown

Biofournil 2507 4th Ave ⊕206/728-1874. This purely French bakery – thick with rustic loaves, baguettes, pastries and sandwiches like Croque Monsieur – is also the single US outpost of an esteemed French breadmaker, so be aware before you burst in asking for a PBJ. Mon–Fri 7am–6pm, Sat & Sun 8am–6pm.

Café Amore 2229 5th Ave ⊕206/728-6033. Fine café near the monorail track, with a good selection of food, such as salads, sandwiches and breakfast frittatas, plus pizza and beer. Wi-Fi Internet access available. Mon–Fri 6am–8pm, Sat 9am–8pm, Sun 9am–6pm.

🏃 **Dahlia Bakery 2001 Fourth Ave** ⊕206/682-4142. Associated with the redoubtable *Dahlia Lounge* (see p.165), this is an excellent spot for upscale baked goods. Serves a scrumptious assortment of pies, pastries, breads, sandwiches, and other concoctions, using only fresh local and regional ingredients. Mon–Fri 7.30am–6pm, Sat 9am–6pm, Sun 10am–4pm.

Macrina 2408 First Ave ⊕206/448-4032. Café in the heart of the action on Belltown's First Avenue, serving coffee and goodies like apricot-nut bread and one mean challah. Mon–Sat 7am–9pm, Sun 8am–6pm. Also in Queen Anne at 615 W McGraw St (⊕206/283-5900). Mon–Sat 7am–7pm, Sun 8am–6pm.

Queen Anne and Seattle Center

Alligator Pear 2523 5th Ave ⊕206/728-5897. One of the better lunch spots along this stretch on the edge of Seattle Center, with good coffee and other beverages, but best for tasty sandwiches using local, organic ingredients; soups, including a succulent sweet potato; and an array of cookies and other sweets. Daily 10am–5pm, weekends opens 9am.

El Diablo Coffee Company 1811 Queen Anne Ave N ⊕206/285-0693, ⓦwww.eldiablocoffee.com. Known for its colorful artwork and furnishings, and for its powerful, eye-opening blends of Cuban-roasted java. Equally good for its savory sandwiches and pastries, plus delicious fruit and chocolate desserts. Mon–Fri 6:30am–11pm, Sat & Sun 6.30am–midnight.

Capitol Hill

Café Venus and the Mars Bar 609 Eastlake Ave E ⊕206/624-4516, ⓦwww.cafevenus.com. Extraterrestrial-themed coffee joint and bar serving entrees like "Space Saucer" pizzas and "Neptune Noodles"; there's a less exciting selection of coffee and teas, though the place is still enjoyable for its New Frontier decor and potent Zotini cocktail – with Kahlua, vodka and Vivace espresso. Mon–Fri 11am–2am, Sat 6pm–2am.

🏃 **Globe Café 1531 14th Ave** ⊕206/324-8815. With its vivid atmosphere and regular poetry readings (see p.194), this is hard to beat for a Seattle experience. Good for its tasty all-vegan menu of full meals, drinks, and desserts, and goofy decor of globes, oddly shaped painted salt shakers, and blackboards for patrons to doodle on. Daily 7am–7pm.

Joe Bar Café 810 E Roy St ⊕206/324-0407. A hotspot for drinking rich coffee, eating savory crêpes, Italian sandwiches, soups, and antipasti, and – most of all – getting the flavor of Seattle's underground art scene, with works by up-and-comers on the walls. Mon 7.30am–5pm, Tues–Fri 7.30am–9.30pm, Sat & Sun 8.30am–9.30pm.

Louisa's Bakery & Café 2379 Eastlake Ave E ⊕206/325-0081. A good place to order breakfast (with savory quiche and French toast), sandwiches, salads, or baked goods. Convivial atmosphere and crowd. Mon–Fri 7am–7pm, Sat 7am–5pm, Sun 8am–2pm.

Piroshki on Broadway 124 1/2 Broadway E ⊕206/322-2820. A small spot in the busiest part of Capitol Hill, with a luscious assortment of meat and veggie piroshkis, as well as sweets like apricot walnut rolls. Mostly takeout, although there are some small tables for eating in the rather cramped premises. Mon–Sat 7am–11pm, Sun 7am–10pm.

Red Line 1525 Olive Way ⊕206/328-9559. A great place to pop in for coffee or knock back a beer. The sandwiches are especially tasty, among them good pastrami, roast beef, pork and even grilled cheese. Daily 6am–10pm, weekends opens 7am.

University District

Black Cat Cafe 5000 30th Ave NE ⊕206/522-5005. A hip and engaging spot for drinking small-batch espresso (Caffe Luca brand), munching on tasty panini and sandwiches, and eating desserts like gelato and raspberry cannoli. Mon & Tues 6am–4pm, Wed–Fri 6am–10pm, Sat 8am–10pm, Sun 8am–4pm.

Burke Museum Café in the basement of the Burke Museum,17th Ave NE and NE 45th St ☎206/543-9854. A fine café with high ceilings, wood-paneled walls, wooden armchairs, and classical music on the stereo, yielding an ambiance that tries to approximate a nineteenth-century drawing room. Offers a good complement of sandwiches, pastries, salads, and espresso beverages. Mon–Fri 7am–5pm, Sat 10am–5pm, Sun 9am–5pm.

Mix Ice Cream Bar 4507 University Way NE ☎206/547-3436. The best place in the U District for ice cream and frozen yogurt, offering a nice variety of flavors and toppings swirled together. The cheesecake-brownie combo is a particularly rich treat. Mon–Thurs noon–11pm, Fri & Sat noon–1am, Sun noon–10pm.

Fremont, Wallingford and further north

Bagel Oasis 462 N 36th St ☎206/633-2676. More imaginative sandwiches than the usual (try the "Rainy Day" combo of portobello mushroom and red peppers), as well as a good variety of bagels, an assortment of spreads, and other baked goods. Mon–Fri 6.30am–4pm, Sat & Sun 7am–4pm.

Erotic Bakery 2323 N 45th St, Wallingford ☎206/545-6969, ⓦwww.theeroticbakery.com. Custom-designed erotic cakes, cupcakes, and chocolates – including the likes of confectionary breasts and phalluses – in a store that also has an extensive selection of risqué greeting cards and naughty novelties. Mon–Sat 10am–7pm.

Mighty O Donuts 2110 N 55th St ☎206/547-0335. A Green Lake favorite for its surprisingly rich and tasty organic vegan donuts. The delicious likes of lemon poppy, coconut, French toast, and glazed are all made

with palm oil. Mon & Tues 6am–noon, Wed–Fri 6am–8pm, Sat & Sun 7am–5pm.

Simply Desserts 3421 Fremont Ave N ☎206/633-2671. Fine Fremont dessert specialist, low in square feet but high in quality; the white-chocolate cakes are a highlight, among the tasty rash of cookies, pies, brownies, etc. Tues–Thurs noon–10pm, Fri & Sat noon–11.30pm, Sun noon–6pm.

Touchstone Bakery 501-A N 36th St, Fremont ☎206/547-4000. Wholegrain organic collective with a small but enticing street counter of pastries that are just as good as those in less health-conscious outlets. Try the orange-oatmeal cookies, or munch on sandwiches, soups, muffins, and pizza. Thurs–Tues 7.30am–6pm.

West Seattle

Alki Bakery 2738 Alki Ave SW ☎206/935-1352. Worth seeking out for the supreme coffee and espresso, and delicious range of baked goods and desserts: eclairs, cookies, donuts, and handpies to make your mouth water. Located along a very popular stretch of beach. Sun–Thurs 7am–9pm, Fri & Sat 7am–10pm.

Husky Deli 4721 California Ave SW ☎206/937-2810. Continental-style sandwiches, meats, cheeses, and desserts, made with gourmet ingredients. Also, rich coffee drinks and the deli's famous ice-cream concoctions, with dozens of different flavors – the various types of chocolate are an undeniable high point. Mon–Sat 9am–9pm, Sun 10am–7pm.

🏃 **Salvadorian Bakery 1719 SW Roxbury St, West Seattle** ☎206/762-4064. More than just a place to snack on bread and desserts, this is a terrific Latin eatery with spicy, very tasty pupusas (which in this form are corn cakes stuffed with anything from pork to peppers) and solid staples like plantains and yucca. Merits a stop if you're in the area. Daily 8am-9pm.

11

CAFÉS | Light meals, bakeries, and desserts

Restaurants

S eattle's **restaurants** encompass a wide range of cuisines, as well as regional or international twists on familiar flavors. The number of culinary approaches is, in fact, considerably larger than one might expect, given the city's limited size compared to the biggest American cities. Asian, seafood, vegetarian, and conventional American cooking are all well-represented, and the number of eclectic international establishments is also on the rise.

The term "**Northwest Cuisine**" is bandied about with regularity in the region, and basically refers to a regional variation on California Cuisine, encompassing a wide array of flavors, gastronomic experiments, and often exotic-sounding dishes made using local, sometimes organic, ingredients. Unsurprisingly, locally caught **seafood** is of a high standard, especially the salmon, though the shellfish is also quite good – much of it caught either in Puget Sound off the banks of western Washington. There's also a handful of quality **steakhouses** in town, with a mix of local favorites and more familiar chain diners. The International District has countless inexpensive East Asian spots, and is particularly strong on **Chinese**, **Japanese**, and **Vietnamese** offerings, though you won't have to look too hard in town for **Thai**, either. **Pan-Asian** cuisine, which fuses different kinds of Asian dishes into the same menu, or mixes Asian and North American styles, has become trendy here in recent years as well. **Vegetarians** will not have a problem, either – the Pacific Northwest is approaching coastal California standards in providing a wealth of meatless alternatives. Even more discriminating vegans will find a few dozen restaurants catering to their needs, widely scattered around the city.

Dining in Seattle is a casual affair, with dress codes rare even in some of the pricier places. **Reservations** aren't a bad idea at the most popular spots, especially on weekends, but mostly it's fine just to show up. Indeed, quite a few places don't take reservations at all. **Non-smoking** laws aren't quite as stringent as they are in California, but most restaurants don't allow it.

Places that open early usually offer **breakfast** – though not only in the morning, but for lunch hours as well, which in Seattle usually run from about 11am to 3pm (see also "Light Meals" in Chapter 11 for more such options). **Lunches** can be anything from humble $5 sandwiches to higher-priced creations that amount to small-scale suppers. If you want to enjoy some of the fancier restaurants without the high cost, lunch prices are often drastically lower than dinner prices. **Desserts** at the same establishments can also get you in the door without blowing a hole in your wallet. If you're on a really tight budget, head for the numerous all-you-care-to-eat **lunch buffets** for $5 or so, many of which can be found at **Indian** restaurants (of which there are numerous good choices). Weekend **brunches** are also popular, though the lines can be considerably lengthy at the best spots.

There are better options for **fast food** in Seattle than elsewhere in the Northwest, especially in **Pike Place Market** – and not simply of the gut-busting chain-burger variety, either. With many tasty ethnic entrees available in the $5 range, it's by far the top place Downtown for a quick bite.

Downtown: Pike Place Market and around

Athenian Inn 1517 Pike Place ☎206/624-7166. A good place for breakfast as well as people watching and checking out views of Puget Sound; try the seafood platter and munch on haddock, herring or halibut if you're coming for a proper meal. Was a shooting location in the film *Sleepless in Seattle*. Mon–Sat 6.30am–6.30pm.

Bacco Bistro 86 Pine St ☎206/443-5443. Step right up to stuff your gut with salmon and crab sandwiches at this affordable bistro. Pastas and paninis offer good value for lunch and weekend dinners. Mon–Thurs 8am-4pm, Fri-Sun 8am-6pm.

Campagne 86 Pine St ☎206/728-2800. Easily the top restaurant in the Market area, and one of the city's best, offering delicacies like potato-wrapped striped bass filet and foie gras parfait in a puff pastry with shallots and turnips. Leans heavily toward seafood specialties, though there are excellent pan-roasted beef entrees and the ever-tasty pomme frites, fried in duck fat. Serves dinner daily from 5.30 to 10pm; the bar is open until midnight. On the ground level, the less-expensive *Café Campagne* has similar dinner hours, but is also a good spot for lunch (Mon–Fri 11am–5pm) and weekend brunch (8am–4pm), albeit with a few more tourists.

Chez Shea 94 Pike St, top floor of Corner Market building ☎206/467-9990. Not surprisingly, given its French-pun moniker, this is a prime place to go for expensive *nouvelle cuisine*, mixed with Northwest ingredients. Offers fixed-price, four- and eight-course dinners ($42–65), including seafood dressed up with elaborate sauces, meat dishes like quail and lamb served in small, succulent portions, and soups and savory pastries. Tues–Sun 5–10pm.

Copacabana 1520 Pike Place, Triangle Building ☎206/622-6359. A Bolivian restaurant that's one of Pike Place's most offbeat eateries, with a concentration on stuffed pies (such as *huminta*, or corn pie) and seafood soups. The outdoor balcony seating has a good view of the human traffic on Pike Place below. Mon–Sat 11.30am–4pm, Sun 11.30am–5pm.

Crêpe de France 93 Pike St, Economy Row ☎206/624-2196. Over a dozen varieties of savory (meat and veggie) and sweet crêpes (notably anything with berry or peach) are whipped up before your eyes at this Pike Place stall with five counter seats; it's a great place for taking in the market ambiance and having a tasty, vaguely Continental experience without spending more than ten bucks. Mon–Fri 10am–5pm, Sat & Sun 10am–6pm.

El Puerco Lloron 1501 Western Ave ☎206/624-0541. A rare authentic Mexican restaurant in Seattle, "The Crying Pig" serves tamales, tostadas, and excellent *chili rellenos* in a cafeteria-style setting with traditional decor. Located on the Hillclimb behind the market. Winter daily 11am–5pm, rest of year Mon–Sat 11.30am–8pm, Sun noon–6.30pm.

Jasmine 1530 Post Alley ☎206/382-9899. A curious blend of the usual Thai staples – tom yum soups, curries, and pad Thai – with unexpected Moroccan and North African offerings – chicken-and-couscous – makes this restaurant a favorite of a small but devoted clan of international foodies. Try the beef over jasmine rice with raisins. Daily 10am–6pm.

Lowell's 1519 Pike Place, main floor of Main Arcade ☎206/622-2036. Among the most popular of the Pike Place restaurants, with cheap prices and waterfront views; it's renowned for its hearty seafood dishes, with basic, all-American breakfasts. There is sometimes a lengthy wait to get a seat on the upper floor, which has the best views. Daily 7am–7pm, lounge open later.

Place Pigalle 81 Pike St ☎206/624-1756. Though tucked unobtrusively in a market alley and therefore easily missed (look for the walkway between the butcher shop and the Pike Place Fish Company), this upper-end French bistro boasts high-quality seafood like mussels, crab and halibut and regionally caught sturgeon – not to mention scrumptious desserts. Patio open in warm weather. Mon–Thurs 11.30am–3pm &

6–10pm, Fri 11.30am–3pm & 6–11pm, Sat 11.30am–3.30pm & 6–10pm.

Sabra 1916 Pike Place ☎206/441-4544. Budget Middle Eastern joint that augments the usual falafel-oriented fare with more unusual dishes, like veggie burgers made from squash. Entrees available for takeout or dining in a small, pleasant outdoor courtyard. Mon–Sat 10am–5.30pm.

Saigon Restaurant 1916 Pike Place, on ground floor of Soames-Dunn Building ☎206/448-1089. One of the best inexpensive places to eat in Pike Place, with a menu of Vietnamese seafood and vegetarian dishes that features some sweat-inducing curries and the always popular *pho* soups; also try the curry tofu soup or the lemon-grass squid. Mon–Sat 11am–6pm.

Sound View Café 1501 Pike Place, Flower Row of Main Arcade ☎206/623-5700. Nothing earth-shattering about the food at this inexpensive cafeteria-style café – just filling portions of healthy soups, salads and sandwiches – but the views of Puget Sound come at a price considerably lower than elsewhere in the market. Mon–Thurs 8am–5pm, Fri & Sat 8am–5.30pm, Sun 8am–3pm.

Downtown: waterfront

Anthony's Pier 66 2201 Alaskan Way ☎206/448-6688, ⓦwww.anthonys.com. Good, expensive seafood – such as shellfish, mahi mahi, and oysters – served in a waterfront restaurant (part of a local chain) with one of the best views of Puget Sound in town. Open Mon–Thurs 5–9.30pm, Fri & Sat 5–10pm, Sun 5–9pm. The restaurant also runs the cheaper *Bell Street Diner* and the takeout-oriented *Anthony's Fish Bar* in the same building. Daily 11.30am–3pm; also Mon–Sat 3–10pm & Sun 3–9pm.

Elliott's Oyster House 1201 Alaskan Way ☎206/623-4340. As the name says, succulent oysters (along with other items like crab and lobster) are the main attraction at this popular waterfront spot on Pier 56, with a dark, handsome interior and nice views of the bay. Be prepared to open your wallet: some of the entrees run up to $40. Sun–Thurs 11am–10pm, Fri & Sat 11am–11pm.

Ivar's Acres of Clams Pier 54 ☎206/624-6852, ⓦwww.ivars.net. A local institution with a chain of several fish bars around town; for sit-down dining, though, stick to either this branch or *Ivar's Salmon House* at Northlake (see p.170). Clams are the things to dig into here; there's also a much cheaper, takeout-oriented fish bar on the same premises. Sun–Thurs 11am–10pm, Fri & Sat 11am–11pm; outdoor fish bar open daily 11am–2am.

▽ Ivar's Acres of Clams

Okinawa Teriyaki 1022 Alaskan Way ☎206/447-2648. For a break from the waterfront seafood (and the high prices), try this small Japanese spot, where you can pick up a piping-hot bowl of ramen or teriyaki noodles for just a few bucks. A good place to fill up if you're on you're way to the ferry just down the road. Mon–Sat 10.30am–8pm.

Waterfront Seafood Grill 2801 Alaskan Way ☎206/956-9171. Ultra-chic hotspot with great bayside views and rich, tender seafood – crab cakes, ahi tuna, and sea bass are the highlights – prepared with meticulous craft and blended with more than a dash of Northwest ingredients. Sun–Thurs 5–10pm, Fri & Sat 5–11pm.

Downtown: Business District

Andaluca 407 Olive Way ☎206/382-6999, ⓦandaluca.com. An elegant slice of Art Nouveau design for a top-shelf Spanish restaurant, located in the *Mayflower Park* hotel. Affordable for its breakfasts of *citrus* pancakes and salmon scrambles, but better for its delicious dishes of paella, beef tenderloin, spicy lamb chops, and even a grilled halibut sandwich; expect to pay twice as much for supper as for lunch. Mon–Fri 6.30am–2.30pm & 5–10pm, Sat 7–11am & 5–11pm, Sun 7am–noon & 5–10pm.

Bambuza 820 Pike St ☎206/219-5555. Jaunty, colorful Vietnamese restaurant with a light and airy atmosphere and a good array of staples – satays, spicy soups, pho – mixed with Northwest seafood. A good culinary fix for an affordable price. Mon–Fri 11am–2.30pm & 4.30–9pm, Sat 4.30–10pm, Sun 4.30–9pm.

Cyber Dogs 909 Pike St ☎206/405-DOGS. Hot, spicy and scrumptious are not words that usually describe vegan cuisine, but this faux hot dog joint (which also offers coffee and Internet access) is an exception. Here you can enjoy meatless wieners that come topped with anything from spinach to sauerkraut to eggplant, and all for less than $5. Located inside the Convention Center. Mon–Fri 8am–midnight, Sat 11am–midnight, Sun 11am–7pm.

Dragonfish 722 Pine St ☎206/467-7777, ⓦwww.dragonfishcafe.com. Good mid-priced, pan-Asian restaurant on the ground floor of the *Paramount* hotel (see review p.147), with dishes such as grilled chicken yakisoba noodles, coconut shrimp rolls, and sugar-snap peas stir-fried with shiitake mushrooms in black beans, garlic, and ginger. Daily 7am–2am.

Earth & Ocean 1112 Fourth Ave ☎206/264-6060. Located off the lobby of the upscale *W Hotel* (see review p.147), this is a marvelous spot for Northwest Cuisine, highlighted by the likes of ahi tuna, crab, octopus and salmon fillets – the "Ocean" part of the equation – but also good for its pasta and steaks. The "Quickie" menu is a three-course meal for $20 (cheap compared to everything else). Mon–Fri 6.30am–10.30am, 11.30am–2.30pm & 5pm–10pm; Sat & Sun 7.30am–1.30pm & 5–10pm (dinner Sun in Mar & Nov).

Hunt Club 900 Madison St, inside the Sorrento Hotel ☎206/343-6156. A swank hotel's even swankier restaurant, where you can delight in venison, braised duck and filet mignon before sampling a complement of profiteroles or cherry bread pudding. You'll get off (relatively) cheap by showing up before 6pm and ordering a six-course meal for a mere $30 a person, Daily 7–10am & 5–9pm; also Mon–Fri 11am–2.30pm

Library Bistro 92 Madison St ☎206/624-3646. A delicious but affordable spot where you can get a helping of French toast or frittatas for breakfast or wait for lunchtime for the pulled pork sandwich with Dr Pepper-infused barbeque sauce. Located in the *Alexis Hotel* (see review p.146). Mon–Fri 7–10am & 11.30am–2pm, Sat & Sun 7.30am–2pm.

Metropolitan Grill 820 Second Ave ☎206/624-3287, ⓦwww.themetropolitangrill.com. A beef-lover's delight, "the Met" has a good choice of top cuts of steak, in a place that's heavy on power suits and has one of the longest bars in Seattle. The filet mignon is a particular standout. Mon–Fri 11am–3pm & 5–10.30pm, Sat 4–11pm, Sun 4–10pm.

Union Square Grill 621 Union St ☎206/224-4321, ⓦwww.unionsquaregrill.com. Another top-notch establishment, great for its barbecued wild-boar ribs, Mexican prawns, grilled King crab and other delights, served in sleekly elegant surroundings with the appropriate pomp and circumstance. Particularly good desserts, too. Daily 5–10pm, also Mon–Fri 11am–3pm.

Wild Ginger 1401 Third Ave ☎206/623-4450. Ever-popular pan-Asian restaurant with extensive daily specials to supplement their already lengthy, ambitious menu. Best to stick with dishes that don't try to do too much at once, like the tuna manada (yellow-fin tuna fried in spicy Indonesian sauce). Excellent food, if somewhat overpriced. Mon–Sat 11.30am–3pm & 5–11pm, Sun 4.30–11pm.

Pioneer Square

Ibiza 528 2nd Ave ☎206/381-9090. A self-proclaimed "dinner club" whose Spanish menu – with its artful selections of spicy squid and clams, croquetas, and rack of lamb – is on the pricey side. More useful to late-night munchers is its tapas lounge, where you can indulge in garlic prawns, empanadillas, and carpaccio for less than $7 a plate. Mon–Sat 4pm–2am.

Il Terrazzo Carmine 411 First Ave S ☎206/467-7797. The height of Italian chic in the area – perhaps the entire city – offering splendid risotto, rack of lamb, gnocchi, and a fine range of pastas, all for exquisitely steep

prices. Mon–Thurs 11.30am–2.30pm &
5.30–10pm, Fri 11.30am–2.30pm & 5.30–
11pm, Sat 5.30pm–11pm.

Jones Barbeque 2454 Occidental Ave S
T 206/625-1339. One of the region's top
barbeque joints, located just a few blocks
south of Safeco Field. If you venture
down here, you can dine on superior ribs,
sausages, and brisket – with the requisite
lip-smacking sauce – and polish it off with a
slice of sweet-potato pie. Adjust your belt a
notch when you finish. Mon–Fri 11am–7pm,
Sat 11am–5pm.

Merchants Café 109 Yesler Way T 206/624-
1515. Local landmark for being the oldest
restaurant on the West Coast, and still
enjoyable for its colorful clientele, warm,
dark ambiance, hearty dishes like beef
stews and chicken sandwiches, and cheap,
stomach-stuffing steak-and-egg breakfasts.
Mon 10am–4pm, Tues–Thurs 9am–9pm, Fri
& Sat 9am–2am, Sun 10am–5pm.

▽ Merchants Café

Trattoria Mitchelli 84 Yesler Way T 206/623-
3883. Another fine Italian eatery in Pioneer
Square, though much cheaper than *Il
Terrazzo Carmine*. Offers a succulent range
of thin-crust pizzas and filling portions of
traditional pastas. Open late to accommodate club-hopping night owls. Sun–Wed
11.30am–11pm, Thurs 11.30am–4am, Fri &
Sat 8am–4am.

Viet Chi 710 Third Ave T 206/622-4180. Good,
inexpensive Chinese and Vietnamese dishes
served mostly to office workers for lunch;
soups and noodles are especially tasty.
Daily 10.30am–5.30pm.

Zaina 108 Cherry St T 206/624-5687. Cheap,
straightforward, well-crafted Mediterranean
fare, including savory gyros, shawarma, and
couscous, along with other familiar staples.
Mon–Fri 8am–7pm.

International District

House of Hong 409 Eighth Ave S T 206/622-
7997. Large restaurant serving tasty, simple
Chinese food; it's open relatively late on
weekends, making it a good option for
dining after events in the Pioneer Square/
Safeco Field area. Also offers excellent dim
sum until 3pm daily. Mon–Sat 9.30am–
1.30am, Sun 9.30am–midnight.

Kolbeh 1956 First Ave S T 206/224-9999. Mid-
priced Persian spot a few blocks south of
Safeco Field, serving kebabs with basmati
rice, as well as tasty lamb, eggplant, and
veggie dishes. The joint really hops on
weekend nights, when there's live music
and belly dancing. Sun–Wed 11am–9pm,
Thurs 11am–midnight, Fri & Sat 11am–2am.

Maneki 304 6th Ave T 206/622-2631. One of
the last holdouts from the old days of the
ID, when Japanese restaurants were much
thicker on the ground. Today, this hundred-
year-old favorite more than suffices, with
its tasty sushi platters, soups, and handcrafted rolls, all for around $7–15. Tues–Sun
5.30–10.30pm.

Phnom Penh Noodle House 660 S King St
T 206/748-9825. Like the name says, an
honest-to-God Cambodian noodle joint that
doles out rich helpings of noodles in various sauces, as well as traditional favorites
like spicy soups and fishcakes. Best of all,
this authentic spot is easy on the wallet
and not overrun by tourists – yet. Daily
8.30am–8pm.

Saigon Bistro 1032 S Jackson St T 206/329-
4939. Old-fashioned Vietnamese favorites
– including hot seafood soups, spicy salads,
rice pancakes, and various noodle dishes
– made well for a mixed crowd of locals and
out-of-towners. Most entrees available for
budget prices. Sun–Thurs 9am–9pm, Fri &
Sat 9am–10pm.

🏃 **Seven Stars Pepper 1207 S Jackson St**
T 206/568-6446. A knockout choice for
hot and spicy Szechuan fixings in the traditional style, with great wontons, seafood hot
pots, and noodle dishes to make you want
to cheer. Don't let the uninspiring strip-mall
site deter you. Sun–Thurs 11am–9pm, Fri &
Sat 11am–10pm.

Tai Tung 659 S King St T 206/622-7372. One
of the district's oldest Cantonese restaurants, with an incredibly extensive menu of
traditional staples, some better than others;
to get a dose of a few things at once, opt

for one of the combo meals, which run around $10. Daily 10am–11.30pm.

Uwajimaya 600 5th Ave S ⊤206/624-6248, ⊚www.uwajimaya.com. Inside the Japanese supermarket-cum-superstore (see p.69), this cafeteria-style spot is a good place to get a cheap assortment of Asian dishes, to eat in or take out. Daily 9am–10pm, Sun closes 9pm.

Belltown

Assaggio 2010 Fourth Ave ⊤206/441-1399, ⊚www.assaggioseattle.com. Pleasant, mid-priced Italian restaurant with a friendly ambiance and a menu featuring such items as pan-seared scallops and potato dump-lings with gorgonzola, among the expected pizzas, pastas, and veal. Mon–Fri 11am–2pm & 5–10pm, also Sat 5–10pm.

Bada Lounge 2230 First Ave ⊤206/374-8717, ⊚www.badalounge.com. The height of neo-yuppie trendiness in the new Belltown. At this retro-modern, self-consciously "futur-istic" joint, the excellent (and moderately priced) pan-Asian seafood – sushi, sashimi, pad thai, etc – is almost as important as wearing the right shade of black. Daily 5pm–2am.

Cascadia 2328 First Ave ⊤206/448-8884, ⊚www.cascadiarestaurant.com. Superb Northwest Cuisine at sky-high prices. Rotat-ing fixed-price menus offer specialties of the region, often including such items as green-curry lamb and whiskey-smoked salmon, matched with top-notch local wines. Mon–Thurs 5–10pm, Fri & Sat 5–10.30pm.

Crocodile Café 2200 Second Ave ⊤206/448-2114, ⊚www.thecrocodile.com. Best known as one of Belltown's prime haunts for alter-native music (see p.182), it's also an affable diner by day, serving the biggest breakfasts in the city. Feast on cheap but hearty diner fare like eggs, salads, sandwiches, and waffles under the gaze of stuffed animals, papier-mâché sculptures, and thrift-store album sleeves. Tues–Sat 11am–11pm, Sun 9am–3pm.

Cyclops 2421 First Ave ⊤206/441-1677, ⊚www.cyclopsseattle.com. Bohemian, but not too cheap, spot where jagged modern artwork overlooks the diner-style booths, and patrons munch on solid dishes like sautéed prawns, potato gnocchi and the chili-laden "Super Bueno Burger." Daily 5–10pm, also weekend brunch 9am–2pm.

Dahlia Lounge 1904 Fourth Ave ⊤206/682-4142, ⊚www.dahlialounge.com. One of Downtown's most established upscale restaurants, best known for its seafood, featuring delicious main courses like Peking duck and Dungeness crab cakes. If you can't afford to drop a wad on dinner, try the adjoining, excellent *Dahlia Bakery* (see p.158). Mon–Fri 11.30am–2.30pm & 5–10pm, Sat 5–11pm, Sun 5–9pm.

Etta's Seafood 2020 Western Ave ⊤206/443-6000. Fine regional fish dominates the menu here, tho most distinctive entree being the King salmon: pit-roasted, rubbed in spices, and served with cornbread pudding. It's among the most expensive items, but worth it. Mon–Fri 11.30am–9.30pm, Sat 9am–3pm & 4–10pm, Sun 9am–3pm & 4–9pm.

FareStart 1902 Second Ave ⊤206/443-1233, ⊚www.farestart.org. Roomy restaurant dedi-cated to providing job training to the home-less, and serving up decent $7 lunches of inventive items such as curry salad, catfish, and zucchini cake. On Thursday nights (by reservation at ⊤206/267-6210), guest chefs from upscale restaurants around town provide something more elaborate for $20. Mon–Fri 11am–2pm. Also an onsite café with similar treats in the new Downtown library (see p.59; Mon–Sat 10am–6pm, Sun 1–5pm).

Flying Fish 2234 First Ave ⊤206/728-8595. Though lacking the eponymous creature on the menu, this is a fine choice for all other kinds of fish, serving up anything from familiar fare like ahi tuna to more adven-turous entrees like monkfish and escolar. It's top-shelf cuisine, even if some of the dishes are saddled with cutesy names like "Wok Lobster." Mon–Fri 11.30am–2pm & 5pm–1am, weekends 5pm–1am.

Lampreia 2400 First Ave ⊤206/443-3301. One of the best and most notable of the high-end eateries along gentrified First Avenue, this Northwest Cuisine spot specializes in über-trendy ingredients like grilled organic polenta and white truffle mushrooms. Expect plenty of attitude if you're not wear-ing the right clothes. Tues–Sun 5–10.30pm.

Lola 2000 4th Ave ⊤206/441-1430. Housed in the fancy *Hotel Andra*, this is the latest gauntlet thrown down to Belltown's many gourmets (and gourmands): a chic, arty spot for Northwest cuisine, where the flavors have a Mediterranean tilt (ouzo kebabs, pork ribs with peaches and mint, spicy leg of lamb, etc). Mon–Fri 6am–midnight, Sat & Sun 4pm–midnight.

Marco's Supper Club 2510 First Ave ☏ 206/441-7801. A local hot spot, and for good reason, with a colorful, eclectic assortment of tasty, upmarket platters like glazed portobello mushrooms with butternut squash, seafood stew rich with mussels, or mojo mahi grilled with black-bean coconut rice, among other rotating temptations. Mon–Fri 11.30am–2pm & Sun–Thurs 5.30–10pm, Fri & Sat 5–11pm.

🏃 **Noodle Ranch 2228 Second Ave** ☏ 206/728-0463. Delicious, informal pan-Asian cuisine starting at $10 and featuring imaginative noodle-based dishes and other creations, served in a casual atmosphere. The green curry is the chef's specialty and packs quite a punch. Mon–Thurs 11am–10pm, Fri 11am–11pm, Sat noon–11pm.

🏃 **Queen City Grill 2201 First Ave** ☏ 206/443-0975. Longstanding favorite for its excellent steak and seafood platters – lobster, crab, tuna, salmon, and the like. Only slightly more affordable than other chic fish-houses in the vicinity, but you can grab a tasty burger for less than $12. Sun–Thurs 4.30–11pm, Fri & Sat 4.30pm–midnight.

Seattle Center and around

Bahn Thai 409 Roy St ☏ 206/283-0444. Relaxed Thai spot with a decorous atmosphere and a long menu of spicy soups, satays, and curry items; the seafood selection is especially varied and good, with imaginative salmon and squid options. Moderate prices are an added plus. Mon–Thurs 11.30am–9.30pm, Fri & Sat noon–10pm.

Bamboo Garden 364 Roy St ☏ 206/282-6616. Looking at the mid-priced menu here, you might not be surprised by the enticing lists of beef-fried rice, Szechuan chicken, and sweet-and-sour pork. However, all the "meat" dishes are made from vegetable-protein products and 100-percent vegetable oil. It's all quite good, and best finished off with a peanut pudding dessert. Daily 11am–10pm.

Chutneys 519 First Ave N ☏ 206/284-6799. The best place in town for a cheap, sit-down Indian meal, great for meat tandooris, kebabs, and vegetarian curries; there's also

a cheap, all-you-care-to-eat lunch buffet, plus locations in Capitol Hill, at 605 15th Ave E (☏ 206/726-1000), and in Wallingford Center, at 1815 N 45th St (☏ 206/634-1000). Sun–Thurs 11.30am–2.30pm & 5–10pm, Fri & Sat 11.30am–2.30pm & 5–10.30pm.

The Sitting Room 108 W Roy St ☏ 206/285-2830. Stylish mid-priced Continental eatery that offers a good selection of European wines and beers to go with the cheese plates, bruschetta, panini, and assorted tarts and cakes for dessert. The cocktails are also a draw, infused with the likes of pomegranate juice and Chartreuse. Tues–Thurs 5pm–midnight, Fri & Sat 5pm–2am, Sun 5–11pm.

Queen Anne

The 5 Spot 1502 Queen Anne Ave N ☏ 206/285-SPOT. The most colorful of Queen Anne's cheap eateries, this Southern-style diner offers "Melting Pot Meals" that include Pumpkin Show Pasta (ravioli in pumpkin-cream sauce), Honey Stung Fried Chicken (dipped in buttermilk and honey), and the Just So Brisket (with a Coca-Cola and onion marinade) – all good, old-fashioned gut-busters. Daily 8.30am–midnight, weekends closed 3–5pm.

Banjara 2 Boston St ☏ 206/282-7752. Terrific mid-priced Indian spot for choice tandoori, vindaloo, stews, and curry dishes, served in a friendly environment. Frequented mainly by locals. Daily 11am–2.30pm & 5–10pm.

Chinoise 12 Boston St ☏ 206/219-6911, ⊛ www.chinoisecafe.com. Popular pan-Asian eatery with an eclectic range of choices – from pad Thai to tempura platters to *udon* noodles – though best for its sushi and sashimi; adventurous diners might try a bite of *unaju* (broiled eel). One of three affordable branches citywide. Daily 11am–3pm & 5–9.30pm.

Ototo Sushi 7 Boston St ☏ 206/691-3838. Sockeye salmon, eel, and flying-fish roe are but a few of the sushi choices you can discover at this solid, mid-priced Japanese restaurant, which also offers good soft-shell crab and veggie rolls, plus a nice ginger-salmon entree. Sun–Thurs 5–10.30pm, Fri & Sat 5–11pm.

Sapphire 1625 Queen Anne Ave N ☏ 206/281-1931. A pan-Mediterranean-styled eatery, picking and choosing dishes around the region, but strong on familiar staples like North African stews, smoked fish, and shawarma, as well as inventive items like orange basil crème brûlée and cod with truffle oil. Something of a cocktail-oriented hipster scene as well, thus the high prices. Sun–Wed 5.30pm–midnight, Thurs–Sat 5.30pm–2am.

Capitol Hill

611 Supreme 611 E Pine St ☎ 206/328-0292. Affordable French crêperie with many savory crêpes, including the *saumon-chèvre*, with smoked salmon and goat cheese, and the *épinard*, with spinach, roasted peppers, cambozola cheese, and walnuts. Don't miss the sweet crêpes, either, rich with butter, fruit, and chocolate. Tues–Sun 5–11pm, also Sat & Sun 9am–3pm.

Bleu Bistro 202 Broadway E ☎ 206/329-3087. Known for its cocktails and nouveau Northwest pasta and sandwiches, served in a low-key, mildly avant-garde environment; there's also a small stage for music and spoken-poetry events. Mon–Thurs 7am–midnight, Fri 7am–2am, Sat & Sun 9am–midnight.

Byzantion 601 Broadway E ☎ 206/325-7580. Arguably the best Greek food in town, reasonably priced and served with enough pita bread to make the prospect of dessert unthinkable. Notably good spinach pie, gyros and souvlaki. Sun–Thurs 11.30am–10pm (Mon opens 4pm), Fri & Sat 11.30am–11pm.

Café Septième 214 Broadway E ☎ 206/860-8858. Large, inexpensive restaurant in the heart of the neighborhood, with booths and sidewalk seating. Serves tasty, somewhat unusual breakfasts and lunches like vegetable fritattas and eggplant steaks, and solid pasta and seafood dishes. Daily 9am–midnight.

Coastal Kitchen 429 15th Ave E ☎ 206/322-1145. One of the most popular mid-priced breakfast and brunch spots in Capitol Hill. The dinner menu somewhat approximates Gulf Coast-style cuisine, with grilled prawns, crab cakes, red-pepper ravioli, and cod-and-chips. Daily 8am–11pm, weekends closed 3–5pm.

Glo's 1621 E Olive Way ☎ 206/324-2577. If you really want to pose as a local, you could do worse than to wait in line outside this ever-packed neighborhood favorite. With its gut-stuffing waffles, hash browns, and omelettes, the place is mostly oriented toward staples – cheap and gratifying fuel for the day's activities. Daily 7am–4pm.

Kingfish Café 602 19th Ave E ☎ 206/320-8757. Southern-styled food, like griddle cakes and beans and rice, in a casual setting, with terrific vintage soul and R&B music playing as you eat beneath large sepia-toned photos. The grilled catfish and shrimp offer a nice change of pace from the usual Seattle fare. Mon & Wed–Sat 11.30am–2pm & 6–9pm, Sun 11am–2pm.

Machiavelli 1215 Pine St ☎ 206/621-7941. Despite the name, no scheming behind this place – just good mid-priced Italian food, served in small portions and featuring tangy and creative pasta sauces. Try the penne with roasted red-pepper pesto, sundried tomatoes, walnuts, and cream. Intimate, cozy ambiance at the foot of Capitol Hill. Daily 5–11pm.

Monsoon 615 19th Ave E ☎ 206/325-2111. Attention from the national food press has given this pan-Asian restaurant a boost in its confidence – and prices. Expect to wait in line on weekends for the scrumptious drunken crispy chicken, Alaskan scallops with black-rice risotto, caramelized Idaho catfish, and ginger pork ribs. The prices still aren't very expensive ($10–20 per entree) – at least not yet. Tues–Sun 5.30–10pm, weekend dim sum brunch 9am–2.30pm.

Noodle Studio 209 Broadway E ☎ 206/325-6277. Curry soups, spicy rice dishes, salad rolls, and, of course, noodles in many different flavors (the five-spice duck is exceptional) are the high points at this appealing Thai joint. Daily 11.30am–10pm.

Piecora's 1401 E Madison St ☎ 206/322-9411. The best pizza parlor in a city not known for its pizza, leaning toward the New York style with rich, flavorful, and gooey pies served in a friendly neighborhood environment. Also with satisfying pasta meals and sub sandwiches. Mon–Thurs 11.30am–11pm, Fri 11.30am–midnight, Sat noon–midnight, Sun noon–10pm.

Queen Sheba 916 E John St ☎ 206/322-0852. Capitol Hill is hardly anyone's first choice for Ethiopian cuisine, but this East African diner almost challenges that claim: with the requisite beef stews, savory *injera* bread, pepper soup, and chicken dishes, this is enjoyable, affordable eating for adventurous eaters. Mon–Fri 4–7pm, Sat & Sun 11am–11pm.

Siam on Broadway 616 Broadway E ☏ 206/324-0892. A crowded and affordable open-kitchen Thai restaurant, with both counter and table seating. Good for digging into familiar noodle and curry dishes that rank among the spiciest in the city. Mon–Thurs 11.30am–10pm, Fri 11.30am–11pm, Sat 5–11pm, Sun 5–10pm.

Teapot Vegetarian House 125 15th Ave E ☏ 206/324-2262. A favorite spot for local vegetarians to dig into Asian-inspired, pseudo-meat meals crafted from vegetable protein, among them such would-be carnivore treats as smoked salmon, crispy duck, and grilled pork. Daily 11.30am–10pm.

Than Brothers 516 Broadway E ☏ 206/568-7218. Specializing in *pho*, a spicy Vietnamese rice noodle soup served in a huge bowl, for less than $6. Other selections are heavy on beef, and the complementary *banh choux à la crème*, a sweet custard puff dessert, is a good treat. Check the website Ⓦ www.thanbrothers.com for all the local branches. Daily 11am–9pm.

Eastlake

14 Carrot Café 2305 Eastlake Ave E ☏ 206/324-1442. This inexpensive place, near the shore of Lake Union, is most popular for its large breakfasts, with weekend crowds often spilling out onto the sidewalk while waiting for the enticing pancakes and omelettes. For something off the wall, try the Tahitian French toast, prepared with tahini. Mon–Fri 7am–3pm, Sat & Sun 7am–4pm.

Chandler's Crabhouse 901 Fairview Ave N ☏ 206/223-2722. Crustacean fanatics will rejoice at this shrine to all things crabby, from crab cakes to cocktails, with especially rich and flavorful *cioppino* (fish stew), sturgeon with peppercorn sauce, and even sushi. A bit expensive, though. Mon–Fri 11am–3pm & 5–10pm, Sat & Sun 10am–3pm & 5–10pm.

I Love Sushi 1001 Fairview Ave N ☏ 206/625-9604. Despite the godawful, tourist-trap-sounding name, this Japanese spot serves up tasty and affordable sushi, sashimi, and rolls to a mainly local crowd. Highlights include the *mirugai* (geoduck clam) and *awabi* (abalone) sushi and the Caterpillar roll (with eel and avocado). The soups, noodle bowls, and sake are also worth a

spin. Mon–Fri 11.30am–2pm & 5–10pm, Sat & Sun 5–10pm.

University District

Agua Verde Paddle Club 1303 NE Boat St ☏ 206/545-8570, Ⓦ www.aguaverde.com. Excellent bayside spot with a convivial atmosphere and nice views of the water; good choice for inexpensive, solid Mexican fare, such as fish and pork tacos, peppery salads, and Mexican barbecued pork ribs. Mon–Sat 11am–9pm.

Araya's 4732 University Way NE ☏ 206/524-4332. Quality Thai restaurant presenting the usual staples – curries, spicy soups, noodle dishes, and the like – made without meat. The real reason to come here, though, is the cheap, all-you-can-eat vegetarian buffet lunch. Mon–Thurs 11.30am–9pm, Fri & Sat 11.30am–10pm, Sun 5.30–9pm.

Bombay Grill 4237 Roosevelt Way NE ☏ 206/548-9999. Simply put, damn good tandoori kebabs and vindaloos, along with more unexpected seafood items like Burmese trout, lobster-tail curry and mussels masala. Don't be alarmed if you hear patrons yelling when you come in: the spicy Chicken Bazari, according to the restaurant, "is known to make patrons stand up and shout." Daily 11.30am–2.30pm & 5–10pm.

Flowers 4247 University Way NE ☏ 206/633-1903. A bar and affordable restaurant that attracts students and would-be bohemians for its quirky decor and rep as a desirable hangout. For food, it leans toward a mish-mash of international fare (samosas to pasta to curry noodles, etc), and also offers a solid lunchtime vegan buffet. Daily 11am–2am.

Saigon Deli 4142 Brooklyn Ave NE, #103 ☏ 206/634-2866. Hole-in-the-wall diner whipping out fine Vietnamese soups and vermicelli noodle dishes; with most dishes under or around $5, you won't go away hungry or broke. Mon–Fri 11am–9.30pm, Sat & Sun 11.30am–9pm.

Tandoor 5024 University Way NE ☏ 206/523-7477. Amid numerous Indian joints offering all-you-care-to-eat buffet lunches, this eatery stands out for having the lowest prices, plus solid standards like curry, tandoori, and vindaloo dishes. Daily 11am–10pm.

Union Bay Cafe 3515 NE 45th St ☏ 206/527-8364. A local hotspot for its refreshing, if expensive, takes on regional

Northwest fare, including good traditional pasta with seafood, lip-smacking items like roasted duck and ostrich, and a truly mean eggplant with polenta. Tues–Sat 5–10pm, Sun 4.30–9pm.

Magnolia

Chinook's 1900 W Nickerson St ☎206/283-HOOK. Popular for both its fresh seafood and its view of the boats in Fishermen's Terminal. The vast menu encompasses many dishes beyond fish, but it's still worth checking out items like the *cioppino* and blackened hallbut tacos. Open Mon–Thurs 11am–10pm, Fri 11am–11pm, Sat 7.30am–11pm, Sun 7.30am–10pm. *Little Chinook's*, next door, is a much less expensive fish bar. Daily 11am–8pm.

Kinnaree 3311 W McGraw St ☎206/285-4460. Fine, inexpensive Thai joint whose menu allows you to order any item in vegetarian, meat, or seafood versions. The green coconut-milk curry and basil rice are both particularly tasty. Mon–Thurs 11.30am–9pm, Fri & Sat 11.30am–10pm, Sun 5–9pm.

Palisade 2601 W Marina Place, in the Elliott Bay Marina ☎206/285-1000. The sea views and quaint atmosphere of this pricey eatery are a big draw, but the core menu items – from Northwest and Italian cuisines – aren't too shabby, either. Indulge in a great prawn platter or Australian rock lobster, sink your maw into the hearty prime rib, or just stick with the fixed-price menu ($26–32 for three courses, before 6pm only). Mon–Thurs 5–9pm, Fri 4.30–10pm, Sat 4–10pm, Sun 4–9pm.

Szmania's 3321 W McGraw St ☎206/284-7305, ⓦwww.szmanias .com. One of the few reasons to journey into Magnolia Village, this is one of the finest restaurants in the city, mixing German, Continental, and Northwest Cuisine on an expensive menu that changes according to the season. The many inventive and tasty entrees range from *prosciutto di parma* to *jagerschnitzel*. Tues–Sun 4.45–10pm, also Tues–Fri 11.30am–2pm.

Ballard

Carnegie's 2026 NW Market St ☎206/789-6643. With a foot in both Parisian and provincial camps, evident in items from rack of lamb to Roquefort tenderloin to good old Coq au Vin, this is one of the area's better

choices for chic French dining. Occupies the converted space of a classic Carnegie Library. Daily 5–9.30pm, weekends until 10pm.

Hattie's Hat 5231 Ballard Ave NW ☎206/784-0175. Legendary favorite for its hefty slabs of meatloaf and hamburgers, 2am nightly bar closing time, and colorful mix of hard-bitten old-timers and grungy hipsters. Better for its local color than its diner-oriented food, though. Mon–Fri 3–10.30pm, Sat 9am–11pm, Sun 9am–10.30pm.

The Hi-Life 5425 Russell Ave NW ☎206/784-7272. Housed in one of Seattle's most historic structures, the Ballard Firehouse, this Northwest cuisine eatery doles out serviceable wood-fired pizzas, French onion soup, steaks, pasta, and the like in a stylish atmosphere in the center of the district. Daily 8.30am–3pm & 5–10pm, weekends until 11pm.

Madame K's 5327 Ballard Ave NW ☎206/783-9710. This one-time bordello now serves up cheap deep-dish pizzas and pastas in hefty portions and rich flavors thick with cheese and sauce. Not subtle in the slightest, but worth it after a day prowling the antique stores. Mon–Thurs 5–10pm, Fri 5–11pm, Sat 4–11pm, Sun 4–9pm.

Ray's Café 6049 Seaview Ave ☎206/789-4130, ⓦwww.rays.com. Always-popular seafood haunt offering high-priced cuisine, such as sablefish and King salmon in its *Boathouse* restaurant on the first floor, and more affordable items like salmon burgers and coconut prawns in the café above. Great waterside views add to the appeal. Daily 11.30am–9pm.

Vera's 5417 22nd Ave ☎206/782-9966. The best place to get the color and flavor of old-time Ballard: the cheap breakfasts and lunches are solid and rib-filling (if nothing too inventive), but the scene inside – stuffed with old junk and a set from the movie *The Sting*, plus grizzled old-timers and newbies – gives the place a strange, almost eerie, appeal. Cash only. Mon–Sat 7.30am–2.30pm, Sun 8am–2pm.

Fremont

Blue C Sushi 3411 Fremont Ave N ☎206/633-3411. The sake and cocktails (with names like "Godzilla") give this place its hip cachet, but the raw fish is the real reason to come. Sushi is prepared in the usual manner and taken from color- and price-coded plates on a belt – fun if you've never tried it before. Mon–Thurs 11.30am–10pm, Fri 11.30am–11pm, Sat noon–11pm, Sun noon–10pm.

El Camino 607 N 35th St ⊤ **206/632-7303.** Mid-to high-priced Mexican fare with a nouvelle twist, featuring elaborately prepared dishes and homemade sodas. The rock shrimp quesadilla, with a margarita, is a nice start; the tamarind-glazed salmon and coconut flan are also worth a go. Sun–Thurs 5–10pm, Fri & Sat 5pm–midnight, Sun also 10am–2pm.

Ivar's Salmon House 401 NE Northlake Way ⊤ **206/632-0767,** ⊛ **www.ivars.net.** One of several restaurants in the *Ivar's* chain (the other notable one being *Acres of Clams*, see p.162), offering sit-down dining and a takeout-oriented fish bar. Smoked salmon is the thing to eat here, and the Sunday brunch (not limited to seafood) is good for indulging on the cheap. Mon–Thurs 11am–9pm, Fri & Sat 11am–10pm, Sun 10am–2pm & 3.30–9pm.

Mad Pizza 3601 Fremont Ave N ⊤ **206/632-5453.** A neighborhood staple serving great pizzas with traditional and exotic (jerk chicken, chorizo, or ricotta) ingredients, most for affordable prices. Something of a lifesaver if you want to duck in for a quick bite, and then head out for hunting art and antiques. Four other Seattle locations. Daily 11am–10pm.

Pontevecchio 710 N 34th St ⊤ **206/633-3989.** Dark, cozy eight-table Italian bistro near the Fremont Bridge, offering expensive but authentic meals of panini and pasta, served with exuberance, plus scrumptious desserts and gelato. Occasional guitar and flamenco dance performances. Mon–Sat 11am–3pm & 6–11pm.

Silence Heart Nest 3510 Fremont Place N ⊤ **206/633-5169.** Having relocated to Fremont from the U District, this Indian-leaning vegetarian spot still offers a bright and airy atmosphere and dishes like meat-loaf, scrambles, omelettes, and sausage – all made without the offending meat. Some of them are quite tasty, too, especially the *masala dosa* – crêpes stuffed with spicy potatoes. Wed–Mon 7.30am–3pm, weekends until 4pm.

Wallingford

Asteroid Café 1605 N 45th St ⊤ **206/547-2514,** ⊛ **www.asteroidcafe.com.** Humble coffee by

by day, groovy Italian spot by night, dishing out primo, upper-end panini and pasta, as well as more unexpected items like Japanese eggplant and grilled quail. Daily 5.30–10pm, weekends until 11pm.

Chile Pepper 1427 N 45th St ⊤ **206/545-1790.** The place to duck into for top-notch, authentic Mexican fare, where they serve piquant mole sauces, nice chicken and pork dishes laden with the epony-mous peppers, and the usual enchiladas and other staples. Not too expensive, either. Mon–Fri 11.30am–9.30pm, Sat noon–10pm.

Dick's Drive-In 111 NE 45th St ⊤ **206/632-5125.** Fifty-year-old fast-food institution serving up sloppy but lip-smacking burgers, rich shakes, and savory fries with just the right crunch – they're among Seattle's best. One of five citywide locations. Daily 10am–2am.

Istanbul Cafe 254 NE 45th St ⊤ **206/675-1998.** One of the many savory and serviceable ethnic eateries along Wallingford's main drag. The meze plates, skewers, salads, and baba ganoush here are all rich and authentic, and the low prices will do nothing to keep you from stuffing your gut until you can barely stand up. Mon–Fri 10am–10pm, Sat & Sun 8am–10pm.

Kabul 2301 N 45th St ⊤ **206/545-9000.** An inexpensive Afghan establishment with a menu of moderately priced kebabs, plus both veggie and meat entrees, Try the *qorma-i tarkari*, an Indian-like stew of cauli-flower, carrots, potatoes, and rice. Live sitar music on Tuesdays and Thursdays. Mon–Thurs 5–9.30pm, Fri & Sat 5–10pm.

Musashi's 1400 N 45th St ⊤ **206/633-0212.** A sushi joint where you can get full for $10 or less on tuna or salmon rolls, grilled vegetable skewers, and much more. As it seats only 25 customers, there's almost always a line out the door; be prepared to wait. Tues–Thurs 11.30am–2.30pm & 5–9pm, Fri 11.30am–2.30pm & 5–10pm, Sat 5–9.30pm.

Green Lake, Greenwood and further north

Carmelita 7314 Greenwood Ave N, Greenwood ⊤ **206/706-7703,** ⊛ **www.carmelita.net.** Mostly organic vegetarian fare including inventive, well-executed dishes like chanterelle risotto, sweet-potato agnolotti, and chickpea and pesto pizzas. Moderate prices, too. Tues–Sun 5–9pm, Fri & Sat until 10pm.

Doong Kong Lau Hakka 9710 Aurora Ave N, Greenwood ☎206/526-8828. Quite a hike out to this inexpensive neighborhood Chinese eatery on the north end of town, but worth it for its massive menu blending authentic entrees with an extra-spicy touch, doing eye-opening things to simple duck, chicken, and noodle dishes. Sun–Thurs 10am–10pm, Fri & Sat 10am–11pm.

Red Mill Burgers 312 N 67th St, Green Lake ☎206/783-6362. Local fast-food joint with a wide variety of classic and adventurous selections to choose from, highlighted by the blue-cheese-and-bacon and red-onion burgers; they make their own tangy mayonnaise, too. Tues–Sat 11am–9pm, Sun noon–8pm.

🏃 **Stumbling Goat Bistro 6722 Greenwood Ave N** ☎206/784-3535. One of those excellent local eateries often unknown to outsiders who, naturally, stumble upon it. The cuisine here is nouveau Northwest, on a rotating menu where you're apt to see anything from potato-leek cake to curry mussels to pork tenderloin. You'll pay top prices, but for a meal you're not likely to forget. Tues–Sun 5–10pm, weekends until midnight.

Superbowl Noodle House 814 NE 65th St, Green Lake ☎206/526-1570, ⊛www.superbowlnoodles.com. Tasty little eatery with authentic won tons, spicy soups and, of course, noodles prepared many different ways. One highlight is the "Heart & Soul Noodles," with green curry and Chinese eggplant. Daily 11.30am–10pm.

Lake Washington and the suburbs

🏃 **BisonMain 10213 Main St, Bellevue** ☎425/455-2033. If you find yourself in this anodyne suburb looking for decent eats, this is one of the best candidates: a local hotspot that serves up good and affordable ribs, pasta, and sandwiches for lunch, then turns around and feeds you succulent, upper-end items like duck breast and rabbit ragout for dinner. Mon–Fri 11.30am–2.30pm & 5.30–9.30pm, Sat 5.30–10pm, Sun 5–9pm.

Cafe Flora 2901 E Madison St, Madison Park ☎206/325-9100, ⊛www.cafeflora.com. One of the best vegetarian restaurants in town, attracting even devout carnivores for its

creative, if expensive, soups, salads, and entrees, like Oaxaca tacos or black-eyed pea fritters; the milk-chocolate cheesecake is equally tasty. A pleasant setting, too, especially the patio wing. Mon–Fri 11.30am–9pm, Sat 5–10pm, Sun 5–9pm.

🏃 **The Herbfarm 14590 NE 145th St, Woodinville** ☎206/784-2222, ⊛www.theherbfarm.com. Internationally famous restaurant specializing in elaborate dinners made with fresh ingredients of the Northwest. Each day's menu is finalized just hours before the meal, though seafood figures prominently in these nine-course, five-hour affairs; the fixed price menu ranges from $169 to $189 per person. Reservations are essential – make them well before your trip. Hours and days vary; often dinner Thurs–Sat at 7pm and Sun 4.30pm.

Hi-Spot Cafe 1410 34th Ave, Madrona ☎206/325-7905, ⊛www.hispotcafe.com. Lunch is served Mon–Fri, but this spot, in a converted house with wooden floors, remains best known for its sumptuous breakfasts (always available), especially fattening creations like the cheese-baked eggs and French brioche toast. An espresso café is downstairs. Daily 8am–2.30pm.

I Love Sushi 11818 NE Eighth St, Bellevue ☎425/454-5706, ⊛www.ilovesushi.com. As with the branch near Lake Union, this fine eatery offers a wide range of affordable Japanese delicacies from the sea, among them fresh salmon, eel, mussels, quail eggs, and geoduck clams. Mon–Sat 11.30am–2pm & 5–10pm, Sun only 5–10pm.

La Medusa 4857 Rainier Ave S, Columbia City ☎206/723-2192. One of the biggest (culinary) signposts of the gentrifying changes in recent years to this formerly sketchy district. This terrific little Northwest restaurant dabbles in Italian and Mediterranean fare, making for such interesting, upscale hybrids as pappardelle with fava-bean cream, pork ribs with tomato jam, and veal meatballs. Tues–Thurs 5–9pm, Fri & Sat 5–10pm.

Salty's on Alki Beach 1936 Harbor Ave SW, West Seattle ☎206/937-1600, ⊛www.saltys.com. A bayside seafood eatery offering a great view of Downtown Seattle and upscale Dungeness crab, lobster, and Alaskan salmon, with a good, if pricey, all-you-can-eat Sunday brunch ($29), plus live jazz on some weekday nights. Hours vary by season; often Mon–Fri 11am–3pm & 5–9pm, Sat 9am–1.30pm & 4–9pm, Sun 9am–2pm & 4–9pm.

Soleil Café 1400 34th Ave, Madrona ☎206/325-1126. Unassuming, inexpensive Mediterranean lunch spot, serving nicely spicy and traditional Ethiopian meals for dinner, such as lamb stews with *injera* bread and other well-prepared staples. Wed–Sun 5.30–9pm, also Sat & Sun 8.30am–2pm.

Waters Lakeside Bistro 1200 Carillon Point, Kirkland ☎425/803-5595, ⓦwww.watersbistro .com. Inside the luxury *Woodmark Hotel* (see p.149), this top-notch restaurant has a superb lakeside setting and patio seating, in addition to excellent Northwest Cuisine that's predominantly seafood-based. Main plates include Dungeness crab cakes, Alaskan prawns and seafood paella. Mon–Fri 6.30am–2pm, Sat & Sun 7am–2pm & 5–9.30pm.

Bars

A lthough Seattle's cafés have a bigger reputation than its **bars**, you won't need to look far to find a good watering hole in any neighborhood. While there are plenty of sedate local taverns, as well as raucous, hell-for-leather joints, the drinking scene in here is actually quite varied. The most interesting casts of characters are found in the more bohemian or culturally diverse zones, such as Belltown, Pioneer Square, Capitol Hill, and Fremont. Some Seattle bars bear a passing resemblance to British pubs, while some seem more like cafés, complete with singer–songwriters, art displays, and DJs; still others cater to discriminating palates by specializing in cigars, wine, or whiskey. Gay and lesbian bars in Seattle are listed on p.198.

Microbreweries are quite popular in the Northwest, and some of them run their own onsite bars (some of which are listed in this chapter). Popular local microbrews include such names as Pyramid, Red Hook, Elysian, and Hale's Ales. Many notable **vintners** are located in the otherwise anonymous Eastside suburb of Woodinville, among them the wineries Chateau Ste Michelle (supposedly the oldest Washington winery), Facelli, Columbia, and Silver Lake, though you needn't visit the 'burbs to have a taste: you can sample the local product at practically any decent restaurant in Seattle. For an onsite tour of any of the above wineries, or for additional information on area vintners, check out Ⓦvintners.net/wawine for a comprehensive listing.

In Washington State, you must be 21 or older to drink legally, so have your ID ready if you look younger than 35 – the state liquor commission can be quite aggressive in making bars enforce its stringent rules. Smokers may find it hard going in Seattle, with many spots having nonsmoking policies. Bars generally close around 2am, when they must by law stop serving alcohol. All establishments with liquor licenses are required to have a minimum of five entrees available for five hours a day, and must also have some type of food available, besides nuts and pretzels, during all the hours they serve alcohol. Depending on the venue, you're likely to come across anything from the familiar buffalo wings and ranch dip to more appealing seafood platters and Northwest cuisine samplers.

Downtown

Alibi Room 85 Pike St #410 ☏ 206/623-3180, Ⓦ www.alibiroom.com. On the lower part of the Pike Place Market, a tightly packed magnet for trendy poseurs and interloping tourists, with dance beats on the speakers (Wed–Sun nights), modish decor, and an onsite script library and independent-film showings. The hipster atmosphere is a bit more inspired than the cocktails, though there are plenty of good local wines and beers available. Daily 11.30am–2am.

Contour 807 1st Ave ☏ 206/447-7704. An arch-trendy spot where the bar food is worth a visit alone for the likes of provolone cheeseburgers and chicken skewers – each less than $2 with drink purchase. Open late, even after the booze stops flowing. Mon 3pm–2am, Tues–Wed 11.30am–2am, Thurs 11.30am–4.30am, Fri 11.30am–7am, Sat 2pm–7am, Sun 2pm–2am.

Green Room 1426 First Ave ⓣ 206/628-3151. Perhaps the greenest bar in the Emerald City, with modern, lime-colored furnishings and a thick crowd of music-lovers – the famed *Showbox* concert hall (see p.183) is directly connected to the bar. Happy hour Tues–Sat 5–8pm. Hours Tues–Sat 5pm–2am, also Sun or Mon if there's a concert at the Showbox.

The Hurricane Cafe 2330 7th Ave ⓣ 206/682-5858. The gut-busting omelettes, chili, pancakes, and burgers are a draw for many young and grungy types, but this 24-hour diner really shines for its bar and lounge, where a good set of scotch, whiskey and wine keeps the revelers busy, and the joint's own Hurricane Mary will make your head spin.

Kells Irish Pub 1916 Post Alley, Pike Place Market ⓣ 206/728-1916, ⓦ kellsirish.com/seattle. Free-spirited Irish bar and restaurant in a central location by the market, with patio seating and nightly performances by Irish-oriented folk and rock groups, though occasional big-names like Liam Gallagher drop by, too. Daily 11.30am–2am.

Pike Pub & Brewery 1415 First Ave ⓣ 206/622-6044, ⓦ www.pikebrewing.com. Small craft brewery serving its own beers, among them a mean stout and porter and the redoubtable Naughty Nellie's Ale, with a large wine list and an extensive fish- and pizza-heavy menu. The sprawling, multileveled premises are slick but unpretentious. Sun–Thurs 11am–midnight, Fri & Sat 11am–2am.

Virginia Inn 1937 First Ave ⓣ 206/728-1937. On the fringes of Pike Place Market, the gritty-looking, old-time *Virginia Inn* hosts a good blend of young professionals and bohemian types, drinking beer of all sorts – microbrew, bottled, and draft. The small outside patio is a great spot for Puget Sound views, although competition for these tables can be fierce. Sun–Thurs 11.30am–midnight, Fri & Sat 11.30am–2am.

Vito's Madison Grill 927 Ninth Ave ⓣ 206/682-2695. An old-style Italian place, with kitschy decor (think red vinyl and lush carpet), a gregarious crowd of graying regulars, and double-barreled drinks that may leave you gasping for air. Later on, a more youthful

contingent takes over, bringing with it kara-oke, techno, and retro-disco music. Mon–Sat 11am–2am.

Pioneer Square

🏃 **Central Saloon 207 First Ave S** ⓣ 206/622-0209, ⓦ www.centralsaloon .com. Bills itself as "Seattle's oldest saloon" (it was established in 1892), and consistently crowded, owing to its location at the epicenter of the tourist district. Every night, the live music ranges from alt-rock to punk to metal and eclectic/acoustic. Daily 11.30am–2am.

Collins Pub 526 2nd Ave ⓣ 206/623-1016. Despite the workaday name, this is Pioneer Square's latest attempt to ride the gentrifying wave. The microbrews, wine, and cocktails are nothing too surprising, but if you want a dash of the upscale (with good bar food) in a sometimes-gritty neighborhood, this fits the bill for discriminating boozers. Daily 11.30am–2am.

Doc Maynard's 610 First Ave ⓣ 206/682-3705, ⓦ www.docmaynards.com. This meeting point for Bill Spiedel's Underground Tours (see p.66) is a good early 1900s-style bar, and a rollicking spot to hear music on weekend nights; at other times, it just serves those waiting to take the tour. Not the place to go if you want to avoid hordes of tourists, but still worthwhile for its boozy, libertine atmosphere and pile-driving rock bands. Wed–Sun 3pm–2am.

J&M Cafe and Cardroom 201 First Ave S ⓣ 206/292-0663. One of the most longstanding watering holes in the district, filled with guzzling regulars during the week, while the weekend brings tear-assing rockers and blues jams. As good a look as you're likely to find of the serious boozing scene in Seattle. Daily 11am–2am.

Larry's Nightclub 209 First Ave S ⓣ 206/624-7665. Part of Pioneer Square's joint cover deal (see p.181), along with several other bars listed here, Larry's is the most blues-oriented spot involved, hosting regional blues performers as well as a little R&B and funk thrown in for good measure. Good drinks and straightforward American food, too. Daily 8am–2am.

🏃 **Owl 'n' Thistle 808 Post Ave** ⓣ 206/621-7777. Guinness is the drink of choice at this Irish pub, with solid bar fare and potent cocktails. Come on weekends for free live music from the Irish-folk house band while during the week a more eclectic selection of rockers, singer-songwriters, and folk artists hold sway. Daily 11.30am–2am.

Pioneer Square Saloon 73 Yesler Way ☎206/628-6444. Part of the restored 1914 brick *Pioneer Square Hotel* (see p.147), this classic watering hole features fifteen micro-brews, an amiable crowd of boozy regulars, and colorful junk behind the bar like an inflatable musician and stuffed chicken. Daily noon–2am.

▽ Bartender at Pioneer Square Saloon

Pyramid Alehouse 1201 First Ave S ☎206/682-3377, ⓦwww.pyramidbrew.com. Across from Safeco Field, an excellent regional brewery with a warehouse-like space that serves a dozen Pyramid brands, including some fruit-flavored varieties and an extra-special bitter (ESB). Mon–Thurs 11am–10pm, Fri & Sat 11am–11pm, Sun 11am–9pm. (See p.73 for brewery tour information.)

Belltown

Axis 2214 1st Ave ☎206/441-9600. This fairly good, if trendy, Northwest cuisine restaurant is capped by a popular bar where you can get $3 pizzas and half-priced appetizers (including honey-walnut shrimp, ahi and mussels) from 5–7pm on weekends or even later on weeknights. The cocktails

themselves are worth a glug, too. Daily 5pm–2am.

Belltown Billiards 90 Blanchard St ☎206/448-6779. The best hangout for those who like to play pool and drink beer – various Seattle Mariners have been spotted inside, along with other athletes. A dozen pool tables are available, going for half-price Mon–Fri 4–7pm. Nightly live music, DJs or special events. Daily 3.30pm–2am.

Lava Lounge 2226 Second Ave ☎206/441-5660, ⓦwww.mamas.com/lavalounge.htm. Belltown's concession to the revival of 1950s tiki-lounge kitsch, with a South Pacific–inspired decor of lava lamps and darkly tropical murals. There's eclectic live music and DJs at night, happy hour from 3–7pm, and a shuffleboard to pass the time. Daily 3pm–2am.

Nite Lite 1926 Second Ave, inside the Moore Theater building ☎206/443-0899. An essential nexus for young and old, where grizzled regulars rub shoulders with black-clad newbies, amid decor like vinyl walls and neon lights that look at least thirty years out of date. The main attraction, of course, is the liquor – strong, dark, and on the rocks. No grasshoppers or pink squirrels allowed. Daily 11am–2am.

Panther Room 2421 First Ave ☎206/441-1677, ⓦwww.cyclopsseattle.com. Attached to the *Cyclops* restaurant (see review p.165), this swinging lounge has excellent, quirky drinks like the appro-priately potent Latin Fireball and similarly fiery Dragon Mary, and even good happy-hour bar fare (most items $2–6; Mon–Fri 4–6pm) like drunken prawns and marsala mushrooms. Mon–Thurs 4–11pm, Fri & Sat 4pm–midnight, Sun 4–10pm.

The Rendezvous 2322 2nd Ave ☎206/441-5823. A converted speakeasy from the Prohibition era that now connects to a performing-arts space (for "improv ritual theater"), offers nightly eclectic music, serves primo bar fare – yam chips, chimichangas, and calamari – and whips up potent cocktails. Come and be wowed by the eye-opening decor and creative atmosphere. Daily 4pm–2am.

Shorty's Coney Island 2222 Second Ave ☎206/441-5449. Although it's on the hippest block of Belltown, *Shorty's* carves its own niche amidst trendy bars and ethnic restaurants with old-fashioned pinball machines, hefty pepper-and-cheese hot dogs and sausages, and gallons of cheap beer. Daily 11pm–2am.

Two Bells Tavern 2313 Fourth Ave ☎ 206/441-3050. A Belltown institution, still drawing arty types – though not as many as it once did – as well as overflow from the Downtown business crowd; microbrews are on tap and burgers are served on French rolls. Daily 11am–2am.

Queen Anne

Chopstix 11 Roy St ☎ 206/270-4444. More geared to out-of-towners than locals, but still occasionally amusing for its postmodern spin on the classic piano bar, where tinklers at the keys will pound out your favorite easy-listening (or even rock) tunes while you sit nursing a Manhattan, Martini, or other drink reminiscent of Dean Martin and his ilk. Tues–Sat 5–10pm; weekends $7 cover.

Hilltop Ale House 2129 Queen Ane Ave N ☎ 206/285-3877. Part of a small local chain of alehouses, where you can load up on tasty Northwest cuisine while enjoying microbrews and imported European beers, too. Sun–Thurs 11.30am–11.30pm, Fri & Sat 11.30am–midnight.

McMenamins Queen Anne Hill 200 Roy St ☎ 206/285-4722. Excellent branch of the regional chain of microbreweries, good for knocking back a Terminator Stout or taking it easy with a light Ruby. Solid all-American fare as well, and convenient Lower Queen Anne location near the Seattle Center. Mon 11am–midnight, Tues-Sat 11am–1am, Sun noon–midnight.

Capitol Hill

Bad Juju Lounge 1425 Tenth Ave ☎ 206/709-9951. Dark, swirling techno beats and eerie artworks are the main draws to this stylish, often-packed hangout, which attracts both slummers and scenesters for its hip ambiance, nightly rock and grunge shows, and bracing cocktails. Mon–Sat 3pm–2am.

Barça 1510 11th Ave ☎ 206/325-8263. Aimed at upscale poseurs and fashionistas, an ultra-chic spot where one can blow wads of cash on imported beers and top-shelf wines. Amid the bar's spotless wood-and-velvet architecture, make sure to wear your best (black) attire and avoid calling the place "Bar-ka" – a move guaranteed to draw sneers. Daily 5pm–2am.

The Bus Stop 508 E Pine St ☎ 206/322-9123. A recent arrival on the drinking scene, in an area for serious boozing, that boasts an eclectic crowd and music selection with solid DJs, and is perhaps best known for its karaoke. Also offers occasional arty performances and, strangest of all, a Tuesday-night knitting circle. Daily 4pm–2am.

Chapel Bar 1600 Melrose Ave, ☎ 206/447-4180, ⊛ www.thechapelbar.com. Few Seattle bars can match the lush, darkly gorgeous atmosphere of this former church mausoleum, which, with its mood lighting, wooden walls and high ceiling with chandeliers, and evocative atmosphere, is reason alone to visit. But the colorful cocktails, decent bar menu (heavy on seafood), and nightly techno DJs don't hurt, either. Sun–Thurs 5pm–1am, Fri & Sat 5pm–2am.

Comet Tavern 922 E Pike St ☎ 206/323-9853. A smoky, rocker's-dive hangout, this is the oldest bar in Capitol Hill – nearly sixty years old. The drinks are nothing surprising, though the grunge atmosphere is, with authentic axe-wielders and bleary-eyed burnouts mixing with youthful hangers-on. The band posters at the front entrance offer a glimpse of the more subterranean musical happenings around town. Daily noon–2am.

De Luxe Bar and Grill 625 Broadway E ☎ 206/324-9697. At the north end of Broadway, one of Capitol Hill's more sedate and engaging spots: it's relatively uncrowded, and offers outdoor seating for drinking and eating good burgers, salads and pasta. Daily 11am–2am.

Eastlake Zoo 2301 Eastlake Ave E ☎ 206/329-3277. A longtime favorite near Lake Union, which numbers grizzled old hippies among its drinkers; one of the better neighborhood bars, favored by those in search of cheap booze and pool – there are four regular tables, plus one for snooker – as well as darts and shuffleboard. Daily 2pm–2am.

Elysian Brewing Co 1221 E Pike St ☎ 206/860-1920, ⊛ www.elysianbrewing.com. Brewpub of one of the better local microbreweries, with a warehouse-type decor that fits in well with the Capitol Hill boho vibe, and flavorful oddities like Zephyrus Pilsner, Night Owl Pumpkin Ale, and Dragonstooth Stout. The menu is pretty good, too, offering sandwiches, curries, and savory tuna fritters. Mon-Fri 11.30am–2am, Sat-Sun noon–2am.

Hop Vine Pub 507 15th Ave E ☎ 206/328-3120. A nice range of quality local microbrews, along with a few wines, accompanied by entertainment from mostly local live acts, with the occasional open-mike event, for little or no cover. Daily 11.30am–2am.

Linda's Tavern 707 E Pine St ☏206/325-1220. One of Capitol Hill's most happening bars, attracting an underground rock crowd with its excellent jukebox, stocked with both rare classics and more current indies. DJs spin two or three nights a week, and the hefty platters of comfort food also have an appeal. Mon–Fri 4pm–2am, Sat 10am–2am.

Satellite Lounge 1118 E Pike St ☏206/324-4019. A relaxed and enjoyable neighborhood haunt that features cheap and tasty all-American bar food, bargain $1–2 beer and well drinks during happy hour (Sun–Thurs 4–7pm, Fri & Sat noon–4pm), and a fun, hip atmosphere in which to drink and be merry. Daily noon–2am.

University District

Big Time Brewery and Alehouse 4133 University Way NE ☏206/545-4509, ⓦwww.bigtimebrewery.com. Relatively long-established microbrewery (circa late-1980s) whose ales are the stock in trade – try the Bhagwan's Best IPA – but featuring other drinks as well, such as the potent Old Wooly Barleywine, all served in a large space with hardwood decor and a shuffleboard in the back room. Mon–Thurs 11.30am–12.30am, weekends until 1.30am.

College Inn Pub 4006 University Way NE ☏206/634-2307. The basement pub affiliate of an adjoining B&B (see review p.151), drawing a young university crowd that's a bit more clean-cut than the norm. A good place to play pool and darts, and knock back big-name or small-batch brews. Mon–Fri 11.30am–2am, Sat & Sun 2pm–2am.

Galway Arms 5257 University Way NE ☏206/527-0404. Straightforward Irish pub that offers hearty stout beers alongside rich stews and other traditional fare; there's also folk and contemporary Irish live music. Generally patronized by an expat crowd, though some students as well. Daily 4pm–2am.

Rainbow Bar & Grill 722 NE 45th St ☏206/634-1761. A few blocks from University Way, dispensing $3 microbrew pints; at 10pm there's often music from an eclectic array of bands, performing rock, jazz, and reggae, for free or a small cover. Daily 3pm–2am, Sun opens 4pm.

Ballard

Hale's Ales 4301 Leary Way NW ☏206/782-0737, ⓦwww.halesales.com. Handcrafted English-style ales from the third-oldest microbrewery in the region, highlighted by the Dublin Style Stout and brews themed after local artworks, such as the Troll Porter (*Fremont Troll*) and the Red Menace Big Amber (Lenin statue). The graceful interior boasts a bar with porcelain tap fixtures. Mon–Thurs 11am–10pm, Fri 11am–midnight, Sat 9am–midnight, Sun 9am–10pm.

Lock & Keel Tavern 5144 Ballard Ave NW ☏206/781-9092. Thankfully, not the kind of place where you'll need to wear the right outfit to order a cocktail, this neighborhood favorite has plenty of space for pool-playing, socializing, and quaffing mixers or microbrews from the long bar in a relaxed, friendly atmosphere. Daily 11am–2am.

People's Pub 5429 Ballard Ave NW ☏206/783-6521, ⓦwww.peoplespub.com. Gut-busting German cuisine and belly-filling drafts straight out of Deutschland, including the likes of Schlenkerla Rauchbier – a smoked beer with an overwhelming flavor – plus wine, scotch, and curious bar fare like deep-fried pickles. Mon & Tues 6pm–2am, Wed–Sun 3pm–2am.

Sunset Tavern 5433 Ballard Ave NW ☏206/784-4880, ⓦwww.sunsettavern.com. Somewhat grungy crowd and tacky furnishings left over from the 1950s, but worth it for the solid collection of beers and enjoyable regional and national bands on stage for nightly blowouts. Mon–Tues 6pm–2am, Wed–Sun 3pm–2am.

Fremont

The Ballroom 456 N 36th St ☏206/634-2575. Although the place has a dance floor and weekend DJ nights (house, techno, and disco), the real focus here is on chugging beer and playing pool. From 4–6pm (and all day Sunday), the nine pool tables are available for half-price, and the place fills up with students, locals, and a few out-of-towners. Daily 4pm–2am.

Dad Watson's 3601 Fremont Ave N ☏206/632-6505. Another outpost of the excellent regional microbrewery chain, featuring excellent craft beers like Hammerhead Ale and the potent Terminator Stout, as well as solid fare like sandwiches, pastas, and especially burgers (try the blue-cheese-dripping Captain Neon for starters). Mon–Fri 11.30am–1am, Sat 11.30am–2am, Sun 11.30am–midnight.

Dubliner 3515 Fremont Ave N ☎206/548-1508. A great place to sit back and drink your troubles away, nursing a Guinness while chowing down on a hearty sandwich, Irish stew, or fish-and-chips. A spirited neighborhood bar that has a lot more color than some of the trendier, newfangled bars nearby. Daily 11.30am–2am.

Red Door 3401 Evanston Ave N ☎206/547-7521. Tap beers from numerous breweries at this amiable local fixture, located right across from the Fremont bridge at the neighborhood's busiest corner, with outdoor seating, good fish-and-chips and sandwiches, and a friendly atmosphere. Daily 11am–2am.

Triangle Lounge 507 Fremont Place N ☎206/632-0880. So named because of the small, triangular outdoor seating area, this tavern is a relaxed affair that attracts a youthful, mildly artsy local clientele, serving grilled fish, potstickers, and black tiger prawns along with microbrews and cider. The outdoor tables are great for people watching on sunny days. Daily 11am–2am.

Wallingford

Al's Tavern 2303 N 45th St ☎206/545-9959. Dive bar and proud of it, *Al's* is a mainstay along Wallingford's main drag, and whether you come here to get sloshed or play pool (both for cheap), you can get a good sense of the boozy old spirit of this neighborhood before the yuppies started colonizing it. Mon–Fri 3pm–2am, Sat & Sun 1pm–2am.

Murphy's 1928 N 45th St ☎206/634-2110. A fine place to go if you're new to Seattle: *Murphy's* pours a nice Guinness, the Irish coffee is good, the atmosphere is convivial, and they have a wide selection of beers from the Northwest. There's often live Irish music on Friday and Saturday nights for a small cover. Daily noon–2am.

SeaMonster Lounge 2202 N 45th St ☎206/633-1824. At this recent arrival on the area's bar scene, the cocktails are inventive and curious (the Oatmeal Nipple for one), but the quirky decor and artworks really make this place stand out – not to mention the nightly selection of oddball music, where you're apt

to hear anything from organ jams to "boom-bap jazz at its best!" Daily 5pm–2am.

Tangletown 2106 N 55th St ☎206/547-5929. Along with terrific drafts from Elysian Brewing – among them a Loki Lager and Perseus Porter – this microbrewery also offers imported brews from Belgium and a nice selection of food – the "Pigs Under a Blanket" omelette and "Green Eggs and Ham" frittata alone merit a brunch-time stop. Mon–Fri 11.30am–2am, Sat & Sun 10am–2am.

Green Lake, Greenwood, and further north

74th Street Ale House 7401 Greenwood Ave N, Greenwood ☎206/784-2955. British-style pub decorated with photos of the UK taverns that inspired it, with a wide selection of draft beers served in "true English imperial 20-ounce pints." Several local microbrews to choose from, and a more extensive and higher-quality menu than most bars in the area. Also worth a stop is its sister bar, *Columbia City Ale House*, in that district at 4914 Rainier Ave S (☎206/723-5123). Both Sun–Thurs 11.30am–11pm, Fri & Sat 11.30am–midnight.

Fiddler's Inn 9219 35th Ave NE, North Seattle ☎206/525-0752. A bit of a jaunt to get to, but proves there's life to the drinking scene beyond the hip central hangouts: a convivial wood-paneled brewpub that's been around since the 1930s and features live music on Sat nights, as well as open mike on Mon nights. Mon–Fri 11.30am–midnight, Sat noon–1am, Sun noon–11pm.

Latona Pub 6423 Latona Ave NE, Green Lake ☎206/525-2238. A nonsmoking tavern often showcasing live jazz, folk, and blues for less than $5 cover, with a rotating selection of exclusively Northwest beers on tap. Cheap pints and appetizers during happy hour, Mon–Fri 5pm–2am, Sat & Sun noon–2am.

Little Red Hen 7115 Woodlawn Ave NE, Green Lake ☎206/522-1168, ⓦwww.littleredhen.com. Burgers and pork ribs, beer-bellied regulars with cowboy hats, and good old macrobrews are but a few of the features of this homespun watering hole – not to mention dance lessons (Sun–Tues 8pm) and karaoke (Wed 9pm), where everyone from old-time hayseeds to smirking hipsters comes to belt out the likes of George Jones and Garth Brooks. Live music shows Thurs–Sun ($3). Sun–Fri 9am–2am, Sat 8am–2am.

Pig 'n Whistle 8412 Greenwood Ave N, Green-wood ☎206/782-6044. If you find yourself this far out in Greenwood - antiquing or just plain lost – you could do a lot worse than to duck into this neighborhood favorite for some heavy, but delicious, chowlike burgers, prawns, and ribs, finished off with a slug of booze or pint of regional beer. Mon–Sat 11.30am–2am, Sun 4–11pm.

Clubs and live music

As you might expect for a city with such a rocking reputation, there are plenty of good nightlife venues in Seattle, and even though the town is hardly one of America's largest metropolises, the scene is not at all sleepy or provincial – and it certainly rewards a spin on the dance floor or a thrash in the mosh pit.

Seattle's **live music** scene got a lot of notice in the early 1990s, when the rock genre of "grunge" – something of a hybrid between classic punk, and experimental pop and noise music – became popular due to the rise of Nirvana and the influence of Sub Pop Records (see "Contexts" for more on the subject). Today, though you may occasionally find a local gig by the likes of grunge stalwarts Pearl Jam or erstwhile Nirvana drummer Dave Grohl's Foo Fighters, the city's many up-and-comers really provide the vitality of today's Marshall-stacked scene. Of course, if you'd rather keep the headbanging to a minimum, there's still a fair amount of good rock 'n' roll and pop music to check out, as well as decent options for blues, jazz, R&B, Cajun, reggae, and acoustic folk.

As for Seattle **clubs**, they're not the raging, all-night, ecstasy-fueled affairs found in, say, California. Rather, they offer a refreshing change for those who want to dance and drink in fairly laid-back surroundings, without the standard dress code and strict door policy standard at clubs in larger, "cooler" cities. With respect to the tunes being spun, the usual disco and funk still blare away at some places, though it's not hard to find more cutting-edge electronic fare – and enterprising DJs are almost as likely to be found in artsy cafés and bars as they are in cavernous danceclub noise cellars.

Live music

Seattle is still the proud home of **alternative rock**, though cynics have been mourning the supposed death of grunge for at least fifteen years – basically, when it left Seattle and achieved national renown. With literally hundreds of bands playing a large and diverse local circuit, the network of venues isn't as extensive as in the 1990s, but there are still plenty of appealing small and informal spots, with the best sites concentrated in and around Downtown, Pioneer Square, and Capitol Hill, with the occasional good show to be found in Belltown (despite the rampant gentrification), the U District, and Ballard.

Along with rock and punk, Pioneer Square is the place to get your fill of the **blues** and, to a lesser extent, **jazz**. Not surprisingly for such a java-fueled town, **folk** and **acoustic** singer-songwriters are easy to find throughout the city, while **reggae** and **world music** groups play with less frequency, but can be seen scattered around on occasion. Check *The Stranger* and *Seattle Weekly* for up-to-date listings; there's also a surprisingly good and updated listing of clubs and events at the Mayor's Office of Film & Music (Ⓦwww.cityofseattle .gov/music).

A good way to see a bunch of bands in one evening is through the Pioneer Square **joint cover night deal**, also called the **Club Stamp** (Ⓦwww.gotstamp .com), which allows you into eight bars and clubs – among them the *Central Saloon, Doc Maynard's, Fenix, New Orleans, J&M Café*, and *Last Supper Club* – for one cover charge of $5 on weeknights and $12 on weekends; pay the fee at the first venue you hit during the evening. Another great way to see a lot of live acts is during one of Seattle's lively **music festivals**. Bumbershoot, held over Labor Day weekend, and the Northwest Folklife Festival, around Memorial Day, are the biggest of these, while the Earshot Jazz Festival, spread out over a few weeks in the fall, also draws major players; see Chapter 17, "Festivals and events," for more info.

The live **venues** reviewed below are broken down by musical style. It's worth noting, though, that cultural barriers are more fluid in Seattle than in many cities, and, as a result, you might well find venues staging something totally off-the-wall or unrelated to their main specialties during your visit; some places are so eclectic that they don't specialize in any one or two genres, and may offer anything from country-punk hoedowns to Theremin concerts, depending on the night. Lastly, keep in mind that if you're **under 21**, you won't be able to enter a music show where liquor is served; there are a few places that put on "all-ages" gigs; check out the "All Ages Action" box in *The Stranger*'s weekly music listings to see what's doing.

Larger venues

Benaroya Hall 200 University St, Downtown ☎206/292-ARTS, Ⓦwww.seattlesymphony .org/benaroya. Downtown's performing-arts showpiece. Although it's best known for performances by the Seattle Symphony (see p.191), the world-renowned acoustics of Benaroya Hall are also put to good use by mainstream artists in folk, pop, and jazz. $15–75.

Key Arena 305 Harrison St ☎206/684-7200, Ⓦwww.seattlecenter.com. This is ground zero for seeing mainstream entertainment in the city, and you'll pay plenty for the privilege. The home of the Supersonics basketball squad (see p.207) also hosts concerts by the top names in rock and pop: tickets start at $25 for a lesser-known band, and can climb up to a stratospheric $300–1000 for the likes of the Rolling Stones or Paul McCartney.

Paramount Theatre 911 Pine St ☎206/682-1414, Ⓦwww.theparamount.com. On the eastern edge of Downtown, this large movie palace, built in 1928 for vaudeville shows and silent films, now seats around three thousand, often hosting well-known rock 'n' roll bands, as well as lectures, classic film

programs, comedians, assorted concerts, and more. It's much more atmospheric and intimate than a sports arena concert. $10–79.

Qwest Field 800 Occidental Ave S, SoDo ☎1-888/635-4295, Ⓦwww.qwestfield.com. Paul Allen's giant football stadium converts into an occasional concert venue, though you're more likely to find convention- and sports-related productions. Tickets usually run $12–80.

South Lake Union Park 860 Terry Ave N ☎206/628-0888, Ⓦwww.summernights.org. The temporary venue, at the south end of Lake Union, for Summer Nights – a series of twenty or so summer concerts by major figures in pop, country, and jazz. Once repair work is complete, the program will be switching back to its original home, Piers 62 and 63 along the waterfront. See the website for the latest news. Mid-June–Aug; $32–58.

Tacoma Dome 2727 East D St, Tacoma ☎253/272-3663, Ⓦwww.tacomadome.org. Easily visible from the I-5 freeway, with its hemispheric wooden roof, the Tacoma Dome seats 20,000, mixing pop, Latin and country concerts into its regular schedule of sports, conventions, and the like. Tickets for popular shows can go for up to $100 and beyond, though they usually fall into the $20–50 range.

White River Amphitheater 40601 Auburn Enum-claw Rd, Auburn ☏ 206/494-2134 or 360/825-6200, ⓦ www.whiteriverconcerts.com. It's quite a trek out to this distant suburb of Seattle and Tacoma, but if you come during spring and summer you can enjoy the big names in country, rock, pop and metal – all in an expansive, scenic setting near the Cascade Mountains, and often for less than the price of a show at Key Arena. April–Oct; $25–85.

Rock, pop, and eclectic

Catwalk 172 S Washington St, Pioneer Square ☏ 206/622-1863, ⓦ www.catwalkclub.net. Once known as a goth hangout and dance club, this energetic, stylish joint is now a rocking spot where you can hear anything from metal to punk and industrial – with an emphasis on alternative rock. $5–10.

Crocodile Café 2200 Second Ave, Belltown ☏ 206/441-5611, ⓦ www.thecrocodile.com. A diner by day (see review p.165) and a hip, intimate rock club by night, this relatively small space is one of the best Seattle spots to see most any kind of music. The action centers on the booth-filled backroom bar, which presents a wide range of acts, from well-known indie fixtures to unknown up-and-comers. Usually $6–12.

El Corazon 109 Eastlake Ave E, Eastlake near I-5 ☏ 206/381-3094, ⓦ www.elcorazonseattle.com. Housed in the old *Graceland* club, this is a spirited, fiery joint for rock, punk, hardcore, metal, and milder variations like emo and shoegazer pop. The emphasis is on the harder stuff, though, and with plenty of all-ages shows, you're bound to get caught up in the raucous, youthful energy. $5–20.

Fenix Underground 315 Second Ave S, Pioneer Square ☏ 206/467-1111, ⓦ www.fenixunderground.com. A popular venue where it's hard to predict what you'll see, from rockabilly and punk to burlesque and 1980s cover bands; the cover charge is usually $5–15. There's also a dance club on the same premises (see review p.185). Both clubs are part of the Pioneer Square Joint Cover program (see p.181).

The Funhouse 206 5th Ave N ☏ 206/374-8400, ⓦ www.thefunhouseseattle.com. Not far from the Seattle Center, this joint scares up punk and hardcore tunes to make the tourists run. If you're not so inclined, you can see some decent, dedicated shows by local thrashers, sometimes for free, rarely more than $8.

Gallery 1412 1412 18th Ave, Capitol Hill ☏ 206/322-1533, ⓦ www.gallery1412.org. There's no simple way to characterize the type of music put on at this performance space – eclectic to say the least. You'll find inventive alt-rock and jangly pop, to be sure, but you'll also come across artists playing free-form jazz, found objects and sound collages – and in February comes the "Seattle Improvised Music Fest." $5–15.

High Dive 513 N 36th, Fremont ☏ 206/632-0212, ⓦ www.highdiveseattle.com. Straight-up club where the acts are mainly regional and play rock in all its variations: thrash, pop punk, grunge, experimental, and anything else that might get the attention of jaded locals. $5–15.

Moore Theater 1932 Second Ave, Belltown ☏ 206/443-1744, ⓦ www.themoore.com. This 1907 former vaudeville auditorium seats nearly 1500, sometimes hosting exciting, up-and-coming bands, but more often estab-lished names in pop, rock and the occasional spoken-word show – anyone from Sheryl Crow to Henry Rollins – along with comedi-ans, dancers, kids' shows, and so on. (See p.188 for more information.) $20–45.

Nuemo's 925 E Pike St, Capitol Hill ☏ 206/709-9467, ⓦ www.nuemos.com. A hard-thrashing, kick-ass venue that has quickly clawed its way up (almost) to the top of the indie-rock heap. Here, the murals and wall art is splashy and irreverent (themed by a creepy clown), the bands are both regional and national – of the punk, goth, rock, and alt-anything variety – and the crowd is lively but not too out of control. $5–18.

The Paradox 1401 NW Leary Way, Ballard ☏ 206/706-6641. ⓦ www.theparadox.org. A longstanding favorite that was forced out of its old home years ago and rooted around until finding this new spot in the same build-ing as a church. Now, this all-ages venue is one of the city's best places to get the feel of the contemporary music scene in all its odd forms – including singer-screamers, math rock, prog-metal, and acoustic punk – for just $7 for most shows.

Premier 1700 1st Ave S ☏ 206/382-7870. ⓦ www.concerteventcenters.com. Somewhat hit-or-miss with its shows, this SoDo club is as committed to hosting football tailgaters as it is to showcasing bands. Concerts run Tues–Sat, and if you come on a good night, you might spot an excellent up-and-comer or decent mid-level rocker; if not, you'll be awash in a sea of obnoxious frat guys and beer-bellied drunks. Free–$20.

Rainbow Bar & Grill 722 NE 45th St, University District ☏ 206/634-1761, Ⓦ www.therainbowlive .com. Good mix of jazz, rock, blues, and hip-hop at this friendly bar (see review p.177) and student-oriented live-music venue. Most of the acts are of the unknown, underground variety, but still fun and compelling. Most shows $3–6.

Showbox 1426 First Ave, Downtown ☏ 206/628-3151, Ⓦ www.showboxonline .com. This 1000-person space across from Pike Place Market is the best place to catch touring acts that have yet to make the bigger arenas, along with well-regarded regional bands, usually with an indie slant. Grab a drink in the venue's adjacent *Green Room* bar (see review p.174) before the show. $10–30.

▽ The Showbox marquee

Sunset Tavern 5433 Ballard Ave NW, Ballard ☏ 206/784-4880, Ⓦ www.sunsettavern.com. Along with being a colorful bar (see review p.177) and karaoke spot, the *Sunset Tavern*'s also a good venue for catching aggressive young rockers and various eclectic acts in nightly performances. $5–10.

ToST N 36th St, Fremont ☏ 206/547-0240, Ⓦ www.tostlounge.com. There's no telling what you'll hear on any given night at this colorful Martini bar and club where the oddball performers mirror the vibrant Fremont scene outside. Avant-rock, spoken word, bhangra DJs, and throat-singing all

have made appearances here – and for a cheap cover ($5–10), you should too.

Jazz and soul

Dimitriou's Jazz Alley 2033 Sixth Ave, Downtown ☏ 206/441-9729, Ⓦ www.jazzalley.com. The best of the big-name jazz venues in Seattle, if a bit mainstream, presenting a steady march of notable out-of-towners; heavy on established veterans, who often headline for two days up to a week. There's also the occasional blues or R&B act. Most shows $20–30.

New Orleans 114 First Ave S, Pioneer Square ☏ 206/622-2563. A compelling spot to catch some solid jazz, Dixieland, and blues, with a little roots-rock and Cajun and zydeco thrown in on occasion. The house bands are free, but regional- or national-level performers cost anywhere from $5–20. The Cajun cuisine isn't bad, either.

Paragon 2125 Queen Anne Ave N, Queen Anne ☏ 206/283-4548, Ⓦ www.paragonseattle.com. Northwest Cuisine restaurant that features periodic performers from Tues–Sat in an intimate, upscale setting. Jazz, soul, and R&B hold sway most of the time, and on Friday nights, the resident DJs play a mix of funk and soul. No cover.

Tula's 2214 Second Ave, Belltown ☏ 206/443-4221, Ⓦ www.tulas.com. Jazz of all stripes every evening, mostly from regional acts, at this highly regarded club. Big-band sessions Sunday nights and live vocal jams some Monday evenings. Also open for food and drink starting at 3pm; after 10pm this all-ages venue becomes 21-and-over only. $5–15.

Blues, roots, and folk

Conor Byrne Pub 5140 Ballard Ave NW, Ballard ☏ 206/784-3640, Ⓦ www.conorbyrnepub.com. There's no question you can have a rollicking good time quaffing Guinness at this top-notch Irish pub, but you should really come for the tunes: blues and bluegrass jams, alt-country and Irish rock, and roots fiddlers and strummers make this spot an excellent choice during the week (when it's free), or on the weekend ($3-7 cover).

Highway 99 Blues Club 1414 Alaskan Way, Downtown ☏ 206/382-2171, Ⓦ www .highwayninetynine.com. Any nightspot that names itself after the grim overhead viaduct must be a place worth a visit, and this rootsy joint certainly is, showcasing regional and national performers in a bare-bones space that's all about the music. No shows Sun, but Wed offers roots, country and zydeco, and there's blues and R&B most other nights. Cover $5–10; $15–20 when a big name's in town.

Tractor Tavern 5213 Ballard Ave NW, Ballard T206/789-3599, W www .tractortavern.com. Roots music of all kinds – zydeco, Irish, blues, bluegrass – is the specialty at the *Tractor*, which also features the occasional high-profile act in rock, jazz and R&B. Often a better choice than similar spots in Pioneer Square. $7–18.

Triple Door 216 Union St, Downtown T 206/838-4333, W www.thetripledoor .net. An attractive modern complex that's the apogee of the folk, roots, alt-country, and blues scene in Seattle: a wonderfully restored former theater that now boasts two glowing venues. The Mainstage has major players and up-and-comers in a moody, dramatic site ($12–25), while the Music-quarium mixes things up with DJs and more experimental fare – it's also free.

World-beat and reggae

Century Ballroom 915 E Pine, second floor, Downtown T206/324-7263, W www.centuryballroom .com. World-music acts from all over the globe visit this spacious ballroom, which has a huge wooden dance floor; cover is usually $10–30. It also holds swing (Sun & Wed 9pm, $5), tango (Tues 9.30pm, $3; and Fri 9.15pm, $7) and salsa nights (Thurs 9pm, $5, and Sat 7.30pm, $7), where you can get a lesson included in the cover charge.

The Mirabeau Room 520 Queen Anne Ave N, Queen Anne T206/217-2800. W www.themirabeauroom.com. Although you can see poetry slams on Tues, comedy on Wed, and burlesque on Thurs, this eclectic spot is also one of the few places to have regular reggae nights (on Mon) and world-beat performers and DJs (on weekends), adding a bit of flash to the staid Queen Anne scene. Free–$15.

Nectar 412 N 36th St, Fremont T206/632-2020, W www.nectarlounge.com. A happening, two-story club that features a mix of DJs and live performers – both of the interna-tional variety. You might hear anything from Latin drumming to Indonesian gamelan (not to mention some funky beats on the turntables), and it's all pretty inexpensive, too. Free–$8.

Serafina 2043 Eastlake Ave E, Eastlake T206/323-0807, W www.serafinaseattle.com. Italian-oriented restaurant that has pleas-ant live Latin, bossa nova and jazz music on Friday through Sunday nights (9pm–midnight). No cover.

Clubs

Though a few of Seattle's **clubs** are the sort of cramped, pretentious spaces you find in most large cities, the majority are very relaxed, with nonexistent dress codes, and all musical tastes and sexual orientations welcomed. Many of the noteworthy clubs are situated in Pioneer Square or Capitol Hill, specializing in varied music and/or DJs on a nightly basis; it's not at all unusual for the same venue to feature goth-industrial, 1980s new wave, and electronica in the same week. With these varied lineups, consulting the entertainment listings in the *Seattle Weekly* or *The Stranger* is essential. Also bear in mind that some clubs that usually present live music, including some listed in the preceding venues section, also feature DJs, either on selected nights or before and/or after shows.

Cover charges are usually in the $5–15 range. Additionally, some clubs have regular free or ultra-cheap nights, and the cover can vary according to the time of the night; early in the evening it may be free, after 9pm $5, and ultimately $10 that same night for the peak crowd. Some prices are listed in the club listings in the alternative weeklies. Gay-oriented clubs are listed on p.198.

Alibi Room 85 Pike St #410, Downtown T206/623-3180, W www.alibiroom.com. Assorted dance beats that make for a refreshing change from the norm, in a space in the bowels of Pike Place Market, where you can either groove to the DJs or hang out in quieter, more intimate spaces and pose with the other hipsters. Rap on Wed; drum-and-bass, jungle and trance on weekends; and eclectic stylings on Sun. No cover, but drinks can be pricey.

Aristocrat's 220 4th Ave S, Pioneer Square ☎206/748-9779, ⓦ www.aristocratsclub.com. One of those clubs in the Square that always seems to be reinventing itself, the latest renovation upping the style quotient on the subterranean club level, where you can hear a solid mix of beats from drum-and-bass to trance to house and rap. $5–10.

Baltic Room 1207 Pine St, Capitol Hill ☎206/625-4444, ⓦ www.thebalticroom .com. Divided into bar, music, and balcony sections, with a view of the Space Needle from the front window. It hosts more music of an eclectic, alternative variety – everything from industrial and electronica DJs to rock and jazz bands – than most DJ-oriented clubs do. Free–$10.

Beso Del Sol 4468 Stone Way N, Wallingford ☎206/547-8087. Usually just a Mexican restaurant, though DJ Fernando spins salsa and other Latin tunes on weekend nights. $5.

Chop Suey 1325 E Madison St, Capitol Hill ☎206/324-8000, ⓦ www.chopsuey.com. An intentionally kitschy dance club and live-music venue decorated with leopard-print designs and Chinese lanterns, presenting an array of DJs on some nights (hip-hop, house, funk), dance bands on others, and a chaotic mix of instruments and turntables on occasion. $3–15.

Club Medusa 2218 Western Ave, Belltown ☎206/652-0981, ⓦ www.clubmedusa.us. Frenetic and occasionally mind-blowing, this spirited hip-hop-disco-funk club gets the patrons fired up with its four-to-the-floor beats and endless energy, closing at 4am on weekends. There's plenty of attitude, though, so if you don't look chic enough, you won't get in. $12–15.

Contour 807 First Ave, Pioneer Square ☎206/447-7704, ⓦ www.clubcontour.com. Fairly cramped space for grooving to house and techno, but fun if you don't mind bumping elbows with your neighbor on the small dance floor. Features a range of DJs Thurs–Sun, hip-hop on Mon, open mike on Wed, and "open decks" (for aspiring DJs) on Tues. Free–$10.

The Element 332 5th Ave N, near Seattle Center ☎206/441-7479, ⓦ www.elementseattle.com. The intent of this club is to provide a posh

setting for weekend DJ and hip-hop shows, as well as Tues Latin spectaculars, with salsa lessons and frenetic performances. Beat-happy tourists, however, will need to look the part of the committed club-hopper (the poorly dressed need not apply) and pony up the $10–15 cover.

Fenix Underground 315 Second Ave S, Pioneer Square ☎206/467-1111, ⓦ www .fenixunderground.com. Dark but engaging music cavern featuring reliable dance DJs devoted to music from the 1970s to today, with specific theme nights thrown in revolving around jungle, drum-and-bass, trance among others. See also its live-music counterpart on p.182. $5–15.

Larry's Nightclub 209 First Ave S, Pioneer Square ☎206/624-7665. Hip-hop and dance DJs, along with R&B and funk musicians and Monday-night reggae. Has courted controversy by offering cheap early-evening drinks ($2 before 11pm nightly) and being the site of a few public fistfights. Still, it's a fixture in the Square, and always a big draw. Free–$10.

🏃 **Last Supper Club 124 S Washington St, Pioneer Square** ☎206/748-9975, ⓦ www .lastsupperclub.com. Moody brick walls give way to three levels and two dance floors alive with computerized lighting effects. This chic spot varies the DJ attack from night to night – trance, acid house, Latin, salsa, and even erotic cabaret. Sometimes it's free, sometimes up to $12.

Lo-Fi Performance Gallery 429B Eastlake Ave E, Eastlake ☎206/254-2824, ⓦ www.lofiseattle .org. Despite their best efforts, Emerald City club-hoppers have let the secret out: this snug space is one of the city's best spots to see enterprising DJs (jungle, experimental, anything creative) in a friendly, mellow environment. There are also occasional retro-rock shows, karaoke and, as the club says, "multi-media installations, sculpture, dance, and avant-garde exploration." Be prepared. $3–15.

Noc Noc 1516 Second Ave, Downtown ☎206/622-4344, ⓦ www.clubnocnoc.com. A stalwart presence on the Downtown scene, which varies the tune from 80s revival on Tues, house and techno DJs Wed–Fri, to the forbidding goth and industrial nights – CrucifiXion and Resurrection – on weekends. Free–$10.

🏃 **Vogue 1516 11th Ave, Capitol Hill** ☎206/324-5778, ⓦ www.vogueseattle .com. One of the older Seattle club-scene institutions, and still packing in youthful, edgy crowds to sounds that vary from new wave and gothic to the more industrial-oriented, ever-popular Sunday Fetish Night; there's also kinkier fare like a vamp drag show and talent contest. $4–10.

The War Room 722 E Pike St, Capitol Hill ☏ 206/328-7666, ⒲ www.thewarroomseattle .com. If you have even a glimmer of interest in the latest hip-hop sounds or the nuances of DJ culture, this is the spot you must seek: a fine, multileveled venue for house

and techno that offers nightly music (and rap on Sat with Yo! Son) and shows with major-name performers, including a few rockers. $10.

Watertown 106 First Ave N, Pioneer Square ☏ 206/284-5003, ⒲ www.watertownbar.com. This neighborhood fixture is well known for hauling out the old favorites of dance music – disco, funk, house, and techno – plus regular hip-hop nights and Tues trance vibes. Free–$5.

Performing arts and film

Seattle's **performing arts** scene is strong and vibrant in many ways: the area has one of the most active **theater** communities of any similar-sized region in the US, both for big-budget and fringe productions, and offers a handful of major **opera**, **classical**, and **ballet** companies. Lesser-known **dance** and **chamber music** organizations stage noteworthy performances as well.

Although you can find the usual run-of-the-mill Hollywood product here as anywhere else, there are a number of venues showing avant-garde or offbeat **films** on a regular basis, mainly at old-time movie theaters and art-houses in historic buildings. The **Seattle International Film Festival** (Ⓦwww .seattlefilm.com) brings hundreds of foreign and independent movies to the area in the springtime. As for **comedy**, the scene in Seattle is quite small, though the city does support a lively **spoken-word** performance schedule, with readings, poetry slams, and other events taking place in bookstores, lecture halls, bars, and cafés.

For **tickets** to the shows and various goings-on listed in this chapter, Ticket Master (Ⓦwww.ticketmaster.com) is the main vendor for many; otherwise, check with the venue. Ticket Window (Ⓣ206/325-6500 or 206/324-2744, Ⓦwww.ticketwindowonline.com) runs the **Ticket/Ticket** service, which sells day-of-show theater and concert tickets at half price. Outlets are at the Pike Place Market information booth, First Avenue and Pike Street; Broadway Market, 401 Broadway E, second level, Capitol Hill; and the Meydenbauer Center in Bellevue, 11100 NE 6th St. They're all open Tues–Sun noon–6pm, with the Broadway location open until 7pm Tues-Sat. Tickets are walk-up and cash-only.

Theater

Seattle is home to a slew of **theaters** and a sizable contingent of actors, directors and other dramatic artists. As such, there's never a shortage of options, from sweeping reinterpretations of the classics and big-budget off-Broadway musicals to tiny experimental works. Prices for a show can vary widely: for prestigious performances at venues in the Seattle Center, tickets can cost more than $50, whereas many smaller shows around town often cost $10 or less. You might even take in a show at a coffeehouse, bar or club – Seattle is well-known for showcasing its cultural offerings in unusual places, and in any venue with artistic pretensions, you're bound to come across something unexpected, and occasionally even rewarding.

Major venues

A Contemporary Theatre (ACT) Kreielsheimer Place, 700 Union St, Downtown ☏206/292-7676, ⓦwww.acttheatre.org. A bit mainstream, though it's one of the heavyweights in town; the mayor has even proclaimed June 29 as "ACT Theatre Day." The fare ranges from warhorses by the likes of Tennessee Williams and Arthur Miller to more current productions with a mildly progressive bent. There are four theaters (the largest named after Paul Allen) with 99 to 387 seats; tickets are $40–60 for most shows, though you can get in for as little as $5 on "pay what you will" nights – usually two performances during a given show's run.

Fifth Avenue Theatre 1308 Fifth Ave, Downtown ☏206/625-1418, ⓦwww.5thavenuetheatre .org. Seattle theater at its glitziest, located in a gigantic 1926 vaudeville house that replicates the throne room of China's Forbidden City. As mainstream as you can get on the West Coast, presenting popular musicals ("Sweeney Todd," "Pippin," etc) with big-name stars and theatrical adaptations of Hollywood movies. $15–75.

Intiman Theatre 201 Mercer St, Seattle Center ☏206/269-1900, ⓦwww.intiman.org. Because it's a respectable institution housed in the Seattle Center, you're rarely going to see anything here beyond the tried-and-true classics and modern re-interpretations of classics. There's usually one (non-controversial) new or recent work per season ($15–49). Offers occasional "pay what you can" nights ($5), similar to those at ACT (see above).

Moore Theatre 1932 Second Ave, Belltown ☏206/443-1744, ⓦwww.themoore .com. Although its musical offerings are a bit more mainstream (see p.182), the Moore's theatrical program is often anything but. Shows range from experimental performance art to multimedia spectacles to impromptu theater and erotic cabaret. Because of the adventurous nature of these shows (along with a few more straightforward productions), they're often quite affordable. $15–40.

On the Boards 100 W Roy St, Queen Anne ☏206/217-9888, ⓦwww.ontheboards .org. Perhaps the best place in town to really get the feel of the creativity bubbling up in the Northwest. In addition to its contemporary dance program (see p.191), this groundbreaking company stages challenging contemporary productions, often mixing dance, multimedia, and theater in the same show. Well worth a look, and affordable too. $12–24.

Paramount Theatre 911 Pine St, Downtown ☏206/682-1414, ⓦwww.theparamount.com. Like the Fifth Avenue (see above), this former vaudeville house is a prime spot to see extravagant musicals as well as big-budget off-Broadway spectacles. Nothing too surprising (the likes of *Annie* and *Beatlemania!*), but highly entertaining on occasion. $50–70. Also has comedy and musical shows that are a bit more varied (see p.181), plus an excellent silent-film series.

▽ Paramount Theatre

Seattle Children's Theatre Seattle Center ☎206/441-3322, ⓦwww.sct.org. Presented in the sizable Martin and cozier Alvord theaters, performances are geared to all ages from toddlers to high-schoolers. The focus is on local works created specifically for youngsters, as well as dramatic adaptations of novels and short stories by the likes of S.E. Hinton and Roald Dahl. Shows run Fridays through Sundays, with matinees. $17–30.

Seattle Repertory Theatre 155 Mercer St, Seattle Center ☎206/443-2222, ⓦwww.seattlerep .org. Seattle's oldest and most established theater company – though hardly staid or dull – mixing revivals of classics with more daring newer works in the Bagley Wright Theatre ($15-46) in the Seattle Center. A second stage in the same facility, the Leo K Theatre ($22-36), puts on contemporary, cutting-edge and smaller-scaled works.

Smaller theaters

Annex Theatre rotating venues ☎206/728-0933, ⓦwww.annextheatre.org. One of Seattle's most established companies for alternative/fringe works. It's unpredictable what you'll see – anything from musical versions of Shakespeare to multimedia meditations on sex. Has outlandish cabaret shows once a month, too ($7). Most tickets $10–15, depending on the site.

ArtsWest 4711 California Ave SW, West Seattle ☎206/938-0339, ⓦwww.artswest.org. Multidisciplinary arts complex that hosts musical performances, art shows, and theatrical productions; the latter tend toward the contemporary, with an assortment of socially relevant and/or irreverent, tongue-in-cheek productions. $12–28.

Book-It Repertory Theatre 305 Harrison St, Seattle Center ☎206/216-0877, ⓦbook-it.org. Gripping theatrical adaptations of classic books and contemporary literature, with most shows taking place at the Seattle Center's own Center House Theatre. $25–40.

Capitol Hill Arts Center 1621 12th Ave ☎206/388-0500, ⓦwww.capitolhillarts.com. A fairly recent venue, housed in a venerable 1917 structure, which showcases inventive music and poetry, as well as eclectic theatre – classics, fringe, protest, experimental, you name it ($20–30). The Lower Level has even farther out material, on an irregular basis, usually for $10.

Consolidated Works 500 Boren Ave N, Eastlake ☎206/860-5245, ⓦwww. conworks.org. Hip arts center whose theatrical shows often involve multimedia – mainly film, music, and the visual arts – with the aesthetic emphasis strongly on the quirky, conceptual, and alternative. See "Capitol Hill" chapter (p.98) for a longer review. Prices vary.

Empty Space 3509 Fremont Ave N, Fremont ☎206/547-7500, ⓦwww.emptyspace.org. Compelling institution that's one of the city's bolder playhouses, featuring "uncommon theatre" and presenting both new material and new takes on classics ($25–30; $10 for students and under-25s); on "pay what you can" nights, you can weasel in for only a buck.

Jewel Box Theater 2322 2nd Ave, Belltown ☎206/441-5823, ⓦwww.jewelboxtheater .com. Part of the Rendezvous Café (see p.175), this theater is a multidisciplinary arts space that hosts a jaw-dropping array of performances – burlesque, experimental theater, noise art, and multimedia works – along with concerts and film screenings. $5–20.

Ned Skinner Theater 2015 Boren Ave, between Downtown and Capitol Hill ☎206/726-5011, ⓦwww.cornish.edu. Hosts quality and somewhat risk-taking modern fare presented by the Cornish College of the Arts. Productions (around twenty annually) range from farce comedy to re-stagings of Shakespearean drama, as well as the occasional musical. The Original Works Festival in February shows off the best of the college's student plays. $7–10.

Nippon Kan Theatre 628 S Washington, International District ☎206/224-0181. One of the most historic theaters in town, built in 1909 and closed and re-opened several times since then. Doesn't have a resident company, but stages works from different local modern and classic troupes. Has been in a state of flux lately, due to fundraising needs, and its schedule has been truncated; for the latest information see ⓦwww.nwaat.com.

Northwest Actors Studio 1100 E Pike St, Capitol Hill ☎206/324-6328, ⓦwww.nwactorsstudio .org. A theater center with two stages that, in addition to offering acting courses, puts on a wide range of performances: comedy, classics, and the avant-garde, plus one-actor shows and impromptu drama. $10–15.

Open Circle 429 Boren Ave N, Downtown
T 206/382-4250, W www.octheater.com. This
fifty-seat theater is one of the city's more
intimate playhouses; its house company
gives several shows and workshops each
year, with everything from Jean Genet revivals to rock musicals. $10–15.

Printer's Devil Theatre rotating venues
T 206/860-7163, W www.printersdevil.org.
Devoted to cutting-edge new work, often
putting on world or Seattle premieres, and
mounting shows at conventional theaters
as well as untraditional spaces like parking
garages, airplane hangars, and, in 2005,
an actual IKEA showroom in Renton. Their
annual "Bonanza" is a blitz of a dozen
productions in as many weeks.

Repertory Actors Theatre rotating venues
T 206/364-3283, W www.reacttheatre.org.
Fairly mainstream company devoted to
staging socially tuned-in, multicultural
performances of off-Broadway revivals,
literary adaptations, and original works;
performances are often held at the Lang-
ston Hughes Performing Arts Center, 104
17th Ave S, in the Central District, and
the Richard Hugo House, 1634 11th Ave,
Downtown (W www.hugohouse.org).

Seattle Shakespeare Company T 206/733-8222,
W www.seattleshakespeare.org. The Emerald
City's official take on the Bard, presenting
heavyweight Elizabethan drama at rotating
venues (often including the Center House in
Seattle Center), as well as other warhorses
from the same era. Veers between faithful
adaptation and modern slash-and-burn
versions. $15–30.

Stone Soup 4035 Stone Way N, Wallingford
T 206/633-1883, W www.stonesouptheatre.com.

Small company specializing in one-act plays,
with improvisational performances the last
weekend of the month; occasional children's
theater as well. $5-20.

Taproot Theatre 204 N 85th St, Green Lake
T 206/781-9707, W www.taproottheatre.org.
Located in a restored 1930s moviehouse
with 228 seats. Offers more family-oriented
fare than the usual Seattle theater, with
frequent revivals of the classics, and Friday-
night improv comedy ($5). Regular shows
$17–30.

**Theatre Off Jackson 409 7th Ave S, Interna-
tional District** T 206/340-1049, W www
.theatreoffjackson.org. The place to go for
irreverent, mainly leftist social satire, readings of classic plays and poetry, and quirky
modern works that are fun but not too out
of the mainstream. Many nights are "pay
what you will"; others are fairly cheap, at
$5–20.

**Theater Schmeater 1500 Summit Ave, First
Hill** T 206/324-5801, W www.schmeater.org.
Although its late-night dramatizations of
Twilight Zone episodes have received most
of the attention, the emphasis here is on
contemporary fringe theater – though classics are often added to the mix. $15–20,
kids free.

**University of Washington School of Drama
4001 University Way NE** T 206/543-4880,
W www.meany.org. A dozen shows from
late October to early June, mostly
presented at Meany Hall and Studio Theatre, Playhouse Theatre, and Penthouse
Theatre (all on the UW campus). Mixes
classics, contemporary works, and
premieres; a bargain at $6–15 a
performance.

Classical music, opera, and dance

Seattle's **classical music**, **opera**, and **dance** institutions often put on
compelling productions, mostly at venues located in the Seattle Center,
though a few alternative sites can also be found scattered throughout the city.
The stunning, high-tech Marion Oliver McCaw Hall is the biggest recent
news on the performing-arts scene (having opened in 2003), giving the
Seattle Opera a prime spot to put on performances, while the much-lauded
Benaroya Hall in Downtown is home to the Seattle Symphony.

Ticket prices are all over the place; as a rule, Benaroya Hall and Seattle
Center performances cost the most, running anywhere from $15–95, while
alternative performances anywhere else often cost a fraction of this – sometimes
below $10 at the smaller places.

Classical music

The Esoterics rotating venues, mainly churches ☎206/935-7779, ⓦ www.theesoterics.org. The most risk-taking and colorful of the city's classical groups doesn't even use instruments – it's a renowned *a cappella* society offering eerie settings of Biblical texts and Latin masses, as well as avant-garde contemporary pieces and international works drawing on cultures of the Middle East and South Asia, among others. $15–20.

Meany Hall 4001 University Way, University District ☎206/543-4880 or 1-800/859-5342, ⓦ www.meany.org. Most of the University of Washington's classical and world music events are staged here, often featuring performers of international renown. The 1200-seat hall is known for its wide proscenium stage; all seats cost the same per each performance, though the best ones are usually taken up by subscribers. Tickets vary widely, from $6–50.

Northwest Chamber Orchestra ☎206/343-0445, ⓦ www.nwco.org. This thirty-year-old company presents concerts at the Nordstrom Recital Hall in Benaroya Hall, as well as the Museum of History and Industry. Fairly affordable tickets ($25–37), with a repertoire ranging from Baroque, Mozart, and Shostakovich to brand-new pieces.

Northwest Sinfonietta ☎253/383-5344, ⓦ www.nwsinfonietta.org. Though based out of Tacoma, this troupe switches venues between Seattle's Town Hall and Tacoma's Rialto and Pantages theaters, offering a broad diet of the classics (2005–06 brought an all-Mozart series), from Baroque to modern – plus the occasional opera. Catch the Sinfonietta in Tacoma if you prefer assigned, rather than open, seating. Tacoma tickets $25–50; Seattle $38.

Orchestra Seattle ☎206/682-5208, ⓦ www.osscs.org. Enjoyable, if unsurprising, fare heavily focused on canonical German works (Bach, Beethoven, and so on), with a larger variety of choral pieces encompassing medieval to early twentieth-century works. Performs at rotating venues, including Meany Hall (see opposite); Town Hall, 1119 Eighth Ave, on First Hill; and Benaroya Hall. $20.

Seattle Symphony Benaroya Hall, 200 University St ☎206/215-4747, ⓦ www.seattlesymphony.org. Under the talented direction of conductor Gerard Schwarz, the symphony is the finest in the region. The Hall also hosts concerts by the likes of the Kronos Quartet, with the requisite light pops fare and odes to Hollywood film music sprinkled in to increase the subscriber base. Well worth a visit, as Benaroya's acoustics are heralded as being among the finest in the world for classical performances. Season Sept–June; $15–90.

Opera

Meany Studio Theater UW School of Music, 4001 University Way ☎206/543-4880, ⓦ www.meany.org. A surprisingly good alternate opera venue that presents classics as well as new works based on classical material (such as a recent setting of Molière's *Tartuffe*). Much cheaper than Seattle Opera, and quite enjoyable to see budding artists at work. $15–20.

Seattle Opera Marion Oliver McCaw Hall, Seattle Center ☎206/389-7676, ⓦ www.seattleopera.org. Previously confined to Mercer Arena, the opera has new digs at McCaw Hall, whose dramatic modernist design and enhanced acoustics promise quite the spectacle (see p.87 for more information). The operatic fare, however, is less surprising – mainly the usual Italian and German heavyweights, though there's a much-heralded production of Wagner's *Ring Cycle* every four years (the next in summer 2009). Season Aug–May; $50–120.

Dance

On the Boards Behnke Center, 100 W Roy St, Queen Anne ☎206/217-9888, ⓦ www.ontheboards.org. In addition to its fine theater program (see p.188), On the Boards also stages cutting-edge dance events, often of a multidisciplinary nature; these are usually held in its own space, though occasional performances are staged in bigger venues such as the Moore Theater (see p.188). Most shows $12–24.

Pacific Northwest Ballet Marion Oliver McCaw Hall, Seattle Center ☎206/441-2424, ⓦ www.pnb.org. When not touring internationally, the Pacific Northwest Ballet puts on around seven programs from September to June. Has an active repertoire of seventy works, the most popular being a December staging of Tchaikovsky's *Nutcracker*, with set and costume design by Maurice Sendak. $20–134.

Spectrum Dance Theater Madrona Dance Studio, 800 Lake Washington Blvd ☎206/325-4161, ⓦwww.spectrumdance.org. Based in Seattle, one of the more prominent jazz dance companies in the US. Gives performances in town – at spots like the Moore and Paramount theaters – when not touring internationally. Tickets vary by show.

Velocity Dance Center 915 E Pine St, Capitol Hill ☎206/325-8773, ⓦwww.velocitydancecenter.org. Hosts dance events in three theaters, but mainly known for its MainSpace Theater. Showcases a wide range of contemporary and international productions, including experimental and classical works, as well as pieces created by students at nearby Cornish College. $15–25.

Film

Although many of its fine old moviehouses have been torn down in the past few decades, Seattle still has enough quality **movie** venues for you to enjoy foreign art films, oddball independent cinema, or mainstream Hollywood flicks in a variety of different settings. The most interesting and atmospheric are the **repertory theaters** in Capitol Hill and the U District, many of which are housed in classic buildings that are either comfortably dilapidated or have been spruced up with renovations by the Landmark chain. Ticket prices are in line with those in most major US cities: around $8–10 for most first-run shows and a few dollars less for matinees. Festival or special-event screenings may cost more, up to $20. There are also several **film festivals** in Seattle, highlighted by the Seattle International Film Festival in the spring. See Chapter 17, "Festivals and events," for details.

911 Media Arts 409 9th Ave N, near Lake Union ☎206/682-6552, ⓦwww.911media.org. Nonprofit media center holding regular screenings of experimental films, videos and multimedia artworks in its visual gallery (Tues–Sat 3–7pm; free). With an erratic but challenging lineup, this is the first place to go for work that's too avant-garde for even the repertory houses.

Admiral Twin 2347 California Ave SW, West Seattle ☎206/938-3456. 1938 Streamline Moderne charmer with a nautical theme: boatlike motifs on the facade, interior designs of whales and etched-in-glass seahorses, and auditoriums called Port 1 and Port 2. Mix of mainstream and alternative films, with *Rocky Horror Picture Show* on the first Saturday of the month at 11.30pm.

Cinerama 2100 Fourth Ave, Belltown ☎206/441-3080, ⓦwww.seattlecinerama.com. Massive facility with state-of-the-art sound and picture quality, as well as a storied history that goes back to the massive, three-projector films of the early 1960s. Features a modern 70mm screen for showing the latest blockbusters and a 90-by-30-foot screen with two thousand vertical panels for experiencing epics old and new.

Consolidated Works 500 Boren Ave N, First Hill ☎206/860-5245, ⓦwww.conworks.org. Multimedia arts complex that shows some of the most avant-garde programs and videos in the Northwest, sometimes in conjunction with other visual art, music, and theater being displayed or performed in the space (see p.189 for full review).

Crest Cinema Center 16505 5th Ave NE ☎206/781-5755. Mainly merits a visit if you find yourself way out in North Seattle; good for catching second-run mainstream and indie fare for super-cheap prices ($3), before those flicks make their appearance on DVD.

Egyptian 801 E Pine St, Capitol Hill ☎206/323-4978, ⓦwww.landmarktheatres.com. Masonic temple built in 1915 that's now the most enchanting cinema in town. The program matches the high standards of the architecture, focusing on offbeat current releases and indie films; hosts much of the Seattle Film Festival, too.

Grand Illusion 1403 50th St at University Ave ☎206/523-3935, ⓦwww.grandillusioncinema.org. Fine old venue for foreign films, cult movies, protest films, and classic Hollywood – though the screening room is a bit on the small side, with just a few dozen seats. Next door is the *Star Life on the Oasis* café (see p.156).

Guild 45th 2115 N 45th St, Wallingford ⊤ 206/633-3353, Ⓦ www.landmarktheatres .com. Pair of quality theaters on the district's main drag: the older venue's a classic, though renovated, 1919 neighborhood moviehouse, and the newer one is a somewhat less distinguished spot built in 1983. Both show a mix of mainstream and independent fare.

Harvard Exit 807 E Roy St, Capitol Hill ⊤ 206/323-8986, Ⓦ www.landmarktheatres .com. Located at the northern edge of Broadway, this classic 1925 building – originally the Women's Century Club and featuring a fireplace and chandelier in the lobby – shows a consistent program of arty and independent current releases.

Neptune 1303 NE 45th St, University District ⊤ 206/633-5545, Ⓦ www.landmarktheatres .com. Lovely little curiosity with aquatic decor inspired by the eponymous Roman god, whose stern visage makes an appearance here and there on the walls. Mainly art and independent films.

Northwest Film Forum 1515 12th Ave, Capitol Hill ⊤ 206/267-5380, Ⓦ www.nwfilmforum .org. Perhaps the city's most prominent film organization, putting on nightly screenings and rotrospectives of international, classic, arthouse, and documentary films, and providing a springboard for up-and-coming visual artists in film and other media.

Seattle Art Museum 100 University St, Downtown ⊤ 206/654-3121, Ⓦ www .seattleartmuseum.org. Presents a good selection of films with an aesthetic bent in its Plestcheeff Auditorium. Program includes director retrospectives, advance screenings of local and indie works, and festivals that highlight a given country's cinema or film genre – the Film Noir Cycle is always a popular event, selling out well in advance.

Seven Gables 911 NE 50th St ⊤ 206/632-8820, Ⓦ www.landmarktheatres.com. Very cozy and attractive 1925 two-story home and former dance hall at the edge of the U District, easily missed if you're not looking for it. Shows mainly independent fare.

Varsity 4329 University Way NE, University District ⊤ 206/632-3131, Ⓦ www .landmarktheatres.com. A trio of theaters from 1940, stacked on top of each other in a vertically oriented complex. Runs one or two art-house movies every day, including old classics, documentaries, foreign films, and newly released independents.

Poetry and spoken word

The popularity of **poetry** and **spoken-word** performances has cooled off in Seattle, with the closures of such fixtures as Dutch Ned's Saloon, among others, in Pioneer Square. Still, several clubs and cafés offer sporadic "**poetry slams**" (see box, p.194) and open mike nights; the big-name published poets tend to do their readings at bookstores or lecture halls. Prices for such events range from nothing at alternative venues to more than $50 at major institutions. The **Seattle Poetry Festival** (⊤ 206/441-4502, Ⓦ www.poetryfestival.org), begun in 1998, is a classic event that's been defunct in recent years, but is due to be revived in 2007.

There are numerous author readings and appearances at local **bookshops**, such as Elliott Bay Book Company, Open Books, and University Book Store (see pp.219–220 and 000 for info). Alternatively, the **Seattle Arts & Lecture Series** (⊤ 206/621-2230, Ⓦ www.lectures.org) presents talks from noteworthy authors from around the globe at venues such as Benaroya Hall and Town Hall. The alternative weeklies – *The Stranger*, *Seattle Weekly* – list most poetry/spoken-word events and author readings; check for current listings.

Capitol Hill Arts Center 1621 12th Ave ⊤ 206/388-0500, Ⓦ www.capitolhillarts.com. A good place to catch what's on the mind of the more alternative- and fringe-minded poets and spoken-word artists on the Hill, typically on the Lower Level of this varied arts space that also hosts theater, music, and dance. $5–15.

The Mirabeau Room 520 Queen Anne Ave N, Queen Anne ⊤ 206/217-2800. Ⓦ www .themirabeauroom.com. Tuesday-night poetry slams (along with open mike sessions) in an eclectic venue that also hosts comedy, burlesque, and music. $4.

Red Sky Poetry Theater 1531 14th Ave, Capitol Hill ☏206/324-8815. Held at the stylish *Globe Café*, this free poetry event showcases the city's up-and-coming bards through slams and open mike events, usually on Sundays at 8pm.

Richard Hugo House 1634 11th Ave, Capitol Hill ☏206/322-7030, ⓦwww.hugohouse.org. A sizable complex with several performing spaces geared toward writers trying out their spoken material, playwrights developing new works, up-and-coming poets declaiming, and visiting authors dropping in to read from their latest works. Free–$5.

Town Hall 1119 8th Ave, First Hill ☏206/652-4255. ⓦwww.townhallseattle.org. At this esteemed venue, housed in a 1922 Romanesque Revival former church, you're likely to see anything – world-beat and chamber music concerts, lectures by science professors, angry manifestos by political activists, poetry readings by avant-garde writers, and more. Tickets vary widely ($5–25) depending on the program.

Comedy

Seattle has few dedicated **comedy** clubs, although regional troupes do occasionally put on shows and improvs at various venues like the Moore and Paramount theaters (check listings in the daily and weekly papers). In addition, performance-oriented taverns and cafés, such the Mirabeau Room (listed above), occasionally hold "comedy nights," involving actual and self-proclaimed comedians.

Comedy Underground 222 S Main St, Pioneer Square ☏206/628-0303, ⓦwww.comedyunderground.com. Features regular house performers, theme-comedy nights, and qualifying "heats" for regional competitions, whose winners sometimes make repeat appearances at the club years later. There's also a branch in Tacoma at 100 S Ninth St (☏253/272-2489). Sun & Tues–Thurs $6–8, Fri & Sat $12–15, Mon open mike $4.

Seattle poetry slams

In the mid-1980s, at the *Green Mill* club in Chicago, **slam poetry** first began when poet Marc Smith decided hecklers could be used to his advantage by asking them to rate his readings on a one-to-ten scale. The genre spread through cities across the US in the 1990s, with Seattle's own Pioneer Square as one of the strongest outposts, especially at the now-defunct Dutch Ned's Saloon. Unfortunately, since that district is now more given over to art of the visual kind (along with music), the public poetry spectacles have moved on to other digs (see p.193 for some good choices).

Today's slams are verbal poetry contests in which competitors read in bang-bang sequence, the winners determined by the audience. If you participate in a Slam, there are four **basic rules**: no props, do your own (original) poem, don't go over three minutes, and check your ego at the door. Judges are chosen from the audience, and could be anyone – from hipsters to Microsoft drones (an occupation bound to draw whoops of disapproval from the crowd). As the night advances, contestants with the higher scores advance to succeeding rounds until only one is left, usually winning a modest cash prize.

While purists may complain that the genre dumbs down poetry to the level of a sporting event, there's no doubt that slams have brought poetry to an audience that would otherwise be loath to seek it out. And the quality of the readings, or at least their amusement value, is fairly high; after all, if you're willing to be graded on your extemporaneous art, there's a fair chance you'll have at least a little talent – or at the very least, a whole lot of gall.

Giggles 5220 Roosevelt Way NE, University District ☏ 206/526-5653, ⓦ www.gigglescomedyclub.com. A mix of national performers you may or may not have heard of (mainly second-tier names) and more energetic local acts. Keep in mind that some shows may cost more than you'd expect, depending on the renown of the comedian. Fri & Sat 8pm & 10pm, starts at $10; open mike Thurs & Sun 9pm, free.

Wiseguys Comedy Cafe 818 112th Ave, Bellevue ⓦ www.wiseguyscomedy.com. While suburban Bellevue isn't exactly known as a hotbed of hilarity, this club does feature many of the regional headliners (if not the bigger names) that make appearances at the city's more central clubs. The shows are hit-or-miss, but might be worth a try if you find yourself across Lake Washington, eager for a chuckle. Fri & Sat 9pm; $10.

Gay Seattle

G ay and lesbian culture in Seattle centers on Capitol Hill, but it's hardly ghettoized anymore, as it tended to be in the 1960s and 70s. Today it's spread widely throughout the metropolis, from Fremont to Belltown to West Seattle – even suburbs like Bellevue. In fact, many gays have moved to Seattle from other parts of the Pacific Northwest (and indeed elsewhere in the US) because of the city's longstanding liberalism and increasingly cosmopolitan character. The gay and lesbian community here has long been among the most organized and politically innovative as well: The Seattle Counseling Services for Sexual Minorities was the first organization of its kind in America when it was founded here in 1969; the city's Lesbian Resource Center is the oldest such agency in the country; and in 1999, the first PTA chapter to represent gay and lesbian parents and teachers was formed here.

The main **publication** serving the community is the weekly *Seattle Gay News* (Ⓦ www.sgn.org), available at newsstands and larger bookshops throughout the city. It includes an events calendar and coverage of both political and arts activity. Although Beyond the Closet, the city's pioneering gay-and-lesbian **bookstore**, closed in 2005, most independent bookstores continue to stock material relevant to the community: Elliott Bay Book Company and University Bookstore (both p.219) are good places to start.

Columbia Funmaps (Ⓦ www.funmaps.com/seattle.htm) publishes a handy map of gay Seattle for visitors ($3), which you can download for free from their website, and the biannual *Pink Magazine* (free; Ⓦ www.pinkmag.com/seattle), available at various cafés and shops throughout town, lists companies that support the community and includes a comprehensive resource directory.

On the last Sunday in June, Seattle's gay and lesbian **Pride Parade and Festival** (Ⓦ www.seattlepride.org) takes over a dozen blocks on Broadway, Capitol Hill's main strip. It's one of the city's most exuberant events, drawing some 75,000 participants and spectators; see Chapter 17, "Festivals and events," for more information.

Finally, there are few explicitly gay hotels in Seattle, as most establishments offer gay-and-lesbian-friendly **accommodation** (see Chapter 10, "Accommodation"). It's only when you get away from the urban area that finding amenable lodging becomes more of a problem – for good choices throughout Washington, check the *Pink Magazine* pages listed above. In the same way, most Seattle **restaurants** cater to gay customers without issue and have a mixed clientele. However, the **bars** and **clubs** noted below (mostly centered on Pike Street in Capitol Hill) cater to gays and lesbians more specifically – which gives them a hip cachet that often attracts hetero crowds once the word gets out.

△ Pride Parade in Capitol Hill

Resources

Aradia Women's Health Center 1300 Spring St, Capitol Hill ☎ 206/323-9388, ⓦ www.aradia.org. Feminist clinic open to all women, though clients can request a lesbian health-care provider if they wish. Confidential HIV testing offered among many other services. **Different Spokes** ☎ 206/254-5529, ⓦ www .differentspokes.org. Seattle's gay-and-lesbian bicycling club, offering a variety of rides in the city and throughout the region (April–Sept Thurs night & Sat & Sun during the day), as well as movies and potluck dinners. Geared to both locals and visitors. **Gay City Health Project 1505 Broadway E, Capitol Hill** ☎ 206/860-6969, ⓦ www.gaycity.org. Organizes social events and services for the gay and lesbian community, ranging from support groups and educational outreach for people with HIV to sporting events, movie nights, cooking events, and yoga. **Ingersoll Gender Center 1812 E Madison St, Capitol Hill** ☎206/329-6651, ⓦ ingersollcenter .org. Support organization centered on transgendered and gender-identity issues, with associated contacts and resources. **Lesbian Resource Center 227 S Orcas St, South Seattle** ☎206/322-3953, ⓦ www.lrc .net. General information on the lesbian community and political groups and events, plus social, governmental, and business resources.

Seattle Commission for Sexual Minorities 700 Third Ave, room 250, Downtown ☎206/684-4500, ⓦ www.ci.seattle.wa.us/scsm. Government entity addressing the needs and concerns of regional gays and lesbians; puts on events, such as the Queer Youth Forum, and provides info on community centers, medical issues, discrimination, and counseling. **Team Seattle 1122 E Pike St, Capitol Hill** ☎206/322-7769, ⓦ www.teamseattle.org. Sports network promoting gay athletics. Hosts summer and winter sports festivals and organizes Seattle's team for the Gay Games.

Bars and clubs

Cadillac Grille/CC Attle's 1501 E Madison St, Capitol Hill ☎206/726-0565. A crowded restaurant and bar with potent drinks and a devoted bunch of regulars (mainly gay men), though not much in the way of atmosphere. Daily 9am–2am.
Changes 2103 N 45th St, Wallingford ☎206/545-8363, ⓦ www.changesinwallingford .com. Friendly, unassuming neighborhood bar with a predominantly gay male-oriented clientele, plus some straight interlopers; known for its colorful karaoke night (Wed & Sun 9pm–1am). Daily noon–2am.
The Cuff 1533 Thirteenth Ave, Capitol Hill ☎206/323-1525, ⓦ www.cuffcomplex.com. Oriented towards the leather-and-Levi's-crowd, this spot can get downright boister-ous at times. Includes a restaurant, a patio, and several bars, plus two DJs spin bass-heavy sounds in the club rooms. Bars daily 2pm–2am, dance club Fri & Sat 9pm–2am.
Elite Tavern 622 Broadway E, Capitol Hill ☎206/324-4470. Somewhat cramped bar with a dreary look, but host to a wide mix of young and older patrons. Come here to drink, not to dance. Daily noon–2am.
Madison Pub 1315 E Madison St, Capitol Hill ☎206/325-6537, ⓦ www.madisonpub.com. Homely neighborhood spot a bit east of the main action in Capitol Hill, attracting regulars for its pool tables, darts, sports trivia, and cozy atmosphere. Also has Wi-Fi Internet access. Daily noon–2am.
Manray 514 E Pine St, Capitol Hill ☎206/568-0750, ⓦ www.manrayvideo.com. One of the most popular spots in town, this upscale "video bar" has retro-60s futuristic decor and 1980s music videos, plus an outdoor patio with a wooden deck and fountain.

Happy hour all day Sunday and karaoke Monday night. Mon–Fri 11am–2am, Sat & Sun 4pm–2am.
Neighbours 1509 Broadway E, Capitol Hill ☎206/324-5358. Broadway's most popular gay disco, and the place to go if you want to dance yourself into delirium to loud, beat-heavy sounds. Increasingly straight in recent years, though still a frequent hangout for drag queens. Sun–Wed 4pm–2am, Thurs 4pm–3am, Fri & Sat 4pm–4am.
R Place 619 E Pine St, Capitol Hill ☎206/322-8828, ⓦ www.rplaceseattle.com. Three-floor bar with pool tables, dance floors, and dart boards, and a prime cruising spot for young, professional gay men. Funky retro-DJs alter-nate with events like underwear contests, amateur strip shows and "porn karaoke." Mon–Fri 4pm–2am, Sat & Sun 2pm–2am.
Re-Bar 1114 Howell St, First Hill ☎206/233-9873, ⓦ www.rebarseattle.com. Draws big gay and straight crowds with an ever-shifting nightly focus that encompasses acid jazz, hip-hop, funk, soul, and Latin. Also some live music from bands you might have heard of, as well as occasional theatrical and spoken-word shows. Daily 10pm–2am.
Seattle Eagle 314 E Pike St, Capitol Hill ☎206/621-7591, ⓦ www.seattleeagle.com. "Seattle's oldest leather bar" attracts a young clientele with an accent on the fetish scene. Theme nights like "Trash," "Meat-rack," and "Tool Shed" bring in an energetic, male-dominated crowd. Daily 2pm–2am.
Sonya's Bar & Grill 1919 First Ave, Downtown ☎206/441-7996. Friendly neighborhood bar in a gentrifying part of town, with a good menu, nice views of Elliott Bay, and a central location near Pike Place

Market. Mon–Thurs 11am–9pm, Fri & Sat 11am–10pm.

Thumper's 1500 E Madison St, Capitol Hill
☎ 206/328-3800. Combination bar/restaurant serving average Northwest Cuisine, with colorful, often drag-oriented, cabaret performances and other shows. Rustic, wood-paneled setting with a fireplace, lounge, patio, and views over Downtown. Daily 11am–2am.

Vogue 1516 Eleventh Ave, Capitol Hill
☎ 206/324-5778, ⓦ www.vogueseattle.com.

Energetic dance club with a mixed gay and straight clientele; hosts fetish fashion shows, drag nights, and other colorful displays. Daily 9pm–2am.

Wild Rose 1021 E Pike St, Capitol Hill
☎ 206/324-9210, ⓦ www.thewildrosebar .com. Seattle's most popular lesbian bar, and a comfortable place for having a bite (the menu has a fairly wide selection), playing pool or darts, or just hanging out. Wednesday is karaoke night. Daily 3pm–2am.

Festivals and events

Festivals in Seattle vary greatly in scale, from the enormous Bumbershoot arts and music festival held around Labor Day to various small, alternative shindigs. A strong sense of neighborhood pride and ethnic identity results in dozens of festivals throughout the year, while several concert series, mostly spanning the summer months, are also worthwhile. The Seattle Center's ongoing Festal series (☏206/684-7200, ⓦwww.seattlecenter .com), devoted to celebrating the cultural diversity of the Pacific Northwest, puts on numerous free mini-fests (several times a month) at Seattle Center, usually celebrating individual ethnicities. With all these options, even a brief stay in Seattle is likely to coincide with an event that piques your curiosity – though many festivals take place from May to September, when the weather isn't so dreary. The timing of each event is given in parentheses at the beginning of the entry.

January

Global Lens (mid) Northwest Film Forum, 1515 12th Ave, Capitol Hill ☏206/267-5380. ⓦwww .seattlefilm.org. A chance to see some of the most compelling works from around the world, particularly from developing countries, in this wide-ranging fest taking place over several weeks, with each film screened several times in one or multiple days. $8–10 per show.

Chinese New Year (late) ☏206/382-1197, ⓦwww.cidbia.org. The International District is at its most colorful around late January to mid February, when parades are staged and dragon costumes come out in full force.

February

Science Fiction Short Film Festival (early) ☏206/724-3428, ⓦwww.sfhomeworld.org. Sponsored in large measure by Paul Allen, this new festival takes place at Cinerama and the Experience Music Project/Sci-Fi Museum, showcasing brief works (under 12 min) that use limited budgets to convey other worlds, speculative ideas, and the like.

Tét in Seattle (early) ☏206/706-2658, ⓦwww .tetinseattle.org. The Vietnamese lunar new year is celebrated throughout Seattle with scrumptious food, traditional music, dance programs, and film screenings, with many events at the Center House in the Seattle Center.

Festival Sundiata (mid) Seattle Center ☏206/329-8086, ⓦfestivalsundiata.org. Held during Black History Month and named after a Mali king who rescued a kidnapped *griot* (storyteller), the largest African-American festival in the Northwest has been going strong for 25 years, with music, workshops, food, crafts, and children's activities – most of them free.

Puyallup Spring Fair (mid) Western Washington Fairgrounds, Puyallup ☏253/841-5045 ⓦwww .thefair.com. All sorts of cheeky, rural-flavored activities taking place on the fairgrounds south of Seattle, including country karaoke, line dancing, all-American food vendors, cowboy poets, swine racing, a petting zoo, and even a curious "Christian talent contest".

March

Irish Week (mid) ☏ 206/684-7200, ⓦ www
.irishclub.org. Focused mainly on the Seattle Center, but also at area bars and parks,
a tribute to Emerald islanders, complete
with hearty Irish food and colorful dancing, lessons in speaking Gaelic, traditional
games, and even a genealogist to help you
trace your roots back to the Olde Country.
Jewish Film Festival (mid) Cinerama and the 5th
Avenue Theatre ☏ 206/622-6315, ⓦ www
.ajcseattle.org or ⓦ www.seattlejewishfilmfestival
.org. A week of Judaism-themed movies and
work by Jewish filmmakers, including Israeli
titles, with overarching social and political
themes.
St Patrick's Day Parade (17th) ☏ 206/684-7200,
ⓦ www.irishclub.org. St Paddy's isn't that big
a deal in Seattle, but there's still a colorful
parade – starting Downtown and heading to
the Seattle Center – and copious amounts
of green beer from Irish pubs.

April

Moisture Festival (early) 4301 Leary Way NW
☏ 206/938-1513. ⓦ www.moisturefestival
.com. Another one of those only-in-Fremont
events, held over several weeks, at microbrewery Hales Ales' own Palladium. Presents
"comedy/varieté" acts that range from
neo-vaudeville shenanigans to outrageous
burlesque and alternative-circus performers.
Somewhat beyond description; must be
seen to be believed. Tickets $10–15.
**Cherry Blossom and Japanese Cultural Festival
(mid to late)** Seattle Center ☏ 206/684-7200.
Free event, usually over a weekend, featuring Japanese historical and cultural exhibits,
food, martial arts, taiko drumming, callig-
raphy, origami, floral arrangement, and tea
ceremonies.
Seattle Poetry Festival (late to early May)
☏ 206/725-1650, ⓦ www.poetryfestival.org. A
week of poetry readings at various venues
throughout the city, culminating in the
Seattle Grand Slam, the ultimate poetry
competition. Will return in 2007 after a
prolonged absence.

May

Seattle International Children's Festival (mid)
Seattle Center ☏ 206/684-7346, ⓦ www
.seattleinternational.org. Multicultural music,
puppets, theater and other antics for the
kids for a week in Seattle, followed by a day
of comparable festivities in Tacoma.
Seattle Maritime Festival (mid) on the waterfront at 2205 Alaskan Way ☏ 206/284-8285,
ⓦ www.boatsafloat.com. Port tours, tugboat
races, boat-building competition, and a
chowder cook-off are on the bill at this free
three-day event. Contact the Odyssey Maritime Museum (ⓦ www.ody.org; see p.155)
for additional information.
University District Street Fair (mid) University
Way ☏ 206/523-4272, ⓦ www.udistrictstreetfair
.org. The biggest event of its kind in Seattle,
a 37-year-old tradition taking over the main
section of University Way with hundreds
of booths, food vendors, eye-popping
costumes, theatrical shows, and lots of live
music and entertainment.
World Rhythm Festival (mid) ☏ 206/781-6680.
ⓦ www.swps.org/wrf. High on the list of Seattlites' most engaging and uptempo events,
featuring drummers and percussionists
from around the world, pounding out their
beats at the Seattle Center in a free-spirited
atmosphere with good ethnic food, ongoing
concerts, and familiar and unusual instruments on display.
Northwest Folklife Festival (late) Seattle
Center ☏ 206/684-7300, ⓦ www.nwfolklife.org.
Memorial Day bash (free, but suggested
donation) attracting 200,000 visitors and
thousands of participants, for all types of
traditional music, including bluegrass, Celtic,
roots and world music, along with crafts,
food, dance, and storytelling. Also watch
for themed benefit auctions for the festival
throughout the year.
Pike Place Market Street Festival (late)
Pike Place Market ☏ 206/682-7453, ⓦ www
.pikeplacemarket.org. A worthwhile event
offering live music on three stages, as
well as food, a beer garden, arts-and-
crafts, and other activities. The 2005 event
featured fifty international chefs competing
to make the world's biggest bowl of clam
chowder, as well as a Chalk Art Zone for
unrestrained children's doodling.

June

**Seattle International Film Festival (early to
mid)** ☏ 206/464-5830, ⓦ www.seattlefilm
.com. More than two hundred films from all
over the world are shown at this prestigious
festival; screenings are often accompanied
by director appearances. Shows take place

at the Egyptian, Harvard Exit, Cinerama, Guild 45th and Paramount theaters and Broadway Performance Hall (see Chapter 15, "Performing arts and film," for contact info), among other smaller venues. Reserve ahead because the prime-time flicks ($8–10) sell out fast.

Fremont Fair & Solstice Parade (mid)
☏ 206/633-4409, Ⓦ www.fremontfair.com. The most enjoyable and bizarre Seattle celebration, with hundreds of arts vendors, plus a parade allowing only human-powered floats and costumes, including nude bicyclists (see p.121 for more info). Followed by a pageant at the end of the route in Gasworks Park.

Northwest New Works Festival (mid) Behnke Center, 100 W Roy St, Queen Anne ☏ 206/217-9888, Ⓦ www.ontheboards.org. The esteemed theatrical/dance group On the Boards (see p.188) holds this three-week festival of innovative contemporary works in dance, drama, film, and multimedia. Prices vary.

Philippine Festival (mid) Seattle Center ☏ 206/684-7200. Lively presentation of the traditional and contemporary culture of the Philippines, featuring music and food of the islands, martial arts, craftworks, dance performances, and many vivid costumes.

Pride Parade and Freedom Rally (last Sun)
☏ 206/324-0405, Ⓦ seattlepride.org. Also known as Gay Pride Parade, a popular event with residents of all sexual orientations, with colorfully garbed participants and a festive atmosphere. Held along Broadway in Capitol Hill.

Rainier Valley Concert Series (June–Aug)
☏ 206/723-SEED, Ⓦ www.seedseattle.org. Summer jazz, including local high-school outfits and the occasional big name, taking place one weekend each month at Seward and Columbia City parks.

July

Independence Day (4th) ☏ 206/684-4075. Fourth of July fireworks along the waterfront at Elliott Bay, Lake Washington, and Lake Union. Gasworks Park (see p.122) is the most popular viewing location, so get there early if you want a good seat.

Bite of Seattle (mid to late) Seattle Center ☏ 206/232-2982, Ⓦ www.biteofseattle.com. Seattle's most popular food festival, drawing around 400,000 visitors, with restaurants setting up booths near five outdoor entertainment stages. Single entrees rarely cost more than $4–7.

Chinatown-International District Summer Festival (mid) Hing Hay Park ☏ 206/382-1197, Ⓦ www.cidbia.org. This spirited weekend

Seattle music festivals

Winter Festival (early Feb) ☏ 206/283-8710, Ⓦ www.scmf.org. Four chamber-music concerts and two recitals at Benaroya Hall, featuring visiting performers and a nice range of classical pieces; tickets $38, or a full package for $134.

Festival of Improvised Music (mid-Feb) ☏ 206/728-1980, Ⓦ www.seattleimprovisedmusic.com. Five days of jazz, improv, experimental and electronic music, presented at Gallery 1412 (see p.182); tickets $10–20.

Seattle Peace Concerts (mid-June to late-Sept) ☏ 206/729-5232, Ⓦ www.seapeace.org. Free rock, blues, zydeco, jazz, and other live music (usually 5–7 acts from noon–6pm) at various local parks throughout the summer; the audience is asked to donate food to the Northwest Harvest organization.

Summer Nights (mid-June to Aug) South Lake Union Park ☏ 206/281-7788, Ⓦ www.summernights.org. Evening waterfront concerts, featuring mostly big-name acts. $42–58. See "Live Music" chapter for a full review (p.181).

Out to Lunch Summer Concert Series (July to early Sept) ☏ 206/623-3206, Ⓦ www.downtownseattle.com. Free weekday music concerts held at dozens of Downtown plazas and parks (usually noon–1.30pm), featuring everything from jazz vibraphonists and "Hawaiian reggae" to lounge music to classical, alt-country, blues and Celtic.

Summer Festival (July–Aug) ☏ 206/283-8710, Ⓦ www.scmf.org. Twelve July chamber concerts by internationally known classical musicians, with most tickets in the $30–40 range and held in North Seattle; followed by five similar performances in August in Redmond.

△ Bite of Seattle festival

event revolves around a pan-Asian street fair full of authentic food, musical performances from taiko drumming to jazz, drill teams, parades, and other programs.
Bellevue Arts and Crafts Fair (late) Bellevue Square ☎ 425/519-0721, ⊛ www.bellevueart.org.

The most prominent Eastside festival, on the last weekend of July, going on sixty years. Features varied entertainment, food, a small film festival, and more than three hundred artists displaying their work – and some 300,000 spectators in attendance.

Sixth Street Arts and Crafts Fair (late) NE Sixth St and 106th Ave NE, Bellevue ☎425/453-1223, ⓦwww.bellevuedowntown.org. Upbeat event featuring live jazz acts in downtown Bellevue, held in conjunction with the Taste of Bellevue foodfest, at which you can sample wide-ranging culinary fare at booths set up by local restaurants.

Seafair (late-July to early-Aug) ☎206/728-0123 ext 108, ⓦwww.seafair.com. Intermittent three-week celebration of maritime culture, featuring vendors selling seafood – raw, baked, and fried – and events at various locations all over town. Includes a marathon and torchlight parade, hydroplane races on Lake Washington, and milk-carton races on Green Lake.

Capitol Hill Block Party (end) ☎206/218-7969, ⓦwww.capitolhillblockparty.com. Upbeat, heel-kicking event with some fifty bands on four stages around the center of this dynamic district. Come to chow down on good eats, bounce around to the local beat, and get a feel for the latest up-and-comers in rock, electronica, and punk. Tickets $12 per day.

August

Best of the Northwest (mid) Magnuson Park ☎206/525-5926, ⓦwww.bestnwcrafts.com. One of several engaging crafts shows spread over a weekend that takes place throughout the year and involves artisans displaying their (buyable) works in glass, pottery, clothing, wood- and metalworks, jewelry, and the like. $6.

BrasilFest (mid) Seattle Center ☎206/684-7200, ⓦwww.brasilfest.com. Colorful costumes, spirited dancing, rousing samba tunes, and plenty of spicy food and enthusiastic performers are the highlights of this yearly Brazilian funfest, each year celebrating a different region of this sizable country.

Chief Seattle Days (mid) Suquamish ☎360/598-3311. Just over the bridge from Bainbridge Island (see p.252), the Suquamish tribe celebrates this weekend festival with Native American food, culture, and canoe races.

Tibet Fest (late) Seattle Center ☎206/444-4059, ⓦwww.washingtontibet.org. Features the art, craftwork and culture of the people of the Himalayas (Tibet and beyond), with *a cappella* singing, theater, music, and food on display – an entertaining and evocative spectacle for those with limited knowledge of the country apart from the Dalai Lama.

September

Bumbershoot (early) Seattle Center ☎206/281-7788, ⓦwww.bumbershoot.org. Mammoth multi-event extravaganza that's one of the city's best parties. Musical acts range from the famous to the obscure, with plenty of film, comedy, and theater thrown in for good measure. All in all, some five hundred acts perform at twenty different venues around town. Day tickets $28, full four-day pass $80.

Puyallup Fair (early to mid) Western Washington Fairgrounds, Puyallup ☎253/841-5045, ⓦwww.thefair.com. Western Washington's biggest county fair, taking place over several weeks about thirty miles south of Seattle. Livestock and home-made crafts displays share space with a rodeo, rides, comedy, food, and mainstream country music. $10.

Salmon Homecoming (early) Piers 62/63 ☎206/386-4320, ⓦwww.nwifc.wa.gov/salmonhomecoming. Held over four days, this mostly free waterfront festival focuses on Northwest tribal groups, with storytelling, food and crafts booths, canoe racing and other cultural exhibits – not to mention the scrumptious salmon bakes.

Festa Italiana (mid to late) ☎206/282-0627, ⓦwww.festaseattle.com. Few can resist the inspired cuisine of Italy, with delicious entrees from the north and south of the country, at this lively festival that involves more than just food; it also features imaginative art and craftworks, classical and modern dancing, traditional musical performers, Catholic masses in Italian, wine-tasting and even a bit of grape-stomping.

October

UW World Series (Oct-May) University of Washington ☎206/543-4882, ⓦwww.uwworldseries.org. A splendid cultural festival that brings international musicians, dancers, acrobats and other performers to the UW campus during the school year. Tickets to popular shows can sell out quickly; shows usually take place at least once a week, for $29–45.

Earshot Jazz Festival (mid to early Nov) ☎206/547-9787, ⓦwww.earshot.org. Daily concerts spread out over several weeks and featuring some 150 performers at a dozen venues. The focus is on progressive contemporary jazz notables with an international reputation. Tickets $10–32, but most are $16–20.

Lesbian and Gay Film Festival (mid to late)
T 206/323-4274, W www.seattlequeerfilm.com.
Runs for a week mostly at the Cinerama
and Harvard Exit theaters, and includes
everything from feature dramas to avant-
garde shorts, encompassing selections from
several continents. Tickets $8–10; all-festival
pass $175.

Dia de los Muertos (early or late Nov)
T 206/684-7200, W www.lacasadeartes.org.
"Day of the Dead," an eye-opening Mexican
celebration of death, with all of its morbid
pageantry, skull decor, dancing skeletons,
macabre attire, and traditional food and
arts-and-crafts. Festivities held at Seattle
Center and at scattered cafés and galleries,
mostly in Capitol Hill.

November

Hmong New Year (early) Seattle Center
T 206/684-7200. A festival honoring the end
of the harvest season for this native people
of Southeast Asia; for outsiders it's a great
opportunity to sample some unfamiliar
cuisine, look at indigenous art-and-crafts
including weaving and a unique sort of
leaf-blowing, and enjoy native dancing and
costumes.

Ballard Jazz Festival (mid) T 206/219-3649,
W www.ballardjazzfestival.com. A fairly
new event that offers mid-level regional
and national performers on a Mainstage
concert and on a Jazz Walk along Ballard
Ave and Leary Way, where you can take
in performances at local clubs and bars
– and even a diner, church, and wine shop.
Passes are $25 for both the Saturday
Mainstage show ($20 alone) and the Friday
Jazz Walk ($15 alone).

**Cultural Crossroads (mid) Crossroads shopping
center, Bellevue** T 425/644-1111, W www
.crossroadsbellevue.com. Three-day multicultural music on two stages (held in and
around a major mall), plus a wide-ranging
food and crafts fair, representing more than
one hundred different ethnic groups.

December

Winterfest (throughout) Seattle Center
T 206/684-7200. A month-long event that
celebrates the holidays with the usual
Christmas-related food, pageantry, and
festivities including ice-skating, tree decora-
tion, and so on.

(17)

Sports and outdoor activities

W ith temperatures that seldom dip below freezing and a close proximity to some of the most scenic mountains and waterways of North America, Seattle is well-suited for year-round **outdoor activities**. The ubiquitous rain hardly stops the pace of hiking, climbing, and biking during the colder months, and most weekend campers and sailors find plenty of opportunities to explore the outdoors, regardless of the weather – though visitors not wanting to get drenched may find it most enjoyable to explore the terrain during the high season, from May to September.

As for **sports**, major franchises didn't arrive here until the 1960s and 1970s, and were slow to catch on, but the city has now embraced its pro teams with enthusiasm, particularly baseball's Mariners and basketball's SuperSonics. Indeed, tickets for such spectator sports are often difficult to come by, and Sonics games are usually sellouts. The prices are often rather steep, too, especially if you want to be close to the action. Baseball remains a better alternative, if only because there are more seats at Safeco Field than at Key Arena, and the Mariners have been woeful in recent years. Seats for weekday and weeknight games are usually available, but for weekend series and key matchups (such as the Yankees and Angels), you'll probably be consigned to the outer reaches of the outfield.

Advance tickets for major Seattle sporting events can be purchased over the phone from TicketMaster (℡206/628-0888, 🅦www.ticketmaster.com), which also sells them in person at a few places throughout the city, including Key Arena and Rite Aid pharmacies, whose central Downtown store is at 319 Pike St (see Chapter 21, "Directory," for more details). TicketMaster charges a fee on top of the ticket price, which can be avoided by contacting the individual teams' box offices, most of which – for the clubs listed below – are located at either Safeco Field, the Seattle Center, or the University of Washington campus.

Baseball

When the Seattle Pilots brought **major league baseball** into town in 1969, the franchise was a miserable failure, lasting only a year before moving to Milwaukee – just long enough for the Pilots' relief pitcher Jim Bouton to pen his classic memoir, *Ball Four*, in which he observed, "A city that seems to care more for its art museums than its ballpark can't be all bad."

Several years later, the **Seattle Mariners** would arrive and face many years of hardship on the field, with success finally coming when the franchise set an all-time record for American League wins in 2001 – though it still failed to win the AL pennant, much less the World Series. Nonetheless, the team's regular-season success enabled it to gain the public funds for an open-air stadium, Safeco Field (see p.73). Naturally, since this fine stadium has opened, the team has gone into a tailspin, finishing 2005 at the bottom of its division.

Tickets – the regular season runs from April to early October – range from $7 for the cheapest seats, in the centerfield bleachers, to $50 for the most expensive, behind the diamond. Call ☎206/622-HITS or visit Ⓦseattle.mariners.mlb .com to purchase tickets; to get tickets in person, drop by the Safeco Field box office or visit one of the six Mariners team shops in the area (see website for details).

Minor league baseball can be seen within thirty miles of Downtown Seattle in both Tacoma, where the winning, triple-A-level **Rainiers** play at Cheney Stadium (April–Sept; $5-12; ☎253/752-7700 or 1-800/281-3834, Ⓦwww .tacomarainiers.com), and in Everett, where the single-A **Aquasox** play at Everett Memorial Stadium (June–Sept; $7-13; ☎206/258-3673, Ⓦwww.aquasox.com). Both teams are Mariner affiliates, and good seats are easy to get; plus, it's outdoors and cheap, offering the chance to see an up-and-comer swing the bat long before he makes his big-league debut.

Basketball

The **SuperSonics** (usually abbreviated to just the "Sonics") are the only Seattle pro team to have won a championship, way back in 1979. Since then, they've been bought by Howard Schultz – mastermind of Starbucks – and have had rather variable seasons, from making it to the NBA finals in 1996 (only to lose to Michael Jordan's Bulls) to failing to make the playoffs on several occasions. They had a surprisingly successful season in 2005, only to lose their coach (and former Sonic) Nate McMillan to their hated Oregon rivals, the Portland Trail Blazers. Now armed with a new coach, they play at Key Arena in the Seattle Center (Oct–May or June; ticket info at ☎206/283-DUNK, Ⓦwww.nba.com/sonics), a 17,000-seat venue where tickets can be hard to get. The range of prices runs from $26–195, from the worst obstructed-view seats to down on the floor at center court (which you won't get unless you know someone).

Also in Key Arena, the **Seattle Storm** began play in the Women's National Basketball Association in 2000, winning a championship in 2004. They're still one of the better teams in the league, and their games can be quite spirited, with the season lasting from May through August, and the playoffs in September. Tickets run $10–39 (info ☎206/217-WNBA, Ⓦwww.wnba .com/storm).

Football

Until the mid-1990s, the **Seattle Seahawks** were among the hottest tickets in town; however, the football squad soon experienced a decade-long stretch of mediocrity, before emerging once again in 2005 as one of the league's premier teams. Several years ago there was even speculation that the franchise would

⑱

be leaving town, until Paul Allen stepped in as a buyer, on the condition that a new open-air stadium be built in the Kingdome's place. After a furious lobbying effort, Allen got his way and Washington voters footed the bill for the new Seahawks Stadium, now Qwest Field (see p.73), which opened in 2002 near Safeco Field. As long as the Seahawks continue to win, **tickets** will be hard to get, and fairly expensive, most recently ranging from $33 to $315 (though this will undoubtedly skyrocket for the 2006 season); call ℡1-888/NFL-HAWK or visit Ⓦwww.seahawks.com to attempt to purchase some.

UW's football team, the **Huskies**, have enjoyed more success than the Seahawks in decades past, though they've been rather woeful in the last few years. They're still a popular draw, however, and play in the Pac-10 Conference at the 72,000-seat Husky Stadium on the edge of campus, near Lake Washington. For **tickets** – which cost $64 for reserved seats – call ℡206/543-2200 or visit Ⓦwww.gohuskies.com; the season runs from September to December or early January, depending on whether the team is in a bowl game. The same ticket office also sells seats for several **other UW sports**, the most popular of which are the men's and women's basketball games; tickets run $15–25 and $10–14, respectively. At all college events, expect a fervent, vocal crowd and don't make the innocent mistake of wearing the opposing team's colors – unless you're prepared to defend your presumed loyalties.

Other spectator sports

Soccer enthusiasts can watch the **Sounders**, the 2005 champions of the A-League, the highest US pro soccer level other than Major League Soccer. They play at Qwest Field (May-Sept; tickets $12–17; ℡206/622-3415 or 1-800/796-KICK, Ⓦwww.seattlesounders.net), though only a limited, lower-tier section is open for soccer seating in this cavernous arena. By contrast, there's no major league **hockey** team in Seattle, but the **Thunderbirds** (Sept–March; tickets $12–30; ℡206/448-PUCK, Ⓦwww.seattle-thunderbirds.com), of the minor Junior A Western Hockey League, play in Key Arena. Finally, in the Tacoma suburb of Auburn, **horse racing** is held at **Emerald Downs** (admission $4; ℡253/288-7000, Ⓦwww.emdowns.com), from mid-April through mid-October.

Biking

Despite its rainy climate, hilly topography, and crowded roads, Seattle is a major draw for **cyclists**: there are about thirty miles of bicycle/pedestrian trails and nearly one hundred miles of marked bike routes. Although you'll have a hard time finding level routes unless you stick close to the lakes, the semi-mountainous terrain guarantees a good workout, and the scenery is often magnificent.

The most popular route is the twelve-mile **Burke-Gilman Trail**, which starts near Eighth Avenue NW and NW 43rd Street in Ballard and follows the banks of the Lake Washington Ship Canal, Lake Union, and western Lake Washington, passing on the way through such areas as central Fremont, Gasworks Park, and the U District. The path is also open to joggers and walkers; at its northern end, it connects to the ten-mile **Sammamish River Trail**, which brings riders over to Marymoor Park (see p.134) on the Eastside. If you follow both trails, the entire journey is 27 miles one-way, making for an excellent workout for cyclists, or slightly more than a marathon for runners who have transportation at the end.

Another good route is the stretch of **Lake Washington Boulevard** that starts at the Washington Park Arboretum (see p.98) and skirts the lake's edge for a few miles before terminating at Seward Park, passing through such attractive districts as Madison Park, Madrona, and Mount Baker. Even better, the southern end of the route is closed to automobiles from 10am to 6pm on the second Saturday and third Sunday of the month between mid–May and mid–September. A tamer experience can be had at fetching **Green Lake** (p.123), where a fine multi-use path circles the lake and draws big crowds on weekends and during the summer – there are even signs marked with the proper lanes for bikes, walkers, and rollerbladers, as if on a freeway.

Far more challenging, and quite stunning, is the **Elliott Bay Trail** along Magnolia Boulevard, which climbs a steep hill from the Magnolia Bridge to Discovery Park, passing gorgeous cliffside views of Puget Sound en route. Another good stretch, if a bit easier, is the **Alki Trail** which takes you around the northern end of the peninsula at West Seattle, terminating along the sands at Alki Beach. For more rural terrain, there's great biking in **Vashon Island** (p.247) and **Lopez Island** (p.264), and good concourses along stretches of Bainbridge and Whidbey islands. See "Out from the city" (pp.233–272) for the countless other options in the terrain beyond the city.

Bike rental and information

At the shops listed below, **rental rates** fluctuate from $5–12 per hour, or $20–45 per day, depending on the proximity of the shop to major attractions and the type of model you're renting.

Aaron's Bicycle Repair 6521 California Ave SW, West Seattle ☎206/938-9795, ⓦwww.rideyourbike.com. Good for renting bikes and acquiring information about the best routes in the city and beyond; also useful as a starting point for trips around West Seattle and Alki Beach. Mon–Fri 11am–7pm, Sat 10am–6pm, Sun noon–6pm.

All About Bike & Ski 3615 NE 45th St, University District ☎206/524-2642, ⓦwww.allaboutbikeandski.com. Based out of University Village, a dealer and renter of bikes, equipment, and tools, along with skiing and snowboarding goods. Mon–Fri 11am–7pm, Sat 10am–6pm, Sun 11am–5pm.

Bicycle Center 4529 Sandpoint Way NE, University District ☎206/523-8300, ⓦwww.bicyclecenterseattle.com. Wide array of models to rent and some of the best prices around ($3/hr, $15/day). Located on the east side of the UW campus, and ideal if you're hitting the nearby Burke-Gilman Trail. Mon–Fri 10am–7pm, Sat 10am–6pm.

Bicycle Paper ⓦwww.bicyclepaper.com. Cycling rides, tours, and races are listed in the free paper available most anywhere sporting gear is sold; much of the same news and articles are available online.

Gregg's 7007 Woodlawn Ave NE, Green Lake ☎206/523-1822, ⓦwww.greggscycles.com. A fine spot for getting a cheap beach cruiser to pedal around the lake (along with faster, sleeker models for more money), with rollerblade rentals for about the same price ($5/hr). Also has a store in Bellevue, at 121 106th Ave NE (☎425/462-1900). Hours for both Mon–Fri 10am–8pm, Sat & Sun 10am–6pm.

Seattle Bicycle Club ☎206/444-4075, ⓦwww.seattlebike.org. Sets up weekend rides around the city, starting from such spots as Gasworks Park and tooling around Lake Washington or Mercer Island, and has information about bike activities and organizations.

Seattle Department of Transportation ☎206/684-7583; ⓦwww.cityofseattle.net/transportation/bikeprogram.htm. Publishes the free and very handy *Seattle Bicycling Guide Map*, which outlines bicycle routes and lists cycling regulations. Other maps offer detailed views of the Burke-Gilman Trail, as well as routes in the University District and Downtown, among many other places.

Critical Mass

European cyclists familiar with stereotypical American attitudes toward transportation (fossil-fueled vs. human-powered) and confrontation (abundant), can find both on display in Seattle at **Critical Mass** (ⓦseattlecriticalmass.org). This high-spirited, often nerve-jangling athletic/protest event meets at Westlake Center at 5.30pm on the last Friday of the month for rides through Downtown (some riders also begin with a pre-ride from the U District to Westlake Center), with the goal of promoting sustainable approaches to transportation beyond automobiles. Born in San Francisco, and now a regular occurrence in many cities around the world, the event gathers enough cyclists passing through major intersections that drivers have no choice but to shut off their engines and wait. Note that, like similar events in California, Oregon, and other US states, such rallies are occasionally prone to run-ins with the police and angry motorists. Staying in the group provides some protection, but keep in mind that Critical Mass originated as something of a radical political statement, so don't come assuming you're in for a joy ride.

Running

Running is a big deal in Seattle in all kinds of weather, and every lunch break finds the waterfront populated with office workers who have changed into athletic gear to take in a few miles of jogging along Elliott Bay or Lake Washington. Seattle's numerous parks and waterside lanes offer many choices for the fitness enthusiast, and some of the better routes are multipurpose biking/running/walking paths, such as the Burke-Gilman Trail (see p.208), the Green Lake path, and most of the other routes described in the "Biking" section above. Discovery Park also has a challenging 2.8-mile loop trail that goes through dense forest and along bluffs with great views of Puget Sound. For more on the various footpaths and jogging routes through the city's parks, the Department of Parks and Recreation offers online info, as well as brochures you can order through the mail or download (☏206/684-4075, ⓦwww.cityofseattle.net/parks/parkguide.htm).

Competitive **races** are held in town throughout the year, highlighted by November's Seattle Marathon/Half-Marathon (fees $60–90; ☏206/729-3660, ⓦwww.seattlemarathon.org), which takes place the weekend after Thanksgiving. The course is one of the best on the West Coast, sending runners on an attractive route that crosses I-90 on the (temporarily closed) freeway bridge and reaches Mercer Island, before heading down to Seward Park and returning to town along Lake Washington Boulevard. *Northwest Runner* (ⓦwww.nwrunner.com), a local periodical available at sporting goods outlets, has a calendar of races in Seattle and the entire Northwest.

Water activities

Watching boats sail through the Hiram M. Chittenden Locks in Ballard is a popular spectator sport, and there are several inexpensive **water activities** centers in Seattle that enable you to get in on the action as well, whether rowing a canoe or trying your luck on a windsurfer. However, **outdoor swimming** is usually not a comfortable proposition in Seattle without a wetsuit, but the hardy do take to the waves at the city's two most popular beaches, **Alki Beach**

△ Kayaking on Lake Union

(p.137) and **Golden Gardens** (p.115) – although the water temperatures are actually warmer, and the crowds thinner, along **Lake Washington**. Alternatively, the city has eight **indoor pools** where you can take a dip for a modest fee, the most conveniently located of these being Queen Anne Pool at 1920 First Ave W, Queen Anne (☏206/386-4282), and Evans Pool on the edge of Green Lake at 7201 E Green Lake Drive N (☏206/684-4961). There's also the heated outdoor Colman Pool, in West Seattle's Lincoln Park, 8603 Fauntleroy Way SW (daily mid-June to Aug; ☏206/684-7494).

Water activities rentals

Agua Verde Paddle Club on Lake Union's Portage Bay, 1303 NE Boat St ☏206/545-8570, ⓦ www.aguaverde.com. Kayak rentals by the hour ($10 single, $15 double, $20 triple), with a third hour for free with the purchase of two hours from Mon–Fri 10am–4pm. Mon–Sat 10am–sunset, Sun 10am–8pm.
Center for Wooden Boats on Lake Union, 1010 Valley St ☏206/382-2628, ⓦ www.cwb.org. Rents sailboats and rowboats for $12.50–46/hr, depending upon the size of the boat and day of the week, with an additional $10 checkout fee for any reservation. (For a full review, see p.98.) Daily noon–5pm.
Green Lake Boat Rentals 7351 E Green Lake Drive N ☏206/527-0171. Rents paddleboats, rowboats, canoes, and single-person kayaks for $10/hr, two-person kayaks for $12/hr, and sailboats and windsurfers for $14/hr. Expect thick crowds on warm summer days. April–Sept daily 10am–6pm.

Mount Baker Rowing and Sailing Center at Stan Sayres Park, 3808 Lake Washington Blvd S, between Mount Baker and Seward Park ☏206/386-1913, ⓦ www.cityofseattle.net/parks/boats. The place to launch anything from a dinghy to a sailboat and take classes on kayaking, canoeing, or general sailing. Mon, Wed & Fri 9am–6.30pm, Tues & Thurs 5.30am–6.30pm, Sat 7am–4pm, Sun 12.30–5pm.
Northwest Outdoor Center 2100 Westlake Ave N, Lake Union ☏206/281-9694 or 1-800/683-0637, ⓦ www.nwoc.com. Rents kayaks by the hour ($12 single, $17 double) and the day ($60 single, $80 double). Hours vary; usually at least Mon–Fri 10am–6pm, Sat & Sun 10am–5pm; closed Mon & Tues in winter.
Urban Surf, 2100 N Northlake Way, Wallingford ☏206/545-9463, ⓦ www.urbansurf.com. Rents surfboards for $15/day, in combo with a wetsuit for only $10 more. May–Sept Mon–Fri 10am–7pm, Sat 10am–5pm, Sun 11am–5pm.

Waterfront Activities Center on the UW campus ☎206/543-9433, ⓦdepts.washington.edu/ima/IMA_wac.php. Rents rowboats or canoes for $7.50 an hour with a valid ID; on weekdays there's rarely a wait, and the marshes of Foster Island are just a few minutes of rowing away. Feb–Oct daily 10am–dusk, except holidays and winter break.

Walking, hiking, and climbing

Walking and especially **hiking** are integral to the Northwest lifestyle, with the best places being a few hours outside of town along the slopes of mounts **Rainier** and **St Helens** (see Chapter 24, "Mount Rainier and Mount St Helens"). A closer option is **Mount Si**, a half-hour's drive east of Seattle, near Snoqualmie Falls. Here, a four-mile climb ascends about 4000 feet to take in glorious panoramas of the surrounding mountains (see p.274 for details).

In the San Juan Islands, **Mount Constitution** on Orcas Island rises nearly 2500 feet, its mountaintop commanding stunning vistas of the surrounding area; also excellent are many of the county parks found elsewhere in the San Juan Islands, and **Fort Ebey** and **Deception Pass** state parks on Whidbey Island (see p.259). Within the urban boundaries, your options are considerably fewer, with most parks simply not designed to provide a vigorous hike; two of the exceptions are **Frink Park**, at 398 Lake Washington Blvd in Madrona (daily 4am–11.30pm; ☎206/684-4075), which offers nicely wooded terrain built around a steep ravine, and West Seattle's **Schmitz Park**, 5551 SW Admiral Way (daily 4am–11.30pm; ⓦwww.schmitzpark.org), a rugged swath of wilderness that's been kept that way by the will of the donor who provided it to the city. Finally, Tacoma's own **Point Defiance Park** (p.240) is one of the region's best, laced with countless trails spread over its 700 acres. For access to the entire Puget Sound area, **trail maps** are found in all good book and outdoor shops; see "Shopping" (p.218) for some of the better bookstore options.

You can **climb** Mount Rainier if you want a truly vigorous workout, as you can with Mount St Helens when it's not rumbling. In the urban area, the outdoors-store REI is a good place to practice your climbing on a 65ft indoor rock "pinnacle," which you can ascend with guidance from the staff (Mon 10am–6pm, Wed–Fri 10am–9pm, Sat 10am–7pm, Sun 10am–5.30pm; $15, or $5 for REI members; climb usually limited to one route or 15 minutes; ☎206/223-1944. ⓦwww.rei.com). For the same price, more serious climbs are offered by Vertical World, 2123 W Elmore St in Fishermen's Terminal (☎206/283-4497, ⓦwww.verticalworld.com), which has 15,000 square feet of space and more than a hundred routes of various degrees of difficulty (Mon, Wed & Fri 10am–10pm, Tues & Thurs 6am–10pm, Sat & Sun 10am–7pm; day-pass $15).

Fitness centers

Working out at the gym is not a big part of the social scene in Seattle, but the frequent rain can make indoor exercise an attractive option for visitors. There are several dozen **fitness centers** in town, many of them Downtown, and with daily or weekly rates often available. If you're looking for particular features, it's worth calling around to the places listed below to see what facilities each offers. If you belong to a gym in your hometown, check to see if your club has a member-swap deal with any Seattle club before you leave. The clubs below are centrally located and offer **free passes**, as noted.

Fitness centers and health clubs

24 Hour Fitness 1827 Yale St, just off I-5, Downtown ☎206/624-0651, ⓦwww.24hourfitness.com. Ten-day pass.

Allstar Fitness 700 Fifth Ave, 14th Floor, Downtown ☎206/343-4692, ⓦwww.allstarfitness.com. Week-long trial membership.

Gold's Gym 825 Pike St, in the Convention Center ☎206/583-0640, ⓦwww.goldsgym.com; also in the Broadway Market, 401 Broadway Ave, Capitol Hill ☎206/322-2322. Day pass.

Pro-Robics 1530 Queen Anne Ave N, Queen Anne ☎206/283-2303, ⓦwww.prorobics.com. Day pass.

Pure Fitness 808 Second Ave, Pioneer Square ☎206/224-9000, ⓦwww.purefitnessclubs.com. Seven-day pass.

Washington Athletic Club 1325 6th Ave, Downtown ☎206/622-7900, ⓦwww.wac.net. $13 for daily guest pass, but many reciprocal memberships at international clubs.

⑱

Kids' Seattle

A lthough Seattle has countless pensioners and families without children, the city is nonetheless very **kid-friendly**: the presence of youngsters in public places and attractions is not just tolerated, it's often encouraged. In Seattle Center, for example, there's a children's theater and museum, an annual children's festival, kid-sized eating tables at the Center House's food court, and a section on the same floor in which the tots can zoom around in toy cars. Seattle's family focus is also enhanced by good public parks and other sites in which to burn off excess energy. One of the best places for doing so is the **International Fountain** (see p.87) at the Seattle Center, which lets kids cool down amid all their antics.

Museums

Not surprisingly, the **Seattle Children's Museum** in the Seattle Center (Mon–Fri 10am–5pm, Sat & Sun 10am–6pm; $7.50 for all ages; ☎206/441-1768, ⓦwww.thechildrensmuseum.org) caters to kids' interests above all else; see p.87 for a full account. Some of Seattle's other top museums – particularly the **Pacific Science Center** in the Seattle Center (p.81), the **Burke Museum** (p.86) in the U District, and the **Museum of Flight** in Tukwila (see p.135) – host a constant parade of boisterous children and school groups, making these institutions feel more like playgrounds, often to the chagrin of adults. Other kid-oriented attractions include the **Seattle Aquarium** at Pier 59 (see p.54) and the **Woodland Park Zoo** (see p.122), both of which balance creature exhibits with programs and discussions to put them in context; the instruments and classical music on exhibit at Benaroya Hall's **Soundbridge** (p.57); and the somewhat less appealing nautical machinery of the **Odyssey Maritime Discovery Center** (see p.55). Further out, the **Museum of Doll Art** in Bellevue (see p.133) and the **Children's Museum of Tacoma** (see p.239) both offer plenty of vivid amusements for the kids, with the former being quite entrancing for adults as well. Finally, the **Seattle Art Museum** (p.56) hosts programs geared at helping kids understand the art on display, and in 2007 will be opening the **Olympic Sculpture Park** (p.55), no doubt inviting questions from the tots about all the strange and wondrous shapes on view.

Parks

Seattle has many **parks** good for all ages and plenty of playground space for toddlers as well. **Green Lake** (see p.123) is the best multipurpose choice of the

214

lot, with an attractive lake, bike path, and public pool, plus boat and cycle rentals available nearby. The most creative option is **Gasworks Park** (p.122), whose "playbarn" is a riot of multicolored pipes and engines; the park's windy hill is also the most popular place in the city to fly **kites** – though its eerie industrial ruins are thankfully off-limits. The much larger **Discovery Park** (see p.109) has spacious fields that are also well-suited for kite-flying and other pastimes, plus a curious onsite fort with old military castoffs that may interest the youngsters. The same is true for such far-flung military-oriented state parks as **Fort Casey** and **Fort Ebey** (p.259) on Whidbey Island.

For a less well-trodden urban park that still offers green space, lakeside views, and a large playground, head for **Seward Park** (p.130), near the southern end of Lake Washington, or, for a singular curiosity that will surely enchant both children and adults, visit **Magnuson Park** (see p.124) for a look at, and a listen to, the strangely harmonious *Sound Garden* kinetic sculpture. Also excellent are the contiguous natural spaces of the **Washington Park Arboretum** (p.98) – which also hosts a fine Japanese Garden – and the marshy trails that run across **Foster Island** (p.100). The **Seattle Parks and Recreation Department** (☎206/684-4075, ⓦ www.seattle.gov/parks) often sponsors kids' activities, especially in summer, from arts-and-crafts to nature walks.

Further away in Bellevue, and usually overlooked by visitors, there's pleasant **Mercer Slough Nature Park** (see p.134), with trails through more than 300 acres of wetlands. Also in Bellevue, the 150 acres of **Kelsey Creek Farm**, in Kelsey Creek Park (daily 9.30am–4.30pm; ☎425/452-7688, ⓦwww.ci.bellevue.wa.us/parks), features ponies, pigs, goats, and sheep that kids can see close up, as well as an old 1888 log cabin that might appeal to older children.

△ Museum of Doll Art

⑲

Beaches and waterways

Seattle does have a few **beaches**, but these are fairly narrow and the water is usually too cold for a dip; there are plenty of athletic activities you can take part in, though, at sites from **Alki Beach** (see p.137) in West Seattle, to **Golden Gardens** (p.115) further north. The best place for family swimming is the outdoor saltwater **Colman Pool** (p.139), though it's open only in the summer. For cheap family thrills, nothing beats aimless cruising around the Puget Sound on the public-transit **ferries**, especially if weather permits, as there's open-air seating on the top deck. The scenic and quick (about a half-hour each way) Seattle–Bainbridge route is the best option, though the Downtown Seattle–Vashon link has the added advantage of being a passenger-only route (see p.34 for more information on ferries). Likewise, watching the boats bob up and down at the **Hiram M. Chittenden Locks** in Ballard (see p.112) is a crowd-pleaser, although children may get bored if the ship traffic is slow. If that's the case, take them to the adjacent **fish ladder**, where they can watch salmon wriggle their way through the Ship Canal. You should check the migration schedule at the locks beforehand, though, to make sure the ladder won't be empty.

Theater and festivals

The **Seattle Children's Theatre**, in the Seattle Center (see p.86), offers half a dozen mainstage productions each year, aimed at a variety of age levels. It's much more engrossing than you might expect, with dramatic adaptations of the works of Roald Dahl (*James and the Giant Peach*, *Matilda*) and Maurice Sendak (*Where the Wild Things Are*), among others. For something more unusual, there's the **Northwest Puppet Center**, north of the U District at 9123 15th Ave NE ($9.50, children $7.50; ☎206/523-2579, ⓦwww.nwpuppet.org); their half-dozen or so shows each season have a multicultural slant that can cover Hindu epics and African-American folktales and various internationally themed shows. They also put on a rather bizarre **marionette opera** ($22) and a seasonal performance of the **Nutcracker** – but if you really want to treat the kids to this December spectacular, Tchaikovsky's masterwork is most vividly on view at the **Paramount Theatre** (p.188), with sets and costumes originally designed by Maurice Sendak. Indeed, the Paramount regularly puts on child-oriented productions, as does the **Stone Soup Theatre** (p.190) in Wallingford. Older kids may enjoy the plays adapted from books like *Little Women* staged at the **Book-It Repertory Theatre** (p.189), which is based out of the Seattle Center; check their respective websites for details. Lastly, the **Seattle International Children's Festival** (☎206/684-7346, ⓦwww.seattleinternational.org) in May has live music, dance, and theater performances also at the Seattle Center.

Shops for kids

Seattle **museum shops** usually have worthwhile kids' sections; the Woodland Park Zoo's gift shop is particularly good, with a lot of wildlife/ecology-oriented books, games, and toys, as is that of the Pacific Science Center. Additionally, **Pike Place Market** (see p.49) is a fail-safe alternative when the kids are restless and you're running short on ideas; there's plenty of food and snacks to replenish the blood-sugar level, plus unpredictable live entertainment including magicians, mimes, and the like – not to mention the always-popular allure of **fish-throwing**.

All for Kids Books & Music 2900 NE Blakeley St, University District ☎206/526-2768, ⓦwww .allforkidsbooks.com. Provides a wide selection of good reading material for kids of varying ages.

Musik Nest 16625 Redmond Way, Redmond ☎425/427-0984, ⓦwww.themusiknest.com. Specializes in puppets of various sizes and musical instruments – to get budding drummers pounding away before they even learn to walk.

Schmancy 1930 Second Ave, Belltown ☎206/728-8008, ⓦwww.schmancytoys.com. An oddball emporium of fun and strange toys: stuffed donuts, friendly trolls and goofy aliens only provide a hint of what's on display. Connected to the fine jewelry store Fancy (see p.222).

Science, Art & More 6417 Roosevelt Way NE ☎206/524-3795, ⓦwww.scienceartandmore .com. Just north of the U District, this store offers quality educational toys illustrating basic concepts in biology, nature, geology, and so on.

Teri's Toybox 420 Main St, Edmonds ☎425/774-3190. Eschews the usual mass-market products for puzzles, creative games, and well-designed clothes, all with a unique or colorful bent.

Top Ten Toys 104 N 85th St, Greenwood ☎206/782-0098, ⓦwww.toptentoys.com. One of Seattle's best spots for acquiring creative amusements, including model trains, colorful dolls and puppets, musical instruments, and inventive board games.

20

Shops and galleries

When it comes to **shopping** in Seattle, you'll probably first be drawn to the glut of centrally located, showy **malls** Downtown, though the stores there are nothing special or unique – mainly chain outlets and the like – and the prices offer few bargains. On the other hand, Seattle's a good place for alternative shopping in all its forms: finding **thrift items**, searching through the racks at **vintage-** and **used-clothing stores**, and hunting for a treasure in a **junk emporium**. The streets of Ballard, Greenwood, Capitol Hill, and Fremont offer the best array of these inspired castoffs.

Seattle has acquired the reputation of a musical capital of sorts since the explosion of alternative rock fifteen years ago, but most of its great **record stores** are now gone, and much of what remains is actually quite ordinary, except for a few hole-in-the-wall places that the true aficionados frequent. **Bookstores** are significantly better, with a good range of establishments from arty specialty shops to clearinghouses for used and remaindered titles. The best book and record stores are generally found in the U District and Capitol Hill.

Most **galleries'** artworks are priced well beyond the reach of the average consumer, but they do form an important adjunct to the Northwest modern-art scene. Their appeal is not limited to collectors, either: anyone with a strong interest in art, particularly **glasswork**, should check them out – and, considering their concentration Downtown, a dozen or more galleries can easily be covered in the same day.

Books

Amid the familiar large **bookstore** chains in Seattle are a smattering of small neighborhood outlets and established specialty shops; most of the used bookstores are comfortably funky and not without their charm – though many have been going under in the wake of Internet sales from larger companies, making Seattle a little less reader-friendly, at least on foot, than it was before the advent of the Web. As a complement to its stores, Seattle excels in **author readings**, especially at Elliott Bay Book Company (see p.219), which has one of the busiest event schedules of any bookstore in the nation; check the local papers and weeklies for listings there and elsewhere.

General

Bailey-Coy Books 414 Broadway E, Capitol Hill ☎206/323-8842. Capitol Hill's top bookstore, with strong gay and lesbian sections, a nice assortment of alternative and left-leaning publications, and a respectable array of art books. The key here is the well-considered selection – you won't have to wade through a bunch of junk to find the good stuff.

Barnes & Noble 600 Pine St, Pacific Place mall, Downtown ☎206/264-0156, ⓦwww.bn.com. The main Seattle branch of the country's biggest chain bookseller, copiously stocked with mainstream fiction and nonfiction. Also another major branch in the University Village Mall, 25th Ave NE and NE 45th St, University District (☎206/517-4107), and countless others in the suburbs.

Borders 1501 Fourth Ave, Downtown ☎206/622-4599, ⓦwww.bordersstores.com. Like Barnes & Noble, a familiar book-retailing giant, with a large selection in all subjects. The corporate atmosphere is eased somewhat with an upstairs café, book readings, and occasional live music. Eight other suburban stores.

Elliott Bay Book Company First Ave S and S Main St, Pioneer Square ☎206/624-6600, ⓦwww.elliottbaybook.com. The best general bookstore in Seattle, with a huge, alternative-leaning selection, a bargain balcony of discounted books (with import volumes and titles you won't see at remainder outlets, and author readings on a near-daily basis, a fine downstairs café, and a decent used selection. See full review, p.69.

Tower Books 701 Fifth Ave N, Queen Anne ☎206/283-4456. A sterile supermarket atmosphere, but the offerings are pretty good, with strong sections on music, graphic novels, comics, and area history and guidebooks. Open every day until midnight.

University Book Store 4326 University Way NE ☎206/634-3400, ⓦwww.bookstore.washington.edu. Despite its institutional odor and department-store ambiance, this is either the best or second-best store (after Elliott Bay) in Seattle. The stock at this massive multi-floor outlet is superb in all categories, from popular to scholarly; also presents an impressive schedule of author readings.

Discount and secondhand

Arundel Books 1001 First Ave, Downtown ☎206/624-4442, ⓦwww.arundelbookstores.com. Centrally located branch of an esteemed LA bookseller, which has a good general inventory on most topics, but is particularly strong on literature, the arts and rare items.

Collins Books 1211 E Denny Way, Capitol Hill ☎206/323-3999, ⓦwww.collinsbooks.com. A valuable selection of mostly non-fiction titles, including selections on history, psychology, medicine, and anthropology (as well as the arts), with a bent toward antiquariana, too.

Half Price Books 15600 NE 8th St, Bellevue ☎425/747-6616, ⓦwww.halfpricebooks.com. National chain that offers a huge selection of remaindered and used books in all categories, as well as a section of half-price, recently published hardbacks and a substantial assortment of used or remaindered CDs, LPs, and cassettes. Three other, more distant suburban stores in the region.

Horizon Books 425 15th Ave E, Capitol Hill ☎206/329-3586. History, politics, fiction, and drama are the focus at this local favorite, which is a good choice for finding obscure titles you might not stumble across elsewhere. Also at 8570 Greenwood Ave N, Greenwood ☎206/781-4680.

Magus Books 1408 NE 42nd St, University District ☎206/633-1800. Has the best used selection in the U District, especially strong in fiction and literature, art, and history, and a helpful staff you can find behind the piles of unprocessed new arrivals.

Seattle Book Center 3530 Stone Way N, Fremont ☎1-866/547-7870, ⓦwww.seattlebookcenter.com. Broad-ranging categories in fiction and nonfiction at this solid Fremont dealer, as well as local history and kids' books.

Twice Sold Tales 905 E John St, Capitol Hill ☎206/324-2421. Offers deep shelves in all subjects, especially fiction, and a comfortable ambiance (in spite of signs reading "If you are an asshole, stay out of our store!"). Open until 1am, and all night on Fridays. There's also a less well-stocked location (with shorter hours) at 1309 NE 45th Ave, University District (☎206/545-4226).

Wessel and Lieberman 208 First Ave S, Pioneer Square ☎1-888/383-3631 or 206/682-3545, ⓦwww.wlbooks.com. Venerable dealer in used and rare items, with the focus on regional history and lore, poetry and literature, and the liberal and fine arts. Worth a visit alone for its solid antiquarian selection.

Specialist

Cinema Books 4753 Roosevelt Way NE, University District ☎206/547-7667. The premiere film bookstore in the Northwest, loaded with material on classic, foreign and art films, and even Hollywood blockbusters; also carries posters and stills.

East West Bookshop 6500 Roosevelt Way NE, University District ☎206/523-3726, ⓦwww.eastwestbookshop.com. New Age bookstore that also peddles crystals, meditation supplies, and incense. Hosts programs and classes on meditation and spirituality.

Flora & Fauna Books 121 First Ave S, Pioneer Square ☎206/623-4727, ⓦwww.ffbooks.net. The life and natural sciences are the main reason to come to this shop, good for its picture-books and scientific tomes on biology, botany, and evolution, as well as fossils and geology.

Left Bank Books 92 Pike St, Downtown ☎206/622-0195, ⓦwww.leftbankbooks.com. The best left-wing bookstore in town, a nonprofit Pike Place Market collective with strong political, historical, feminist, gay, and literature sections, as well as a good rack of underground zines.

Metsker Maps 1511 Pine St, Downtown ☎206/623-8747, ⓦwww.metskers.com. Recently relocated to Pike Place Market, but still the best place to go in town for maps, including hiking and nature trails throughout Puget Sound; there's a quality selection of travel books, too.

The Mountaineers ☎206/223-6303, ⓦwww.mountaineersbooks.org. An online dealer in nature-oriented travel books, mountaineering literature, and outdoor guides; check website for information on author lectures and public discussions throughout the city on those topics.

Old Seattle Paperworks 1514 Pike Place, Downtown ☎206/623-2870. The emphasis at this market shop is on quirky and bizarre note cards and posters – particularly the latter, chock full of images of artists and art movements from the twentieth century, forgotten ads for soap and soda, and glaring propaganda in brash colors.

Open Books 2414 N 45th St, Wallingford ☎206/633-0811, ⓦwww.openpoetrybooks.com. One of the very few poetry-only bookstores in the US, carrying some six thousand new, used, and out-of-print titles. Also hosts frequent readings, and is known for its inspired, discriminating selection of top-notch poets.

Peter Miller Books 1930 First Ave, Belltown ☎206/441-4114, ⓦwww.petermiller.com. Not a good place to come if you're looking for a bargain, but still quite appealing for its superlative collection of art, architecture, graphic design, and photography books – many of them glossy, sizable volumes that can easily run in the $100+ range.

Recollection Books 6512 Roosevelt Ave NE, University District ☎206/783-1686, ⓦwww.eskimo.com/~recall. The place to go if you're

hunting for tales of the Chicago Seven, the writings of Malcolm X, or the finer points of electric blues. Leans toward leftist and black history, musical culture (and counterculture), and hobbies like gardening and fishing.

Revolution Books 1833 Nagle Place, Capitol Hill ☎206/325-7415. Small store a block from Broadway with a leftist bent, its shelves stocked with various tracts on Marxism, radical environmentalism, anti-consumerism, and so on.

Seaocean Book Berth 3534 Stone Way N, Fremont ☎206/675-9020, ⓦwww.seaoceanbooks.com. The sea in all its glory is the focus here, whether you're into ships, shipwreck diving, nautical tales and lore, naval battles, explorers, or oceanography.

Seattle Art Museum Store 100 University St, Downtown ☎206/654-3120. Small but well-stocked store, with interesting art books of all types (many of which are difficult to find elsewhere in the city), as well as a few titles of regional interest on local art, travel, and history.

Seattle Mystery Bookshop 117 Cherry St, Pioneer Square ☎206/587-5737, ⓦwww.seattlemystery.com. Offers a good range of new and used mysteries, true-crime tales, and thrillers, in both hardcover and paperback.

Wide World Books & Maps 4411 Wallingford Ave N, Wallingford ☎206/634-3453, ⓦwww.travelbooksandmaps.com. Seattle's only exclusively travel-oriented bookseller, with an excellent selection of guides, travel literature, maps, and accessories.

Wit's End 4262 Fremont Ave N, Fremont ☎206/547-2330, ⓦwww.booksatoz.com/witsend. Fremont dealer in coffee and tea, as well as worthwhile liberal-arts titles in several categories – history, sociology, fiction, kids' books, and native cultures.

Newsstands

Broadway News 204 Broadway E, Capitol Hill ☎206/324-7323. Vends thousands of magazines and newspapers, ranging from mainstream to ultra-alternative. Also in Fremont, as the Fremont News, at 3416 Fremont Ave N (☎206/633-0731).

Bulldog News 4208 University Way NE, University District ☎206/632-NEWS, ⓦwww.bulldognews.com. Perhaps the best of Seattle's newsstands, also serving coffee and baked goods. A neighborhood fixture that's a prime spot for hanging out.

First & Pike News 93 Pike St in Pike Place Market ☎ 206/624-0140. A great source for international and out-of-town newspapers, in an irresistible location on the market's most prominent corner, at First Ave.

Clothing and accessories

While Seattle doesn't offer too many designer boutiques where it's worth dropping a wad, the city is a great place for **secondhand** and **vintage** clothes shopping. Places like Capitol Hill and Fremont are the obvious choices for this type of merchandise, just as Pike Place Market is the place to pick out wearable crafts like jewelry and tie-dyed shirts.

New

Barneys New York 1420 Fifth Ave, Downtown ☎ 206/622-6300. If for some reason you're struck by the need to spend a huge amount of money at this national emporium for upscale suits, dresses and shoes, Seattle has a branch – naturally, on 5th Avenue.

Betsey Johnson 1429 Fifth Ave, Downtown ☎ 206/624-2887. Local outpost of the designer women's chain, whose clothes are known for their vivid color and sometimes garish designs.

Byrnie Utz Hats 310 Union St, Downtown ☎ 206/623-0233. Longstanding haberdashery favorite and a good spot for a chapeau, with one of the largest selections of men's and women's hats and caps on the West Coast.

Cibola 1501 Pike Place no.521, Pike Place Market ☎ 206/682-5640, ⊛ www.geocities .com/cibolaclothing. Natural-fiber clothing and accessories for men and women, with an earthy flair and neo-hippie style.

John Fluevog Shoes 205 Pine St, Downtown ☎ 206/441-1065, ⊛ www.fluevog.com. One of the premier stops for footwear with a hip, youthful bent – the perfect look for a 22-year-old with a pocketful of credit cards. Located on the outskirts of Pike Place Market.

Maggie's Shoes 1927 First Ave, Pike Place Market ☎ 206/728-5837. Italian shoes and bags for men and women. A new collection is handpicked from Milan every season, and the prices are lower than you may find for comparable items in bigger cities.

Metro 231 Broadway E, Capitol Hill ☎ 206/726-7978. Not for the faint of heart, but perhaps a required stop if you're doing some serious clubbing. Loaded with the likes of lace body-stockings, vinyl dresses and masks, kick-ass funk boots, and, of course, leather in all its forms.

Nordstrom Rack 1601 Second Ave, Downtown ☎ 206/448-8522, ⊛ www.nordstrom.com. Features many of the same designers found in Nordstrom's main shopping center a few blocks away (see p.222), but with prices slashed by 30–75 percent. Often has clearance or end-of-the-season deals – prepare to fend off the hordes.

Pendleton Northwest 1313 Fourth Ave, Downtown ☎ 206/682-4430, ⊛ www.nwpendleton .com. All kinds of thick wool clothing and blankets, much of it handcrafted in a unique style and made in the eponymous Oregon town. Also in Tacoma at the Washington State History Museum, 1911 Pacific Ave (☎ 1-800/593-6773).

Rockin' Betty's 113 Broadway E, Capitol Hill ☎ 206/709-8821. The pinnacle of hip, cheap, and sexy, this affordable boutique is aimed at serious club kids, with funky platform shoes, cheesy t-shirts, and quirky plastic purses and accessories.

Trendy Wendy 211 Broadway E, Capitol Hill ☎ 206/322-6642. A good spot to pick up bargain-priced designer duds and quality lesser-known labels, all in the range of $30–80. Solid selection of women's attire, jewelry, and accessories.

20

▽ Trendy Wendy

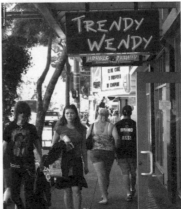

Used and thrift

Atlas Clothing 1515 Broadway E, Capitol Hill ☏ 206/323-0960. Retro-chic in spades, stuffed with gear that wouldn't look out of place at a 1970s disco or a 1980s new wave concert. Has everything from checkerboard shirts to neon pants, with an especially smart set of sneakers.

Buffalo Exchange 4530 University Way NE, University District ☏ 206/545-0175, ⓦ www .buffaloexchange.com. Seattle branch of the vintage clothing chain, which has stores throughout the West; good for shoes, accessories, and interesting castoff dresses and shirts.

Fancy 1932 2nd Ave, Belltown ☏ 206/443-4621, ⓦ www.fancyjewels.com. An essential spot for anyone into cool and unique jewelry (and money to spend on it): rocket-shaped earrings, mood and "space" rings, necklaces and bracelets with bizarre slogans, and much more.

Fritzi Ritz 750 N 34th St ☏ 206/633-0929. The most flamboyant of the Fremont used-clothing outlets. Its old-fangled duds – everything from swanky dresses to bowling shirts – are appropriately stylish or kitschy, and labeled by the era from which they hail.

Isadora's Antique Clothing 1915 First Ave, Downtown ☏ 206/441-7711, ⓦ www.isadoras .com. Vintage clothing for men and women

spanning the 1880s to the 1950s. Strong in suits from the 1940s and 1950s, as well as old-fashioned evening gowns and tuxedos.

Le Frock 317 E Pine St, Capitol Hill ☏ 206/623-5339, ⓦ www.lefrockonline.com. Despite the tongue-in-cheek name, this is an excellent spot for a stylish array of vintage attire (with truly classy dresses and suits), as well as current designer labels at knocked-down prices.

Pretty Parlor 6729 Greenwood Ave N, Greenwood ☏ 206/789-8788, ⓦ www.prettyparlor .com. Zingy, eye-opening items that'll make you feel comfy at a retro-cocktail scene or a postmodern go-go. Fun and stylish clothes from the last five decades, as well as contemporary, handcrafted items.

Red Light 4560 University Way NE, University District ☏ 206/545-4044, ⓦ www.redlightvintage.com. A hip hangout, as well as the biggest vintage-clothing store in Seattle, though not very discriminating, selling everything from bell bottoms and skatewear to leg warmers and old Nike shoes. Also in Capitol Hill at 312 Broadway E (☏ 206/329-2200).

Vintage Chick 303 E Pine St, Capitol Hill ☏ 206/625-9800, ⓦ www.vintagechick.com. Funky, chic, and off-kilter fashion for men and women at this high-profile retro-vendor. Decent coats and accessories, too.

Department stores and malls

Downtown Seattle's compact cluster of **department stores** and **malls** seems unremarkable to everyone but longtime residents, who remember a time not so long ago when there were few such behemoths in the Business District. The center of the city's retail universe is Nordstrom, which sits on a huge lot in the Downtown core. The venerable department store draws hordes of regional consumers, many of whom spill over into the area's shops, restaurants, and parks. For numerous tourists, it's hard to resist making this the first stop in town.

Department stores

Bon-Macy's Third Ave and Pine St, Downtown ☏ 206/506-6000, ⓦ www.macys .com. More renowned for versatility than originality, this vendor (formerly the Bon Marché, now hybridized with the giant Macy's chain) is nonetheless one of the better department stores in the city center, with a full range of affordable clothes and merchandise.

Eddie Bauer 1330 Fifth Ave, Downtown ☏ 206/622-2766, ⓦ www.eddiebauer.com. The original flagship store of the outdoor clothing and equipment chain, established in the 1920s. Still focuses on outdoor gear, but offers plenty of other kinds of clothes as well.

Nordstrom 500 Pine St, Downtown ☏ 206/628-2111, ⓦ www.nordstrom.com. Like it or not, this is the first place in Seattle most tourists visit after Pike Place Market. This multifloor giant has extensive women's clothing and shoe sections, and a reputation for good customer service. Discounted stock is available a few blocks away, at Nordstrom Rack (see p.221). **REI 222 Yale Ave N, just off I-5** ☎206/223-1944, ⓦ www.rei.com/stores/seattle. An essential stop for outdoorsy types, this massive complex is loaded with clothing, books, and backpacks; it also has outdoor test trails for the mountain bikes on sale, a simulated rain room for testing rain gear, in-store how-to clinics, and a waterfall by the entrance. If the hordes of shoppers grow tiresome, take a break by climbing up the store's famed "Pinnacle" rock wall (see p.212).

Malls

Bellevue Square Bellevue Way between NE Fourth and NE Eighth aves, Bellevue ☎425/454-2431, ⓦ www.bellevuesquare.com. More than two hundred shops, including branches of Nordstrom and Macy's department stores, restaurants, toy stores, and much more. Little to distinguish it from any other super-mall, though.

Broadway Market 401 Broadway E, Capitol Hill ☎206/322-1610, ⓦ www.broadwaymarket.com. Smaller-scaled with more neighborhood vendors than the Downtown malls, but has fallen on hard times lately. Scattered mix of beauty and fitness centers, fast-food and sit-down restaurants, and a half-price ticket outlet.

Crossroads NE 8th St and 156th Ave, Bellevue ☎425/644-1111, ⓦ www.crossroadsbellevue .com. Nearly a hundred restaurants, stores, newsstands, coffeeshops, and fast-food outlets in a mall three miles east of Bellevue Square. Something of a community center

(the frequent site of city festivals and the like) and occupying several square blocks, it's a sizable complex that's easy to get lost in. **Northgate Mall 401 NE Northgate Way, North Seattle** ☎206/362-4777. Massive and some-what depressing, this monster complex is five miles north of town and draws hardcore shoppers to Macy's, JC Penney, and Nord-storm, as well as chain retailers like Ann Taylor, Gap, and Express.

Pacific Place 600 Pine St ☎206/405-2655, ⓦ www.pacificplaceseattle.com. Another big mall with the familiar array of retailers on three levels, plus a sky-bridge to the adja-cent Nordstrom (see p.222).

University Village NE 45th St at 21st Ave NE, U District ☎206/523-0622, ⓦ www.uvillage.com. A mall complex housing the usual suspects – Gap, Eddie Bauer, Barnes & Noble, Pottery Barn, etc – but with the advantage of being in a favorable location near the university, and built around an open-air site for some fresh, non-stagnant air.

Uwajimaya 519 Sixth Ave S, International District ☎206/624-6248, ⓦ www.uwajimaya.com. Most of the first floor is given over to Asian foodstuffs, while most of the second floor is occupied by Kinokuniya Books, one of Japan's largest book chains. Mixed in are electrical appliances, dishes, and five-and-dime knickknacks. Definitely worth a browse.

Westlake Center Pine St between Fourth and Fifth aves, Downtown ☎206/467-3044, ⓦ www .westlakecenter.com. In many ways unavoid-able, smack in the center of Downtown, Westlake Center is big and crowded, with four levels and more than eighty shops; few are very original, though Fireworks (see p.227) provides an interesting diversion.

Food and drink

Options for **food and drink** include the standard array of supermarket chains as well as friendlier local businesses that are more likely to have a less predictable selection of goods. **Pike Place Market** is the biggest and most central spot for fruit, vegetables, seafood, bread and pastries, and so on; every week **Organic Wednesdays** (June–Oct 10am–4pm, also **Summer Sundays** June–Sept 10am–4pm) offers a nice selection of organically grown produce.

For a breath of fresh air with your food shopping, small open-air **farmers' markets** are held in the warmer months in places like Olympia (see p.244) and Bainbridge Island (see p.250). In town, the best of these are held in the U District, at the northwest corner of 50th and University (late-May to early-Nov Sat 9am–2pm), and in Ballard, NW 56th Street at 22nd Avenue NW (May–Nov

Sun 10am–4pm; Dec–Mar at 5330 Ballard Ave, Sun 11am–3pm; Ⓦwww .fremontmarket.com/ballard).

If you want to take home some of Seattle's trademark beverage, the chain **coffee** outlets all sell their java in handy bags – though you may be better off sticking to the local brews, of which Vivace is arguably the best; it's sold throughout the city, not only at the eponymous café (see p.155).

Delis and groceries

DeLaurenti Specialty Food and Wine 1435 Pike St, in Pike Place Market ☎206/622-0141, Ⓦwww.delaurenti.com. An excellent specialty food store, with luscious Mediterranean cheeses and meats, baked and deli goods, and wines.

PCC Natural Markets 600 N 34th St, Fremont ☎206/632-6811, Ⓦwww.pccnaturalmarkets .com. Local health and wholefood chain, administered by the Puget Consumers Co-op; you don't have to be a member to shop here, although the prices are lower if you are. Other branches at 7504 Aurora Ave N, Green Lake (☎206/525-3586), and 2749 California Ave SW, West Seattle (☎206/937-8481), plus four others further out.

QFC 1401 Broadway Ave E, Capitol Hill ☎206/860-3818, Ⓦwww.qfconline.com. Omnipresent, centrally located supermarket chain that's a cut above most others in quality. Other locations at 416 15th Ave E, Capitol Hill (☎206/322-5020), and 100 Republican St, near the Seattle Center (☎206/285-5491).

Roxy's Deli 462 N 36th St, Fremont ☎206/632-3963, Ⓦwww.hotpastrami.com. You can tell from the website name what this place is all about – not to mention bagels, omelettes, lox, Reubens, and the rest of your deli faves. As close to Gotham as you're going to get in Seattle.

Tan Dinh Deli 1212 S Main St, International District ☎206/726-9990. An authentic, lip-smacking joint that only the locals seem to know about, probably because it's in a strip mall. Still, a solid choice for noshing on egg rolls, soups, and noodle dishes, as well as picking up a host of Asian desserts and spices, for not more than a few bucks.

Uwajimaya 519 Sixth Ave S, International District ☎206/624-6248, Ⓦwww.uwajimaya .com. The largest Asian supermarket in the Northwest, where you can buy everything from noodles and sushi to teas and teapots. See full review, p.69.

Vios Cafe and Marketplace 903 19th Ave E, Capitol Hill ☎206/329-3236. A great place to fill up on cheap, delicious Greek and Mediterranean fare – whether from the grocery or the deli – including tasty lamb burgers and baguette sandwiches, as well as good salads and desserts.

Beverages and spirits

Bottleworks 1710 N 45th St no 3, Wallingford ☎206/633-BIER, Ⓦwww .bottleworks.com. The pinnacle of Seattle beer stores, with more than four hundred brews from twenty different countries. Especially strong for regional Northwest beers.

Caffè Appassionato 4001 21st Ave W, near Magnolia ☎206/281-8040, Ⓦwww.caffeappassionato.com. Specialty gourmet coffee company that sells about thirty varieties from different regions of the world. Also at 4518 University Way NE, University District ☎206/545-4865.

Champion Wine Cellars 108 Denny Way, near the Seattle Center ☎206/284-8306, Ⓦwww .championwinecellars.com. Offers a good variety of wines from Washington State and around the world.

Good Coffee Company 818 Post Ave, Downtown ☎206/622-5602. Coffee-seller near Pike Place Market whose estimable java is almost as appealing as its collection of vintage coffeemakers on display.

Lighthouse Roasters 400 N 43rd St, Fremont ☎206/634-3140, Ⓦwww.lighthouseroasters .com. Local favorite for fine house coffee and espresso, including the savory Captain Bert's Breakfast Blend, all available to take home or for guzzling on the spot.

Teacup 2207 Queen Anne Ave N, Queen Anne ☎206/283-5931, Ⓦseattleteacup.com. Stocks more than a hundred varieties of tea in bulk and also packed with tea-serving paraphernalia. Offers classes and tastings on weekend afternoons.

Washington State Liquor 1201 Second Ave, Downtown ☎206/464-7910. The most centrally located of all the state-controlled liquor stores, which are the only ones allowed to sell spirits. There's a fairly predictable, high-priced selection of booze.

Gourmet supermarkets

ChefShop 305 9th Ave N, Lake Union ☎206/286-9988, ⓦchefshop.com. An Internet food company's retail store, carrying a wide range of upscale food choices, from Continental chocolates and rare mushrooms to spicy herbs and chutneys, plus countless varieties of rice, pasta, and sweets.

Metropolitan Market 2320 42nd Ave SW, West Seattle ☎206/937-0551, ⓦwww.metropolitan-market.com. A gourmet superstore with one of the biggest and best selections in town – a 24-hour emporium

of French cheeses, exotic meats, esoteric cookware, and just about anything else you need for whipping up a stylish and expensive feast.

Trader Joe's 112 W Galer St, Queen Anne ☎206/378-5536, ⓦ www.traderjoes.com. The top choice for affordable gourmet grub, this West Coast–based chain peddles a nice assortment of international entrees, cookies, and soups, along with its own branded wines, pastas, sauces, and even truffles. The most centrally located of six branches in the Seattle Metro area.

Whole Foods 1026 NE 64th St, University District ☎206/985-1500, ⓦwww.wholefoods.com. The local entry in a gourmet chain that's good for quality products at midrange prices, including bulk grains and cereals, copious vegetarian selections, a sizable array of fresh organic produce, free-range chicken, and hormone-free beef.

Music

You'll have no trouble finding current major-label **music** releases and prominent indie recordings in Seattle – but the range of imports, reissues, out-of-print LPs, and non-rock music is somewhat disappointing, with some of the better stores from the glory days closing in the last decade or so. However, some of the Portland stores to which Seattle music fans previously made a three-hour trek (eg, Everyday Music) have opened branches here, thus broadening the local LP and CD selection. Beyond this, there are some specialty stores with unusual concentrations if you've got time to browse, particularly if you're into vinyl, old-school punk, or dance music.

General

Cellophane Square 4538 University Way NE, University District ☎206/634-2280. A fairly good all-around rock store with many new and used CDs. Low on exotic items, but well-stocked with current indies. Also carries soul, hip-hop, folk, blues, reggae, and world music.

Easy Street Records 20 W Mercer St, Queen Anne ☎206/691-3279, ⓦwww.easystreetonline.com. One of the city's top choices for alternative music (CDs and LPs), this sizable store also features concert gear and in-store performances, which are potentially excellent in a music city like Seattle. Well-known for its similarly indie-minded branch in West Seattle, 4559 California St SW (☎206/938-EASY), with its own café.

Everyday Music 112 Broadway Ave E, Capitol Hill ☎206/568-3321. One of the essential

choices for used music, with plenty of space, an eclectic selection, and loads of racks featuring all genres. Not much atmosphere, but if you find that long lost record, who cares?

Sonic Boom Records 3414 Fremont Ave N, Fremont ☎206/547-2666, ⓦwww.sonicboomrecords.com. Top-notch favorite for indies, focusing on national groups and rising local talent; there's both vinyl and CDs, along with in-store performances

▽ Sonic Boom Records

and frequent appearances by area musicians. Also at 2209 NW Market St, Ballard (☎206/297-2666), and a brand-new location in Capitol Hill at 514 15th Ave E (☎206/568-BOOM).

Tower Records 701 Fifth Ave N, Queen Anne ☎206/283-4456, ⓦwww.towerrecords.com. If you've gotta have that new Coldplay CD as soon as it's out, this chain will have it, along with just about every major-label release and many prominent indie ones. Otherwise, it's only recommended for its wide range of music magazines. Another branch in the U District at 4518 University Way NE (☎206/632-1187).

Specialty and LPs

Bop Street 5519 Ballard Ave NW, Ballard ☎206/297-2232. Features a very considerable stockpile of LPs (33 1/3, 78s, and some CDs): vintage rock, soul, jazz, and novelty. The warehouse atmosphere may not be too inviting, but you can find a hidden gem if you're lucky.

Bud's Jazz Records 102 S Jackson St, Pioneer Square ☎206/628-0445. Though this basement store is a bit cluttered, it's easily the best place to buy jazz in Seattle, with a large section devoted entirely to local practitioners, plus all the big names; there's a solid blues selection too.

Electric Heavyland 252 NE 45th Ave, Wallingford ☎206/545-2800, ⓦwww.electricheavyland.com. Music to thrash by, at this emporium for anything heavy – from grindcore to death metal – with some psychedelia thrown in, too. Also offers a curious onsite art gallery, whose paintings make more sense after you've been moshing all night.

Jive Time 3506 Fremont Ave N ☎206/632-5483, ⓦwww.jivetimerecords.com. A hotspot for vinyl of all kinds – skater punk, free jazz, hillbilly, retro-pop, prog-metal, and more

– with many bargain-bin prices as well as a good selection of rarities. An old-time favorite that, unlike some stores, continues to rock on. Also in Capitol Hill at 411 E Pine St (☎206/329-5168).

MusicWerks 612 E Pine St, Capitol Hill ☎206/320-8933, ⓦwww.musicwerks.com. Pronounce the "w" like a "v" and you're in business: this joint is all about Teutonic thumping and beat-aggression – better-known as goth, darkwave and industrial. Visit in your darkest shade of black.

Singles Going Steady 2219 Second Ave, Belltown ☎206/441-7396. One of the few remaining emblems of the old Belltown, before the yuppies arrived. Offers an extensive collection of vintage and current punk-oriented indie rock, mostly on vinyl. Especially strong on out-of-print/limited-edition seven-inches and punk collectibles.

Sub Pop Mega Mart 1514 Pike Place Market #14 ☎206/652-4356, ⓦwww.subpop.com. Tiny store dedicated to bands on the Sub Pop label, as well as the few indies it distributes. Good for fanzines, books, and Sub Pop posters too.

Wall of Sound 315 E Pine St, Capitol Hill ☎206/441-9880. Well-considered selection of new and used underground CDs and LPs, encompassing world music, experimental, noise/ambient, electronica, dub, jazz, and more, with lots of indies and imports that you can listen to first.

Zion's Gate 1100 E Pike St, Capitol Hill ☎206/568-5446, ⓦwww.zionsgate.com. Sharing space with an art gallery, this small shop specializes in electronica – ragga, dub, house, jungle, and techno; heavy on vinyl, limited-editions, and imports.

Specialty stores

Seattle caters to every interest with its countless **specialty stores**, several of which are well-known for their wide selection of colorful castoffs and eye-popping curiosities. These junk emporia are the highlights of shopping without a purpose or a schedule, and their appeal is typically much more enjoyable and lower-key than the aggressive consumerism of Downtown's shopping malls. Along with these shops, there are also good choices in town for finding everything from kites and condoms to retro–mod furniture and glassworks.

Archie McPhee 2428 NW Market St, Ballard ☎206/297-0240, ⊛www.mcphee .com. Legendary clearinghouse for all kinds of antique junk, novelty trinkets, and cultural detritus, with a heavy emphasis on lounge-lizard and Tiki decor. See p.114 for a full review.

Area 51 401 E Pine St, Capitol Hill ☎206/568-4782. Loaded with ultra-modern furniture, various sleek household items, and plastic doodads from the mid-twentieth century. The prices for these pieces may be steep, but the place – a de facto museum of Bakelite, formica, polyurethane, and neon – easily merits a trip.

Deluxe Junk 601 N 35th St ☎206/634-2733. The most amusing of Fremont's thrift shops demands a look around even if you have no intention of buying anything, with its odd collection of miscellany such as toy electric guitars, old typewriters, leopard-patterned furniture, and truly astounding kitsch. Plus, there's a statue of a lascivious, humanoid French fries box out front.

Filson 1555 Fourth Ave S, Pioneer Square ☎206/622-3147, ⊛www.filson.com. You don't have to be in a grunge band to wear plaid – this is the spot to get the best woolen shirts, parkas, breeches, and rugged gear and accessories for fishing, hunting, and hiking. The store started during the Klondike Gold Rush and the historical displays bear testimony to that heady era.

Fireworks 210 First Ave S, Pioneer Square ☎206/682-9697, ⊛www.fireworksgallery.net. Imaginative assortment of unusual jewelry, hand-painted furniture, glass, ceramics, and prints, as well as novelties like fetching ladybug and frog umbrellas. There are other branches in the malls at University Village, 2625 NE University Village (☎206/527-2858); Bellevue Square, 196 Bellevue Square (☎425/688-0933); and Westlake Center, Downtown (☎206/682-6462).

Fremont Antique Mall 3419 Fremont Place N ☎206/548-9140. No visit to Seattle would be complete without a stop in this sizable underground space stuffed with all manner of treasures and assorted junk: movie posters, Hawaiian shirts, 1970s LPs, Bakelite jewelry, forgotten toys, and many other items too numerous to mention.

Glass Eye Gallery 1902 Post Alley, Pike Place Market ☎206/441-3221, ⊛www.gegallery .com. Unlike the glassworks that you'll see in most galleries, much of what's on sale here is affordable. Small, but rich and lustrous, pieces range from "fireball" marbles to heart pendants with wings (or horns) to kaleidoscopic paperweights and glass icicles.

Goodwinds Kites 3420 Stone Way N, Wallingford ☎206/633-4780, ⊛www.goodwindskites.com. Not just a big selection of kites, but also windsocks, flying toys, and kite-making accessories. Located just a few blocks north of Gasworks Park (see p.122), whose hills are among the most popular kite-flying sites in Seattle.

John's Music Center 4501 Interlake Ave N, Wallingford ☎206/548-0916, ⊛johnsmusic .com. The "Conga Capital of the Northwest" specializes in exotic drums from all over the world, as well as ethnic wind and string instruments.

Re-Soul 5319 Ballard Ave, Ballard ☎206/789-7312, ⊛www.resoul.com. The name's a pun in more ways than one: retro-flavored designer shoes are a big deal at this chic emporium, which also sells modernist antiques and contemporary artisans' work in furniture, glass, jewelry, and assorted geegaws like clocks and bird-feeders. It's all very hip, and expensive.

Scarecrow 5030 Roosevelt Way NE, University District ☎206/524-8554, ⊛www.scarecrow .com. Seattle's best independent video store, with a huge selection of films for rent or purchase. Especially strong on cult items, as well as foreign and art films.

Thriftko 124 N 85th St, Greenwood ☎206/789-5357. Fabled junk emporium where you can find anything from a dingy lampshade to a mohair jacket or an earthenware jug – all for not more than a couple bucks. A spot that's quietly popular with the bohemian set, who come here to snap up retro-chic bargains before they find their way to the bigger-name vintage shops.

Traditions & Beyond 606 Twelfth Ave S, Pioneer Square ☎206/621-0655, ⊛traditionsandbeyond .org. Intriguing shop specializing in both traditional and contemporary Native American arts-and-crafts, from glassworks and wooden carvings to dolls and musical instruments; all profits go to scholarships for Native American students.

Specialty stores

SHOPS AND GALLERIES

⑳

Art galleries

The focus of Seattle's **art gallery** scene is located in Pioneer Square and Belltown, though you can also find pockets of interest in districts like Capitol Hill, Fremont, and Downtown. Most galleries rotate their stock while seeking out new items, so it pays to check back regularly to discover the latest ideas bubbling up in Seattle's creative community. One stand-out of the local art world is **glasswork**, much of it coming from **Dale Chihuly** and the **Pilchuck Glass School** he helped found (see box on p.229).

In Pioneer Square, the first Thursday evening of every month is **Gallery Walk**, when dozens of galleries hold openings between 6 and 8pm; a similar event takes place in Ballard on the second Saturday of the month from 6 to 9pm. To find out what's showing around town, check current listings in the papers or in the free regional art magazine *Art Access* (Ⓦ www.artaccess.com). Typical gallery hours are approximately Tuesday to Saturday 11am to 5pm, with some open for shorter hours on Sunday.

Pioneer Square

4Culture 101 Prefontaine Place S, near Third Ave and Yesler Way ☎ 206/296-7580, Ⓦ www.4culture.org. The public gallery of a municipal arts organization, where you're apt to see anything from the latest abstraction to curious installations to oddball performance works.

Bemis Building 55 Atlantic Ave S, near Safeco Field ☎ 206-381-8457, Ⓦ www.ouchmyeye .com. Eclectic venue that hosts thirty artists' studios and puts on regular shows every month or two, as well as participating in the First Thursday Gallery Walk.

Foster/White 123 S Jackson ☎ 206/622-2833, Ⓦ fosterwhite.com. Half a dozen rooms showcase eclectic, sometimes superb, work by Northwest artists that occasionally outclasses what's at the Seattle Art Museum or the Henry Art Gallery. Also at 1331 5th Ave, Downtown ☎ 206/583-0100.

G Gibson Gallery 300 S Washington St ☎ 206/587-4033, Ⓦ www.ggibsongallery .com. One of the more noteworthy galleries around, with a focus on photography and related fine art; the rotating exhibits may include historic works by Robert Mapplethorpe, Richard Misrach, and Imogen Cunningham.

Glasshouse Studio 311 Occidental Ave S ☎ 206/682-9939, Ⓦ www.glasshouse-studio .com. Small space displaying pieces by renowned and less well-known glass artists. You can watch artists at work in the studio at the rear, and a small selection of irregular pieces is sometimes offered for discounted prices.

Greg Kucera Gallery 212 Third Ave S ☎ 206/624-0770, Ⓦ www.gregkucera.com. Small exhibits of major international names are housed in a 4200-square-foot space. Heavy bent toward mid-century modernism, abstraction, and color-field painting.

Howard House 604 Second Ave ☎ 206/256-6399, Ⓦ www.howardhouse.net. Combines the usual media, like painting and photography, with sculpture in ceramics, glass, and metal, all of it with a strong avant-garde or conceptual bent.

SOIL Artist Cooperative 112 Third Ave S ☎ 206/264-8061, Ⓦ www.soilart.org. Well-regarded for its compelling, sometimes shocking contemporary artworks and use of mixed-media techniques and inventive assemblages.

Belltown and around

Auto Gallery of Seattle 3025 First Ave, northeast of Belltown ☎ 206/448-1247, Ⓦ www .autogalleryseattle.com. Doubles as a showroom for upper-end used cars and an exhibition space for local artists, with much painterly and photographic realism.

Center on Contemporary Art 410 Dexter Ave N ☎ 206/728-1980, Ⓦ www.cocaseattle.org. A small space given over to rotating exhibits of work – paintings, videos, sculptures, and multimedia pieces – that are more irreverent than what's found in other contemporary galleries. See p.80 for a review.

Pitcairn Scott 2207 Second Ave ☎ 206/448-5380, Ⓦ www.pitcairnscott.com. Plenty of brooding color studies and mixed-media assemblages on view, most with an eye to the mainstream upper-middle-class art buyer.

Roq La Rue 2316 Second Ave ☎206/374-8977, ⓦwww.roqlarue.com. Presenting a vivid parade of brightly colored, bizarre works with themes taken from pop culture and mass entertainment; styles frequently involve grotesque caricature or satirical visual puns.

Suyama Space 2324 Second Ave ☎206/256-0809, ⓦwww.suyamapetersondeguchi.com/art. Features challenging avant-garde and conceptual installations. It's located in an architectural office, so you'll have to buzz the front door to get in.

Other areas

Consolidated Works 500 Boren Ave N, East-lake ☎206/860-5245, ⓦwww.conworks.org. Hip arts center that features a wide range of multimedia pieces and presents some of the most challenging contemporary work in town; it's especially well-suited for large pieces and installations. Also hosts a theater, cinema, and dance space. See p.98 for a full review.

Edge of Glass 513 N 36th St, Fremont ☎206/632-7807, ⓦwww.edgeofglass.com. Displays work by local glass artists, including bowls, vases, hand-blown paperweights, and jewelry, some of it affordable. Also holds daily glassblowing demonstrations; call ahead for times.

Photographic Center Northwest 900 Twelfth Ave, First Hill ☎206/720-7222, ⓦpcnw.org. The gallery of Seattle's foremost photography school exhibits both nationally known and emerging artists, with art available for purchase if you spot a master in the making.

Dale Chihuly and the Pilchuck School

In the museums and galleries of the Seattle area, you're bound to encounter numerous references to the **Pilchuck Glass School** and its co-founder, **Dale Chihuly**. Perhaps the most renowned glass artist in the world, Chihuly helped establish the school with other kindred spirits in the early 1970s as an experiment in communal workmanship and art-making. Located in the foothills of the Cascade Mountains, about fifty miles north of Seattle, the school is now a leading generator of glass-art talent. Typical works are displayed all over Tacoma and in many interior spaces in Downtown Seattle, providing an easy (and free) way to take in some of the more astonishing colors and contortions that the artists have blown and crafted. The Pilchuck Glass School is not open for public visits, but the institution does hold an annual, five-hour **Open House** ($20) on a Sunday in late July; call ☎206/621-8422 ext 44, or check ⓦwww.pilchuck.com for details and reservation information; there are also exorbitantly priced "**auction weekend tours**" for getting up-close looks at the pieces over the course of four days ($1750).

The school's website offers details on where to see the Pilchuck's product around town, but the best place to view Chihuly's own work is in Tacoma – his home town – at the city's Downtown art museum, in the lobby of the federal courthouse at Union Station, and at the Bridge of Glass and adjacent Museum of Glass (see p.237). Interestingly, in 1996 Chihuly also installed a dozen 1200-pound chandeliers around the canals, archways, and plazas of Venice, Italy, and the following year gave a glass-blowing demonstration at a private party for Bill Gates and influential political/business bigwigs from around the world. For an extensive look at the highlights of his oeuvre, check out the four films in the *Chihuly Collection* (see p.309).

Naturally, the overwhelming media attention has led to a backlash among the more irreverent sectors of the alternative-arts world; the *Lava Lounge*, for one, held a "**smash a Chihuly**" raffle that gave the public a chance to bash an actual Chihuly piece to bits in front of an audience, and some critics have charged that Chihuly's work is more like industrial design than real art – the same charge once lobbed at another artist, Alexander Calder, famed for his giant black- and red-steel "Calder-mobiles" gracing the lobbies of countless corporate offices and upscale hotels – not unlike Chihuly's work today

Rainier Square Gallery 1333 Fifth Ave, level 3, Downtown ☎206/667-9184, ⓦwww .seattlearchitecture.org. Hosting the ongoing exhibit "Blueprints: 100 Years of Seattle Architecture," which employs detailed text and vintage city photos, as well as models, artworks, sketches, and blueprints from Seattle's urban-design history.

Washington State Convention and Trade Center Eighth Ave and Pike St, Downtown ☎206/447-5000. In addition to works on loan from various museums, the center exhibits numerous pieces by relatively unknown artists from the Northwest, throughout the Galleria level and in cases on floors 1–5.

William Traver Gallery 110 Union St, second floor, Downtown ☎206/587-6501, ⓦwww .travergallery.com. A sizable, lofty space well-suited for contemporary sculpture and multimedia pieces. A branch in Tacoma, at 1821 E Dock St (☎253/383-3685), is next to the Museum of Glass (see p.237).

Directory

Airport Seattle-Tacoma International Airport, known as Sea-Tac ☎206/433-5388 or 1-800/544-1965, ⓦwww.portseattle .org/seatac. Located fourteen miles south of Downtown Seattle near I-5 freeway. See "Getting there," pp.19–24, for information on national and international airlines.

Banks Hours vary, but most banks are open at least Monday to Friday 10am–5pm, sometimes with Saturday hours. Central Downtown branches include: Bank of America, 701 Second Ave ☎206/358-0500, ⓦwww.bankofamerica.com; KeyBank, 700 Fifth Ave ☎206/684-6507, ⓦwww.keybank .com; Union Bank of California, 910 Fourth Ave ☎206/587-6100, ⓦwww.uboc.com; US Bank, 1301 Fifth Ave ☎206/344-2395, ⓦwww.usbank.com; Washington Mutual, 1201 Third Ave ☎206/461-6475, ⓦwww .wamu.com; Wells Fargo, Westlake Center, 1620 Fourth Ave ☎206/287-0039, ⓦwww .wellsfargo.com. Also Umpqua Bank at 11100 NE 8th St, Suite 200, Bellevue ☎425/732-6016, ⓦwww.umpquabank.com

Coast Guard Search-and-rescue emergencies ☎206/217-6001.

Consulates Australia, 401 Andover Park East, in Tukwila, south of Downtown ☎206/575-7446, by appointment only; Canada, 600 Stewart St no.412 ☎206/443-1777, ⓦwww .can-am.gc.ca/seattle; New Zealand, 6810 51st Ave NE ☎206/525-0271, information only, no consular services; UK, 900 Fourth Ave #3001 ☎206/622-9255, ⓦwww .britainusa.com.

Crisis Clinic For resources and support for emotional crisis and trauma, disabilities, and other services, contact ☎206/461-3222, ⓦwww.crisisclinic.org.

Currency exchange Most large Downtown banks will change foreign currency and travelers' checks. American Express checks should be cashed at their Downtown office at Azumano Travel, 600 Stewart St (Mon–Fri 9am–5pm; ☎206/441-8622, ⓦtravel .americanexpress.com). Travelex (ⓦwww .travelex.com) changes money at Sea-Tac Airport in the Main Terminal (daily 6am–10pm; ☎206/248-0401), and in the North Satellite at Gate D (daily 6am–6pm; ☎206/248-7484), and in Bellevue at 10630 NE 8th St (Mon–Fri 8.30am–5pm; ☎425/462-2817).

Dentist referral The Seattle/King County Dental Society, 2201 Sixth Ave, Suite 1306 (☎206/443-7607, ⓦwww.skcds. org), provides a referral service to low-cost dental clinics around town. The most central and convenient such clinic is at 720 Eighth Ave S #100, International District (Mon–Fri 8am–6pm; ☎206/461-3235, ext. 6024).

Directory assistance Local ☎411; long distance ☎1 + area code + 555-1212.

Drugs Although hard drugs carry stiff penalties and jail time, possession of less than 40 grams of marijuana is treated as a misdemeanor in Washington, punishable by up to 90 days in jail and a $1000 fine – though not often prosecuted. However, if you're a foreign national, even a minor drug bust could be a convenient excuse for the authorities to boot you from the country – or worse, place you on the government's "watch list" barring re-entry.

Electricity 110V AC. European appliances typically require two-pin plug adapters for lower US voltages.

Emergencies/hotlines ☎911. For urgent, non-emergency matters, ☎206/625-5011.

Food safety To check a restaurant's safety or cleanliness record, or to report a vendor in violation of health standards, call King County's Food Protection Program at ☎206/296-4600, or check out online reports at ⓦwww .metrokc.gov/health/foodsfty.

Hospitals The best overall choice is Northwest Hospital, 1550 N 115th St, North Seattle (☎206/364-0500, ⓦwww.nwhospital.org); or for minor injuries, Country Doctor Community Clinic, 500 19th Ave E, Capitol Hill (☎206/299-1600, ⓦwww.cdchc.org). Women can also use the Aradia Women's Health Center, 1300 Spring St, Downtown (☎206/323-9388, ⓦwww.aradia.org).

Internet access Available from cyber-oriented coffee shops (see "Cafés," p.153) and city libraries. Except for libraries, expect to pay around 10–15¢ per minute to browse the Web.

Laundromats 12th Avenue Maytag Laundry, 1807 12th Ave, Capitol Hill ☎206/328-4610; Fremont Avenue Laundromat, 4237 Fremont Ave N, Fremont ☎206/632-8924; Seattle's Nicest Laundry, 5020 Roosevelt Way NE, University District ☎206/524-7855, and 333 NW 85th St ☎206/784-9020. Check also in the *Yellow Pages* for a given neighborhood.

Left luggage You can leave luggage at Sea-Tac Airport at Ken's Baggage, under the escalator between baggage-claim carousels 9 and 13 (☎206/433-5333; daily 5.30am–12.30am), or in storage lockers at Greyhound, 811 Stewart St (☎206/628-5526).

Legal advice Seattle King County Bar Association Lawyer Referral & Information Service (☎206/623-2551, ⓦwww.kcba.org) does pro bono work and provides legal referrals.

Library The newly rebuilt central branch of the Seattle Public Library is Downtown at 1000 Fourth Ave (Mon–Wed 10am–8pm, Thurs–Sat 10am–6pm, Sun 1–5pm; ☎206/386-4636, ⓦwww.spl.org). See p.56 for a full review. Also worth a look is the Ballard branch (p.114).

Pharmacies The prescription department is open 24 hours a day at Bartell Drugs, 600 First Ave N, Queen Anne (☎206/284-1353, ⓦwww.bartelldrugs.com). Check website for many other Seattle locations, with regular business hours.

Police stations West Precinct, 810 Virginia St (☎206/684-8917); East Precinct, 1519 12th Ave (☎206/684-4300); North Precinct, 10049 College Way N (☎206/684-0850); South Precinct, 3001 S Myrtle St (☎206/386-1850); Southwest Precinct, 2300 SW Webster St (☎206/733-9800). See ⓦwww.cityofseattle.net/Police/contact.htm for more information.

Post offices Generally open Monday to Friday, 9am to 5pm and Saturday mornings. The main post office is Downtown at 301 Union St (Mon–Fri 7.30am–5.30pm; ☎206/748-5417). For other branches call 1-800/275-8777 or visit ⓦwww.usps.com.

Tax Sales tax in Seattle is 8.8 percent, one of the highest in the US, applied to everything except groceries, and a Food & Beverage Tax (mainly for restaurants) bumps the total up to 9.3 percent; it's similar throughout the rest of the metropolitan area. There's also a steep hotel tax of 16 percent in Seattle (it's 4-6 percent less in surrounding areas and Puget Sound).

Telephones Public phones are plentiful throughout the city; if you need more privacy, duck into a shopping center or big hotel. Local calls cost 50¢, and considerably more (often at least $1 per call) in major hotels.

Tickets Most big entertainment and sporting events go through TicketMaster (☎206/628-0888, ⓦwww.ticketmaster.com), which charges a variable, often high service fee, and pre-sells tickets at Key Arena (see p.181) and Rite Aid pharmacies, whose central Downtown store is at 319 Pike St. Meanwhile, Ticket/Ticket (☎206/325-6500 or 206/324-2744, ⓦwww.ticketwindowonline.com) offers day-of-show theater and concert tickets for half-price; see "Performing Arts and Film," (p.187) for more information on both services.

Time Seattle is on Pacific Standard Time (PST), three hours behind Eastern Standard Time (EST) in the US, and eight to nine hours behind Greenwich Mean Time, depending on whether Daylight Savings Time is in effect.

Tipping Generally 15 percent for restaurants, though upscale eateries may expect closer to 20 percent (still, it's up to you) and many restaurants will slap a flat 18 percent charge on parties of six or more. Generally $1 per carried bag at hotels and $1 per day for maid service (both with a minimum $2 tip).

Travel agents STA Travel, 424 Broadway E, Capitol Hill (☎206/329-4567, ⓦwww.statravel.com), and 4311 University Way NE, University District (☎206/632-2448), is a good general source of discount flights and related information. See "Getting there," (pp.19–24) for more information on travel agents.

Travelers Aid 909 Fourth Ave, Downtown (Mon–Fri 9am–4.30pm; ☎206/461-3888). Temporary shelter for abused women and the unexpectedly homeless.

Out from the city

Out from the city

Tacoma and Olympia

L
ocated thirty and sixty miles south of Seattle, respectively, **Tacoma** and **Olympia** are independent cities that have almost been completely enveloped by the Seattle metropolitan sprawl, so that the entire stretch of interstate between these three cities now resembles one long, linear suburb. If you're in the Seattle area for more than a week, Tacoma and Olympia should merit at least a day-trip for their renovated historic architecture, interesting museums, and appealing parks. Moreover, they're the only cities in the region – or any place further south along I-5 in Washington, for that matter – with anything resembling the cultural attractions of their neighbor to the north.

Tacoma

Long a workaday mill and port town with a notably foul stench, **TACOMA** was never a big draw for outsiders, except perhaps for its massive **Tacoma Dome**, 2727 East D St (information at ☎253/272-3663, ⊛www.tacomadome .org), a wood-roofed athletic and concert venue that, viewable from the I-5 freeway, is the city's most prominent sight – if not its most inspiring. Nowadays, though, Tacoma's dismal reputation is on the upswing, as all but one of its smelly pulp mills have closed, and the city's eyesore of a copper-smelter was brought down over a decade ago.

More importantly, thanks to skyrocketing real-estate prices in Seattle, Tacoma has become a popular housing alternative (though this has only led to even worse traffic congestion between the cities). The resulting influx of middle-class families, young people, and artists has rejuvenated the old burg, so much so that the city – to the amazement of Northwesterners – has actually become a minor tourist attraction. The town also has some degree of historic relevance: Downtown is perched above Puget Sound at **Commencement Bay**, a deep harbor whose appeal helped Tacoma to be chosen as the western terminus for the Northern Pacific Railroad's transcontinental route in 1873, snatching the line from the grasp of Seattle, which had to wait until 1906 for its own rail station.

Arrival and information

Tacoma is well-served by local and regional **mass transit**: Amtrak (☎1-800/ USA-RAIL, ⊛www.amtrak.com) pulls in at Freighthouse Square, 1001 Puyallup Ave; Pierce Transit (☎253/581-8000, ⊛www.ptbus.pierce.wa.us) runs frequent

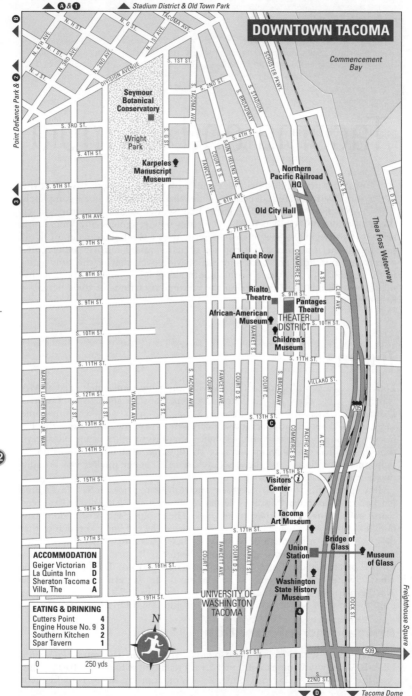

DOWNTOWN TACOMA

Stadium District & Old Town Park

A & 1

B

Point Defance Park & 2

2

3

Commencement Bay

N. H ST.
N. G ST.
TACOMA AVE.
N. 1ST AVE.
N. H ST.
N. G ST.
N. 4TH AVE.
N. 3RD AVE.
N. 2ND AVE.
N. 1ST AVE.
N. J ST.
DIVISION AVENUE
S. 1ST ST.
S. 2ND ST.
S. BROADWAY
S. STADIUM
SCHUSTER PKWY.

Seymour Botanical Conservatory

Wright Park

S. 3RD ST.
S. 4TH ST.
S. 5TH ST.

Karpeles Manuscript Museum

S. G ST.
TACOMA AVE.
SAINT HELENS AVE.
FAWCETT AVE.
COURT D. S.

S. 4TH ST.

Northern Pacific Railroad HQ

S. 6TH AVE.

Old City Hall

S. 7TH ST.

Antique Row

Rialto Theatre

Pantages Theatre

African-American Museum

THEATER DISTRICT

Children's Museum

COMMERCE ST.
A ST.
CLIFF AVE.

S. 9TH ST.
S. 10TH ST.
S. 11TH ST.

MARKET ST.

S. 8TH AVE.
S. 9TH ST.
S. 10TH ST.
S. 11TH ST.

DOCK ST.
E D ST.

Thea Foss Waterway

VILLARD ST.

705

MARTIN LUTHER KING JR WAY
S. J ST.
S. I ST.
YAKIMA AVE.
S. TACOMA AVE.
S. G ST.
FAWCETT AVE.
COURT E
COURT D S.
COURT C
S. BROADWAY
COMMERCE ST.
PACIFIC AVE.
A CT.

S. 12TH ST.
S. 13TH ST.
S. 14TH ST.
S. 15TH ST.
S. 16TH ST.
S. 17TH ST.
S. 18TH ST.
S. 19TH ST.

C

Visitors' Center

Tacoma Art Museum

Bridge of Glass

Union Station

Museum of Glass

UNIVERSITY OF WASHINGTON TACOMA

Washington State History Museum

4

Freighthouse Square

DOCK ST.

509

S. 22ND ST.

N

0   250 yds

D

Tacoma Dome

ACCOMMODATION
Geiger Victorian   B
La Quinta Inn   D
Sheraton Tacoma   C
Villa, The   A

EATING & DRINKING
Cutters Point   4
Engine House No. 9   3
Southern Kitchen   2
Spar Tavern   1

Seattle Express bus services between Seattle and Tacoma ($3), as well as local routes ($1.25); while Sound Transit (☎1-800/201-4900, ⊛www.soundtransit .org) offers Seattle-bound express buses ($3) and the Sounder commuter rail (rush hour only; 1hr trip; $4) from a station at the Tacoma Dome; Sounder and Amtrak rail routes terminate at Seattle's King Street Station (see p.70). The **Tacoma Visitors' Center**, 1516 Pacific Ave (Mon–Sat 9am–5pm, Sun noon–5pm; ☎253/627-2836, ⊛www.traveltacoma.com), has maps and literature about the history and attractions of the area, along with walking guides, which can prove especially helpful when exploring local architecture.

Accommodation

Devoe Mansion 203 133rd St E ☎253/539-3991, ⊛www.devoemansion.com. Four elegant rooms in a 1911 Colonial Revival mansion named after a local women's-rights pioneer. Known for savory breakfasts, set on a beautifully presented table underneath an antique chandelier. Located just south of Downtown Tacoma, on several parklike acres. $115.

Geiger Victorian 912 North I St ☎253/383-3504, ⊛www.geigervictorian.com. The quintessential B&B, in this case an Eastlake Victorian from 1889, loaded with all the chintz and antiques you'd expect, plus a fireplace, claw-footed tubs in the rooms, and a hand-painted ceiling in the Virginia Mason suite – by far the most unique room ($149); other rooms $99–119.

La Quinta Inn 1425 E 27th St ☎253/383-0146, ⊛www.laquinta.com. A basic and clean chain motel, just a few blocks from the Tacoma Dome, with a heated pool, complimentary breakfast, and high-speed Internet access. The least expensive, but still more than adequate, accommodation close to Downtown. $99.

Sheraton Tacoma 1320 Broadway Plaza, between 13th and 15th sts ☎253/572-3200 or 1-800/845-9466, ⊛www.sheratontacoma.com. One of the plushest hotels in town, next to an enormous convention center; ask for a room with a view over Commencement Bay. Suites with parlors are available for $229; otherwise $118.

The Villa 705 N Fifth St ☎253/572-1157 or 1-888/572-1157, ⊛www.villabb.com. This Renaissance Revival mansion, surrounded by luxurious gardens, has been converted into a B&B with plenty of creature comforts; some of the five rooms (named after Italian towns) have private verandas with views of Commencement Bay and the Olympic Mountains. About a mile northeast of Downtown. $135.

The Museum and Bridge of Glass

A large part of the reason for Tacoma's recent turnaround is the **Museum of Glass**, 1801 E Dock St (Wed–Sat 10am–5pm, Sun noon–5pm, summer open daily; $10, kids $4; ☎1-866/4-MUSEUM, ⊛www.museumofglass.org), an institution like no other in the region. The $63-million facility sits alongside an inlet of Commencement Bay, across from the city's old railyards and dockside terminals. In homage to Tacoma's history, the museum's main identifying feature is a towering, metal-shingled cone that vaguely resembles an antiquated smokestack

– though the institution is anything but old-fashioned. Predominantly featuring glassworks (but also mixed-media assemblages, installation and conceptual art, and even painting and sculpture), the museum's bent is toward contemporary work, often showcasing the vivid, flowery designs of pre-eminent Tacoma glassblower **Dale Chihuly**. In fact, inside the museum's "Hot Shop," you might find Chihuly himself or another glass artist creating a new piece before an amphitheater full of visitors

Outside, you can see his striking designs writ large on the **Bridge of Glass** (ⓦwww.chihuly.com/bridgeofglass). This open walkway, which runs across a train line and over Interstate 705 from the museum's front plaza, is structurally unexceptional, but is marked by three sections that display the artist's work in its full glory: an overhead skylight, called the **Seaform Pavilion**, filled with colorful glass shapes resembling shells, urchins, and the like; a pair of crystalline **blue spires** that look like rock-candy towers as they sit directly over the freeway; and the **Venetian Wall**, a series of glass vases and sculptures in viewing boxes, which is best seen in the morning when the rising sun illuminates the back of the glassworks to great effect.

Pacific Avenue

Crossing over the Bridge of Glass from the museum, you reach **Pacific Avenue**, the main cultural drag of downtown Tacoma, and the axis of the city's recent rejuvenation. While not exactly a strip pulsing with commercial and creative energy, such as Broadway on Capitol Hill, it does offer some interesting diversions that can be worth your time if you're in the area.

On the west end of the Bridge of Glass, **Union Station**, no. 1717 (Mon–Fri 10am–4pm), the earliest and most visible example of Tacoma's rebirth, is a 1911 Baroque Revival treasure with a copper dome and marble-faced lobby. Graced with even more Chihuly glassworks – especially beautiful are the 27 orange-and henna-hued glass butterfly shapes in the **Monarch Window** – this elegant old station hasn't hosted an arriving train in twenty years. Instead, it's been reborn as a federal courthouse, renovated for $57 million, and as a station on the **TacomaLink trolley** (Mon-Fri 5.30am-8pm, Sat 8am-10pm, Sun 10am-8pm; free), connecting the Tacoma Dome with the Theater District – a good way to get around town if you don't feel like walking.

Adjacent to the north side of Union Station is the **Tacoma Art Museum**, at no. 1701 (Tues–Sat 10am–5pm, Sun noon-5pm; $7.50; ⓣ253/272-4258, ⓦwww.tacomaartmuseum.org), where the minor pieces by Picasso, Degas, Renoir, and Frederic Remington aren't too inspiring, but the building itself – a gleaming steel-and-glass creation by Antoine Predock – is quite a marvel. The other highlight is, not surprisingly, the **art glass** on display, much of it created or inspired by the work of Chihuly and his Pilchuck School. The temporary exhibits are fairly wide-ranging, anything from installations to native tribal works to classic photography, though the museum's limited space means there aren't more than a few taking place at any one time.

On the south side of Union Station, the excellent **Washington State History Museum**, no. 1911 (Mon–Sat 10am–5pm, Thurs open until 8pm, Sun noon–5pm; $7, free Thurs 5–8pm; ⓣ253/272-3500, ⓦwww.wshs.org/wshm), has a huge array of exhibits on regional history, its **Great Hall** incorporating large galleries that re-create the milieu of frontier towns and different historical periods with walk-through cabins, a Depression-era lunch counter, and other interactive models; further compelling exhibits cover subjects such as alcoholism among Native Americans and the 1919 general strike in Seattle. The museum is also constructing a huge **model railroad**, due to be the largest such display in the state, showcasing the glory days of trains in the 1950s, when Tacoma was an industrial powerhouse – and, incidentally, visited by almost no tourists.

Another demonstration of the local commitment to historic preservation can be seen at the **University of Washington, Tacoma** (Ⓦwww.tacoma.washington .edu). Across Pacific Avenue from Union Station, the university features a handful of old grain and grocery warehouses that have been cleverly converted into classrooms and offices. Even more conversions are planned for the future, while an active railway, crossed by overhead walkways, continues to run directly through the middle of campus.

The Theater District and around

Seven blocks north and two blocks west of Pacific Avenue lies the heart of Tacoma's **Theater District**, yet another refurbished area that began to breathe life back into the city in the early 1990s. The action centers on the complex of three major performance houses for drama, symphonic music, opera, and pop concerts, collectively known as the **Broadway Center for the Performing Arts**, 901 Broadway (☎253/591-5894, Ⓦwww.broadwaycenter.org). Two of these spaces occupy stunning old moviehouses, the **Pantages** and the **Rialto**, landmarks with terracotta facades and copious historic-revival decor.

Just north of the Broadway Center you'll find **Antique Row**, on Broadway between S Seventh and S Ninth streets, where fifteen dealers in historic collectibles, old-fashioned curiosities, and various worn-out junk have set up shop; it's a good place to pick up a forgotten LP, modernist chair, or creaky butter churn, if you're in the market for such items.

To the northeast is the classically designed **Old City Hall**, 625 Commerce St, a striking 1893 Renaissance Revival edifice with a bell tower that looks as if it's been plucked straight from Tuscany; the building's now used as office space. Across the street, the 1888 **Northern Pacific Railroad Headquarters** is another grand Italianate creation, topped by a high tower and cupola, which casts an imposing shadow over this part of town, though Tacoma is hardly a railway colossus anymore.

A few lesser-known museums are also in the immediate vicinity, including the **Children's Museum of Tacoma**, 936 Broadway (Tues–Sat 10am–5pm, Sun noon–5pm; $5; ☎253/627-6031, Ⓦwww.childrensmuseumoftacoma.org), where the youngsters can play puppeteer, gardener, or artist, with all the requisite props. One block over, the **African-American Museum**, 925 Court C (Mon & Wed 1-4pm, Thurs–Sat 10am–6pm; $3.50; ☎253/274-1278, Ⓦwww .aamuseumtacoma.org), is a good place to get a better sense of regional and national black history, with displays on Dr Martin Luther King Jr, as well as African-American pioneers, soldiers, and civic leaders from Washington state's past.

Wright Park

Northwest of the Theater District, **Wright Park**, at Sixth Avenue and South G Street, occupies about ten city blocks; it was laid out in 1886, and still retains a measure of its late-Victorian design and style. With seven hundred plants in more than a hundred varieties, it's an excellent spot to stroll, pitch horseshoes, or do a little lawn bowling. Even better, the park features the compelling **Seymour Botanical Conservatory**, 316 South G St (Tues–Sun 10am–4.30pm; donation; ☎253/591-5330), a 1908 glass-and-steel structure that holds some two hundred different species, from lilies to ferns and bromeliads – but especially orchids, of which there are some two hundred varieties.

Across the street from the conservatory, the grandly Neoclassical **Karpeles Manuscript Museum**, 407 South G St (Tues–Sun 10am–4pm; free; ☏253/383-2575, ⓦwww.karpeles.com), with its six Roman Revival columns, is one of seven museums established by David Karpeles throughout the US to showcase his immense collection of manuscripts. It's worth a look to the serious bibliophile: among his holdings are the conclusion page of Darwin's *The Origin of Species* and a study page for Karl Marx's *Das Kapital*. However, what you'll see depends on the temporary exhibits on display (typically on view for three months), which in the past have covered everything from diplomatic records and famous proclamations to literary first editions and noteworthy diaries and memoirs.

The Stadium District and Old Town Park

Immediately north of Division Avenue from Wright Park begins the **Stadium District**, a neighborhood of Victorian architecture whose centerpiece is the stunning **Stadium High School**, 111 North E St, a monumental three-story French chateau – originally built in 1891 as a hotel, though it never opened – that would seem borrowed from a fairytale if it weren't swarming with teenagers.

If you have a particular zeal for nineteenth-century history, head further west to **Old Town Park**, 30th St at Carr St, which offers a good account of Tacoma's past at the **Job Carr Cabin Museum**, 2350 N 30th St (Wed–Sat 1–4pm, summer opens at noon; free; ☏253/627-5405, ⓦwww.jobcarrmuseum .org). Housed in an 1864 log home that was built in the first decade of the area's settlement, the museum displays old documents and antiques from the town's pre-industrial days. Beyond the cabin, Tacoma's **old town** (ⓦwww .oldtownbusinessdistrict.com) has some predictably antiquated structures, but is really only worth seeking out if you want a stiff drink at the classic *Spar Tavern* (see p.242).

Point Defiance Park

About four miles north of Downtown, off Ruston Way at Pearl Street, picturesque, 700-acre **Point Defiance Park** is one of the largest urban parks in the US. Its **Five-Mile-Drive** loop has fine viewpoints of Puget Sound at various vistas and park-access points, from which you can lose yourself on the numerous trails. There are also some fine gardens here, featuring everything from Japanese plantings to dahlias, fuschias, irises and roses; a model pagoda with a waterfall; and a replica Shinto shrine with a Torii gate carved in cypress. You'll also find a worthwhile **zoo** and **aquarium** in the park, 5400 N Pearl St (hours vary, generally daily 9.30am–5pm; $8.75; ☏253/404-3636, ⓦwww.pdza.org); the former holds interesting displays of arctic creatures like polar bears, as well as red wolves and a beluga whale, along with an **Asian Forest** exhibit that's home to Bamboo, an irascible elephant recently relocated from Seattle's Woodland Park Zoo, where she wasn't too popular with the other pachyderms. The aquarium is a bit more predictable, with tidepools, otters, and octopi – though the **South Pacific** section is highlighted by a nicely menacing selection of sharks brought from ocean reefs down under.

If you can't get enough history, signs on the Five-Mile-Drive will direct you to **Fort Nisqually**, 5400 N Pearl St (April–May Wed–Sun 11am–5pm; daily June–Aug 11am–5pm; Sept–March Wed–Sun 11am–4pm; $4 Mar–Oct, rest

Green
(and blue)
Seattle

Seattle enjoys a picturesque natural setting few cities can match. The scenic waters of Puget Sound lap along the city's western shores, urban parks such as Washington Park Arboretum and Discovery Park exhibit the spectacular lush vegetation that define the verdant Pacific Northwest, and the majesty of Mount Rainier dominates the skyline – on sunny days, that is. To fully appreciate the splendor of Seattle's great outdoors – an essential experience to nearly any Northwest visit – requires a leisurely course, whether in a boat, on a bike, or on foot.

On the trail

An extensive network of paved, dirt, and rocky **trails** lace throughout and around the city, making it almost impossible to list all the stellar options for cycling and hiking. Residents take full advantage of it; indeed, the locally based Cascade Bicycle Club is the largest of its kind in America, while the Olmsted-designed parks system means no one has to leave the city limits for a relaxed stroll or strenuous ramble. Nature lovers find many of the region's **endemic species** along the wayside, too, with groves and glades overlooked by Western red cedar, Sitka spruce and Douglas fir, or vine maple and Pacific yew trees (many of them visible in Seattle's own Washington Park Arboretum). **Bird-watchers** near the Puget Sound shoreline glimpse the magisterial blue heron or the black-and-white-winged guillemot – as well as more familiar finches, wrens and hummingbirds – while bald eagles make their nests atop spruce, fir, and cedar trees. To best experience the natural bounty, bring along a comprehensive nature guide to the region and expect to spend plenty of time looking at Dungeness crabs by the shore, otters on the riverbanks, and hawks and falcons soaring overhead – just don't expect to make a fast pace on the trail while you're at it.

Still, gung-ho hikers can't leave before taking at least one trek up a **mountain** in the nearby Cascade Range. The obvious place to start is **Mount Rainier**, an imposing lure that looms in the background of many picture-postcard views of Seattle. The hiking trails are among the best to be found in the country, with eclectic terrain from shady forest glades and deep, craggy ravines to austere glaciers and icy basaltic peaks.

Seattle's best hikes

Several of the Seattle area's numerous **hikes** stand out for their scenic splendor and native features, and are well worth the trek if you have the time – or in some cases, the endurance.

Best beach walk: Lopez Island At its southern end, this rugged island in the San Juans features expansive vistas of Puget Sound, protected sea lions and tidepools in Shark Reef Park, and an engaging walk over wave-polished pebbles at Agate Beach.

Best mountain trek: Wonderland Trail Signature trek looping around Mount Rainier, which can take up to two weeks to traverse in full, but is well worth hiking even a short segment on its beauteous course, past glacier-fed rivers and stunning alpine lakes and meadows.

Best nature hike: Foster Island Trail An elevated wooden path cuts through a nicely preserved wetland buzzing with wildlife and passing kayakers, and into the woody confines of Washington Park Arboretum.

Best urban jaunt: Burke-Gilman Trail Sixteen miles of curving concourse, often past strikingly beautiful terrain, mostly along the northern shore of the Ship Canal and the northwestern edge of Lake Washington.

Most surreal hike: Ape Cave An eerie, hollowed-out lava tube created thousand of years ago by Mount St Helens, where basaltic walls rise overhead as the broken ground, dead-quiet atmosphere, and chilly air add to the alien volcanic landscape.

The still-active volcanic peak of **Mount St Helens** is pretty much on par with Rainier, though with recent bursts of seismic activity, the mountain's climbing opportunities have often been curtailed or at least limited. You can still hike on the volcano's lower slopes without a permit, taking varying paths along forest groves, rock-strewn rivers, or fields of ashen tephra – though some of St Helens' most unexpected landscapes can be found underground, where there's a spellbinding network of lava tubes and caves.

On the water

Synonymous with natural beauty and excellent sightseeing, Puget Sound is the area's defining body of water, but you don't have to sail across it to find out just how much all the waterways influence daily life. With Downtown Seattle's waterfront aimed more at industrial and tourist activities, the city's most engaging axis of waterborne travel is the **Lake Washington Ship Canal**, which links that eponymous lake on the east to Lake Union, Salmon Bay and, on the western side, Puget Sound. While there are plenty of operators giving official tours through the canal, the best way to traverse the channel is either with your own motorized craft or by paddling along in a canoe or kayak; you can rent both at the Waterfront Activities Center on the University of Washington campus. **Lake Union**, near Downtown Seattle, is if anything even more eclectic in its array of watercraft – yachts from private clubs bob along the gentle waves, as do old-fashioned dinghies and steam-powered antiques from the Center for Wooden Boats. Sign up for a cruise there and experience the lake the way Seattle's founders might have, tackling the current in a handcrafted slip – though the seaplanes landing overhead provide a distinctly modern touch.

Still, the lakes do take a backseat to **Puget Sound**, a huge maritime inlet lined by many of Washington State's most vibrant communities and home to over 700 islands. Unlike similarly ballyhooed bodies of water such as San Francisco Bay or the Great Lakes, this one is attractive throughout (with minimal industrial ugliness and overdevelopment). With few bridges crossing the Sound, the essential way to go is by ferry, which can take you as far as Victoria, British Columbia. More active pursuits exist too: renting space on a fishing charter, taking your kayak around the wilder stretches of Whidbey Island and the San Juans, enjoying a pleasant journey by canoe along the shore of Vashon and Bainbridge islands, or even breaking out water skis, treating the Sound, as many do, as one big, beautiful lake.

Kayaking on Puget Sound

Watery vistas

If you want to get a full sense of Seattle's watery context, head to these breathtaking **vistas**:

Discovery Park This park's shoreline (especially near its signature lighthouse) feels wholly removed from Seattle's urban hubbub, and provides a good deal of solace with its rocky shores and bayside channels – views spectacularly enhanced at sunset.

Kerry Park On its high slope, this Queen Anne park is perhaps the top choice for seeing Seattle in stunning relation to Elliott Bay.

Puget Sound's islands Good views can be found at Deception Pass on Whidbey Island and throughout the San Juans – but perhaps best at Mount Constitution on Orcas Island.

Riding a ferry An engaging trip that will take you past the striking waterside topography of Puget Sound; one of the best such journeys connects Seattle to Bremerton across the breadth of the Sound in one lovely hour.

Deception Pass Bridge, Puget Sound

of year $3; ⓦwww.fortnisqually.org), a reconstruction of a fur-trading outpost begun in the 1830s, with homes and storehouses that illustrate the stark lifestyles of residents of the original fort. If you have any illusions about those good old days, docents in period clothing will provide a lesson in just how much work went into sewing garments, cooking food, weaving baskets, and smithing metal during that hardscrabble era.

Another glimpse of the region's harsh historical conditions is provided at the **Camp 6 Logging Museum** (grounds daily dawn–dusk; interior exhibits April–Oct Wed–Sun 10am–4pm; free; ☎253/752-0047, ⓦwww.camp-6-museum .org/c6.html), located near the fort, on the southern boundary of the park. The museum has antique equipment and photos, but most vividly displays the crude bunkhouses, dangerous-looking tools, and industrial-age rail cars that made up the working life of loggers. It's best to visit on spring and summer weekends, when the steam locomotive rides are running ($4).

Pacific Rim Bonsai Collection

For a very different sort of experience, head eight miles north of Tacoma, just off I-5 at a marked exit, to the **Pacific Rim Bonsai Collection** (March–Sept Fri–Wed 10am–4pm, Oct–Feb Sat–Wed 11am–4pm; free). Created by the Weyerhaeuser timber-products company, perhaps as a bid for better public relations, it's nevertheless well worth a look for its fascinating selection of sixty-odd specimens. Bonsai are plants that, through heavy pruning and having their root structure confined to small containers, are maintained in miniature, almost sculptural form by artisans who typically hail from East Asia, where the craft is very much an art form. The plants here are no match for those in Japan and China, but they do sport some rather intriguing features, and are fairly unusual to be seen in the Pacific Northwest. Highlights include the pale-pink weeping branches of the Tamarisk, the elegantly gnarled branches and horizontally splayed greenery of the Formosan Juniper – a quintessential Bonsai look – and, as one of the most unusual items, the Sumac's single thin black trunk, twisted up to support a few vivid red and green sprigs at the top.

Next to the Bonsai Collection is a more familiar selection of blooms, at the **Rhododendron Species Collection** (March–May Fri–Wed 10am–4pm, June–Feb Sat–Wed 11am–4pm; $3.50; ⓦwww.rsf.citymax.com), where lovers of that particular flower can get a glimpse of some ten thousand of them spread over 22 acres in a pleasant wooded setting.

Eating and drinking

Antique Sandwich Company 5102 N Pearl St ☎253/752-4069. The budget sandwiches are just OK here, but the ambiance at Point Defiance Park, in which it's located, is inviting. The restaurant is a good place to catch an acoustic concert by a local performer or listen to self-styled singers take part in Tuesday's open mike night. Daily 7am–7.30pm.

Cutters Point 1936 Pacific Ave ☎253/272-7101. Central branch of an estimable local chain that serves up prime varietal coffees in a cozy environment and has tasty baked goods and snacks. Convenient to the major

sights in the area. Mon–Thurs 6am–9pm, Fri 6am–7pm, Sat & Sun 8am–7pm.

Engine House No. 9 611 N Pine St ☎253/272-3435. This convivial tavern with fire-station decor is a better place for drinking local microbrews or hearing live music than for eating. The menu is heavy on the usual burgers and pizza. Sun–Tues 11.30am–midnight, Wed & Thurs 11.30am–1am, Fri & Sat 11.30am–2am.

Polynesian Grill 10518 S Tacoma Way ☎253/584-6494. Although located a fair distance from the city center, in South Tacoma, this humble spot serves up some

22

of the area's best pork ribs, barbecued chicken, and Hawaiian and Filipino cuisine, all with a heavy dose of island spices – and karaoke (in the adjacent bar). Daily 11am–9pm.

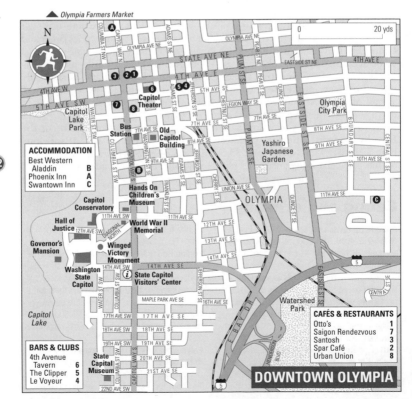 **Southern Kitchen 1716 Sixth Ave** ☎253/627-4282. Gumbo, catfish, hush puppies, candied yams, and fried okra are just a few of the things you can stuff your gut with at this award-winning local favorite – about as close to Dixie as you're going

to get in the Pacific Northwest. Mon–Sat 7am–8pm, Sun 10am–6pm.

Spar Tavern 2121 N 30th St ☎253/627-8215, Ⓦ www.the-spar.com. Classic brick diner and watering hole near the bayfront around Old Town Park, serving up burgers, seafood, and a good range of local micro-brewskis, plus blues on Sunday nights. Kitchen open Mon–Fri 11am–midnight, Sat & Sun 9am–midnight; bar open daily 11am–2am.

Olympia

Unlike most small-town state capitals, Washington State's **OLYMPIA** has more to offer than just legislative buildings and run-of-the-mill bars and diners catering to politicians and lobbyists. In fact, thanks to its quality nightlife scene and proximity to Seattle – just an hour north on the I-5 freeway – the town doesn't shut down on the weekends, either, and makes a good base for exploring the **Washington Cascades** and **Mount Rainier**.

▲ *Olympia Farmers Market*

ACCOMMODATION
Best Western
 Aladdin   B
Phoenix Inn   A
Swantown Inn   C

BARS & CLUBS
4th Avenue
 Tavern   6
The Clipper   5
Le Voyeur   4

CAFÉS & RESTAURANTS
Otto's   1
Saigon Rendezvous 7
Santosh   3
Spar Café   2
Urban Union   8

DOWNTOWN OLYMPIA

22

Olympia became the capital of the Washington territory in 1853, and though it was quickly superseded commercially when railways were placed elsewhere, it became state capital in 1889 when Washington finally entered the Union, nearly three decades after its neighbor Oregon. Today, the city has a regal **state capitol** and a surrounding **capitol campus**, but it also has an eccentric streak, due in part to the presence just outside town of Evergreen State College, an untraditional school that allows students to design their own courses of study. Cartoonist Matt Groening (creator of *The Simpsons*) went to Evergreen, as did Sub Pop Records co-founder Bruce Pavitt and numerous semi-famous indie rockers; Kurt Cobain even lived in Olympia for several years before his rise to fame in Nirvana – not surprising since there are more than a few decent rock bands still making the town their home.

Arrival and information

Greyhound drops off in the town center at 107 Seventh Ave SE (☎360/357-5541, ⓦwww.greyhound.com), just north of the capitol campus, and runs **buses** from Seattle to Olympia, a 2hr trip, several times a day. **Amtrak** (ⓦwww.amtrak.com) pulls in at the nearby town of Lacey, 6600 Yelm Hwy SE, and connects to Seattle and Portland. For getting around town, Intercity Transit (☎360/786-1881, ⓦwww.intercitytransit.com) serves the Olympia area (75¢ tickets, $1.50 daily pass). The **state capitol visitors' center**, Capitol Way at 14th Avenue (daily 8am–5pm; ☎360/586-3460, ⓦwww.ga.wa.gov/visitor), is stocked with maps and brochures to set you on your way.

Accommodation

Best Western Aladdin 900 Capitol Way ☎360/352-7200 or 1-800/367-7771, ⓦwww.bestwestern.com. A predictably clean (if generic) motor lodge near Olympia's center, with a gym, hot tub, heated outdoor pool, and breakfast buffet. $72.

Millersylvania State Park Tilley Rd ☎360/753-1519, ⓦwww.parks.wa.gov. Ten miles south of Olympia, this 840-acre campground, with rugged facilities designed during the New Deal era, has 135 tent sites, 52 RV hookups, and four primitive sites. Located near a beach, with eight miles of hiking and bike trails. $15–21.

Phoenix Inn 415 Capitol Way ☎360/570-0555, ⓦwww.phoenixinnsuites.com. Perhaps the best choice overall for affordable luxury and convenience, with fridges and microwaves in each room, as well as an onsite pool, hot tub, gym, and wireless Internet access. $109.

Swantown Inn 1431 11th Ave SE ☎360/753-9123, ⓦwww.swantowninn.com. One of the very few B&Bs in Olympia that offer more than a room or two. This inn has four units in a striking 1887 Eastlake Victorian, with wireless Internet, savory breakfasts, simple, old-fashioned decor, and views of the Capitol. $99.

Downtown Olympia and Capitol Lake

The centerpiece of **Downtown Olympia** is the **Old Capitol Building**, Washington at Seventh Ave (Mon–Fri 8am–5pm; free; ☎360/586-3460), a Romanesque Revival jewel featuring gothic turrets and stone arches overlooking the pleasant green square of **Sylvester Park**, named after Olympia's founder. Surprisingly, the Old Capitol was first constructed as a local county courthouse in 1892, but taken over by state politicians less than a decade later in order to secure a cheap but impressive legislative building; it looked more magnificent then, with no less than eight towers and a high bell tower – which an earthquake and fire destroyed, respectively, decades later. Nowadays this truncated Capitol acts as the home of the state educational bureaucracy. A few blocks east, the **Yashiro Japanese Garden**, Ninth Ave at Plum St (daily dawn–dusk; free; ☎360/753-8447), is a small refuge with a pagoda, fish pond, and waterfall that provides a brief respite on your travels; two blocks north of the Old Capitol, the stylish, classic **Capitol Theater**, 206 E Fifth Ave (☎360/754-3635, ⓦwww.olyfilm.org), is home to the Olympia Film Festival in early November, and regularly hosts rock bands and other acts on weekends. A block away, the focus of Olympia's live-music scene is along **East Fourth Avenue**, where you can dance or rock hard at Le Voyeur, no. 404 (☎360/943-5710); The Clipper, no. 402 (☎360-943-6300); and the 4th Avenue Tavern, no. 210 (☎360/786-1444).

Three blocks further west from here, at **Capitol Lake**, you'll find the waterfront **Olympia Farmers Market**, 700 N Capitol Way (Apr–Oct Thurs–Sun 10am–3pm, Nov–Dec Sat & Sun only; ☎360/352-9096, ⓦwww.farmers-market .org). There's a nice selection of fruits, vegetables, herbs, pastries, and baked goods on offer, as well as items like handcrafted soaps and puzzles.

The Washington State Capitol

Just south of Downtown, starting at 14th Avenue and Capitol Way, the capitol campus comprises several blocks of government buildings, dominated by the Capitol itself, the **Washington State Legislative Building** (tours daily on the hour 10am–3pm; self-guided visits daily 10am–4pm; ☎360/753-2580), an imposing Romanesque Revival pile with the sort of towering columns and striking dome you might expect. The original territorial capitol was constructed here in 1856 as a modest wooden structure that didn't take long to decay, at which point operations were moved to the Old Capitol; the present structure, finished in 1928, is, at 287 feet, the tallest all-masonry domed building in the US, and the sixth-tallest in the world.

△ Washington State Legislative Building

The Legislative Building has a nicely opulent design highlighted by 42 granite steps, symbolizing Washington's status as the 42nd state granted admission to the Union; six gargantuan bronze entry-doors decorated with scenes from state history; a rotunda with a five-ton Tiffany chandelier; and a large circular Russian Circassian Walnut table in the State Reception Room, whose base was carved from a single tree trunk in the shape of eagles' legs. The building was damaged by a 2001 earthquake, which had its epicenter in nearby Nisqually, but was refurbished to deal with the damage (after it had just been upgraded before the earthquake) and re-opened in 2004.

Around the capitol campus

Across from the Capitol, the **Hall of Justice** (Mon–Fri 8am–5pm; same information as above) is the Neoclassical home of the state supreme court, with an elegant colonnade clad in sandstone, its suitably imposing Roman architecture echoing its neighbor's nicely. The two buildings are accessible via Capitol Way, which, at 14th Ave, hosts the Capitol's **visitors' center** as well as **Winged Victory** – a striking bronze memorial commemorating Washington's fallen soldiers in World War I with the winged figure herself, several soldiers from different service branches, and a nurse. Memorial Day events and others typically take place around this 1938 statue, no doubt because the **World War II Memorial**, not far at Capitol Way and 11th Ave, is a much more abstract bronze-and-granite affair that's not quite so triumphant, poignantly engraved with the names of six thousand deceased soldiers from the state.

Next to the Capitol, the **governor's mansion** (Wed, by reservation only at ☎360/902-8880) is a redbrick neo-Georgian house that was erected as a temporary structure in 1908 and slated for demolition soon after. Surprisingly, the building has lasted nearly a century, and has even been renovated and expanded several times. Its current resident is Christine Gregoire, who won Washington's heavily disputed 2004 election by a mere 129 votes in a re-count. On the northern side of the campus, the **Capitol Conservatory and Gardens**, 11th Ave at Water St (Mon–Fri 8am–3pm; free; ☎360/586-TOUR), is worth a look for its eclectic selection of plants from tropical to northern regions, many of which are grown here to decorate other gardens on the campus site.

Across from the campus at 11th Ave and Capitol Way, the **Hands On Children's Museum** (Mon–Sat 10am–5pm, Sun noon–5pm; $7; ☻www.hocm.org), with its art studio and science-oriented games and puzzles, offers solace for the tots who've seen too many Greek columns and statues for one day. Eight blocks south of the capitol campus, the **State Capital Museum**, in the Renaissance Revival-styled Lord Mansion at 211 W 21st Ave (Tues–Fri 10am–4pm, Sat noon–4pm; $2; ☎360/753-2580, ☻www.wshs.org/wscm), houses two floors of marginally interesting exhibits. The detailed but dry overview about the history of Olympia on the ground floor is outshone by the Native American displays and temporary exhibits on state politics and the Puget Sound region upstairs.

Wolf Haven International

About ten miles south of Olympia along Old Highway 99, **Wolf Haven International** (tours on the hour March–Jan Wed–Mon 10am–3pm, summer also 4pm; 1hr length; $8; ☻www.wolfhaven.org) is a nonprofit organization offering sanctuary to more than forty wolves who are not able to survive in the wild. The guided tours let you walk within yards of the unexpectedly friendly animals, and the tour guides occasionally let loose with full-throated imitation wolf howls, setting off a blood-curdling frenzy of mournful baying among the resident lupines. The exchange is even more surreal during a "**howl-in**" (July to early Sept, biweekly Sat 6–9pm; $12), a combination of storytelling and music that draws upon wolf-related myths and legends and involves howling at the wolves until they respond in kind. A half-hour tour is also part of the event, sometimes with nature-related movies and cocktails; to **camp** afterwards, add $13 per person (by reservation only at ☎360/264-4695). The institute also hosts affordable **group presentations** for ten or more people (May–Aug, hours vary; reserve two weeks in advance; $8), which focus on wolves from different parts of the world, and the current challenges these creatures face from human encroachment.

Eating and drinking

Otto's 111 N Washington St NE ☎ 360/352-8640. Popular, reliable bakery that offers cheap and healthy breakfast and lunch dishes plus good bagels; the other branch is in San Francisco. Daily 7.30am–2pm.

Saigon Rendezvous 117 Fifth Ave SW ☎ 360/352-1989. Good mix of Chinese, Thai, and Vietnamese food (with a few veggie options) that's reasonably priced and well-portioned. Right in the city center. Mon–Sat 10.30am–10pm, Sun 11.30am–9pm.

Santosh 116 Fourth Ave W ☎ 360/943-3442. Extensive menu of decent Indian dishes, and an all-you-care-to-eat lunchtime buffet for around $10. Sun–Thurs 11am–9.30pm, Fri & Sat 11am–10pm.

Spar Café 114 Fourth Ave E ☎ 360/357-6444. Old-time American diner cuisine in a funky 1930s-era setting, with a long, curving counter, old photos of Olympia on the wall, and a backroom lounge for smokers and drinkers. Also with blues and jazz on Saturday nights. Sun–Thurs 6am–10pm, Fri & Sat 6am–11pm.

Urban Onion 116 Legion Way ☎ 360/943-9242. Serves up delicious, inexpensive burgers for the vegetarian and carnivore alike. Mon–Wed 7am–9pm, Thurs 7am–10pm, Fri 7am–11pm, Sat 8am–11pm, Sun 8am–9pm.

23

Puget Sound

The grand waterway of **Puget Sound** marks the western boundary of the Seattle metropolitan area. From north to south, the Sound covers about a hundred miles, and is dotted throughout by numerous islands, ranging in size from the largest in the continental US to tiniest waterlogged plots. Many of these islands make great getaways: **Vashon**, **Bainbridge**, and **Whidbey islands** all have a more relaxed pace than Seattle and are served frequently by ferry. On the mainland of the Olympic Peninsula, the Victorian burg of **Port Townsend** has some notable historical sights and good nightlife; while east of Whidbey, artsy **La Conner** makes for another pleasant waterside diversion. Further up the Sound, the more distant **San Juan Islands** offer some of the most tranquil settings in all of western Washington, a good stopover especially if you're on your way to Victoria, British Columbia.

Vashon and Maury islands

A half-hour from Seattle by ferry, **VASHON ISLAND**, spread over 48 square miles, lures visitors with its sizable parks, open fields, rocky beaches, and rural roads. The main highway runs across the narrow island, while a sliver of sandbar and fill connect it to adjoining **MAURY ISLAND**, less than half the size of its neighbor, with much of the same scenery. The islands' attractive vistas and low-key atmosphere are their main appeal, and the lone spot worth seeking out, for its striking views of downtown Seattle and Mount Rainier, is the beachside setting of the **Point Robinson Lighthouse** (tours by reservation only at ☎206/463-9602). Located on the eastern end of Maury Island off Point Robinson Road, this tiny beacon has been shining for ninety years; if you're really into the setting you can stay for a week at the adjacent **lighthouse keeper's quarters** ($800–950; info at ☎206-463-9602).

Vashon Island is well connected to the Seattle metro region, the Kitsap Peninsula, and Tacoma. You can bring over a **car** via West Seattle's Fauntleroy ferry terminal, but the best way to explore Vashon Island is to take a **bike** on the ferry that leaves from the Downtown Seattle terminal – though you should note that only ten bicycles are permitted on this passenger-only boat (see Basics, p.34, for complete ferry information). The connections to Tacoma and the Kitsap Peninsula take you to Point Defiance Park (see p.240) and Southworth, respectively. Alternatively, you can rent a **bike** from Vashon Island Bicycles, in the north-central part of the island at 9925 SW 178th St (☎206/463-6225) – they go for $5 an hour, $20 a day, and $50 for a three-day weekend. For an entirely

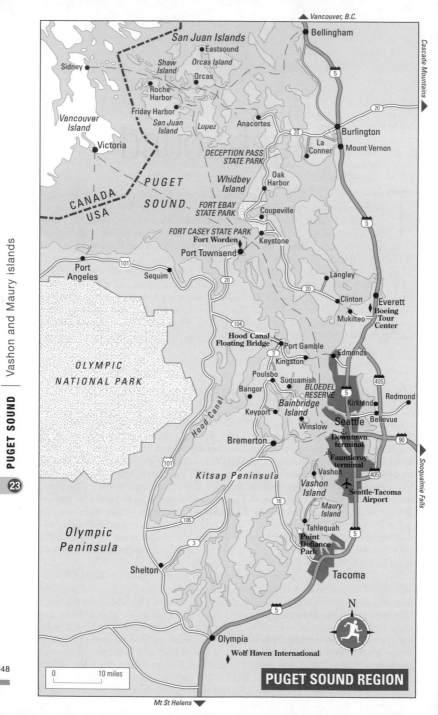

Vancouver, B.C.

Bellingham

San Juan Islands

Eastsound

Orcas Island

Sidney

Shaw Island

Orcas

Cascade Mountains

5

20

Roche Harbor

Friday Harbor

San Juan Island

Vancouver Island

Lopez

Anacortes

20

La Conner

Burlington

Mount Vernon

Victoria

P U G E T

DECEPTION PASS STATE PARK

5

Whidbey Island

Oak Harbor

S O U N D

CANADA

USA

FORT EBAY STATE PARK

Coupeville

FORT CASEY STATE PARK
Fort Worden

Keystone

Port Angeles

Port Townsend

101

Sequim

20

Langley

20

Clinton

Everett
Boeing Tour Center

Mukilteo

104

Snoqualmie Falls

OLYMPIC

NATIONAL PARK

Hood Canal Floating Bridge

Port Gamble

3

Kingston

Poulsbo

Suquamish

BLOEDEL RESERVE

Edmonds

405

Redmond

Bangor

Keyport

Bainbridge Island

Kirkland

Bellevue

Hood Canal

Winslow

Seattle

Downtown terminal

Fauntleroy terminal

90

Bremerton

Kitsap Peninsula

Vashon

101

Vashon Island

405

16

Maury Island

Seattle-Tacoma Airport

106

3

Olympic Peninsula

Tahlequah

Point Defiance Park

5

Shelton

Tacoma

N

5

Olympia

Wolf Haven International

0   10 miles

PUGET SOUND REGION

Mt St Helens

different view of the two islands, you can rent a **boat** at Puget Sound Kayak, on an inlet on the island's east shore, at 8900 SW Harbor Drive ($14–25 per hour, $40–65 per day; ☎206/463-9257), and explore the beaches and coves in a single- or double-seat kayak, canoe or rowboat.

Vashon

A sleepy hamlet for most of Seattle's history, Vashon Island's main town of **VASHON** is increasingly a preserve for Seattle yuppies, whom longtime residents say you can count by the increasing number of Mercedes and Jaguars loading onto the ferries. Although companies like the ski-manufacturer K2 have their headquarters here, the burg is mainly useful to visitors as a base for exploring the rest of the two islands. If you happen to be here during July, you can check out the **Strawberry Festival**, an annual event showcasing natural foods (highlighted by the eponymous berry) and featuring spirited parades, upbeat music, and locals garbed in all manner of colorful costumes.

The one way in which bucolic Vashon defies the usual small-town stereotypes is with its engaging **gallery** scene – there are a number of good art spaces here, some of them run by current or former Seattlites, and you're apt to see more than the anodyne landscapes you might expect. Anything from performance to functional to installation art, as well as painting, sculpture and photography is likely to be on view at galleries in or around downtown along Vashon Highway SW. Some of these include the Blue Heron, no. 17600; Gallery 070, no. 17633; and Silverwood, no. 23927. During the first two weeks of May and December, a **Studio Tour** lets you peek inside the studios of forty artists, while the **Gallery Cruise** (first Fri of month; free) is another public event with food, music and showings of the town's latest artwork (info for both at ⓦwww.vashonalliedarts.org).

Accommodation

All listings below are on Vashon Island; Maury Island has few amenities.

Artist's Studio Loft 16529 91st Ave SW ☎206/463-2583, ⓦwww.asl-bnb.com. This splendid B&B offers four swanky rooms and cottages with tasteful modern furnishings, fireplaces, and kitchenettes, as well as onsite gardens and a hot tub in a tranquil natural setting. $95.

AYH Ranch Hostel 12119 SW Cove Rd ☎206/463-2592, ⓦwww.vashonhostel .com. Offers dorm beds in pseudo-historic log cabins, tepees and covered wagons for $16, or private rooms for $70.

Lavender Duck 16503 Vashon Hwy SW ☎206/463-2592, ⓦwww.vashonhostel .com/ldmain.html. Vashon's most affordable non-hostel accommodations, with four serviceable, if rather basic, rooms in a 1986 farmhouse. $70.

Swallow's Nest Guest Cottages 6030 SW 248th St ☎206/463-2646, ⓦwww .vashonislandcottages.com. Eight bird-themed cottage units with varying amenities, from utilitarian to elegant Victorian decor; located in four separate sites throughout Vashon, including an entire house ($125 per floor). Rooms start at $85.

Eating and drinking

Casa Bonita 17623 100th Ave SW ☎206/463-6452. A good Mexican restaurant – a rarity in the area – with large, inexpensive portions of enchiladas, fajitas, and the like. Daily 11am–10pm.

Express Cuisine 17629 Vashon Hwy SW ☎206/463-6626. Very informal setting, with large shared tables and delicious, filling dishes, dominated by seafood staples but with assorted ethnic items –

23

such as Caribbean jerk chicken – included as well, for moderate prices. Wed–Sun 5–10pm.

Hardware Store 17601 Vashon Hwy SW ☎206/463-1800. A former hardware vendor now converted into a dining spot for nouveau American cuisine, with espresso bar, local art on display, and wine, furniture and other items for sale. Wed–Mon 9am–9pm.

Rock Island Pub & Pizza 17322 Vashon Hwy SW ☎206/463-6814. Gourmet pizzas and microbrews for moderate prices. Tues–Sat 11am–9.30pm.

Sound Food 20312 Vashon Hwy SW ☎206/463-3565. Straightforward, inexpensive veggie and vegan sandwiches, salads, and pastries in an agreeable setting. Mon–Thurs 7am–8pm, Fri 7am–9pm, Sat & Sun 8am–8pm.

Bainbridge Island

The highlight of visiting **BAINBRIDGE ISLAND** is just getting to it on the ferry ride from Seattle – just east across the Sound – which sweeps by the Magnolia bluffs on the outward journey and offers a close-up view of the cityscape upon the return (see Basics, p.34, for ferry information). Despite the island's touristy shops and galleries near the ferry dock, it's not entirely welcoming to outsiders: public transit is sparse, there are no budget accommodations (other than the hardscrabble state park campsite in the north), and the island's narrow roads aren't great for biking. There are some artsy stores and comfortable diners in **Winslow**, a small harborside town, and the **Bloedel Reserve** provides some interest as well for its floral blooms. Even better, the island serves as a gateway to the north part of the Kitsap Peninsula (see p.251). Bainbridge Island's **visitors' center** is located in Winslow at 590 Winslow Way E (☎206/842-3700, ⓦwww.bainbridgechamber.com).

Winslow and the Bloedel Reserve

Bainbridge's single noteworthy town, **WINSLOW** features restaurants, boutiques, and antique shops on its main block of **Winslow Way**. There are galleries here, too, though the work therein is not quite as interesting or adventurous as that found on Vashon Island. Still, Bainbridge Arts and Crafts, 151 Winslow Way E (☎206/842-3132, ⓦwww.bainbridgeartscrafts.org), and the Island Gallery, 106 Madison Ave (☎206/780-9500, ⓦwww.theislandgallery.net), display inventive pottery, jewelry, sculpture, and the like. On the plaza behind City Hall (which is on Madison Avenue), the **farmers' market** sells produce and crafts on Saturday mornings (9am–1pm) from May to September.

A car is necessary to reach Bainbridge Island's only official attraction, the **Bloedel Reserve**, 7571 NE Dolphin Drive, off the Agatewood Road exit of Hwy-305 (Wed–Sun 10am–4pm; $10; by reservation only at ☎206/842-7631, ⓦwww.bloedelreserve.org). Sited on the former grounds of a lumberman's estate, this conservatory contains nearly 150 acres of gardens, ponds, meadows, and wildlife habitats, including 84 acres of second-growth forest and rhododendrons, along with three hundred varieties of trees and 15,000 cyclamen plants. It's often perfectly quiet except for the birds (there's a refuge with swans, blue herons, and more), while the geometric Japanese garden and forest-enclosed reflecting pool add to the ethereal aura.

Accommodation

The island is loaded with one- and two-bedroom units, detached cottages, and the like for rent. Bainbridge Vacation Rentals (☎206/855-9763,

@ www.bainbridgevacationrentals.com) provides the rundown on many such rentals: anything from a simple studio to a several-story house, from one night to a month, running anywhere from $100 per night to $1000 a week.

Fay Bainbridge State Park off Sunrise Drive NE ☎206/842-3931, @ www.parks.wa.gov. Seventeen-acre campground on the northeast tip of Bainbridge Island, with 36 very basic sites and a beach with good views of the surrounding area. Closed mid-Oct to mid-April (but open for day use year-round). $15–21.

Furin-Oka 12580 Vista Drive NE, 3 miles north of Winslow ☎206/842-4916, @www .futonandbreakfast.com. Stylish replica of a Japanese guesthouse located in a bamboo grove, with traditional amenities like a soaking tub, kimonos, and *shoji* screens. Japanese or American breakfasts available. $159.

Island Country Inn 920 Hildebrand Lane NE, just north of Winslow ☎206/842-6861, @www.nwcountryinns.com/bainbridge.html. Bainbridge's only hotel, this worthwhile choice has 46 rooms, all with queen- or king-sized beds; there's also a pool and Jacuzzi. Rooms $109; suites with microwaves and fridges for $30–50 more per night.

Eating and drinking

Harbour Public House 231 Parfitt Way SW, Winslow ☎206/842-0969, @ www.harbourpub .com. Renovated 1881 house now used for serving up the usual range of seafood, salads, burgers, and beer – most of it quite serviceable. Tues–Sun 5–10pm.

San Carlos 279 Madison Ave N ☎206/842-1999. A nice touch of nouveau Mexican and Southwest US fare transported to Puget Sound. Quite good for its mid-priced ribs, chili, garlic prawns, and chimichangas. Daily 5–10pm.

Sawatdy Thai Cuisine 8770 Fletcher Bay Rd NE ☎206/780-2429. On the opposite side of the island from Winslow, Bainbridge's best Thai restaurant is good for traditional, inexpensive staples like spicy soups and noodle dishes. Tues–Fri 11.30am–1.30pm & Tues–Sun 5–9.30pm.

Winslow Way Cafe 122 Winslow Way, Winslow ☎206/842-0517. One of the pricier local restaurants, but also among the best; good for gourmet pizza, pasta, and seafood. Sun–Thurs 4.30–9.30pm, Fri & Sat 4.30–10.30pm.

The Kitsap Peninsula

From the northern part of Bainbridge Island, you can cross over on the Agate Pass Bridge to the **KITSAP PENINSULA**. While not too far from Seattle itself, Kitsap feels a world away, with all the small-town charms (and limitations) of other parts of the Olympic Peninsula – of which this peninsula is itself an extension. So irregular is its shoreline you could almost mistake it for another large island, if not for the peninsula's narrow southern stretches linked by Highway 3 to Olympia much further south. However, unless you're camping at one of the remote state parks (check @ www.parks.wa.gov for the rundown), there's little reason to stay overnight here, and Kitsap's sights are best explored on a day-trip leading up to Port Townsend (see p.253).

Suquamish

From Bainbridge Island, the village of **SUQUAMISH** is just a few miles north of Hwy-305 near the Port Madison Indian Reservation. Seattle's namesake, **Chief Sealth**, is buried here in **St Peter's Churchyard**, 7076 NE South St (daily dawn–dusk), his grave marked by two large dugout canoes atop wooden beams. The sight is quite dramatic – by far the greatest memorial to Sealth in the region – and you may even find the Chief's headstone marked with ceremonial necklaces, beads, and other native honors. Half a mile away, **Old Man House Park** (daily 8am–dusk) was where the Suquamish people's 500ft by 50ft **longhouse** stood, the longest one ever constructed on Puget Sound; it was burned down by the government in 1870. Today, the park is a pleasant little spot that provides a nice respite with its picnic tables and good views of the Sound. For more on the tribe, the **Suquamish Museum**, off Hwy-305 on the way to Poulsbo, at 15838 Sandy Hook Rd (daily May–Sept 10am–5pm; Oct–April Fri–Sun 11am–4pm; $4; ⊛www.suquamish.nsn.us/museum), movingly recounts the native population's forced Americanization after whites had established dominance in Puget Sound. The museum also presents exhibits on the games, craftwork, and culture of the tribe, along with a selection of vintage photographs of its members from the early twentieth century.

Poulsbo to Port Gamble

As you continue north, you'll come to **POULSBO**, a bizarre sort of tourist trap with coffee-shop Viking signs, gabled roofs, and Scandinavian foodstuffs on display. Founded by Norwegians, it has exploited its heritage by revamping the cafés and souvenir shops along its main route, Front Street, in "little Oslo" kitsch. Needless to say, locals take every opportunity to dress up in fancy Nordic duds, especially during mid-May's **Viking Fest** (☎360-779-3378, ⊛www .vikingfest.org). Heading north, you soon rejoin the main road – Hwy-3 – and reach the **Hood Canal Floating Bridge**, which crosses over to the Olympic Peninsula. More than a mile in length, the bridge used to be billed as an engineering miracle – until a chunk of it floated out to sea during a violent storm in 1979. These days it's mainly known for its traffic, which can be hellish if you're coming back to Seattle at the end of a weekend or holiday – expect to wait for miles going eastbound if you're unlucky enough to be here when endless "marine traffic" keeps the drawbridge raised.

Just a few miles north of the east side of the bridge, **PORT GAMBLE** is a nicely preserved community built in the 1850s as part of a sawmill complex – a mill that lasted until 1995, when its operator shut it down. Still, the charming old houses and Carpenter Gothic–styled **St Paul's Episcopal Church** remain, and the little town retains a good measure of the New England sea-village atmosphere its creators intended – in fact, many of the first residents came straight from Maine. It shouldn't take long to wander the handful of streets and main buildings found here; to get started, visit the **Port Gamble Historic Museum**, directly facing the bay near the general store (May–Oct daily 10.30am–5pm; $2.50; ☎360/297-8074, ⊛www.ptgamble.com/museum), for a **walking map** and background on the history of this quaint little town.

Keyport and Bremerton

Once you reach Hwy 3 from Poulsbo, there are two main reasons for heading south toward Olympia – either to complete a grand loop of the Puget Sound region, or to go back to Seattle from Bremerton, taking in a magnificent **ferry ride** (see "Basics," p.34) that lasts an hour and takes you past the verdant, craggy bays and inlets around the Kitsap Peninsula and Bainbridge Island. On the highway which runs south to the outskirts of Bremerton, military enthusiasts will be keen to visit **KEYPORT**, site of the **Naval Undersea Museum**, just east of Hwy-3 on Hwy-308 (June–Sept daily 10am–4pm; Oct–May closed Tues; free). Operated by the US Navy, it displays an imposing array of nautical weaponry, from torpedoes to depth charges to aquatic mines and various other bombs and destructive gadgets.

Ten miles further south along Hwy-3, a turnoff leads three more miles east to **BREMERTON**, a rough-edged shipyard town that, apart from its ferry terminal, draws visitors for its **Bremerton Naval Museum**, 402 Pacific Ave (Mon–Sat 10am–4pm, Sun 1–4pm; donation suggested; ☎360/479-SHIP), a mildly interesting assortment of historic weaponry and model ships, and the warship **USS Turner Joy**, 300 Washington Beach Ave (summer daily 10am–5pm; $7; ☎360/792-2457), the most conspicuous sight in the area. This 1959 destroyer – which you can tour and poke about its crew cabins, torpedo launchers, and other elements – is most notable for being involved in the 1965 Gulf of Tonkin incident, which became President Lyndon Johnson's thin excuse for Congress to escalate the war in Vietnam.

Port Townsend

Once you cross the Hood Canal Floating Bridge and continue westbound along Hwy-104, then north on Hwy-20, you reach **PORT TOWNSEND**, alive with brightly painted Victorian mansions, convivial cafés, and a vigorous cultural scene. A wannabe San Francisco since the mid-nineteenth century, the town's economic clout developed through the timber industry and a busy seaport in the last half of the 1800s. The town was well-poised for Puget Sound supremacy in the late 1880s and early 1890s, when confident predictions of a railway terminus lured the rich here, who set about building extravagant Gothic

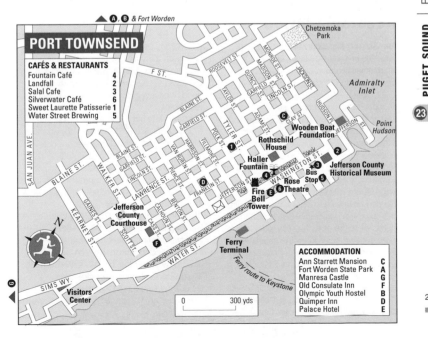

homes on the bluff above the port. Unfortunately for the investors, the railway never happened, and the town was left with a glut of stylish residences overlooking a small, hapless business district.

In more recent times, this combination has turned out to be Port Townsend's trump card: since the old mansions were restored in the 1960s, the town has mellowed into an artsy community with a good degree of charm. Choices for accommodation are varied, with tourists in search of Victoriana filling plush B&Bs, and the nearby nineteenth-century **Fort Worden** providing ample **camping** and **youth hostel** facilities. Port Townsend also puts on several big **music festivals** throughout the year, most notably the Festival of American Fiddle Tunes in early July, a Jazz Festival in late July, and a Blues Festival in early August. The programs are organized by a nonprofit arts organization, Centrum, based in Fort Worden (☏360/385-5320 or 1-800/733-3608, ⓦwww.centrum .org); book accommodation well ahead of time if you plan on attending any of these festivals.

Arrival and information

Port Townsend is thirty minutes by **ferry** from Keystone on Whidbey Island near Fort Casey (see Basics, p.34 for ferry information), or accessible by land over the Hood Canal Bridge from the Kitsap Peninsula (see p.252). Pick up information at the **visitors' center**, half a mile south of the town center on Hwy-20 at 2437 Sims Way (daily 9am–5pm; ☏360/385-2722, ⓦwww .ptguide.com). To get around, you can rent a **bike** from PT Cyclery, 252 Tyler St (Mon–Sat 9am–6pm; ☏360/385-6470, ⓦwww.ptcyclery.com), for $7 per hour or $25 a day, and get information on area cycling trails; or hop around on a Jefferson Transit **bus** ($1.25 for unlimited daily rides; ☏1-800/371-0497, ⓦwww.jeffersontransit.com), with eight major routes serving the area.

Accommodation

Ann Starrett Mansion 744 Clay St ☏360/ 385-3205 or 1-800/321-0644, ⓦwww .starrettmansion.com. One of the town's most imposing Victorian mansions, an 1889 Queen Anne with elegant ceiling frescoes, a splendid spiral staircase, and antique furnishings. Nine ornate and comfortable doubles and suites, starting at $115. Also offers a pair of two-room suites in a Downtown cottage ($125–145).

Fort Worden State Park off Cherry St north of Downtown ☏360/385-4730, ⓦfortworden .org. The old military compound of Fort Worden has two campsites: one has thirty units near the conference center ($22 per night), while the other has fifty sites in a more enticing location by the seashore ($27). Elegant, former military houses and apartments are also available for nightly rent, starting at $113.

Manresa Castle Seventh and Sheridan streets ☏360/385-5750 or 1-800/732-1281, ⓦwww.manresacastle.com. Quasi-French

castle from 1892 that's now an elegant hotel with thirty rooms that range from cozy single units ($99) to swanky suites in the tower ($189). Also has a surprisingly good, if pricey, nouvelle Northwest cuisine restaurant.

Old Consulate Inn 313 Walker St ☏360/385-6753 or 1-800/300-6753, ⓦwww.oldconsulateinn .com. Dating from 1889, this elegant uptown villa, with its spiky tower and wraparound veranda, has seven plush suites ($130 and up, plus one rather small room for $99), as well as a grand piano and an old organ. Add $15–20 for high season.

Olympic Youth Hostel 272 Battery Way, Fort Worden State Park ☏360/385-0655, ⓦfortworden.org. Up the hill from the Parade Ground in Fort Worden, with dorm beds, private rooms, and a kitchen. An all-you-can-eat pancake breakfast is included. Check-in 5–10pm; early check-out at 9.30am. $17 dorms, private rooms $25.

Palace Hotel 1004 Water St ⓣ360/385-0773, ⓦwww.palacehotelpt.com. The best bet for staying Downtown, this refurbished Victorian charmer has an elegant lobby and in-room antique decor, claw-footed tubs, and excellent views of the Sound. The basic rooms are ultra-cheap ($59 with shared bath), and even the two-room suites are affordable ($109 and up).

Quimper Inn 1306 Franklin St ⓣ360/385-1060 or 1-800/557-1060, ⓦwww.quimperinn.com. Delightful 1888 B&B decked out in Colonial Revival style, restored and furnished with period decor; has five comfortable guestrooms. $98.

Downtown

Port Townsend's physical split – half on a bluff, half at sea-level – reflects its Victorian-era social divisions, in which wealthy merchants built their homes uptown, and the working class were stuck with the noise and ruckus of the port below. **Downtown** is the commercial center of Port Townsend, its shops and cafés located on and around **Water Street**, which sports an attractive medley of 1890s brick and stone buildings. The main route into town, Sims Way, leads right to this historic stretch, and the ferry pulls in just a few blocks south as well.

Along Water Street, there are many fine bookstores, coffeehouses, and antique shops that are worth a browse, and also not to be missed is the splendid little **Rose Theatre**, near the fountain at 235 Taylor St (ⓦwww.rosetheatre.com), a restored 1907 gem that plays independent and art films. Just two blocks away along the wharf, you can take a break at any of the **landings** to watch the ferries, fishing trawlers, and pleasure cruisers go about their business in the Sound. There are few other official sights in the vicinity, but for **City Hall**, 540 Water St, a boxy Italianate structure that's now being restored to its early condition, so as to once again hold the **Jefferson County Historical Museum**, temporarily relocated to 210 Polk St (Mon–Sat 11am–4pm, Sun 1–4pm; $3; ⓣ360/385-1003, ⓦwww.jchsmuseum.org), the best place to get the skinny on the town's interesting history. Although the exhibits are in flux during the restoration, you're apt to spot such items as a photographer's chair draped with bear and buffalo skins; unusual late nineteenth- and early twentieth-century two-necked harp guitars; and displays on native peoples in the area, nautical activities, and the port's appearance (along with Fort Worden's) in such Hollywood films as *An Officer and a Gentleman*.

Further north, it's just a couple of minutes' walk to **Point Hudson**, where the old Coast Guard Training Station has been turned into a marina. Here, the Wooden Boat Foundation, at 380 Jefferson St, holds the annual **Wooden Boat Festival** (ⓣ360/385-4742, ⓦwww.woodenboat.org), a three-day weekend event in September with more than 150 wooden boats of all kinds on display.

The upper town

Above downtown is the uptown bluff, which is only accessible by road on its north and south ends – also by staircase off Taylor Street, which leads past the incongruous **Haller Fountain**, decorated with a nude sculpture of "Venus rising from the sea." The **upper town** is conspicuously marked by the looming **Fire Bell Tower**, its wooden red frame rising 75 feet in a picturesque, but no longer purposeful, manner. It was built in 1890 to summon volunteer firemen during powerful blazes with a 1500-pound brass ringer, but it's been nearly eighty years since it stopped working – still, it's relevant enough to Port Townsend's image to have been architecturally restored in 2004. In the blocks around the tower are some of the big wooden mansions it was no doubt put there to save, including the **Ann Starrett House**, 744 Clay St (see "Accommodation," p.254), which swarms with gables, boasting an octagonal tower and an impressively ornate elliptical staircase that has to be seen to be believed; it was built in 1889 near the end of Port Townsend's boom. The 1868 **Rothschild House**, at Franklin and Taylor streets (Mon–Sat 11am–4pm, Sun 1–4pm; $4; ☎360/385-1003), predates the high times, its plankboard frame and simple columns making it resemble a sedate Colonial Revival farmhouse. More impressive than either – or practically anything else in the region – is the grand **Jefferson County Courthouse**, Walker and Jefferson streets (Mon–Fri 9am–5pm; ⊛www.co.jefferson.wa.us), a towering red Romanesque Revival edifice with a clock tower that looks like a medieval Italian version of Big Ben.

Fort Worden

Two miles north of downtown Port Townsend, along Cherry Street, **FORT WORDEN** (☎360/344-4400, ⊛www.fortworden.org) was one of a trio of coastal fortifications (including Fort Casey, across the sound; see p.259) built at the beginning of the twentieth century to protect Puget Sound from attack by the new steam-powered battleships. Used by the army until 1953, then employed as a juvenile detention center for the next twenty years, Worden is now an expansive state park. Just beyond the main gates is the large, green **Parade Ground**, where soldiers once marched; it's lined on one side by the barracks, a series of plain wooden buildings that are rented as vacation units (see "Accommodation," p.254). The *Olympic Youth Hostel* and the **visitors' center**, 200 Battery Way (summer daily 10am–4pm, March–April & Nov Sat & Sun only; ☎360/344-4458), are also found here.

Across from the Parade Ground, the century-old Officers' Row culminates in the sedate **Commanding Officers' House** (June–Aug daily 10am–5pm; March–May & Sept–Oct Sat & Sun noon–4pm; $2), a 1904 Colonial Revival home whose interior has been carefully decked out in full retro-Victorian style, its upper story adorned with stern-looking portraits of most of the 33 commanders who called the place home. Beyond the Parade Ground, old bunkers radiate out across the park – though the most diverting are down along the seashore, including the massive concrete gun emplacements of the **Kinzie Battery**, which date from the 1890s. If you're really intrigued by these deadly relics, you can take a trail and go poking around **Artillery Hill**, where the guns sit silently under heavy tree cover. The park's **Coast Artillery Museum** (summer daily 11am–4pm, rest of year Sat & Sun noon–4pm; $2) provides more information on the Fort's strategic value and heavy weaponry.

Also along the shore – but much nearer to the Parade Ground, at the end of the wharf – is the small **Marine Science Center**, 532 Battery Way (April–May & Sept–Oct Sat & Sun noon–4pm, June–Aug Wed–Mon 11am–5pm; $5; ☎360/385-5582, ⊛www.ptmsc.org/index.html), which has large tanks in which you can touch tidepool creatures and observe local animals and plants; you can also review a timeline of Puget Sound natural history.

Don't leave the area before you've had a chance to see one of Port Townsend's visual icons, the **Point Wilson Lighthouse**, a 1913 column at the end of Quimper Peninsula off Harbor Defense Way, just beyond Fort Worden (grounds tours Wed 11am–4pm; donation suggested). Even today, the isolated beacon still guides ships through the Admiralty Inlet of Puget Sound, giving you a sense of the rugged maritime atmosphere of a century ago (even though the light's been automated for thirty years).

Eating and drinking

Fountain Café 920 Washington St ☎360/385-1364. Mid-priced seafood and pasta specialties like oyster stew and wild mushroom risotto in a small spot a short distance from the waterfront. Daily 5–9pm & Wed–Sun 8am–3pm, Mon & Tues 11.30am–3pm.

Landfall 412 Water St ☎360/385-5814. Pleasant dining on the Point Hudson waterfront, with an imaginative menu of seafood and vegetarian dishes, as well as fresh salmon and tasty fish tacos and onion burgers. Moderate prices, too. Daily 7am–2pm.

Salal Café 634 Water St at Taylor St ☎360/385-6532. Very popular spot renowned for its breakfasts – blintzes, omelets, frittatas, and crêpes – and also good for its solid lunchtime burgers and pastas. Serves up a mean tofu stroganoff, too. Daily 7am–2pm.

Silverwater Café 237 Taylor St ☎360/385-6448, ⓦwww.silverwatercafe.com. Well-regarded for its seafood dishes – such as Northwest floribunda and ahi tuna with lavender pepper – the café also has mid-priced pasta and vegetarian selections. Mon–Fri 11.30am–8.30pm, Sat 11.30am–9.30pm, Sun 5–8.30pm.

🏃 **Sweet Laurette Patisserie** 1029 Lawrence St ☎360/385-4886, ⓦwww.sweetlaurette.com. One of the best bets for French-style baked goods in town, with elaborate (and expensive) cakes that resemble artworks, and more affordable scones, pies, and pastries, plus savory omelets, panini, and croissant sandwiches. Mon–Fri 7am–5pm, Sat 8am–5pm, Sun 8am–3pm.

Water Street Brewing 639 Water St ☎360/379-6438. Funky live-music joint showcasing blues and rock bands, and boasting great microbrews, solid staples like fish-and-chips, and a wonderful old wooden bar with an enormous mirror to boot. Sun-Thurs 11.30am–9.30pm, Fri & Sat 11.30am–10pm.

Whidbey Island

The largest island in the continental US – nearly fifty miles from southern to northern tip – **WHIDBEY ISLAND** is a winding, serpentine stretch of land that covers much of the Sound. Not easily seen in full on a short ferry trip, it requires at least a solid day to appreciate its diverse qualities. The island's small towns of **Langley** and **Coupeville** are both pleasant stops, while **Fort Casey**, **Fort Ebey**, and dramatic **Deception Pass State Park** are more enticing with their remote wooded trails and stark cliffside vistas.

△ Walkway along Puget Sound

Arrival and information

Ferries to Whidbey Island leave from **Mukilteo**, about thirty miles north of Seattle off I-5, a little southwest of Everett (see p.140). The twenty-minute ferry ride (see "Basics" for ferry information; p.34) terminates at **Clinton**, a tiny town near Whidbey's southern edge; from there, Hwy-525 snakes through the middle of the island to Deception Pass at the top, turning into Hwy-20 halfway through the journey.

Island Transit has a **free bus service** running the length of the island on eleven different routes – you'll need to take routes #1 and 4 to go the full distance (daily except Sun; ☎360/678-7771, 360/321-6688 or 1-800/240-8747, ⓦwww.islandtransit.org), but bringing a **car** is advisable if you want to visit Whidbey's less accessible attractions. The Central Whidbey Chamber of Commerce runs the **visitors' center** in Coupeville, 107 S Main St (☎360/678-5434, ⓦwww.centralwhidbeychamber.com), with all the requisite brochures on island attractions and the many B&Bs; a free **visitors' guide**, with a detailed **map** of the island, can also be picked up on the ferry.

Accommodation

Anchorage Inn 807 N Main St, Coupeville ☎360/678-5581 ⓦwww.anchorage-inn.com. One of the better deals around – seven affordable B&B rooms, decorated in a mild Victorian style, in a pleasant setting with a view of the Sound ($85). Adjacent cottage ($160 per night) is an 1883 charmer with two bedrooms. Special discounts for art students and ministers.

Captain Whidbey Inn 2072 W Captain Whidbey Inn Rd, Coupeville ☎360/678-4097 or 1-800/366-4097, ⓦwww.captainwhidbey.com. Out of the way, but worth it, with quiet, wooden-walled rooms overlooking Penn Cove, cottages and chalets in the forest, and a restaurant, *The Cove*, renowned for its seafood. Four- to six-day package trips include cruises on the Inn's *Cutty Sark* ship ($1950 and up). Rooms $85, cabins $175, cottages $275.

Country Cottage of Langley 215 Sixth St, Langley ☎360/221-8709 or 1-800/718-3860, ⓦwww.acountrycottage.com. Five rooms in a restored 1920s farmhouse, on a bluff above Langley and the Puget Sound. All rooms have CD players and fridges ($139); the more expensive suites have Jacuzzi tubs and fireplaces ($179).

Deception Pass State Park 5175 N Hwy-20 ☎360/657-2417, ⓦwww.parks.wa.gov. One of the most popular state parks in the US, Deception Pass is spread over 4000 acres and has around 250 tent sites, as well as primitive grounds. It fills up quickly in the summer months, so call ahead. $15–21.

Ebey's Landing National Historic Reserve Fort Casey and Fort Ebey state parks, north of Keystone ☎360/678-4636, ⓦwww.parks.wa.gov. Two parks built around old defense installations, with good hiking trails, and a mix of trailer, tent and primitive campsites. Reservations taken at Fort Ebey; closed Nov–Feb. $15–21.

The Inn at Langley 400 First St, Langley ☎360/221-3033, ⓦwww.innatlangley.com. One of the poshest stopovers on the Sound, built into a bluff overlooking the water. Starting at $250/night, all 26 rooms have porches with waterfront views; the suites and private cottages cost about twice as much. You can save $50 by coming during the week in the offseason.

Langley and Coupeville

The ferry from Mukilteo lands at sleepy, unexceptional Clinton. A slightly more interesting first stop is **LANGLEY**, a well-heeled seaside village just a few miles away off Hwy-525, with a stretch of wooden storefronts set on a picturesque bluff overlooking the water. First Street is lined with antique stores and galleries such as the **Artists' Cooperative of Whidbey Island**, no. 314

(☎360/221-7675), and the various artisans at the **Hellebore Glass Studio**, no. 308 (☎360/221-2067, ⊛www.helleboreglass.com).

In the island's center, **COUPEVILLE** is Washington State's second-oldest city and Whidbey's most historic district, with several dozen buildings from the late nineteenth and early twentieth centuries, its neighborhoods dotted with vintage Victorian homes – leftovers from its days as a flourishing seaport. It was settled back in the 1850s by sea captains and merchants attracted by the protected harbor in **Penn Cove**, and by the plentiful oak and pine trees. The several blocks of waterfront on **Front Street**, between Main Street and the pier, feature most of Coupeville's shops and eateries, making for a quick, enjoyable stop. There are a few classic structures worth a look, too, with the 1886 **Loers House**, Eighth St at Grace St, a mix of traditional Victorian architecture with an onion-domed turret.

The **Island County Historical Museum**, 908 NW Alexander St, at Front St (summer Wed–Mon 10am–5pm, rest of year Fri–Mon 10am–4pm; $3; ⊛www.islandhistory.org), can give you the lowdown on the local heritage, though one of the most historic buildings, **Alexander's Blockhouse**, just outside the museum, can be seen on its own for free. This creaky wooden structure was built by settlers in 1855 to defend themselves from attack by Skagit Indians – which never occurred.

Fort Casey and Fort Ebey state parks

Coupeville is part of **Ebey's Landing National Historical Reserve** (information at ☎360/678-3310, ⊛www.nps.gov/ebla), a series of farms, forests, and privately owned land named after one of the island's first white settlers, **Colonel Isaac Ebey**, who, in an 1851 letter to his brother, described his new home as "almost a paradise of nature... I think I could live and die here content." Ebey did get part of his wish: in 1857 he was slain by Alaskan Tlingit in revenge for killing one of their chiefs.

On the western side of the island are two state parks in the reserve: the first, **FORT CASEY STATE PARK** (daily 8am–dusk, winter open Sat-Sun only), three miles south of Coupeville, was built at the beginning of the twentieth century to guard the entrance to Puget Sound, though it was soon obsolete. Check out the grim cluster of dark **gun batteries**, whose artillery emplacements can be freely explored, along with the eerie, bomb-shelter-like **bunkers** underneath. Much cheerier is the squat but charming **Admiralty Head Lighthouse** nearby (Sept–Dec & March–May weekends 11am–5pm, June–Aug daily; donation suggested), one of several lighthouses on Whidbey Island. A half-mile south of Fort Casey, the **Keystone ferry landing** will allow you to make the short trip to Port Townsend (see p.253), just across Admiralty Inlet to the southwest; see Basics, p.34, for ferry information.

The second of the state parks in the reserve, seven miles north along the beach from Fort Casey, **FORT EBEY STATE PARK** (summer 6.30am–dusk, winter 8am–dusk; ☎360/678-4636) offers an attractive shoreline and plenty of opportunities for hiking, biking, and fishing. An abandoned gun and bunker emplacement also remains here, built in 1942 to defend against possible attack from the Pacific; the eerie atmosphere is enhanced by the remote location and heavy forest cover.

Deception Pass State Park

Beyond Ebey's Reserve, contemporary military matters dominate the economy of **Oak Harbor**, Whidbey's largest – and most unappealing – town. You'd do better to head further north on Hwy-20, where **DECEPTION PASS STATE PARK**, (summer 6.30am–dusk, winter 8am–dusk; ☎360/675-2417), sprawls over four thousand acres of rugged land and sea that's great for hiking, fishing, birdwatching, scuba diving, and so on. The park occupies land on both Fidalgo and Whidbey islands, which are separated by Deception Pass itself, a narrow gorge spanned by an arching steel bridge. The turbulent waters below the bridge were originally thought to be a small bay when charted by the Spanish, but the British later discovered that the passage was actually a deep channel, and gave the site its current name.

Grab a map from the Whidbey-side park office and head to the **Lighthouse Point Trail** that begins near the **interpretive center** (summer 8am 5pm; free), and meanders along beach and forest for nearly a mile, leading to rocky bluffs with good views of the pass. The center has a small but interesting exhibit and video on the creation and history of the Civilian Conservation Corps (CCC), one of the programs initiated by President Franklin Roosevelt in the 1930s to create jobs and, at the same time, conserve the nation's natural resources. Most of the two-and-a-half million men who joined the corps were young, hungry, and in need of the steady meals (and $30/month pay) the organization provided. In Washington State, the CCC built most of the structures in about a dozen state parks, including the trails and facilities in Deception Pass State Park itself.

Eating and drinking

Christopher's Front Street Café 23 Front St, Coupeville ☎360/678-5480. Fine lunches, dinners, and microbrews; the place strikes a good balance between basic diner food and ritzier dining, with its panini, seafood, pastas, and steaks. Lunch Mon–Fri 11.30am–2pm, Sat & Sun noon–2.30pm, dinner 5–9.30pm, closed Wed.

🏃 **The Cove 2072 W Captain Whidbey Inn Rd, Coupeville** ☎360/678-9325, ⓦwww .whidbeyscoverestaurant.com. Located at the *Captain Whidbey Inn*, this is one of the island's best and most expensive restaurants, serving fine seafood, including locally harvested mussels and fresh herbs and vegetables from its gardens. Reservations essential. Thurs–Sun 11am–2pm & Wed–Sun 5–9.30pm.

Knead & Feed 4 Front St, Coupeville ☎360/678-5431. Cozy bakery offering inexpensive homemade breads, pies, and cinnamon rolls, plus an onsite espresso bar for tasty gourmet coffee. Mon–Fri 8am–3pm, Sat & Sun 8am–4pm.

Langley Village Bakery 221 2nd St #1, Langley ☎360/221-3525. Great baked goods, pizza, and soups, either to go or dine-in at the several small tables. Daily 7.30am–5pm.

Neil's Clover Patch Cafe 2850 SR 525, Langley ☎360/321-4120. Buffet spot with gut-busting weekly specials of fish-and-chips and pork ribs, with hefty staples like eggs and steak the rest of the time. Daily 6.30am–8pm, Wed–Sat closes at 9pm.

Toby's Tavern 8 Front St, Coupeville ☎360/678-4222. Seafood, burgers, and microbrews at this wharfside joint, plus solid, belt-loosening pastrami sandwiches and French dips. Daily 11am–9pm, bar closes at 10.30pm.

Village Pizzeria 108 First St, Langley ☎360/221-3363. Well-regarded pizza joint that serves up piping hot strips of pepperoni-and-cheese, as well as more exotic offerings with clams and pesto. No credit cards. Daily 11.30am–9pm.

La Conner

Across Skagit Bay from the northeastern corner of Whidbey Island is quaint **LA CONNER** – not a foreign name, but an honorary acronym to the town founder's wife, Louise A. Conner. Replete with touristy, yet amiable, souvenir shops

23

and cafés, the downtown area is sited along the waterfront of the **Swinomish Channel**, a sheltered inlet between the San Juan Islands and Puget Sound.

Before the area was diked and drained, the surrounding Skagit delta was a marsh prone to flooding; the original trading post here was built on a hill to avoid the soggier ground. When the railroads reached the Pacific Northwest in the 1880s, La Conner was all but abandoned – though in the 1930s, artists such as Morris Graves became attracted by its isolation, cheap land, and the unusual light patterns of its landscapes. Kindred spirits – such as fellow painter Guy Anderson – followed, and the backwater town became both an artists' colony and the hangout of oddballs and counterculture types. Since the 1970s, though, when the waterfront was spruced up with new shops and amenities, the town has traded on its offbeat reputation to pull in the tourist dollar. As such, it's hard, nowadays, to get a glimpse of anything vaguely "alternative," unless you count the town's several **art galleries**, though even they offer mostly tasteful, unadventurous pieces aimed at visiting urbanites.

Arrival and information

La Conner is located about an hour's drive north of Seattle off of Hwy-20, or by bridge from Whidbey Island along the same highway. La Conner's **visitors' center**, a short walk from the waterfront at Morris and Fifth streets (Mon–Fri 10am–4pm, Sat 11am–3pm; ☎360/466-4778, ⊛www.laconnerchamber.com), issues free town **maps**, and has a comprehensive list of accommodation. Lodgings can get scarce during the two-week **Skagit Valley Tulip Festival** in April, so book ahead.

Accommodation

Heron Inn 117 Maple Ave ☎ 360/466-4626, ⊛www.theheron.com. A mix between a familiar B&B and a boutique hotel, offering twelve units (starting $79) with swanky modern furnishings, fireplaces and Jacuzzis, nice mountainside views, and suites for about $40 more.

Hotel Planter 715 S First St ☎360/466-4710 or 1-800/488-5409, ⊛www.hotelplanter.com. Plush, modern queen beds and doubles in a stylishly remodeled Victorian inn, complete with antique decor and a hot tub. $89.

Katy's Inn 503 S Third St ☎360/466-3366 or 1-800/914-7767. Attractive old B&B with wraparound porch and wooden balcony, antique pump organ, two standard rooms,

and two slightly more expensive suites. $70–80.

La Conner Channel Lodge 205 N First St ☎360/466-1500, ⊛www.laconnerlodging.com. Lavish waterside doubles with fireplaces and balconies, featuring an adjacent dock ($135). Also operates the *La Conner Country Inn,* 107 S Second St (☎1-888/466-4113), offering 28 mostly double rooms with fireplaces, at considerably cheaper rates ($82).

Wild Iris Inn 121 Maple Ave ☎360 466-1400 or 1-800/477-1400, ⊛www.wildiris.com. Twelve fancy suites ($149) with DVD players, hot tubs, fireplaces, and decks, along with several smaller, but still comfortable, rooms that sport fewer amenities ($109).

The town

Lined by pleasant boutiques and eateries, the highlight of La Conner's attractive waterfront is its excellent **Museum of Northwest Art** (**MoNA**), 121 S First St (Tues–Sun 10am–5pm; $5; ☎360/466-4666, ⊛www.museumofnwart.org), which showcases the work of the region's painters, and is far more engaging than most of the bland galleries elsewhere around town. The first floor is given over to temporary displays, while the second holds the permanent collection – a bold sampling of modern art, including work by the likes of Morris Graves, William

Morris, Dale Chihuly, and especially Guy Anderson, whose paintings are of particular note for their naked human figures adrift against somber landscapes.

A few blocks away, at 703 S Second St, the Gaches Mansion – the MoNA's former home – now holds the **La Conner Quilt Museum** (Wed–Sat 11am–4pm, Sun noon–4pm; Dec Fri–Sun only, Jan closed; $4; ☎360/466-4288, ⓦwww.laconnerquilts.com), which presents a rotating display of quilts from around the world, with antique, handwoven items mixed with more bizarre modern creations. If anything, the museum's grand edifice is just as interesting as its collection, an odd mix of Eastlake and other Victorian architecture styles, with a touch of Tudor Revival in its half-timbered dormers and fairytale tower.

Eating and drinking

Cafe Culture 109 E Commercial St ☎360/421-0985. Well-regarded combo coffeehouse and art gallery that serves up solid espresso but is best for its regular exhibitions of international artwork and compelling local pieces. Daily 7.30am–4pm.

Calico Cupboard Café and Bakery 720 S First St ☎360/466-4451. Affordable breakfasts and lunches in a tearoom-like atmosphere located in a classic 1887 structure. Try the banana-coconut griddlecakes, a savory omelet, or a fudge pie from the takeout bakery. Mon–Fri 7.30am–4pm, Sat & Sun 7.30am–5pm.

La Conner Brewing Company 117 S First St ☎360/466-1415. Located next door to the art museum, offering a wide, inexpensive range of good beers – highlighted by a tasty lambic framboise – and savory gourmet pizzas. Daily 11.30am–10pm for dining; bar 11.30am–midnight.

La Conner Seafood & Prime Rib House 614 S First St ☎360/466-4014, ⓦwww .laconnerseafood.com. Good seafood, burgers, and steaks are the focus of the mid-priced menu here, highlighted by its crab cakes, salmon-and-chips, and fresh clams and oysters. Outdoor seating and nice waterside vistas, too. Daily 11.30am–9.30pm.

The San Juan Islands

Northwest of Whidbey Island, midway between the Washington coast and Canada, the **SAN JUAN ISLANDS** scatter across the eastern reaches of the Strait of Juan de Fuca and, for many people, are the highlight of the Puget Sound region. Tailor-made for strolling, cycling, and naturewatching, the idyllic San Juans are the breeding grounds of rare native birds and sea creatures: white-headed bald eagles circle over treetops, and Orca ("killer") whale pods pass close to shore. As a convoluted maze of green islands, with myriad bluffs and bays, the San Juan archipelago has 743 islands, but only about 170 of them are actually visible during high tide, and only sixty of those are populated. Unless you've got your own boat or quite a bit of money, your visits will be restricted to the four islands served by Washington State Ferries: **San Juan**, by far the largest, offers historic state parks and a thriving port, Friday Harbor; **Orcas** is the most scenic, especially in the mountainous interior of Moran State Park; **Lopez** is the most sedate and quiet, its flat and largely empty roads a haven for bicyclists; and **Shaw**, by contrast, has barely anything – or anyone – to see.

The area was first seen by European eyes by explorer **Juan de Fuca**, now believed to have been a Greek sailing for the Spanish, who in 1592 claimed to have found an inlet at 47 degrees north latitude while searching for the mythical "Northwest Passage" that would connect the Pacific and Atlantic oceans. This claim went unacknowledged until 1787, when Englishman **Charles Barkley** found a strait at the location and named it in honor of de Fuca. It was the Spanish, though, who first fully explored the strait in 1790 under **Manuel Quimper**, accounting for the Spanish names that grace several of the islands.

Getting to the islands: Anacortes

Washington State Ferries (☎206/464-6400 or 1-888/808-7977, ⓦwww.wsdot .wa.gov/ferries) departs for the San Juans from the small port of **ANACORTES**, just west of La Conner on Hwy-20. The town is reachable via **Airporter Shuttle** (6am–11.30pm; 3hr trip; $33 one-way, $61 round-trip; ⓦwww.airporter .com), which runs twelve lines daily from Sea-Tac Airport and two from Downtown Seattle (2.25pm & 4.25pm), with a westbound connection in Mount Vernon. Anacortes has several decent places to **eat** before getting on the boat: try *Geppetto's*, 3320 Commercial Ave (☎360/293-5033), with good Italian takeout food and baked goods, or *La Vie En Rose*, 418 Commercial Ave (☎360/299-9546, ⓦwww.laviebakery.com), serving tasty deli sandwiches, desserts, and breads. If you need to **stay** overnight to catch a crack-of-dawn ferry, Commercial Avenue is lined with numerous budget hotels, the least generic of which is the hot tub-equipped *Islands Inn*, no. 3401 (☎360/293-4644, ⓦwww.islandsinn .com; $58), offering bayside views and fireplaces, while the *Majestic Hotel*, no. 419 (☎360/293-3355; $95), is a lovely option from 1889, newly reopened and refurbished, with old-fashioned decor and a good restaurant and bar.

There are about a dozen Washington State **ferries** daily, the earliest of which leaves around 5.30am; see Basics, p.34, for full schedule and prices. If you're

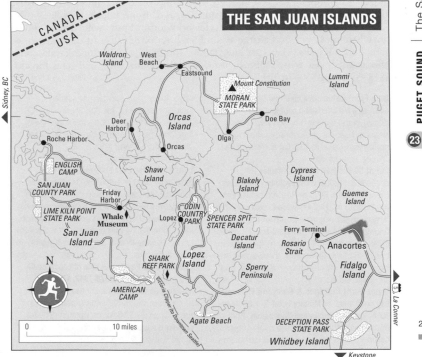

bringing a vehicle, you should probably come early – ideally two hours in advance – as the lines at the port can be long during the high season. A passenger-only alternative is the *Victoria Clipper* (☎360/448-5000 or 1-800/888-2535, ⓦwww.victoriaclipper.com), which runs from Pier 69 in Seattle to San Juan's Friday Harbor ($42–45 one-way, $60–68 round-trip), with a four-hour layover there. Boats leave once daily from mid-May to mid-September, and weekends only April to mid-May and late September. While a day-trip to the islands is manageable, it's better to stay in the San Juans overnight; be sure to **book** accommodation well in advance.

Lopez Island

The first stop on the Anacortes ferry route, which runs east of the islands through the **Rosario Strait**, is usually **LOPEZ ISLAND**, the most pastoral and uncrowded of the three main islands; its farms formerly supplied much of western Washington with meat and fruit products. Although today it's not the agricultural power it once was, there are still plenty of orchards and cattle around, if little else. There isn't much to do here except hike, camp, and bike, which is a large part of its appeal: Lopez is virtually undeveloped, with a resident population of less than two thousand. In as much as the island has a base, it's the little roadstop of **Lopez Village**, down Fisherman Bay Road about five miles from the ferry stop.

Getting around and accommodation

The best way to explore small, mostly flat Lopez is by **bicycle**. Rentals are available in Lopez Village from The Bike Shop on Lopez (☎360/468-3497), or further south at 2847 Fisherman Bay Rd, from Lopez Bicycle Works (☎360/468-2847, ⓦwww.lopezbicycleworks.com); both will deliver bikes anywhere on Lopez, and charge around $5/hour or $25/day. At the latter location, Lopez Kayaks (May–Oct only; ☎360/468-2847, ⓦwww.lopezkayaks.com) also arranges **sea trips** ($35/2hr tour, $75/3hr 30min tour) and rents **kayaks** ($15–35/hr or $30–70/day).

Blue Fjord Cabins 862 Elliott Rd ☎1-888/633-0401, ⓦwww.interisland.net/bluefjord. A quiet retreat in the woods, offering two cozy, secluded cabins at reasonable rates. $89 spring and fall; add $10 for summer rates. Closed Nov–March.

Inn at Swifts Bay 856 Port Stanley Rd ☎360/468-3636, ⓦwww.swiftsbay.com. The most luxurious B&B on Lopez, nestled at the bottom of a little-traveled road near the ferry; turn left one mile south of the dock, and it's on the right, just past the fire station. Only a few minutes' walk from the beach, the *Inn* has five units ($95, three suites starting at $155) with hot tubs, fireplaces, and an onsite sauna.

Lopez Farm Cottages & Camping Fisherman Bay Road south of Military Road ☎1-800/440-3556, ⓦwww.lopezfarmcottages.com. For about twice the price of the more basic campgrounds on Lopez, these campsites have a few more modern amenities, including showers, for $33 (open May–Oct 1). Five comfortable cottages – each with fireplace, porch, and deck – are available year-round, varying from $100–180 according to season.

Lopez Islander 2847 Fisherman Bay Rd ☎360/468-2233 or 1-800/736-3434, ⓦwww.lopezislander.com. The only luxury hotel on Lopez has thirty spacious rooms (most with sunset views), swimming pool, and hot tub, starting at $89 – with campsites for $25–35. Lopez Bicycle Works and Lopez Kayaks are also at the site.

Odlin County Park north side of Lopez, south of Upright Head ☎360/378-1842, ⓦwww.co.san-juan.wa.us/parks. By the beach, just a mile from the ferry, with numerous hiking trails. Charges $16 for campsites ($19 for premium sites on the beach), or $11 for those without a vehicle.

Spencer Spit State Park Baker View Rd
☎360/468-2251, ⓦ www.parks.wa.gov. Thirty-
four tent sites (along with three primitive
ones; no vehicles) at an isolated park with
good hiking, clamming and crabbing. The
best place to camp on Lopez, so reserve
ahead in peak season. Closed Nov–Feb.
$15–21.

The island

In Lopez Village, there are few traditional sights except for the **Lopez Island Historical Museum**, 28 Washburn Place (May–Sept Fri & Sat noon–4pm; donation suggested; ⓦwww.rockisland.com/~lopezmuseum), which has an interesting selection of bric-a-brac from the past – old gillnets, hand-carved canoes, stuffed birds – and will give you an introduction to the native tribes and early pioneers who populated the Lopez, as well as an overview of the island's limited attractions. If you're interested, here you can pick up a useful map of a **driving tour** of the area's historic sites and homes.

The top destination here is **Shark Reef Park** (☎360/378-8420), at the island's southwest tip on Shark Reef Road, accessible via Fisherman Bay and Airport roads. A ten- to fifteen-minute walk through dense forest is rewarded by beautiful rocky vistas at the water's edge, from where you can spot the occasional sea lion past the tidepools. Also on the island's southern end is **Agate Beach**, whose shoreline is actually strewn with fat little pebbles that make a memorable sound at high tide. Back on the northeast side of the island, **Spencer Spit State Park**, in addition to its campsites (see "Accommodation," opposite), also offers good hiking among the trees, clamming and picnicking, and, along the spit, sunbathing on a slender strand of sand that juts out from the shore.

Eating and drinking

Bay Café 9 Old Post Rd, Lopez Village ☎360/468-3700, ⓦ www.bay-cafe.com. The only spot in Lopez for elegant dining, and the eclectic seafood entrees – seafood curry and risotto cakes, in the $17–20 range – are worth it. Reserve in advance; live jazz on Sunday nights. Days and hours vary by season; usually Wed–Sun 5.30–10pm.
Holly B's Bakery 165 Cherry Tree Lane, Lopez Village ☎360/468-2133. Small stop for tasty, inexpensive cinnamon buns, breads, pastries, pizza and light snacks. April–Oct

Wed–Sat 7am–5pm, Sun 7am–4pm; Nov Thurs–Sun only.
Isabel's Espresso Village House Building, Lopez Village ☎360/468-4114. One of the better spots to have your coffee in town, with juice drinks, chai, iced tea, sweets, and some lunch items, too. Days and hours vary by season.
Love Dog Cafe 1 Village Center, Lopez Village ☎360/468-2150. Deli sandwiches, seafood and pasta are the main draw at this unassuming spot with a relaxed patio. Mon–Fri 8am–8pm, Sat & Sun 8am–9pm.

Orcas Island

The most alluring destination in the San Juans for striking scenery, horseshoe-shaped **ORCAS ISLAND** teems with rugged hills and leafy timber that tower over its leisurely roads, craggy beaches, and abundant wildlife. It's not only the island's fairly rustic topography that keeps the hordes away, but also that it hasn't been fully exploited as a tourist destination. You can come here and easily find a quiet cove or tranquil setting and peaceably spend the day. Nonetheless, while not completely overridden with outsiders, its enviable qualities have not escaped the notice of the larger world, either: though there are only 3500 full-time island residents, there are three times as many property owners. Yet, despite being much busier than Lopez, Orcas's holiday resorts are so well tucked into distant coves that the island's peace and quiet is hardly disturbed.

Arrival, information, and accommodation

Ferries dock in tiny **Orcas**, and down the main road of Horseshoe Highway is the slightly larger town of **Eastsound**. Maps and island **information** are available at the Chamber of Commerce, N Beach Rd in Eastsound (☎360/376-2273, ⒲www.orcasisland.org), next to *Bilbo's Festivo* restaurant (see opposite). You can rent **bikes** (for $30 per day) in Orcas from Dolphin Bay Bicycles, just up from the dock (☎360/376-3093, ⒲www.rockisland.com/~dolphin), or in Eastsound from Wildlife Cycles, 350 N Beach Rd at A St (☎360/376-4708, ⒲www.wildlifecycles.com), and cycle north through the island's fetching farm country – the onetime heart of the state's apple orchards, until Eastern Washington came to the fore.

Beach Haven Resort 684 Beach Haven Rd ☎360/376-2288, ⒲www.beach-haven.com. An appealing refuge three miles west of Eastsound, with beachfront log cabins, cottages, and a lodge amid wooded grounds (rates start at $100–125). While remote, it's not undiscovered; reservations for summer stays (one-week minimum) are needed a year in advance.

Doe Bay Village & Resort Doe Bay Road, turn right at the sign for Doe Bay Natural Foods Café & General Store ☎360/376-2291, ⒲www .doebay.com. Eight dormitory hostel beds for $25/night (or private rooms for $65), plus yurts ($75) and various types of cabins for about two to three times as much – some with microwaves and wood stoves. Hot tub and sauna use included (except for hostelers); $35 campsites cover a single tent (for two persons).

Moran State Park off Horseshoe Hwy southeast of Eastsound ☎1-800/452-5687, ⒲www .orcasisle.com/~elc. Great park with four different developed campgrounds, some with yurts and cabins, most with showers and restrooms, and others with kitchens.

There's a primitive campsite as well. $15–21, plus $7 registration fee.

Orcas Hotel at the ferry landing in Orcas ☎360/376-4300, ⒲www.orcashotel.com. A restored Victorian inn with twelve units, the plushest with Jacuzzis, balconies, and harbor views ($142); the rooms on the sides and in the back don't have these amenities, though they're considerably less expensive ($89).

Outlook Inn 171 Main St, Eastsound ☎360/376-2200, ⒲www.outlook-inn.com. Pleasant late-Victorian complex spread over three buildings and offering basic waterside rooms and suites with hot tubs, fireplaces, and balconies, plus onsite restaurant and lounge. $74, or $54 with shared bath. Add $30–100 per unit in high season.

Rosario Resort & Spa 1 Rosario Way ☎1-800/562-8820, ⒲www.rosario.rockresorts .com. Former Seattle mayor and wealthy shipbuilder Robert Moran built this elegant waterside mansion that now serves as an ultra-swanky resort – expensive even by island standards. $149, or $199 high season.

The island

While **Orcas** will most likely be your first stop on the island, it's really just a street with a few simple shops. **Eastsound**, ten miles in on the main road, is a slightly larger town that offers more, including a handful of decent restaurants. Not far from the Chamber of Commerce in Eastsound, the **Orcas Island Historical Society & Museum**, 181 N Beach Rd (daily 10am–3pm, Fri 1–6pm, closed Mon; donation suggested; ⒲www.orcasisland.org/~history), provides an overview of the island's Native American and pioneer background, but is most interesting for its site: the museum is spread over six interconnected log cabins which were originally constructed in the 1880s and 1890s by homesteaders carving out a space on the isolated terrain.

Past Eastsound, it's a few miles to the gates of **Moran State Park** (⒲www .orcasisle.com/~elc), encompassing five thousand acres of forest and lakes and thirty miles of trails. Overlooking the expanse is **Mount Constitution**, at 2409ft the highest point on the island; a tough but exhilarating four-mile trail

23

leads from Cascade Lake on the Horseshoe Highway to the top of the mountain (also accessible by car via a five-mile paved road). The steep path twists around creeks, fields, and thick foliage, and there's a fair chance of spotting some of the nearly two hundred species of birds on the island. At the summit, the stone **Mount Constitution Tower** has an intriguing rugged design – resembling a medieval fortress from the Crusades. The panoramic views here are as good as you'd expect, looking out as far as Vancouver Island, and back towards snow-capped mounts Baker and Rainier.

If you've had your fill of hiking, the best place to unwind on Orcas – even if you're not staying there – is at **Doe Bay Village & Resort** (see "Accommodation," opposite). Perched at one of the calmest spots in the San Juans, it's a lovely place, built on a secluded bay, with echoes of its previous incarnation as a New Age-flavored "human potential center" still hanging around its cabins, cottages and hostel dorms. Its open-air, mineral spring-fed hot tubs are available for day use by non-guests ($10). A more adventurous dip into the water can be had from Shearwater Adventures, on kayak trips that leave from Doe Bay, Deer Harbor Marina, and *Rosario Resort* ($49/half-day, $85/full day; ☎360/376-4699, ⓦwww.shearwaterkayaks.com), yielding closer views of the island's population of bald eagles, seals, and whales.

Eating and drinking

Bilbo's Festivo North Beach Rd and A Street, Eastsound ☎360/376-4728. Inexpensive Mexican entrees and tasty desserts, dished out in an affable setting; reservations are advised, as this is a popular spot. Daily 5–9pm, also summer 11.30am–2.30pm.

Café Olga corner of Olga Rd and Doe Bay Rd, on the eastern side of the island ☎360/376-5098. Succulent soups and sandwiches, as well as fruit pies, served indoors and on an outdoor porch, with an adjoining art gallery. March–Nov daily 10am–6pm.

Christina's 310 Main St, Eastsound ☎360/376-4904, ⓦwww.christinas.net. Well-regarded local favorite that offers some of the most chic

dining in the San Juans, serving up nouveau Northwest fare and seafood for around $30 an entree. Thurs–Mon 5.30-10pm.

The Kitchen 249 Prune Alley, off Horseshoe Hwy north of Orcas ☎360/376-6958. Appetizing pan-Asian fare, such as seared salmon, chicken teriyaki, and spring roll wraps; most everything's cheap and tasty. Mon–Sat 11am–3pm & 5–7pm.

Portofino Pizzeria A St, Eastsound ☎360/376-2085, ⓦwww.orcasonline.com/~portofino. Handcrafted pizza, hot and cold sandwiches, focaccia, and calzones, using fresh local ingredients. Mon–Sat 11.30am–8pm, Sun 4–8pm.

San Juan Island

SAN JUAN ISLAND holds the San Juans' only incorporated town, **Friday Harbor**, whose wharfside blocks seem more commercially active than the rest of the islands put together. The rest of San Juan Island is rural and sparsely populated, with plenty of good scenery, hiking, and even a few cultural sights – most notably, a **whale museum** and two national historic parks, **American Camp** and **English Camp**, which were military bases during a land dispute between the UK and the US in the 1800s.

Arrival, information, and tours

Ferries arrive at Friday Harbor, where San Juan Transit maintains a **visitors' center**, in the Cannery Building next to the terminal at 91 Front St (Mon–Fri 9am–4.30pm; ☎360/378-8887, ⓦwww.sanjuantransit.com) – it's a good place to pick up info and a **map** of the island's irregular main roads. The main office of the **San Juan Island National Historical Park**, First and Spring streets (Mon–Fri 8.30am–4.30pm; ☎360/378-2240, ⊛www.nps.gov/sajh), is not a visitors' center per se, but its staff is happy to answer questions about the island.

A **car** is the best way to check out the scattered points of interest on San Juan; you can either bring one over by ferry or rent one in Friday Harbor. M&W, 725 Spring St (☎1-800/323-6037, ⊛www.sanjuanauto.com), is a local outfit renting vehicles for $40–80, depending on the season. From April to September, the **San Juan Shuttle** stops at most of the island's principal attractions ($4/one-way, $7/round-trip, $10/day-pass, $17/two-day pass, or $17 for a 2hr guided bus tour; ☎360/378-8887 or 1-800/887-8387, ⊛www.sanjuantransit .com). **Bikes** ($30/day) and **scooters** ($50/day) can be rented at Island Bicycles, 380 Argyle St (Thurs–Sat only; ☎360/378-4941, ⊛www.islandbicycles.com), while **mopeds** are available from Susie's Mopeds, corner of First and A streets, across from the ferry departure lanes ($20/hour or $60/day; ☎360/378-5244 or 1-800/532-0087, ⊛www.susiesmopeds.com). To get on the water, San Juan Safaris (☎360/378-1323 or 1-800/450-6858, ⊛www.sanjuansafaris.com) runs April-to-September **sea kayak treks** and **whale-watching cruises** ($59 each) from Friday and Roche harbors; and Island Dive & Watersports (☎360/378-2772, ⊛www.divesanjuan.com) has half-day **scuba-diving** charters ($79 per person) and guided **shipwreck diving tours** ($120).

Accommodation

It's essential to **book** ahead in summer for rooms in Friday Harbor, especially during the popular **San Juan Island Jazz Festival** (☎360/378-5509), held the last weekend in July.

Hotels and B&Bs

Friday's 35 First St, Friday Harbor ☎360/378-5848 or 1-800/352-2632, ⊛www.friday-harbor .com/lodging.html. Convenient to the ferry, this renovated 1891 hotel has an agreeable ambiance and a range of rooms from economy ($59) to suites ($159) – the more spacious of which will set you back at least $200.

Harrison House 235 C St, Friday Harbor ☎360/378-3587, ⊛www.harrisonhousesuites .com. Popular B&B in a verdant setting, with kayaks and mountain bikes for island use, and four sizable suites ($150, plus a smaller studio for $125) with Jacuzzis, kitchens, fireplaces, and one to three bedrooms each. Add $40–100 more in high season.

Hotel de Haro 248 Reuben Memorial Drive, Roche Harbor ☎360/378-2155 or 1-800/451-8910, ⊛www.rocheharbor.com. Located in the *Roche Harbor Resort*, this elegant 1886 complex offers standard rooms with shared bathrooms ($75), as well as four upscale suites and quaint cottages with antique decor ($129). Add $25 (for basic rooms) to $100 (for cottages) in the high season.

Wharfside slip K-13, port of Friday Harbor ☎360/378-5661, ⊛www.slowseason.com. Two private staterooms on a 60ft-sailboat in the harbor make for an interesting change of pace from the usual B&B. Offers morning breakfast cruises around the harbor in summer, though this can raise the cost up to $300; otherwise $150–265, depending on the room and season.

Wildwood Manor 5335 Roche Harbor Rd, Roche Harbor ☎360/378-3447 or 1-877/298-1144, ⊛www.wildwoodmanor.com. Old-fashioned Victorian estate with three rooms – Pink, Blue, and French – offering the standard B&B amenities in an appealing forested location with fine views of the area. Rates start at $135–180, depending on the room and season.

Campgrounds and hostels

Lakedale Resort 4313 Roche Harbor Rd, between Roche Harbor and Friday Harbor ☎360/378-0944 or 1-800/617-2267, ⊛www .lakedale.com. A range of accommodation, from simple campsites ($21–26) to tasteful lodge rooms ($137–209) and individual log cabins ($177–279); offers guest-only lake activities such as swimming, fishing, and kayaking.

Pedal Inn 1300 False Bay Drive, five miles from the Friday Harbor ferry dock ☎360/378-3049. Hiker and cyclist camp with primitive facilities, but onsite showers and laundromat, for only $5 per person. April–Oct only.

San Juan County Park 380 West Side Rd, on the western edge of the island ☎360/378-1842, ⓦwww.co.san-juan.wa.us/parks/sanjuan.html. Appealing for its rugged bluffs and rocky beaches, this park offers campsites with fire rings and picnic tables, as well as a

boat launch. $25–34. Come by foot, bike or kayak, and it's only $6. Reserve ahead in high season.

Wayfarer's Rest 35 Malcolm St, Friday Harbor ☎360/378-6428, ⓦwww.rockisland .com/~wayfarersrest. The island's only hostel, reachable on foot from the ferry, with bunk rooms for $22/night or private rooms for $55/night. Full kitchen facilities and herb garden; advance booking is advised.

Friday Harbor

With a population of nearly two thousand, **FRIDAY HARBOR** is by far the biggest town in the San Juans. When it became the county seat in 1873, after the Pig War ended (see box, p.270), it had a population of just three people. Thanks in part to a protected harbor and good anchorage, by the turn of the century the town's residents numbered up to four hundred, and it continued to grow through the first half of the 1900s, until a postwar decline refocused the town toward tourism and real estate.

With its numerous cafés and restaurants, the **waterfront** area is the handiest place to eat before touring the island. The area's highlight is the **Whale Museum**, 62 First St (daily: July & Aug 9am–6pm; rest of year 10am–5pm; $6; ☎1-800/946-7227, ⓦwww.whalemuseum.org), which has a small collection of whale skeletons and displays explaining the creatures' migration and growth cycles. There's also a listening booth for the different kinds of whale songs, along with walrus, seal, and dolphin soundtracks. Short documentaries are shown about research expeditions, and the museum monitors cetacean activities on a "**whale hotline**" (☎1-800/562-8832), to which you can report any sightings. The local orcas (or "killer whales") are protected by a ban on their capture, instituted in 1976, but they're still threatened by pollution.

The volunteers here can give you additional information on the nearly one hundred whales that roam the 200-mile radius of San Juan Island – best seen at **Lime Kiln Point State Park** (daily 8am–dusk), known to some as "Whale-Watcher Park," on the island's western side at 6158 Lighthouse Rd. Named after the site's former lime quarry, this is where orcas come in summer to feed on migrating salmon, and there's usually at least one sighting a day in June and July. If you're really interested in seeing the whales up-close, San Juan Safaris (see above) runs good whale-watching cruises.

American Camp and English Camp

At San Juan's southern tip is **AMERICAN CAMP** (dawn–11pm; free; ☎360/378-2902, ⓦwww.nps.gov/sajh), a national park that played a role in the infamous Pig War (see box, p.270). Morale among the US troops stationed here was quite low, and it's not hard to see why: the windswept, rabbit hole-strewn fields are bleak and largely shorn of vegetation. A self-guided, one-mile **trail** begins from the parking lot, passing the camp's few remaining buildings and what's left of a gun emplacement. Costumed volunteers re-enact life in both camps during the summer; drop in at the **visitors' center** for details (summer daily 8.30am–5pm; rest of year Thurs–Sun 8.30am–4.30pm; free).

On the island's western side is **ENGLISH CAMP** (same information as American Camp), the site of the only foreign flag officially flown by itself on American soil. Here, forests overlook pleasant green fields and big-leaf

23

The Pig War

Both English Camp and American Camp were established on San Juan Island as the result of the **Pig War**, a dispute in which not a single shot was fired at a person – the lone casualty was a pig that belonged to the British. The swine's demise, however, sparked conflict over a long-simmering border dispute between the US and the UK (which still ruled Canada).

The **Oregon Treaty of 1846** had given the United States possession of the Pacific Northwest south of the 49th parallel, extending the boundary "to the middle of the channel which separates the continent from Vancouver's Island." There were, however, two channels – Haro Strait and Rosario Strait – between Vancouver Island and the mainland, and San Juan Island lay between them. Citing different interpretations, both the British and Americans claimed the island and began settling it in the 1850s.

In 1859, American settler **Lyman Cutlar** shot the aforementioned British pig, which was rooting in his garden. When the British threatened to arrest him, 66 American troops were sent in; the governor of British Columbia responded by sending three warships. Eventually, US President James Buchanan sent Winfield Scott, commanding general of the US Army, to cool things down. An agreement was reached allowing for joint occupation of the island until the dispute could be settled (or, more importantly for the US, until the Civil War had ended). This co-ownership ultimately lasted for twelve years, during which a number of deaths resulted from the tough conditions faced by the forces on both sides, though none from warfare. Finally, the dispute was ended when it was referred in 1871 to Kaiser Wilhelm I of Germany, who ruled in favor of the US.

maple trees near the shore, where four buildings from the 1860s and a small formal garden have been restored. A slide show in the barracks (summer daily 9am–5pm; free) explains the Pig War – a tale that you will no doubt have fully memorized over the course of your visit. From here you can hike an easy loop to **Bell Point**, a promontory with expansive waterside views, or retreat to the parking lot to mount the short but steep one-mile wooded trail to **Young Hill**, passing the small **English Camp cemetery** on the way. The 650ft summit has views over much of the island, and looks out to the shore of British Columbia, not more than ten miles away.

Roche Harbor

At San Juan's northwest tip is **ROCHE HARBOR**, established in the 1880s around the limestone trade, and highlighted by the gracious white **Hotel de Haro** (see "Accommodation," p.268), built over the harbor in 1886 to house visiting lime-buyers. The hotel's now part of the *Roche Harbor Resort*, and unless you're staying there, it's only worth a quick peek at the building and a stroll around the minuscule wharf and general area.

A less prominent, but no less interesting, site in the vicinity is the **Roche Harbor Cemetery** (daily dawn–dusk), accessible by turning off Roche Harbor Road just before the arch welcoming visitors to town; you can park at the small lot nearby. A few yards further down the road, a small footpath leads into the cemetery, where signs guide you to the haunting **mausoleum** of John Stafford McMillin, founder of the *Hotel de Haro*. Set far back from the street in the woods, with seven stately pillars surrounding a chipped round table and chairs honoring various members of the McMillin clan, one almost expects wolves to commence howling at any moment. For an explanation of all the

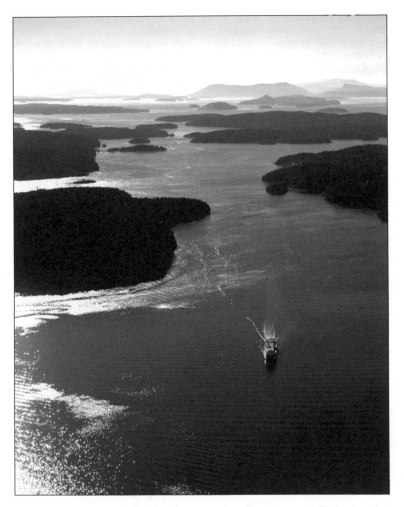

△ The San Juan Island

weird, complicated Masonic symbolism behind the design of the site, check out ⓦwww.rocheharbor.com/walkingtour.html, which informs us that the site is still unfinished, perhaps thankfully, because Mr McMillin "did not see fit to install the bronze dome with its Maltese Cross."

Eating and drinking

Bella Luna 175 First St, Friday Harbor
ⓣ360/378-4118. Hefty Italian and American fare, best for pizzas, pastas, and breakfasts, which include frittatas and English muffins smothered with veggies, eggs, and hollandaise sauce. Daily 7am–10pm & noon–10pm.

Cannery House 174 First St, Friday Harbor
ⓣ360/378-2500. Interesting menu of assorted fresh, affordable seafood, soups, sandwiches, and homemade breads; good views of the harbor, too. Daily 11am–3pm, also summer 5–8pm.

Friday Harbor House **130 West St, Friday Harbor ☎360/378-8455.** Swank, elegant spot for dining on Northwest Cuisine, but particularly good for its sizable wine list, hard ciders, and well-made cocktails. Daily 5.30–10pm.

Garden Path Café **in Churchill Square at 232 A St, Friday Harbor ☎360/378-6255.** Simple, straightforward salads and sandwiches – the big bonus is the view of the harbor, with both indoor and patio seating. Mon–Fri 8am–3pm & 5–9pm, Sat 7am–2pm.

McMillin's **248 Reuben Memorial Drive, Roche Harbor ☎360/378-5757, ⓦwww.rocheharbor.com/dining.html.** The finest of several eateries at Roche Harbor Resort. Though the pricey steak and seafood entrees are rather straightforward, the prime rib and crab are worth the splurge, and the place offers pleasing waterside vistas. Daily 5–10pm.

San Juan Donut Shop **209 Spring St, Friday Harbor ☎360/378-5059.** The most popular breakfast place in town (and not just for donuts), opening early to serve eggs and muffins to diners on their way to the crowded morning ferries. Daily 6.30am–3pm.

Thai Kitchen **42 First St, Friday Harbor ☎360/378-1917.** Reasonable Thai food, good for tasty staples like spring rolls and pad Thai. Located on the main drag, near the Whale Museum. Tues–Fri 11.30am–2.30pm & 5–9pm, Sat–Mon 5–9pm.

Mount Rainier and Mount St Helens

The striking **Cascade Mountains**, pushed up by tectonic forces some 35 million years ago, extend north–south from Canada down toward Oregon. The most-visited peaks in the range are Mount Rainier and Mount St Helens, two giants that may look the picture of serenity, but still conceal a colossal and dangerous volcanic power. Indeed, the threat of further eruptions is far from over: Mount St Helens exploded in 1980, annihilating trees and wildlife over a massive area and raining down ash all over the Northwest, and in 2005 again showed signs of rumbling to life.

Mount Rainier National Park, a comfortable day-trip from Seattle, is an imposing but readily accessible peak, its wide summit easily visible from Seattle on clear days. A visit to the **Mount St Helens National Volcanic Monument**, 165 miles south of the city, will require more time and planning. Mount St Helens is also less conventionally beautiful, though certainly just as dramatic, with the devastation from its eruption a quarter-century ago still quite apparent. A closer taste of the Cascades can be had at spectacular **Snoqualmie Falls**, a monumental torrent just under an hour's drive from the city.

Snoqualmie Falls

Twenty-five miles east of Seattle along I-90, **Snoqualmie Falls** (☎425/831-5784, ⊛www.snoqualmiefalls.com), which exceeds even Niagara Falls by a hundred feet in height, is a favorite weekend getaway for city-dwellers. Fans of David Lynch's cult TV series *Twin Peaks* might recognize the falls – it was pictured in the show's dreamlike opening sequence. The flow, actually controlled by the local power company, cascades 270ft down from a solid-bedrock gorge, spewing out a dense, almost choking mist in places. An **observation platform** is just across from the parking lot, cantilevered over the gorge to provide can't-miss shots for amateur shutterbugs. For an equally dramatic and less crowded viewpoint, take the half-mile **river trail**, which leads from the platform to the bottom of the falls, though its steep grade should be avoided if you're wearing shoes without good traction. Between the platform and the

waterfall, the **Salish Lodge** (☎425/888-2556 or 1-800/826-6124, ⓦwww
.salishlodge.com; $279), the grand wooden structure featured in many *Twin
Peaks* episodes, is worth a splurge if you have the money to spend on a nice
room.

Several miles south of the falls, in the town of North Bend, you can grab a
slice of the famous cherry pie at the legendary **Mar-T Cafe**, now known as
Twede's, 137 W North Bend Way (☎425/831-5511), where *Twin Peaks* agent
Dale Cooper always took care to enjoy a "damn fine cup o' coffee." If you're
not interested in TV-related tourism, you may enjoy **hiking** some of the
nearby trails, the best of which are close to North Bend, at **Mount Si**. A good
choice is the steep, four-mile climb up to Mount Si's peak, which begins on
Mount Si Road. Towering trees shade the trail most of the way to the stony
area near the 4000ft summit, where great views of the surrounding mountains
(including Mount Rainier) can be had. The hair-raising walk to the top of the
nearby "Haystack" outcropping is not advised for casual day-trippers. Another
good hike is the less steep, but still challenging, route up neighboring **Little
Si**, accessible from a trail that begins near the junction of Mount Si Road
and 434th Avenue. The five-mile round-trip takes you up to Little Si's 1600ft
peak, in the process winding its way past much striking scenery – huge Ice
Age-era boulders, dark, primeval-looking forests, and, in the spring, meadows
flush with wildflowers.

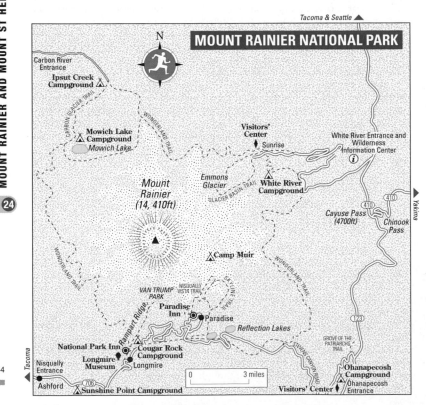

△ Mount Rainier

Mount Rainier

Set in its own national park ninety miles southeast of Seattle, glacier-clad **Mount Rainier** is the tallest and most accessible of the Cascades, and a major Washington landmark – lurking in the background of countless Seattle cityscape photos. To Native Americans living nearby, it spawned a complex mythology, appearing as a jealous wife who was magically metamorphosed into a giant mountain vengefully protective of its higher ridges and peaks. On no account would the local **Klickitat** have ventured up the slopes into this hostile spirit country, where the hazards were inscrutable to human eyes – apt considering the summit is wreathed in clouds much of the time. The Klickitat called it *Tahoma* ("Snowiest Peak"), and there have been moves to revive the original appellation if for no other reason than to end the dire puns about the name describing the weather (though the mountain's name is actually pronounced "ray-NEER"). The mountain acquired its current moniker when explorer George Vancouver named it after one of his cronies, eighteenth-century British rear admiral, **Peter Rainier**, who never even saw it.

If you're visiting during the long winter season, Mount Rainier sees heavy snowfall, and along with it a steady stream of snowshoers, snowboarders, and cross-country skiers. There are both marked and unmarked trails on novice, intermediate, and advanced routes, varying in length from one to ten miles; check with park staff for current routes and availability, which depend on snow conditions.

As spring takes hold, the snow-line creeps up the mountain, unblocking roads and revealing a lattice of **hiking trails**, which at the higher elevations are rarely clear before mid-June. July and August are the sunniest months, when the air is crisp and clear, meadows sprout alpine flowers, and wildlife emerges, with deer, elk, and mountain goats at the forest edges and small furry marmots scurrying between their burrows.

Arrival and information

Rainier National Park is roughly square in shape, with an entrance at each corner. The nearest of these entrances to Seattle is **Nisqually**, at the park's southwest corner. There are also two entrances on the park's eastern flank, **Ohanapecosh** to the south and **White River** in the north. **Carbon River**, the fourth and least-visited entrance, is in the park's more remote northwest corner (information for each of these is provided on the following pages).

If you're coming in by **car**, head south from the city on I-5, taking Exit 127 onto Hwy-512 East; after a few miles, follow Hwy-7 south to Hwy-706, where you'll enter the park just short of **Longmire**, a small cluster of buildings that includes the **Longmire Museum** (May to mid-Oct 9am–5pm, mid-Oct to Dec 9am-4pm; ☎360/569-2211 ext 3314). The museum offers information on the mountain and area wildlife, and sells **park permits** ($10 per vehicle, or $5 each for those on foot, bike, or motorcycle) good for a week inside the park. Be aware that road access depends on weather conditions – with flooding and wind damage constant concerns – so unless you're traveling in the height of summer, call ahead to the National Park Service for details (☎360/569-2211, ⊛www.nps.gov/mora).

Next door to the Longmire Museum, the **Wilderness Information Center** (June to mid-Oct 7.30am–5pm; ☎360/569-HIKE) has plenty of information on the park's network of **trails**, over three hundred miles in all, ranging from easy walks through the forests of the lower slopes to steep treks up to Rainier's 14,411ft summit. Longmire's *National Park Inn* (see "Accommodation," opposite) is the only place in the park to rent **skis** and **snowshoes** in winter, starting at $15 and $12 per day, respectively.

Other than a car, alternate ways to reach the park include the **Rainier Shuttle** (☎360/569-2331), which runs a May-to-October three-hour bus from Sea-Tac Airport to Paradise, a small town on the southern side of the park ($46 one-way), and the **Ashford Mountain Center Shuttle** (van rental $210–320; ☎360/569-2604, ⊛www.ashfordmountaincenter.com), which is better if you're in a group of up to four people and need to travel from Sea-Tac to other destinations in the park. **Gray Line** operates ten-hour, round-trip sightseeing tours to Paradise from Downtown Seattle (May–Sept; $54; ☎360/624-5077 or 1-800/426-7505, ⊛www.graylineseattle.com). In all cases advance reservations are required.

Accommodation

The park offers two splendid **lodges**, though the *Paradise Inn* – a stately 1917 timber hotel – will be closed for renovation until 2008. There are also six **campgrounds** ($10–15), which are on a first-come-first-served basis, except for Cougar Rock, in the southwest part of the park, and Ohanapecosh, in the southeast (reserve for both at ☎1-800/365-CAMP). The only campgrounds open throughout the year are Sunshine Point, adjacent to the Nisqually entrance, and Ipsut Creek, five miles east of the Carbon River entrance – though they only offer 18 and 29 campsites, respectively. **Wilderness permits** (free, or $20 by reservation at ☎360/569-2211 or ⊛reservations.nps.gov) are required for heading into the backcountry with your gear. If all else fails, there's standard motel **accommodation** in Ashford, just outside the Nisqually entrance, as well as the more distinctive choices listed below.

Mountain Meadows Inn 28912 SR 706 E, Ashford ☎360-569-2788, ⊛www .mountainmeadowsinn.com. Six cozy, antique-laden rooms with various historic themes (Early Colonial, Native American, etc), some detached from the main house, offering kitchenettes and claw-foot tubs. Onsite hot tub also available for use by all guests. $139.

Mounthaven 38210 SR 706 E, Ashford ☎360/569-2594 or 1-800/456-9380, ⊛www .mounthaven.com. Ten cabins, some with fireplaces, kitchenettes, fridges, wood stoves, and porches, on six acres lying between two mountain creeks. $109. Hot tub (for a fee) and playground; minimum two-day stay on weekends. Also seventeen full-hookup RV sites for $25.

National Park Inn at Longmire in Mount Rainier National Park ☎ 360/569-2275, ⊛ rainier .guestservices.com. Currently the only park lodge open. Comfortable accommodation in a classically rustic lodge, with 25 guestrooms and a restaurant, plus cross-country skiing and snowshoe rentals. Open year-round, with complimentary breakfast included in winter and spring; reservations essential. $98, add $34 for private bath.

Stormking Cabins 37311 SR 706 E, Ashford ☎ 360/569-2964, ⊛ www.stormkingspa.com.

Not exactly roughing it, but if you want the feel of a real wood cabin nestled in a forest glade – a cabin that also includes a kitchenette, hot tub, fireplace, and mosaic floor – then these four luxury units will more than suffice. Two-night minimum stay. $155. Also offers spa treatments ($50+), and sauna and hot tub rentals ($15 per hour) to non-guests.

Whittaker's Bunkhouse 30205 SR 706 E, Ashford ☎ 360/569-2439, ⊛ www .whittakersbunkhouse.com. A favorite among local climbers and hikers, this old loggers' bunkhouse has dorm beds ($30), double rooms with private baths ($80), and a hot tub. Located next to the Rainier Shuttle stop, with an espresso bar and Wi-Fi Internet access.

Nisqually entrance trails

After passing through the **Nisqually entrance**, and beginning at Longmire, you'll find the **Trail of the Shadows**, a popular half-hour jaunt around the alpine meadow where James Longmire, a local farmer, built a now-defunct mineral springs resort at the end of the nineteenth century. Although it's no match for the area's higher, steeper, and more inaccessible trails, it's still a pleasant walk through meadow and forest in the shadow of mountain peaks, passing an early homestead cabin along the way. Leading off from this loop are more strenuous hikes, such as the five-mile **Rampart Ridge Trail**, which takes you on a climb through thick trees to the ridge – created by an ancient lava flow – from where you'll have a good view of Mount Rainier.

The Trail of the Shadows loop also intersects with the 93-mile **Wonderland Trail**, which encircles the mountain. It's an essential route for serious nature enthusiasts in excellent physical condition; hiking the length of it will take you ten to fourteen days. A hardy but manageable branch of the trail (four to five hours one-way) begins back in Longmire near the Wilderness Information Center (see opposite). From there, head two miles northeast through old-growth forest to the Cougar Rock campground; as the trail meanders to Reflection Lakes, five miles east, it crosses over the Nisqually River – with its muddy-gray, glacier-fed waters – then follows Paradise River by some lovely waterfalls.

Keep in mind that, although trails around Longmire are free from snow earlier than those at higher elevations, in midsummer you'll probably want to drive further up the mountain, where much of the snow, still many feet deep even in June, will have melted enough to allow passage that's impossible at other times of the year.

Trails from Paradise

From Longmire it's just eleven miles through the thinning forest, and past waterfalls of glacial snowmelt, to **Paradise**, where the **Jackson visitors' center** (May to mid–Oct daily 10am–6pm; mid–Oct to Dec 10am–5pm; ☎ 360/569-2211 ext 2328) has films and exhibits on natural history and offers a circular observation room for viewing the mountain. From Paradise, both the 1.2-mile **Nisqually Vista Trail** loop and the five-mile **Skyline Trail** climb the mountain, providing

24

gorgeous views of its craggy peak and glistening glaciers. The park rangers also offer a summer program of **guided walks**, and from late December to early April two-hour guided snowshoe walks leave from the visitors' center (weekends only 10.30am & 2.30pm; limited to 25 people on a first-come-first-served basis; $1 for snowshoe rental, or bring your own).

Paradise is the starting-point for **climbing Mount Rainier**, a serious endeavor involving ice axes, crampons, and a degree of danger. It usually takes two days to get to the summit – with its twin craters rimmed with ice-caves – and back. On the first day climbers aim for the base camp at **Camp Muir**, ready for the strenuous final assault and the descent to Paradise on the second. You have to **register** with the rangers, paying $30 per person, and an additional, flat $20 for the climbing party (information at ☏360/569-HIKE or 360/569-2211, ext 3314). Unless you're very experienced, the way to do it is with the Rainier Mountaineering guide service in Paradise (☏360/569-2227, ⊛www.rmiguides .com), which offers three-day courses – one day's practice, then the two-day climb – from mid-May through September for $795. Equipment rental (lug-sole climbing boots, ice axes) costs extra, and reservations with advance payment in full are required.

The rest of the park

In summer, it's possible to drive about an hour from Paradise along rugged **Stevens Canyon Road** to the park's southeastern corner, cruising around hillside ridges on a winding concourse with plenty of switchbacks. Here, the **Ohanapecosh entrance** and **visitors' center** (July–Oct daily 9am–5pm; ☏360/569-6046) is set in deep forest, near the gurgling Ohanapecosh River. Amongst several trails hereabouts, one of the most enjoyable is the **Grove of the Patriarchs**, a 1.3-mile loop along an islet in the Ohanapecosh River, with ancient groves of giant Douglas fir, western hemlock, and red cedar trees.

North from Ohanapecosh, in the park's northeast corner, is the **White River entrance** and the **Wilderness Information Center** (July–Oct daily 7.30am–4.30pm; ☏360/569-6046), which gives out trail information and issues backpacking and climbing permits. Six miles west of here, at the White River picnic area and campground, you can reach any number of trails leading around mountain ridges and the lower reaches of glaciers, or pick up the Wonderland Trail, which leads around the dramatically sited Shadow and Frozen lakes, offering astounding views of the volcanic terrain. Eleven miles further up the mountain from the White River entrance, along another winding route full of switchbacks, the **Sunrise visitors' center** (July–Sept daily 9am–5pm; ☏360/663-2425) has wonderful views of **Emmons Glacier**, the huge tongue of ice on the mountain's northeastern side, and of the Rainier summit. The hardiest hikers can get a better look on the **Glacier Basin Trail**, a seven-mile slog with striking summer views of wildflowers, craggy peaks, and mountain goats.

The last and least-frequently visited of the national park's four entrances, the **Carbon River entrance** (no visitors' center), lies in the northwest corner of the park, and isn't linked by road to the other three. Hwy-165, the paved approach road, runs as far as the ranger station, which serves as the trailhead for the short and easy **Carbon River Rainforest Trail**, which nudges into Mount Rainier's one and only chunk of temperate rainforest. As evocative as the forest's moss-covered spruces and canopies of greenery are, it's a long way to go for a trail that's just a third of a mile long. Rugged types should consider the seven-mile round-trip **Carbon Glacier Trail**, beginning four miles east of the Carbon River entrance at the Ipsut Creek Campground. The trail is high-lighted by a suspension bridge that crosses a river below the mouth of the dirty, crumbling Carbon Glacier – the glacier of lowest elevation in the US outside of Alaska, and the source of the Carbon River itself.

Mount St Helens

The native Klickitat knew **Mount St Helens** as "Tahonelatclah," or "Fire Mountain" – and, true to its name, in May of 1980 the mountain exploded, leaving a blasted landscape and scenes of almost total destruction for many miles around. Slowly but surely, second-growth forests have emerged and the ash has partly disappeared beneath new vegetation. Even so, much of the land continues to bear witness to the incredible force of the eruption, with once-pristine valleys sheared by mudflows, mangled trees ripped from their roots, and entire mountainsides that still resemble a post-nuclear wasteland. And recent tremors and small billows of steam and ash haven't given any assurance that the mountain is finished with its violent business.

Arrival and information

Mount St Helens is a major tourist attraction, with most people heading for the two **visitors' centers**, Coldwater Ridge and the smaller Johnston Ridge Observatory, which overlook the blast zone from the northwest side of the mountain. Either destination is at least three hours from Seattle, south down I-5 and then east along either Hwy-504 or -503. It's a time-consuming trek, and an overnight stay at minimum is necessary if you want to get a feel for the area; if you want to explore more sites or take some lengthy hikes you should set aside a few days.

The best time to visit is during the week, as traffic can clog the access roads on summer weekends. During the summer, the east side of the mountain can be reached along scenic but rough forest roads from US-12 to the north and Hwy-14 in the south. To check conditions, and for general information, call the **Mount St Helens Visitors' Center**, five miles east of Castle Rock at 3029 Spirit Lake Hwy (daily 9am–5pm, summer closes 6pm; ☎360/274-0962, ⓦwww.fs.fed.us/gpnf/mshnvm). The one-day **Monument Pass** ($3 single visit, $6 multiple visits) allows entry to the Coldwater Ridge and Mount St Helens visitors' centers, and the Johnston Ridge Observatory; while the **Northwest Forest Pass** ($5) is good for other sites such as the Ape Cave, Lava Canyon, etc, and is available through putting money in drop boxes at site parking lots.

Permits are required for those interested in **climbing** the mountain above 4800 feet (lower-level routes don't require them), where the majority of routes up to the summit begin, and only one hundred of them are issued per day from April to October ($15). Half are booked far ahead of time, but fifty are set aside for distribution by lottery one day in advance. To enter the lottery, you have to be at *Jack's Restaurant* (☎360/231-4276), five miles west of Cougar, a tiny settlement on Hwy-503, at 6pm. The rest of the year, things ease up, though all prospective climbers still have to register at *Jack's* before they go. The climbing route begins at the **Climbers' Bivouac**, at the end of a narrow, winding road high up the mountain, and the round trip takes between seven and twelve

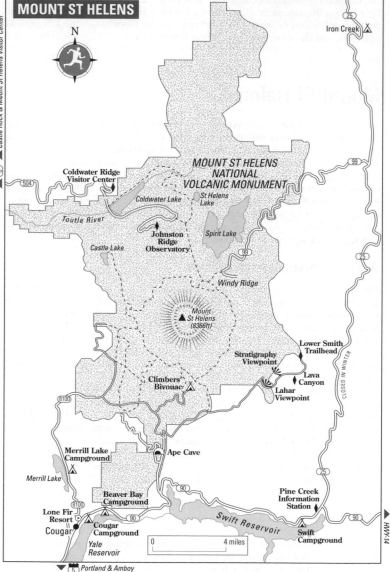

hours. The climb takes you to the crater rim, but the crater itself – a jagged cauldron of rock and steam – is out of bounds (though geologists and other scientists are allowed to visit it by helicopter).

Note that with the increased seismic activity on the mountain in 2005, the park service has been frequently disallowing climbing above 4800 feet. Check or call for details on the latest conditions.

Accommodation

If you're keen to avoid a long drive, or want to have time for a decent hike, then **staying** overnight in the area is a good choice. There's motel accommodation beside the junction of I-5 and Hwy-504 in the uneventful town of **Castle Rock**, but your best bet may be to aim for the hamlet of **Cougar**, which straggles along Hwy-503 nearer the mountain.

Though there aren't any campgrounds within the national monument, there are **private campgrounds** operated by the PacifiCorp energy company, in the vicinity of Cougar (June–Aug only; ☎503/813-6666 for reservations): the Cougar campsite, located on Yale Reservoir just north of the village (reservations required; 60 sites; $15); Beaver Bay, about a mile north on 503 (first-come, first-served; 78 sites; $15); and Cresap Bay, accessed by turning right at *Jack's Restaurant* while going east on 503, and continuing on for two miles south (reservations required; 73 sites; $15). Inside the park, **wilderness camping** is allowed below 4800 feet, and at Climbers' Bivouac – the only permit required is the Northwest Forest Pass ($5; see p.279).

Ike Kinswa State Park 14 miles east of I-5 (Exit 68) on Hwy-12, near Mossyrock ☎360/864-2643, Ⓦwww.parks.wa.gov. Located north of the mountain, and spread over 450 acres. Terrific for its boating, fishing, and watersports, and has more than a hundred campsites. Summer 6.30am–dusk, rest of year 8am–dusk. $15–21.

Lone Fir Resort 16806 Lewis River Rd (Hwy-503) in Cougar ☎360/238-5210, Ⓦwww.lonefirresort.com. Seventeen basic motel rooms, half with kitchens and microwaves, plus a swimming pool. Located along a central route on the south side of the mountain; $45. Also has RV and tent camping for $15–21.

Mount St Helens Motel 1340 Mt St Helens Way in Castle Rock, near the junction of I-5 and Hwy-504 ☎360/274-7721, Ⓦwww.mtsthelensmotel.com. Standard motel accommodation located a bit east from the main mountain attractions. Queen-sized beds in every room. $49.

Seaquest State Park at Silver Lake about five miles east of I-5 on Hwy-504 ☎1-800/452-5687, Ⓦwww.parks.wa.gov. Across the road from the Mount St Helens Visitors' Center, an excellent, scenic choice for birdwatching, cycling, hiking, and fishing, with 55 tent sites on 475 acres. Open daily: summer 8am–8pm; rest of year 8am–5pm. $15–27.

Silver Lake Motel & Resort Hwy-504 six miles east of I-5 in Silver Lake ☎360/274-6141, Ⓦwww.silverlake-resort.com. Convenient for mountain access and bass fishing (you can cast a line from your balcony). Offers clean, comfortable motel rooms with kitchenettes (seasonal $95–110), cabins with kitchens ($65), 11 RV hook-ups ($25), and 22 campsites ($16).

The northwest slope

The obvious introduction to Mt St Helens, especially from Seattle, is on Hwy-504 (heading east from I-5), which takes you past some of the most dramatic volcanic scenery, on the **northwest slope** of the mountain. The road runs through dark-green forests, past **Silver Lake** and **Toutle River Valley**, until bald, spiky trees signal a sudden change: beyond, thousands of gray tree-shards still lie in uniform rows, knocked flat in different directions back in 1980 when blast waves bounced off the hillsides. It's a weird and disconcerting landscape, the matchstick-like flattened forest left to rot, regenerating the soil and providing cover for small animals and insects. There are several good vantage points as you progress up the road – notably at **Hoffstadt Bluffs**, where you can make out the path taken by the avalanche of debris that swept down the valley – to the **Coldwater Ridge visitors' center** (May–Sept daily 10am–6pm, reduced winter hours; ☎360/274-2131), which has interpretive exhibits and a film detailing the eruption.

24

Eight miles further along Hwy-504, the low-slung **Johnston Ridge Observatory** (May–Oct daily 10am–6pm; ☎360/274-2140) – named after David Johnston, a government geologist who died at the location during the eruption – is as close as you'll get to the mountain by car, since the observatory lies at the end of a dead-end road. The views here, over the still-steaming lava dome and pumice plain, are quite extraordinary. Again, interpretive displays, a video, and a fifteen-minute film give the background. Outside the center, the half-mile paved **Eruption Trail** leads to slightly higher viewpoints marked with interpretive displays; there's also a short, dusty, and, in places, steep hiking trail that takes you toward **Spirit Lake**, with much longer and more strenuous side trails leading up toward the edge of the crater peak.

The south and east slopes

Interstate 5 intersects Hwy-503 twice before it reaches Portland, Oregon, and either exit will do to access the fascinating **south slope** of the mountain – the side seen mainly by locals, since most tourists head to Johnston Ridge. The highway leads both to **Cougar**, where there's a good motel and a campground, and nearby **Beaver Bay**, which has only a campground. Beyond Cougar, it's ten miles further along Forest Road 83 to the **Ape Cave**, a rocky, tube-like lava cavern – the longest in the continental US – channeled two thousand years ago by the rushing molten lava of an eruption. Despite the compelling name, there are no oversized primates lurking inside; the place was named after the St Helens Apes, an outdoors group for local youth. In the cave, there are two subterranean routes to choose from: the three-quarter-mile lower trail, where you have to return to the entrance to get out, and the much more difficult one-and-a-half-mile upper trail, which emerges higher up the mountain. For a less strenuous jaunt, the quarter-mile **Trail of Two Forests** elevated boardwalk, off the road shortly before Ape Cave, has a 55-foot crawl through a lava tunnel; bring a flashlight.

Ranger-led **tours** (late-June to early-Sept daily 10.30am–4.30pm, on the hour), pointing out all kinds of geological oddities you'd otherwise miss, leave from **Apes Headquarters** (late-June to early-Sept daily 10am–4pm) beside the cave. Lanterns can be rented until 4pm for $3.50 at the headquarters, or from *Jack's Restaurant* back in Cougar, for $10, plus a $20 deposit. Also, keep in mind that it's much colder in the cave than outside, so bring extra clothing.

Climbers' Bivouac to Lava Canyon

Further up the mountain, **hiking trails** climb and traverse the south side of Mount St Helens, exploring its every nook and cranny. Take detailed **advice** from the rangers before you set out on all but the shortest of walks, and remember to pack plenty of water. The most popular climbing route begins at the **Climbers' Bivouac** trail base, high up the mountain at the end of USFS road 830; it takes you to the crater rim and back in seven to twelve hours. Climbing is hedged with restrictions, though (see p.279).

Further east begins an excellent loop drive on Forest Road 83, leading you past the highlights of the south slope. The first of these is the **Lahar Viewpoint**, which gives you a good look at how this side of the mountain was changed by mudflows both ancient and recent – the 1980 blast carved up many landscapes in the vicinity, exposing their basaltic rocks and geologic layers. Indeed, a short distance away, the **Stratigraphy Viewpoint** provides a look at one such vivid vista, where volcanic flows are revealed in bright horizontal bands of orange and yellow tephra (hardened ash). At the end of the loop, the **Lava Canyon**

The eruption of Mount St Helens

From its first rumblings in March 1980, **Mount St Helens** drew the nation's attention as one of the rare examples of (recent) volcanic activity in the continental US. Residents and loggers were evacuated and roads were closed, but by April the entrances to the restricted zone around the steaming peak were jammed with reporters and sightseers. The mountain didn't seem to be doing much, however, and impatient residents demanded to be allowed back to their homes. Harry Truman, operator of the *Lodge at Spirit Lake*, famously refused to move out and became a national celebrity – lauded for his "common sense" by Washington's governor.

Waiting at the barriers, a convoy of homeowners was about to go and collect their possessions when the **explosion** finally came on **May 18** – powered by subsurface water heated to boiling by geothermal activity, and causing a chain reaction that blew apart the peak not upwards but sideways, ripping a great chunk out of the northwest side of the mountain. An avalanche of debris slid into Spirit Lake, raising it by two hundred feet and turning it into a steaming cauldron of mud, as dark clouds of ash buried Truman and suffocated loggers on a nearby slope. Altogether, 57 people died on the mountain: a few were there doing their official duties, such as brave geologist David Johnston, but most had ignored the warnings. The wildlife population was harder hit: about a million and a half animals – deer, elk, mountain goats, cougars, and bears – were killed, and thousands of fish were boiled alive in sediment-filled rivers. There were dire economic effects, too, as falling ash devastated the land, and millions of feet of timber were lost.

For decades after, the mountain remained fairly quiet, with second-growth forests and groundcover taking root, and early colonizing plants and animals taking advantage of the relative lack of competition and predation. On October 1, 2004, though, the mountain rumbled back into everyone's consciousness, with small bursts of steam and ash that continued throughout the month. Despite predictions, however, no eruption came – that is, until **March 8, 2005**, when a minor, but actual, eruption at dusk clouded the skies with ash, creating a plume that reached a jet-level height of 36,000 feet in a few minutes. Since then, seismic activity and small hiccups of ash and steam have occurred, making the US Forest Service understandably nervous about letting hikers get too close to the forbidding crater.

Even if you want to keep your distance from this fearsome giant, the mountain's presence is unmistakable in the region, and not just up-close on the forest-service roads. Indeed, looking north from southwest Washington and Portland, Oregon, you can't help but notice the looming silhouette of a ruined gray mound over the horizon, the charred remains of what was once a lively and romantic winter playground.

24

has several short trails leading past harrowing drop-offs near gigantic igneous rocks, past striking waterfalls, to dramatic, mudflow-scoured landscapes. If you want to give yourself a scare, traverse the hanging **suspension bridge** that leads over the canyon's sheer-rock gorge, your heart skipping a beat with every rickety bounce.

Windy Ridge

Simply put, the **east slope** of Mount St Helens has the most striking, almost unbelievable views of the volcano's tremendous power, yet it is also the most difficult – or at least the most unpleasant – to reach. From Hwy-503, near where Forest Road 83 branches away, you'll need to travel 53 switchbacking, nausea-inducing miles to curve around the eastern side of the mountain. You can also travel there via the northern slope, but in the end it's no quicker. Along the way, you can check conditions at **Pine Creek Information Station** (summer daily 9am–6pm) and then head north along Forest Road 25, before making the final push up Forest Road 99 to **Windy Ridge**, a rocky outcrop with breathtaking views of the crater from the northeast. A short hike from here also leads to the long, circular trail around the summit and the somewhat easier hike down past Spirit Lake to Johnston Ridge – though check with rangers about the latest conditions, since bad weather and seismic activity can keep many trails, especially on higher elevations, closed for months at a time.

On Windy Ridge, the devastation wrought by the 1980 eruption is even more startling: entire slopes denuded of foliage, colossal tree husks scattered like twigs, and huge dead zones where anything alive was vaporized. The former resort area of **Spirit Lake**, below the ridge, is one such area: the lake's once deep-blue water boiling away during the cataclysm, as a violent cascade of burning rock and mud filled it with dark volcanic debris.

Windy Ridge can also be accessed from the north from **Randle**, which provides access to what remains of Spirit Lake and passes through lava flows with numerous fine viewpoints en route.

Contexts

Contexts

A brief history of Seattle

n the annals of the 150-year **history** of Seattle, the official story is based as much on myth as fact: from virgin forests and uncut wilderness emerged white settlers who, emboldened by the heroic feats on the Oregon Trail, ultimately brought into being the modern state of Washington. Because of its importance to the Klondike Gold Rush and its abundance of fish and lumber, the Emerald City became a regional commercial powerhouse, later emerging as a national leader in aerospace and high-tech, thanks in no small part to the federal defense budget that, directly or indirectly, engendered both. And there was also that business with the World's Fair.

You could easily get by on a visit knowing only this pocket history of the city and little more. However, the reality is naturally richer, and more contradictory – namely, how such an industrial and military giant could also birth such a vigorous labor movement and activist counterculture; how a quintessential timber town could also be present at the rise of the modern environmental movement; and, perhaps most curiously, how a city with such dreary weather throughout much of the year could attract newcomers by the score – many fleeing from the much sunnier confines of California.

Geologic origins

Most of central and western Washington did not exist 200 million years ago. Then, the western edge of North America lay on what is now the far east of the state, around Spokane. With the ongoing process of **continental drift**, in which chunks of the earth's crust are forever in motion, colliding with and splitting from one other, the land mass of modern Washington began to grow – though in a rather surprising way.

Much of the state was formed when island "**micro-continents**" originating in the South Pacific collided with the northwestern edge of North America over the course of 150 million years, slowly adding to the land mass until the rough contours of the state as we know it today emerged about fifty million years ago. The Seattle area itself, known to geologists as the **Puget Sound Lowland**, may have originated as part of a tectonic rift or fault, though this is still somewhat unclear: the local topography is built on glacial debris – gravel, till, and sand – that's more than a half-mile deep in places, making the area difficult to study. The debris also adds an element of danger to this **earthquake**-susceptible terrain; nothing here is built on bedrock, and the ground can become quite unsteady during a major quake, as residents experienced as recently as 2001. Moreover, plate tectonics are never far from one's mind when, a hundred miles to the south, the tremors and steam belches of Mount St Helens continue unabated, a vivid reminder of just how shaky the ground can be in these parts.

Native peoples

Long before European explorers and white settlers showed up, the Pacific Northwest was occupied by a variety of **native peoples**. The majority of these

C

groups arrived during the most recent Ice Age, some twelve to twenty thousand years ago, when a temporary **land bridge** across the Bering Strait allowed passage from Asia into North America. Eventually, some of these groups made it south to the Pacific Northwest, establishing their own tribes and nations. Those who settled in the Seattle area were of the **Coast Salish** group, Native Americans who depended on fishing and gathering for their essentials, and who frequently lived in **longhouses** – structures, sometimes several hundred feet in length, in which entire Indian tribes lived in a communal fashion. Today, few records remain of their culture, which was largely wiped out by the white settlers, who came bearing guns and deadly foreign germs.

One intriguing mystery from this early age has emerged in recent years, however, when **Kennewick Man** was discovered in 1996 near the Columbia River. This Ice Age-era specimen showed few chromosomal links to modern native peoples, and scientists claim he may even be an unexpected proto-Caucasoid migrant – whose genetic kin, the first time around at least, did not successfully invade and colonize the region.

Exploration and conflict

What is now the Pacific Northwest was unknown to **Europeans** until the search for the legendary **Northwest Passage** – a long-hoped-for channel that would connect the Pacific and Atlantic oceans – fired the imaginations of European explorers in the 1500s and 1600s. One of these explorers, **Juan de Fuca**, a Greek navigator sailing for the Spanish, claimed at the end of the sixteenth century to have found an inlet at 47 degrees latitude in the Northwest. However, his discovery was not officially recognized, and it wasn't until 1787 that English captain **Charles Barkley** found and named the **Strait of Juan de Fuca** in the San Juan Islands, in approximately the same location as the waters de Fuca claimed to have visited. The Spaniard **Manuel Quimper** explored the San Juans in 1790, but Puget Sound wasn't charted until a couple of years later, by **Peter Puget** under the command of **George Vancouver**, whose primary mission was to settle territorial disputes with Spain. By 1795, as a result of Vancouver's efforts, the British assumed control of the region, at least for a few decades.

American presence in the Sound was initiated by the **Pacific Fur Company** in the early nineteenth century, and was soon countered by the British-held **North West Fur Company**, resulting in several decades of uneasy relations in what would become Oregon and Washington. During the US presidential campaign of 1844, the distant region even became a national cause celebre, with supporters of jingoistic candidate James K. Polk shouting "54'40 or fight!" – referring to the geographic parallel many Americans imagined as their northern border by right of manifest destiny. Polk's territorial ambitions, however, were sated with the Mexican-American War, and the Anglo-American hostility largely ended in 1846, when the territory known as Oregon country was divided on the **49th parallel**, in the middle of the channel separating the continent from Vancouver Island. The British received the portion north of the parallel, while ownership of San Juan Island itself remained in dispute. The **Pig War** of 1859, in which British and American camps on San Juan Island nearly came to armed conflict over the shooting of a pig by an American settler (see box, p.270), was finally resolved by arbitration in favor of the US in 1872.

Founding and settlement

Seattle was officially **founded** by white pioneers at roughly the same time that other major (non-Spanish) West Coast cities were established, and it would later find industrial and commercial success through extractive industries. However, it was a long time before the city began to wield notable influence in international business and the arts, or to project a truly distinct identity.

In 1846, there were as yet no white settlements in Puget Sound except for a small community in **Tumwater–Olympia**, which was founded by migrants on what would become known as the Cowlitz Trail, a northern spur of the Oregon Trail. Four years later, a small group of pioneers from Illinois led by Seattle founder **David Denny** were advised to settle in Puget Sound by a traveler they met during their journey west. On November 13, 1851, most of them landed on the western edge of what is now West Seattle, where they were greeted by **Chief Sealth** of the Duwamish-Suquamish peoples.

It was not a promising start for what would become the biggest city in the Pacific Northwest: many in the landing party were sick, they landed in the midst of a rainstorm, and Denny, who had arrived a few weeks before the main group, had yet to finish building shelter for them. The settlement of about two dozen people, half of them children, was named New York by one of the men, Charles Terry, after his home state. Soon, though, the name was unofficially, derisively, altered by the settlers to "New York-Alki" – in native slang, "New York by-and-by" – later assuming its current moniker of **Alki Beach**.

In early 1852, settlement members **Arthur Denny**, Carson Boren, and William Bell claimed land to the north, nearer to the deepwater harbor of Elliott Bay. Help soon arrived with **Henry Yesler**, who chose Seattle as the location for Puget Sound's first **steam sawmill**. The area around Seattle, **King County** (named after William Rufus King, a US vice president in the 1850s), was recognized by the federal government, and Seattle became its county seat. By 1853 there were 170 Seattle residents, many of whom worked at Yesler's mill.

Washington territory governor **Isaac Stevens** negotiated land treaties with the Indians in the mid-1850s, designed to keep the natives on small reservations that would not impinge upon the most desirable land. He was aided by Chief Sealth, who helped arrange treaties in lieu of armed conflict. Still, there were several skirmishes, culminating in an Indian attack on Seattle in January of 1856 that resulted in few casualties, though many homes were burned. This so-called **Indian War** slowed population growth in the area, with some settlers leaving for less risky territory to the south.

In a strange interlude in the 1860s, **Asa Mercer** tried to boost the city's population and morale by arranging for the passage of unmarried women from the East Coast to Seattle, where men outnumbered women by about ten to one. An initial scheme brought about a dozen women to Seattle from Massachusetts, but his attempt on a larger scale failed. Contracting a ship in New York City for five hundred passengers, he managed to secure fewer than one hundred, and only a few dozen of these were potential brides. After sailing all the way around South America's Cape Horn, the ship's captain also refused to take them any further than San Francisco. Mercer finally got a few of the brides-to-be to Seattle, but stiffed a number of local bachelors who had paid for their wives in advance – though he did manage to marry one of them himself.

The railroad era and the Great Seattle Fire

Seattle became an incorporated city in 1869. Four years later, the **Northern Pacific Railroad** chose Tacoma's Commencement Bay as the western terminus of its transcontinental line, taking the wind out of Seattle's sails by dashing its hopes of becoming a great overland freight depot. Undaunted, some citizens raised money for their own railroad through Snoqualmie Pass to Walla Walla, and even built the first few miles of tracks with their own hands – but the impetus soon waned. Indirectly, though, their goal was accomplished: in the 1880s, Henry Villard of Northern Pacific bought the Seattle–Walla Walla railroad line and built a track that facilitated connections between Seattle and the transcontinental line. And in 1893, the **Great Northern Railroad** made Seattle its Pacific terminus, though it would be another thirteen years before its **King Street Station** was finished – only to be topped five years later by the much more elegant **Union Station**, the monument of the rival Union Pacific.

A few years before the apex of the railroad era, Seattle's growth was set back, at least temporarily, by the **Great Seattle Fire of 1889** (see box, p.67), which destroyed much of Downtown, mostly around today's Pioneer Square – which had long before replaced Alki Beach as the town's population center and hub of settlement. The fire caused $15 million in damage, but the city quickly rebuilt, this time using much safer building materials, including the magnificent neo-Romanesque stone facades that still grace businesses there today. Between 1880 and 1890, the population of Seattle increased by about ten times, to a little over 40,000. Still, the city wasn't without major problems, including rampant civic corruption, anti-Chinese rioting, prevalent prostitution, and an erratic infrastructure that at one time included a sewer trench that ran uphill along First Avenue. It was, in large measure, a formerly small town now bursting at the seams.

Boomtown I: the Klondike Gold Rush

In July of 1897, the discovery of **Klondike gold** in northwestern Canada inspired a wave of zealous prospectors, and Seattle was in the fortunate position of being the closest American port of any appreciable size. The town was inundated with starry-eyed fortune-seekers, their dreams fired up by tales and legends of those who had found unimaginable wealth and glory up north. Taking a page from the profiteers who founded true fortunes a half-century earlier in the San Francisco Gold Rush – namely tool-sellers and outfitters like Leland Stanford – the Seattle Chamber of Commerce created the **Bureau of Information** for drawing gold-diggers to Seattle. Cleverly conceived by publicists like the well-named **Erastus Brainerd**, the bureau's campaign placed numerous ads in newspapers and magazines across the nation extolling the wonders of the **Seattle–Klondike connection**. (Eventually, even one of Seattle's mayors caught gold fever, quitting his job to take part in the frenzy.)

The gambit paid off. While predictably few of the incoming fortune-hunters who set off from Seattle returned with pots of gold, thanks to the massive influx of ship and rail traffic throughout the town, business boomed in banks and shops and the shipbuilding and real estate industries. The most far-reaching effect of the gold rush was a dramatic rise in Seattle's **population**, as many would-be prospectors settled in the city, either by choice or necessity. By 1900, the city had 80,000 residents; by 1910, that number had tripled.

Growth in the Progressive Era

Seattle's position as an emerging major American city during the **Progressive Era** solidified with the **Alaska–Yukon–Pacific Exposition** of 1909, which drew nearly four million visitors over a five-month period.

The University of Washington campus was developed around the expo buildings by the **Olmsted brothers**, John Charles and Frederick Law Jr, sons of landscape architect Frederick Law Olmsted, who designed New York City's Central Park. The two were renowned park planners, responsible for greenspaces from LA to Portland, and had been hired earlier, in 1903, to design a system of parks and boulevards for Seattle. The result was a city where you could travel from Green Lake through the Washington Arboretum down to Seward Park without ever leaving the grass. In 1910, Seattle citizens approved $2 million worth of **park bonds**, fueled not just by a desire for more greenspace, but also a need to plan new neighborhoods that had recently been annexed: Ballard, West Seattle, and South Seattle.

Cultural entertainment also began to prosper during the era, exemplified by such early venues for theater and vaudeville as the (extant) Moore and (demolished) Pantages theaters. However, alongside the growth and good times, houses of **gambling** and **prostitution**, which adjoined many entertainment establishments, were flourishing on Downtown's **Skid Road** (see box, p.64). In 1915 the state of Washington voted for **Prohibition**, and Mayor **Hiram Gill** personally led raids on places that sold hard liquor. The bootleggers got back at him by providing testimony in a federal grand jury indictment of Gill and others for conspiracy to violate interstate commerce law. Though found not guilty, Gill was impeached, but the city council refused to remove him. This was very much in character with Gill, who in the 1910s was elected three times, recalled twice, and defeated twice.

More level-headed reform was championed in the subsequent decade by **Bertha Knight Landes**, who in 1926 became the first woman mayor of a major US city. She balanced her desire for greater law enforcement and vice control with a dedication to improve public parks and health programs – but still was ousted after one term.

Industrial progress and the strike of 1919

An important local trade development came in 1917 with the completion of the **Lake Washington Ship Canal** in Ballard, which allowed passage from Lake Washington to Lake Union and Puget Sound. The canal's **Ballard Locks** ensured that the lakes would remain freshwater, crucial for salmon to spawn there, while the docks and wharves created employment for many locals, notably the numerous Scandinavians who had settled in Ballard.

With large numbers of Seattle residents employed in **shipping** and **manufacturing** (particularly timber products), unions gained strength here in the early twentieth century, including the leftist **International Workers of the World** (IWW), better known as the **Wobblies**. In early 1919, a shipyard strike in Seattle set off a wave of sympathy strikes by other unions, which led, on February 6, to the first **general strike** ever called in a US city. Fifteen hundred soldiers were brought in from nearby Fort Lewis, but no violence occurred before the largely unsuccessful strike quietly ended five days later. Some of the strike's advocates, such as newspaper reporter **Anna Louise Strong**, had hoped that the strike would bring the management of industry into the hands of workers. She was thus viewed as a socialist agitator, and, along with other staff of the *Union Record* paper, was indicted for sedition – although the charges were eventually dropped. The IWW, meanwhile, was torn by internal policy disputes in the 1920s, and never regained the stature it had enjoyed during World War I.

From the 1930s through the 1950s, the most influential labor organizer in Seattle was **Dave Beck**, who eventually became president of the Teamsters. An effective organizer – by the end of World War II, Seattle was 95 percent unionized – Beck was no radical, seeking any solution other than a strike, and was seen by some as too chummy with local business. His influence was greatly eroded when he was found guilty of income-tax evasion, for which he served jail time in the early 1960s.

World War II to the Vietnam War

Seattle's shipping and timber industries were hit hard by the **Great Depression**, but **World War II** reinvigorated the port. The war also boosted the city's small black population, as African-Americans moved to Seattle (and other West Coast cities) to work in war-related industries. Simultaneously, the Japanese-American population, previously Seattle's largest minority, was persecuted and depleted as a result of President Roosevelt's **Executive Order 9066**, which interned members of the community in detention camps.

The war brought tremendous growth to the area's **defense industry**, particularly aviation companies like **Boeing**, which was founded in Seattle in the 1910s. The early 1940s saw such great demand for military planes that by 1944 Boeing employed 50,000 workers – though the end of the war nearly killed the operation. The company's diversification, particularly into **commercial jetliners**, started it down the road toward lasting success. In 1947, around one in five of Seattle's manufacturing workers were employed by Boeing; by 1957, the ratio was one in two. The talent needed to run the company – particularly engineers and technicians – also gave rise to a significant culture of technology in the area. This marriage of a vibrant economy and technology was celebrated by the **Century 21 Exposition** (also known as the **World's Fair**) in 1962, for which Seattle's most recognizable symbol, the **Space Needle**, was built, and which finally gave the city the glimmer of an international presence.

The political movements sweeping much of America in the 1960s were mirrored in microcosm in Seattle. In 1962, City Councilman **Wing Luke** became the first elected Asian-American official in the Northwest, while sit-ins by blacks a few years later led to the approval of a fair housing ordinance. There were also **Vietnam War protests** on the UW campus, including one demonstration that blocked rush-hour traffic on I-5 to protest the US invasion of Cambodia, and continued Downtown, where paint bombs were thrown and windows broken at Seattle's federal courthouse. As a result, the leaders of the group that organized the protest – who came to be known as the **Seattle Seven** – were charged with conspiracy to damage federal property, though a mistrial was eventually declared.

The 1970s and 1980s

In the 1970s Seattle began to establish itself as one of the most desirable places to live in the US. Both **Pike Place Market** and **Pioneer Square** – the city's two most historic areas – were rescued from the brink of destruction and renovated into the thriving spots they are today. The **Forward Thrust** plan, devised by attorney and activist James Ellis, pushed through bonds approving funding for community centers, parks, and a domed sports stadium, the **Kingdome**, which was completed in the mid-1970s. However, the city was still extremely dependent on the fortunes of the area's biggest employers, and sharp cutbacks at Boeing in the early 1970s resulted in a deep **recession** that saw unemployment rise to twelve percent – double the national average.

Not long after, though, Seattle crystallized its international image with the rise of software giant **Microsoft** in the 1980s and the **Starbucks** empire the decade following. Microsoft, which actually started up in 1975, was one of the great business success stories of the late twentieth century, controlled by the world's richest man, **Bill Gates**, and inspiring literally hundreds of computer- and software-focused companies to choose Puget Sound as their base (many, indeed, founded by ex-Microsoft employees). The company garnered headlines for creating a fresh crop of **Microsoft millionaires** (boosted by their stock holdings), who were willing to adopt a casual, yet still ruthless, approach to achieving corporate dominance, while also investing in public arts and culture.

At the same time, a thriving **alternative rock scene**, largely developed on the **Sub Pop** label in the mid-to-late 1980s, burst into international prominence with the chart-topping success of grunge bands like Nirvana, and a frenetic music scene grew in the once-decrepit Belltown district. The other arts began to thrive as well, evidenced by numerous offbeat **theater companies** and **galleries**, as well as dramatically expanded **art museums** – so much so that Jane Alexander, chair of the National Endowment for the Arts, was moved to call Seattle the "Athens of the West" in 1997. This was certainly a far cry from 1943, when the then-conductor of the Seattle Symphony, Sir Thomas Beecham, dismissed the city as an "aesthetic dustbin."

Boomtown II: the 1990s

By the 1990s people began moving to the Seattle metropolitan area in force, especially to suburban Bellevue and Redmond, and **housing prices** rose sharply. Though the population within the city limits remained stable at around half a million, Seattle's infrastructure felt the strain of development in its outly-ing areas – the **mass transit** system began to be overstressed, and **traffic** turned nightmarish, especially in the inter-suburban commute.

Meanwhile, the explosion of a well-funded arts and culture scene resulted in the construction of the Seattle Symphony's **Benaroya Hall** and the **Experi-ence Music Project**, along with an expanded **Henry Art Gallery**. These institutions elevated the city's profile, and other museums took advantage of the good times by doubling in size or undergoing major renovations. Population growth fueled economic expansion as well. Seattle had re-established itself as a top port in the 1960s, and by the 1990s it was the US leader in container tonnage exports to Asia. In addition, **Fishermen's Terminal**, redeveloped in 1993 at a cost of $13 million, became key to Washington State's $1.5 billion-per-year fishing industry, and tourism emerged as a $10 billion-a-year industry – one of the state's five largest.

But uncomfortable political tempests swirled, too, in the battle over the construction of two new sports stadiums to replace the Kingdome: **Safeco Field** and, more notoriously, **Seahawks Stadium** (now Qwest Field), which was financed at huge public expense thanks to Microsoft co-founder Paul Allen's elaborate PR campaign. Transportation funding emerged as another point of contention, with a thirty percent cut at the end of the decade further exacerbating transit problems. If that weren't enough, a ballot measure designed to curb local taxes (including the notoriously steep vehicle-registration fee) created even more difficulties for state and local funding.

By the end of the decade, some of Seattle's biggest claims to fame had lost the world's attention: the grunge rock explosion had subsided; Starbucks, thanks to its global success, grew to be seen as a symbol of sterile American hegemony; and the public's fascination with the area's high-tech industries waned, espe-cially as Microsoft fought with the Justice Department over anti-trust infringe-ment. Closing out the century, the city hosted the **World Trade Organization conference** in late 1999. Originally envisioned as an opportunity for Seattle to showcase its rising role in international global trade and world affairs, the week turned into a PR nightmare when **riots** broke out between police and anti-globalization protesters, putting the city in the headlines once more – this time in an unfavorable light (see box, opposite).

The paradox of growth

Things worsened for Seattle at the end of 2000, when the **high-tech bubble** burst, and the national economy turned sour. Countless Seattle firms went out of business or suffered through some of the toughest years they had ever expe-rienced. Even Boeing began laying off thousands of workers, and also moved its corporate headquarters to Chicago. What was a national recession became something closer to a regional depression for many industries here, as Washing-ton and Oregon became the country's leaders in unemployment (still remain-ing near the top, or bottom, in 2005).

The February 2001 **earthquake** only made things worse, adding to the dreary outlook with a slew of damaged or shuttered businesses, including many in Pioneer Square. In combination with a weak local economy, the decrease in public revenue through reduced taxes, and slash-and-burn ballot measures caused **widespread cutbacks** in funding for the arts, parks, social programs,

C

Political protest in the Pacific Northwest

The Pacific Northwest has a long and rich history of **political protest**. In the early twentieth century, a fervent brand of civil disobedience took root here, centered on class and economic issues. After the **labor movements** of the first half of the twentieth century (see p.292) and the Vietnam **war protests** of the late 1960s and early 1970s (see p.293), the focus turned more toward environmental and consumer issues – not surprising, as the region hosts such corporations as the timber giant Weyerhaeuser and retail monoliths like Nike, Microsoft, Costco, and Starbucks.

The 1975 publication of Ernest Callenbach's highly influential book **Ecotopia** was a key event of this shift in focus. The book imagined an environmentally conscious chunk of the US – from northern California to the Canadian border – seceding from the nation and establishing an earth-friendly oasis. While the premise of the novel was fanciful, its effect was prescient. Along with Edward Abbey's *The Monkey Wrench Gang*, the text became a touchstone for a wave of sometimes radical environmentalism, and later on, **Deep Ecology**. Although unfamiliar to much of America, the "deep ecologists" of the 1980s were quite active regionally, advocating a back-to-nature ethic that involved rejecting the supposed taint of much of modern life. The group **Earth First!** was the most visible of these leftist collectives, engaging in actions from sit-ins at timber company offices to allegedly "spiking" trees with metal rods, thus destroying any chainsaws that might be used to try and cut them down (and perhaps severing a lumberjack's arm in the process).

By the 1990s, former Earth Firsters and other militant progressives formed splinter groups like the **Earth Liberation Front** (ELF), whose alleged vandalism of car dealerships and business offices ignited such anger among Washington, DC, politicians that some branded the group terrorists on a par with al-Qaeda, with the FBI following suit. Although the members of such groups formed only a small, if highly visible, minority among the Pacific Northwest's political activists, many other progressives shared the same anger at the timber industry for damaging the land and at multinational corporations for (as they saw it) reducing the world to a homogenized wasteland of fast-food and chain stores. This anger reached boiling point at the height of the late-1990s bubble economy, during the 1999 **World Trade Organization conference**.

Initially, the demonstrations against the conference were peaceful, with many protesters treating the event like an absurd parade, dressing up in endangered-turtle costumes and the like. All this changed on November 30, when dissenters occupied major intersections, leading to the cancellation of the conference's opening ceremonies. Police responded by showering them with pepper spray, and by nightfall, Mayor Paul Schell had declared a state of emergency, asking the governor to bring in the National Guard. The next day, Schell cordoned off a 50-block zone in Downtown, and some six hundred protesters were arrested – some for their mere presence in the area, and some for smashing windows and looting stores like Starbucks and McDonald's. With the help of tear gas, rubber bullets, concussion grenades, and wooden clubs, police herded demonstrators onto Capitol Hill, where clashes continued well into the night, and intermittently over the next few days.

In the ensuing political fallout, Seattle police chief Norm Stamper retired, and Schell was heavily criticized for his handling of the situation (leading in part to his re-election defeat). The debacle had a more important effect, however: these days, global economic conferences are no longer held in open, democratic cities where people might wave placards, heckle the delegates, or throw rocks and break windows. Instead, the financial fate of the "free world" is – ironically – decided in authoritarian enclaves like Singapore, where a shouted insult will land you in jail, and freedom of choice is strictly limited to supermarkets and shopping malls.

and business development. By 2002 the bloom was officially gone from Seattle's monumental economic growth, and the years since have been marked by inertia as high-tech industries re-trench, Boeing continues to lay off workers or transfer them elsewhere, and the once-abundant money for arts and culture has become much more difficult to find. However, like so much that characterizes the region, Seattle's travails are built on a **paradox**.

Simply put, despite all of its problems, Seattle is still one of the most attractive cities to live in for young, enterprising workers – or, as media reports have dubbed them, the "**creative class**." Even though such migrants have to cope with a housing stock that has nearly doubled in price in five years (even as real wages increase by only half that amount), terrible traffic congestion, a disappearing manufacturing base, and a climate that can best be described in the autumn and winter as dismal, they continue to come in droves – often taking a pay cut in the process, going from a mid-level manager in, say, Cincinnati, to a barista in Seattle. The contradiction is one that has puzzled economists, some of whom chalk it up to the **dynamic aura** that still surrounds the city – a glow that has as much or more to do with independent rock, funky art galleries, and freewheeling culture as it does with Microsoft, Boeing, and Starbucks. Indeed, it's not surprising that the previous addresses of many young arrivals are not, as you'd expect, in Idaho or Montana, but New York and California. And if anything, the only real challenger to Seattle's growth comes from its longtime rival to the south, Portland, which, with its unaffordable increases in housing costs, sky-high unemployment, gloomy weather, and disappearing industries, has become an even bigger draw for young and creative types – many of them refugees from Seattle.

The rise of alternative rock

L ong after the supposed demise of the grunge movement, it's still taken for granted that Seattle is one of the country's best spots for discovering the latest in **underground rock** bands and checking out what trends are bubbling under the surface of American culture. In this it has something in common with San Francisco and Los Angeles, but unlike those cities Seattle was never a leader in mainstream commercial music (psychedelia, arena rock, heavy metal); instead, it has always had a separate, sometimes indefinable, identity. Perhaps the only real comparison to Seattle, as a musical bastion, is Austin, Texas, which in the last three decades has done with country and roots music what Seattle has done with rock: create space for a viable, **alternative music** scene that the rest of the country only later catches up to, and intermittently embraces.

Tangled roots

Unlike a lot of cities with a notable musical pedigree, urban Seattle itself has not always been the epicenter of the **regional sound** it's known for. Rather, while the city boasts the recording studios, publications, promoters, and DJs that provide the essential tools for the movement, the dance halls, clubs, and bands themselves have come from throughout Western Washington, from Aberdeen to Bellingham, with a particular concentration in Olympia – almost as much of a music center as Seattle, especially during the 1990s.

The **roots** of Seattle-area rock 'n' roll, however, can be traced back long before that, to 1957, the year Richard Berry wrote **Louie Louie**, which was to become the Pacific Northwest's anthem – not for the lyrics (thought to be incomprehensible or pornographic, depending on your politics), but simply because so many regional bands would later become famous recording it. The first was the **Wailers**, who in 1960 carried on the work of popularizing the tune (at least locally), which Berry had begun doing years earlier in area bars and clubs. As a rousing, incoherent call-to-arms, *Louie Louie* was hard to beat – then or now – and other Northwest bands that would ride it to fame include **Paul Revere and the Raiders** and the **Kingsmen** – both of them actually from Portland.

Regardless of their background, groups like the Wailers, Raiders, Kingsmen, **Dynamics**, and **Sonics** – the latter as forerunners of the modern punk style – became famous throughout Western Washington for their simple, driving rock melodies and wildly kinetic shows at venues like the Parker Ballroom in North Seattle and, especially, the **Spanish Castle Ballroom** between Seattle and Tacoma. It was at the latter concert hall that these groups gave some of their most inviting performances, drawing young musicians to sit in with them onstage, perhaps playing the rhythm line and picking up a few chords. Among them was a 17-year-old **Jimi Hendrix**, who immortalized those early years with his own *Spanish Castle Magic*.

Free Expression Art

Despite his talent, Hendrix never found his way here as a headliner, and indeed had to seek the comforts of far-off England to become an international sensation. He did, however, hone his craft in Seattle, playing basic rock 'n' roll and watching audiences scream with delight for hard-charging groups like the Wailers. But Seattle was hardly a hotbed of musical invention, and in fact was downright conservative in many ways.

In **the 1960s** the Seattle scene was largely confined to copycat groups mimicking the latest styles of the day – be they surf tunes, Beatlesque melodies, psychedelia, hard rock, proto-metal, or anything else. The area's potential was certainly evidenced, though, with the rise of musical events such as the **Sky River Rock Festival**, beginning in 1968, and the **Seattle Pop Festival**, in 1969. However, as much as those events drew local crowds and showcased notable outsiders like Led Zeppelin, Steve Miller, Chuck Berry, and Ike and Tina Turner, they couldn't disguise the provincialism of the Seattle scene – its hometown groups were still minor by comparison, and the region itself even seemed inimical to rock music. Indeed, it wasn't until a few years later that a major festival could even be held in Seattle proper, instead of many miles outside of the city in sleepy farm country.

Bumbershoot held great promise when it was first put on as the blandly titled **Festival '71**, taking place in the Seattle Center just as the World's Fair had done nine years prior. Tens of thousands of people showed up to experience "**Free Expression Art**" with far-out electronic music, loopy art shows, oddball decor, and an uneven representation of local bands – which included hillbilly country jams. The curious character was no doubt due in part to its patronage by the mayor (thus keeping out any acts that were too outlandish) and the fact that the Seattle scene still hadn't ripened into anything considered a movement, or produced any truly great bands.

Outside influences

The years between the first **Bumbershoot** (which continues to this day in better and louder form) and the late 1980s brought great **influences** to the bands that would later become pioneers of the Western Washington sound – though typically these were touring bands from outside the region. Although it was certainly true that native rock groups like **Heart** could fill arenas and sing cigarette-lighter-raising anthems, they were few and far between and, in any case, had little positive impact on the burgeoning punk-based sound that would come to characterize grunge.

Seattle had some of its first **punk bands** on the scene in 1976, right after punk's emergence in London and New York, though they were little known beyond the region. Rather, it was the usual suspects – Sex Pistols, Ramones, Germs, Cramps, Dead Kennedys, Black Flag, Bad Brains – that had an early, groundshaking effect on Seattle music: if Seattle music found its own way in later years, it was with this kind of punk as a cornerstone, in combination with another, less heralded influence – what was in the 1980s known as **college rock**, later morphing into alternative or indie.

Although college rock (so called for its heavy, often singular, airplay on college-radio stations) was hardly confined to rock alone, and could encompass the country-flavored meanderings of R.E.M. or the oddball funk of Fishbone, it was particularly influential to the local sound with its harder, angrier edges. Potent outsider groups like Sonic Youth, My Bloody Valentine, Dinosaur Jr, Hüsker Dü, the Jesus and Mary Chain, and, most of all, the Pixies, had an immeasurable effect in Emerald City bars and clubs. And with his mix of flowing verses mixed with thrash-guitar choruses and the occasional scream, the Pixies' **Black Francis/Frank Black** emerged as a spiritual godfather on

C

records such as *Surfer Rosa* and *Doolittle*. If anything, those records marked the real birth of the Seattle sound, particularly in the mind of a young Kurt Cobain, who traced back the core elements of his own sound to Black's *Gouge Away* – as beautiful and terrifying as a rock anthem could be.

The Puget sound

The British magazine *Melody Maker* first recognized the area's considerable musical potential with a 1989 showcase article, "Seattle, Rock City." The real commercial impact of this Puget sound, however, came two years later with **Nirvana**'s release *Nevermind*, which solidified the international awareness of what was called **grunge** and changed the face of Western popular music. With the band's anthem, *Smells like Teen Spirit*, and even better songs like *Come as You Are*, *In Bloom*, and *Lithium*, a new, hybridized form of rock music took root – a blend of punk ferocity and classic, melody-based songwriting, in direct contrast to the blues-based hard rock and heavy metal of the time. Public Enemy No.1 in this regard was Led Zeppelin, who, for whatever their merits, had done the most to enforce and entrench the grinding macho "cock rock" sound that more introspective performers like Cobain despised.

Nirvana, of course, did not emerge *sui generis* from the ashes of 1970s punk and 1980s college rock, and was followed in due course to national renown by the likes of Pearl Jam, Alice in Chains, Soundgarden, the Screaming Trees, Green River, and several others, even as earlier bands from the 1980s like Mudhoney gained long-overdue attention. Many of these groups did not even come from Seattle proper, but hailed from other places in **Western Washington** such as Olympia or, in the case of Nirvana, tiny Aberdeen. It was in Seattle, though, that it all came together, with promotion in free music papers like *The Rocket* (1979–2000) and the particular support of the label **Sub Pop**, which was a phenomenon in its own way (see p.78 for its history). Soon after the group's national conquest, Sub Pop sold Nirvana's recording contract to Geffen Records, which, ironically, had first risen to glory in the 1970s on the heels of the Eagles, the very type of stadium rock band Nirvana was in pure revolt against.

The grunge legacy

It's difficult to overstate the **impact** grunge, or alternative or indie, music had on **rock-music history**. Indeed, the concept of an artistically viable, fairly uncompromised musical form suddenly being accepted by the masses was, to put it mildly, a bit strange. It seemed that overnight mass-market channels such as MTV had gone from playing cheesy videos by New Kids on the Block and hair-metal lipstick-rockers like Poison to the hazy gloom of Soundgarden's *Black Hole Sun* and Pearl Jam's *Alive*. The record industry, at least for a few years, seemed to change with the same speed, and a flood of imitation, Seattle-styled bands was soon on the charts. Some strands of grunge would develop into the dry, bummer-oriented sound of **emo**, while others would evolve into less commercial, more experimental variants. In any case, the creative vitality of the scene – which many local musicians had feared was being diluted with national exposure – was already on the decline when Kurt Cobain **committed suicide** on April 4, 1994, in his Madrona home (see p.128 for details). In less than three years Nirvana had gone from

Northwest obscurity to playing international stadiums; Seattle's form of **alternative rock** had become canonical; and the creative side of modern music (as opposed to the pop-oriented or bubblegum variety) was permanently changed. The specific type of rock subgenre called grunge may have met its end in the mid-1990s, and commercial radio may have soon reverted to its bloodless pop form, but independent music would continue to make strides, in Seattle and beyond.

The regional wave

Even though indie bands love to bemoan the latest death of rock, in 2005 the **independent music** scene is still vital and compelling in the Northwest, perhaps benefiting from the demise of grunge in not having to live up to a presumed "sound." Seattle still plays host to many solid local and national bands at tubthumping clubs like *Nuemo's* and *El Corazon* (see p.182 for a list), even though most of the old stalwarts have shut down – except for the *Crocodile Café* and the *Showbox*. In Olympia, too, the scene is plenty inviting if you want to see local bands on the rise, as that small town has produced its own pioneers, among them **Sleater-Kinney** (named after a freeway exit) and **Bikini Kill**. Even suburban Issaquah has engendered what may be independent rock's biggest band of the moment, **Modest Mouse**, which, despite its early avant-garde rock and punk stylings, has become a huge national draw with a somewhat more approachable sound. True to the Northwest form, though, the hummable melody of a song like *Ocean Breathes Salty* soon reveals a darker current, as the singer's friend is lost beneath the waves: "Won't you carry it in? In your head, in your mouth, in your soul…"

Books

U nfortunately, some of the best **books** on Seattle and the Pacific Northwest are either long out of print or confined to the shelves of research libraries. That said, most are available for cheap prices online and there are also many volumes in print concerning the city and Puget Sound that are well worth reading before your visit. Publishers are listed US/UK, unless there is only one, in which case this is indicated. While all the books below are worth a look, we do have our favorites – highly recommended choices are indicated by a 🏃.

History and society

Kurt E. Armbruster *Orphan Road: the Railroad Comes to Seattle 1853–1911* (University of Washington Press, US). History of the long, tortuous process of bringing railways to the region, including the story of how Tacoma was initially chosen as a rail terminus over Seattle. Many good black-and-white photos.

Pierre Berton *The Klondike Fever* (Carroll & Graf, US). Thorough, readable account of the characters and events of the 1890s gold rush, from a Canadian writer's perspective.

Rob Carson *Mount St. Helens: The Eruption and Recovery of a Volcano* (Sasquatch, US). Excellent historical overview (from 1990) covering the devastation wrought by the volcano in May 1980; tracks the subsequent rebirth of the surrounding landscape over the next twenty years – though for the latest seismic news you'll have to check government websites (see p.279).

Gregory Dicum and Nina Luttinger *The Coffee Book: Anatomy of an Industry from Crop to the Last Drop* (New Press, US). Since there are currently no probing volumes on *Starbucks*, this wide-ranging guide – covering the often exploitative system used to turn third-world beans into industrial brews – will suffice, giving the reader a sense of the darker undercurrents of the coffee biz.

Paul Dorpat *Seattle, Now & Then* (Tartu, o/p). Excellent photo book that cogently illustrates the development of Seattle neighborhoods over the last century, with striking images providing dramatic comparisons and contrasts. Easily available online.

🏃 **Timothy Egan** *The Good Rain: Across Time and Terrain in the Pacific Northwest* (Knopf, o/p). One of the key books about the region, an evocative work focusing on the Northwest's beleaguered ecology, social and environmental leaders, and industries that have reshaped the landscape.

Robert L. Friedheim *The Seattle General Strike* (University of Washington Press, US). Hard to find, but still the most complete documentation of the 1919 strike, an epic battle between labor and industry – though perhaps a bit dry and detailed for the casual reader.

🏃 **T.M. Sell** *Wings of Power: Boeing and the Politics of Growth in the Northwest* (University of Washington Press, US). Although there are plenty of glossy, coffee-table books fawning over the company's prowess, this impressive tome broadens the scope by describing Boeing's impact on the politics, culture, and economy of Washington, and how the region's biggest industrial employer can also be its most controversial.

William Speidel *Sons of the Profits*
(Nettle Creek, o/p). Full of rich,
humorous, bite-sized facts and stories
about the corruption that was rife
among Seattle's founders between
1850 and 1900.

David Takami *Divided Destiny: A
History of Japanese Americans in Seattle* (University of Washington Press,
o/p). The story of early Japanese
immigration to the region, followed
by confinement in internment
camps, and later recovery and social
renewal.

Janet Thomas *The Battle in Seattle: the Story Behind and Beyond the
WTO Demonstrations* (Fulcrum, US).
Excellent opinionated analysis of the
motives behind the 1999 protests and
discussions of some of the key participants – of whom the author was one.

James R. Warren *King County and
its Queen City Seattle: an Illustrated
History* (Windsor, o/p). Coffee-table
hardback mixing concise historical text with superb vintage photos
and diverting sidebars on women's
suffrage, black pioneers, and the like.

Biography and oral history

Walt Crowley *Rites of Passage*
(University of Washington Press,
o/p). Vividly detailed and historically
astute memoir of left-wing activism
and counterculture in 1960s Seattle,
written by the editor of an underground newspaper of the time, who
went on to become one of the city's
most renowned journalists.

Sandra Haarsager *Bertha Knight
Landes of Seattle: Big-City Mayor*
(University of Oklahoma Press,
US). Straightforward, rigorously
researched biography of the Seattle
politician who in 1926 rose from the
scene of activist women's clubs to
become the first woman mayor of a
large US city.

Warren Jefferson *The World of Chief
Seattle: How Can One Sell the Air?*
(Book Pub Co, US). Fine historical
portrait of the city's namesake and
his Duquamish-Suquamish tribe,
from the injustice visited on them
by white settlers to their vibrant
modern society and lifestyle. Also
worthwhile is Albert Furtwangler's
Answering Chief Seattle (University
of Washington Press, US), about the
curious history of the chief's famous
farewell speech.

**Stephen Manes and Paul
Andrews** *Gates* (Touchstone, US).

Frustratingly, this insightful and
balanced bio of Bill Gates, Microsoft's co-founder and the richest man
on the planet, is now almost fifteen
years old and hasn't been updated. It's
still the best read on the early years
though; to pick up the story in the
modern era, try *Microsoft Rebooted*
(Doubleday, US) by Robert Slater.

Murray Morgan *Skid Road:
An Informal Portrait of Seattle*
(University of Washington Press,
US). Fascinating stories and anecdotes on the history of the city,
focusing on key figures and inci-
dents from the early days, particularly the colorful characters who
founded Seattle.

**Braiden Rex-Johnson and Paul
Souders** *Inside the Pike Place Market*
(Sasquatch, US). Photo-filled profile
of Pike Place Market at the end
of the twentieth century, with the
stories and sketches of many who
work there.

Ron Strickland *River Pigs and
Cayuses: Oral Histories from the Pacific
Northwest* (Oregon State University
Press, US). Fascinating tales of the
long-lost professions and people that
shaped the region, from cowboys
and lumbermen to pirates and
blacksmiths.

Travel and specialist guides

David D. Alt and Donald W. Hyndman *Roadside Geology of Washington* (Mountain Press, US). A fine volume that points out and analyzes everything from the rock visible at highway roadcuts to the reasons for the area's earthquakes, with good discussion of the unsteady sediments underneath the Puget Sound region.

Tom Douglas et al. *Tom Douglas' Seattle Kitchen* (Morrow, US). As good a guide as you're likely to find – with scrumptious recipes, too – on nouveau Northwest cuisine, penned by the master-chef/guru of the Seattle dining scene, who has some four swanky restaurants in his domain.

Timothy Egan *Wild Seattle: A Celebration of the Natural Areas in and Around the City* (Sierra Club, US). A visual celebration indeed, presenting eye-opening images of the region's splendid, verdant setting and the urban area's swath of greenery. A good companion to many of the Puget Sound sights described in this guide, with a text by one of Washington's best writers.

Cathy McDonald and Stephen R. Whitney *Nature Walks in and around Seattle* (The Mountaineers, o/p). Guides to several dozen walks in parks, forests, and wetlands in Seattle and environs, from favorites like the Discovery Park loop trail to obscurities like West Hylebos Wetlands State Park.

Marge and Ted Mueller *The San Juan Islands Afoot & Afloat* (The Mountaineers, US). Trails, parks, campgrounds, and water activities in the San Juans, by authors who have written similar guides to the North, Middle, and South Puget Sound areas. Last updated in 2004.

Andy Perdue *The Northwest Wine Guide: A Buyer's Handbook* (Sasquatch, US). One of the more current overviews of the major vintners in the region, with the history, price range, and character of each of the given wineries. Useful if you want to know what's good to guzzle when you arrive here.

Roger Sale *Seeing Seattle* (University of Washington Press, o/p). More than two hundred pages of suggested walking tours of the city and its varied neighborhoods by one of Seattle's leading historians, with some off-the-beaten-path routes and opinionated background.

Robert Spector *Space Needle: Symbol of Seattle* (Documentary Media, US). Short, straightforward account of the creation of the city's icon, with accompanying photographs.

Music

James Bush *Encyclopedia of Northwest Music* (Sasquatch, o/p). Broad reference that has short bios and discographies of numerous Northwest musicians of all styles, as well as essays on major regional musical movements.

Kurt Cobain *Journals* (Riverhead Press, US). Controversial reproduction of the Nirvana frontman's diaries, complete with random thoughts, creative ideas, and various doodles, plus brickbats for more aged rockers like Pete Townsend and other musical targets.

Charles R Cross *Room Full of Mirrors: A Biography of Jimi Hendrix* (Hyperion, US). Though it's courted controversy for saying that Hendrix skirted military service by claiming to be gay, this lengthy bio may well end up being the defining tome on Seattle's legendary guitarist. Especially good info about Jimi's myriad struggles in Seattle during his early years.

Paul de Barros *Jackson Street After Hours: the Roots of Jazz in Seattle* (Sasquatch, o/p) Initially a government-funded oral history project, this long-overdue volume nicely covers the Seattle jazz scene from the 1930s through the 1950s, with great photos and illustrations.

🏃 **Clark Humphrey** *Loser* (Feral House, US). The definitive account to date of Seattle rock, starting from its pre-rock origins in jazz/R&B, but focusing mainly on the punk and post-punk periods of the last thirty years.

Dave Marsh *Louie Louie* (Hyperion, o/p). Unusual biography of a song, tracing, in often hilarious detail, the way the garage-rock anthem *Louie Louie* went from an obscure R&B tune to the signature song of many Pacific Northwest bands.

Kim Neely *Five Against One: the Pearl Jam Story* (Penguin, US). Four-hundred-page bio of Seattle's second-most-famous rock band, sometimes painting singer Eddie Vedder in a less-than-flattering light. Detailed and engagingly written.

Charles Peterson *Screaming Life: a Chronicle of the Seattle Music Scene* (Harper Collins, o/p). Eye-opening photographs of alternative's glory years, with images of most of the key participants and the stories associated with them. Peterson's more recent volume, *Touch Me I'm Sick* (Power-House, US) adds even more imagery of grunge power from the movement's peak.

Art and architecture

🏃 **Steven C Brown et al.** *Native Visions: Evolution in Northwest Coast Art from the 18th to the 20th Century* (University of Washington Press, US). Terrific images and learned commentary on the vivid, striking works of local tribal artists, some of which are visible in metro-area museums, parks, and galleries.

Jeffrey Carl Ochsner *Shaping Seattle Architecture* (University of Washington Press, o/p). Comprehensive study of Seattle architecture from the 1850s to the present, covering not just famous landmarks, but also typical business and residential developments; a must for serious architecture enthusiasts.

Jeffrey Carl Ochsner and Dennis Alan Andersen *Distant Corner: Seattle Architects and the Legacy of H.H. Richardson* (University of Washington Press, US). A penetrating look at the architecture of Pioneer Square, and how a brief historical opportunity

– rebuilding after a massive fire and the rise of a Romanesque Revivalist – could reshape an entire district in one architect's image.

Tina Oldknow *Pilchuck: a Glass School* (University of Washington Press, o/p). Illustrated history of the founding and evolution of the alternative art center that's become an international phenomenon, having the most profound effect on art in Washington State over the last quarter-century.

Lara Swimmer *Process: Seattle Central Library* (Documentary Media, US). A fine photographic overview and history of what may be Seattle's most important building, Rem Koolhaas's strange and beautiful geometry of glass and steel, which also happens to be stuffed with books.

Ellen Harkins Wheat *Jacob Lawrence: American Painter* (University of Washington Press, US). Originally a catalog for a major exhibition at the Seattle Art Museum, illustrating the pioneering work of Lawrence, who was based in Seattle starting in the early 1970s.

Sally B. Woodbridge and Roger Montgomery *A Guide to Architecture in Washington State* (University of Washington Press, o/p). Although published in 1980, still the most useful and handy guide to the metropolitan region's architecture, which covers half the book and is presented in a manner that's more insightful and less gushing than more contemporary guides.

Fiction and literature

Sherman Alexie *Indian Killer* (Warner, US). Acclaimed story of a Seattle serial murderer and the community's reaction to the crimes, as a framework for reflections on interracial relations. The author's more recent *Ten Little Indians* (Grove, US) is a compelling set of short stories realistically depicting modern native life.

Lynda Barry *Cruddy* (Simon and Schuster, US). Affecting, sometimes shocking, memoir of a teenage girl in early 1970s Seattle, told with much dark humor and vivid descriptions, enhanced further by the author's own lurid, striking illustrations.

Matt Briggs *The Remains of River Names* (Black Heron Press, US). Modernist presentation of a dozen stories set in Seattle and throughout Washington State in the 1960s and 1970s, focusing on the members of a single family and told from the first-person perspective of each.

Charles Burns *Black Hole* (Pantheon, US). If there's such a thing as an essential Northwest graphic novel, this is it: a dark, mesmerizing view of Seattle in the 1970s, as suburban teens are terrorized and transformed (in unexpected ways) by a particularly surreal disease. A striking mix of evocative black-and-white imagery and clever social commentary.

Michael Byers *The Coast of Good Intentions* (Mariner, US). Slow, evocative portraits of the overcast atmosphere and fractured characters populating the Emerald City. Spellbinding writing, a bit on the depressing side.

Ernest Callenbach *Ecotopia* (Heyday, US). Highly influential fantasy of the Pacific Northwest breaking away from the US and establishing a progressive, ecologically friendly utopia. While not too realistic, the book has served as loose inspiration to countless nature-lovers and environmental activists.

Raymond Carver *What We Talk About When We Talk About Love* (Harvill/Vintage); *Cathedral* (Panther/Vintage); *Fires* (Vintage, US); *Elephant* (Vintage, UK); *Where I'm Calling From* (Harvill/Vintage). Northwest-born and -raised writer whose regionally set short stories are superbly written, terse, and melancholic tales of everyday life and disintegrating family relationships. Best-known poetry volume is *A New Path to the Waterfall* (Atlantic Monthly Press, US).

Douglas Coupland *Microserfs* (Regan/Flamingo). Curious novel/journal, by the coiner of the term "Generation X". Focuses on six Microsoft workers who all live together and are trying to make it in the shadow of Bill.

G. M. Ford *Black River* (Avon/Eos). Gripping thriller about Seattle-based reporter and crime novelist Frank

Corso, who becomes immersed in tracking down an evasive and thoroughly dangerous mobster in the Emerald City.

David Guterson *Snow Falling on Cedars* (Vintage/Bloomsbury). Well-regarded, but sometimes long-winded and repetitive, tale of life and death on a rural Puget Sound island. Made into an uneven movie.

J. A. Jance *Breach of Duty* (Avon/ Eos). In one of many mysteries from this local author, homicide detective Jonas Piedmont Beaumont investigates the murder of a woman burned to death in her bed, in a first-person narrative that features plenty of Seattle references only longtime residents will recognize.

Richard Powers *Plowing the Dark* (Picador, US). Ambitious novel with nods to suspense and science-fiction genres, tying together the destinies of an American hostage in Beirut and the employee of a Seattle-based virtual-reality developer.

Lee Williams *After Nirvana* (Perennial, o/p). Dark portrait of the lives of four homeless street kids living in the Seattle demimonde, where drugs and prostitution are commonplace and a morbid humor often creeps into the grimmest predicaments.

Tobias Wolff *This Boy's Life* (Grove, US). Set in 1950s Washington State, a mournful, forceful memoir relates a painful, brutal upbringing. A sharp, self-deprecating humor infuses the book as it does Wolff's *In Pharaoh's Army* (Picador/ Vintage), culled from his Vietnam War experiences.

Seattle on film

The first major **movie** shot on location in Seattle was *Tugboat Annie* in 1933, and it was thirty years before the next, the Elvis Presley vehicle *It Happened at the World's Fair*. With Seattle's increased cachet and profile, shoots are more commonplace today, although the **Puget Sound** area is probably better-known for hosting television series: *Twin Peaks* was set in Snoqualmie Falls, twenty five minutes away; *Northern Exposure* was shot in Roslyn, seventy miles east; and the hit sitcom *Frasier* was set, though not shot, in Seattle. The now-outdated book *Seattle on Film* by Randy Hodgins and Steve McLellan (True Northwest, o/p) is the best guide to the city's Hollywood history before the mid-1990s. Films below are listed with their director and the year of their release.

The urban area

Cinderella Liberty (Mark Rydell 1973). James Caan is a sailor on leave, and Marsha Mason his love interest, in a film with many location shots of a pre-gentrified, down-at-heel Belltown. More interesting as a period piece than great cinema.

Dogfight (Nancy Savoca 1991). Shot on location in Seattle, which is somehow passed off as 1963 San Francisco in this offbeat film about an unlikely romance between a folk-singer and a serviceman about to go to Vietnam.

The Fabulous Baker Boys (Steve Kloves 1989). Mainstream hit starring Jeff and Beau Bridges as a fading lounge jazz act, and Michelle Pfeiffer as the new singer who drives a wedge between them.

House of Games (David Mamet 1987). Mamet's first, perhaps best, foray into film directing. A modern film noir about a psychologist who gets drawn into a ring of con men, making effective use of dark, gritty Seattle locations.

It Happened at the World's Fair (Norman Taurog 1963). Typically dispensable Elvis Presley film – flimsy plot, mediocre music, and a spectacular location, in this case Seattle's World's Fair. Features young tyke

Kurt Russell in a bit role attacking Elvis.

Last Days (Gus Van Sant 2005). Revolving around the middling, suicidal end of Seattle rock-star "Blake," this thinly veiled portrait of Kurt Cobain's demise is strikingly well-acted, visually evocative, and amazingly tedious.

Little Buddha (Bernardo Bertolucci 1994). Uneven flick (with Keanu Reeves as Siddhartha) about a Seattle boy thought by local Tibetan monks to be the reincarnation of a lama. Less than half is set in Seattle, but Bertolucci wanted the city as a backdrop for its architecture and overcast light.

Money Buys Happiness (Gregg Lachow 1999). A whimsical, slightly surrealistic study of an especially troubled day in the life of a married couple; shot in Seattle neighborhoods, it includes a memorable scene in the U District's *Allegro Espresso Bar* (see p.156).

The Parallax View (Alan Pakula 1974). Political-paranoia thriller starring Warren Beatty as an investigative reporter determined to find the real killers of a high-ranking politician. Most of it doesn't take place in Seattle, but the opening sequence, an assassination at the top of the Space Needle, is dazzling.

Singles (Cameron Crowe 1992). Romantic, early-1990s look at young Seattleites in a Capitol Hill apartment building, with cameos by members of Pearl Jam and Soundgarden. Crowe set his 1989 debut, *Say Anything* (a mismatched high-school romance with John Cusack), in Seattle as well, establishing his template for mildly sentimental tales of young urban life.

Sleepless in Seattle (Nora Ephron 1993). Sappy smash in which a widowed Tom Hanks falls for reporter Meg Ryan, with help from his son and talk radio. Great location scenes, including a long comic exchange with Rob Reiner in Pike Place Market's *Athenian Inn*.

The Slender Thread (Sydney Pollack 1965). Little-seen drama inspired by the real-life activities of the Seattle Crisis Clinic. Sidney Poitier stars as a University of Washington psychology student dealing with an attempted suicide by Anne Bancroft.

Trouble in Mind (Alan Rudolph 1985). Odd, self-consciously arty film of murky crime schemes and romantic tangles that makes good use of the grayest aspects of Seattle (called *Rain City* here).

Twice in a Lifetime (Bud Yorkin 1985). Gene Hackman plays the lead role in this low-key film about the breakup of a marriage in a working-class family. Shot mostly in Ballard.

Wargames (John Badham 1983). Now-dated, mildly amusing nuclear-war fantasy set in Seattle, with Matthew Broderick as the teenage whiz-kid who almost starts an atomic holocaust.

Western Washington

Five Easy Pieces (Bob Rafelson 1970). Classic "dismal Northwest" piece that takes middle-class piano-prodigy drop-out Jack Nicholson from the sun-baked oilfields of Texas north to visit his family in Washington's San Juan Islands – the change of scenery and climate perfectly conveying his cruel malaise.

McCabe & Mrs Miller (Robert Altman 1971). Perhaps the greatest film ever made about the pioneer history of the Northwest, starring Warren Beatty and Julie Christie. Set in the Washington frontier town of "Presbyterian Church" at the beginning of the twentieth century, where an unexpected three-day blizzard provided Altman with an unforgettable cinematic climax.

An Officer and a Gentleman (Taylor Hackford 1982). Debra Winger and Richard Gere military melodrama filmed at Fort Lawton in Port Townsend, though Louis Gossett Jr has the best role as a tough-as-nails drill sergeant.

The Ring (Gore Verbinski 2002). Formulaic remake of a popular Japanese horror film, in this case concerning a reporter who visits Western Washington to investigate a mysterious videotape that causes death to those who watch it. It's already had one sequel and more are on the way.

Snow Falling on Cedars (Scott Hicks 1999). Based on the novel (see p.306) about a 1954 murder on a fictional Puget Sound island and the ensuing trial, which digs up wounds dating back to the internment of the community's Japanese-Americans during World War II. Only a few beach scenes were actually shot in Puget Sound.

This Boy's Life (Michael Caton-Jones 1993). Based on Tobias Wolff's book (see p.306) and set in the small North Cascades town of Concrete, Washington. Stars Leonardo DiCaprio as the victim of abusive patriarch Robert De Niro.

Twin Peaks: Fire Walk with Me (David Lynch 1992). A full-length "prequel" to the television series *Twin Peaks*. A big flop when released and something of an artistic disappointment as well, considering the director's background.

Documentaries

The Chihuly Collection (various 2003). A set of interesting, compelling documentaries about Tacoma's favorite son, the region's most renowned glassblower, making his various artworks in Seattle and installing them in places like London, Chicago, and Jerusalem.

Hype (Doug Pray 1996). Witty documentary about the explosion of the Seattle alternative rock scene in the late 1980s and early 1990s, with interviews with most of the major musicians and scenesters, as well as live footage of all the knowns and unknowns.

Kurt and Courtney (Nick Broomfield 1998). Controversial, sometimes hilarious, guerilla documentary on real and imagined mysteries surrounding the death of Kurt Cobain. Worthwhile not so much for investigative reporting (there are virtually no substantiated revelations) as for the interviews and confrontations with hangers-on from the grunge scene.

Streetwise (Martin Bell 1985). Gritty documentary examining (some might say exploiting) the plight of Seattle's homeless street kids. Not without its moments of tenderness and wit, though.

Triumph of the Nerds (Robert X. Cringely 1996). Informative three-hour TV documentary about the rise of Bill Gates, Steve Jobs, and the other techno-nerds who created modern computing. Followed two years later by a sequel, *Nerds 2.0.1: a Brief History of the Internet*.

C

Travel store

Visit us online

www.roughguides.com

Information on over 25,000 destinations around the world

- **Read** Rough Guides' trusted travel info

- **Share** journals, photos and travel advice with other readers

- Get exclusive Rough Guide **discounts** and travel deals

- Earn membership points every time you contribute to the

  Rough Guide community and get free books, flights and trips

- Browse thousands of **CD reviews** and artists in our music area

ONLINE

TRAVEL

Africa & Middle East

Cape Town & the Garden Route
Egypt
The Gambia
Jordan
Kenya
Marrakesh DIRECTIONS
Morocco
South Africa, Lesotho & Swaziland
Syria
Tanzania
Tunisia
West Africa
Zanzibar

Travel Theme guides

First-Time Around the World
First-Time Asia
First-Time Europe
First-Time Latin America
Travel Online
Travel Health
Travel Survival
Walks in London & SE England
Women Travel

Maps

Algarve
Amsterdam
Andalucia & Costa del Sol
Argentina
Athens
Australia
Baja California
Barcelona
Berlin
Boston
Brittany
Brussels
California
Chicago
Corsica
Costa Rica & Panama

Crete
Croatia
Cuba
Cyprus
Czech Republic
Dominican Republic
Dubai & UAE
Dublin
Egypt
Florence & Siena
Florida
France
Frankfurt
Germany
Greece
Guatemala & Belize
Hong Kong
Iceland
Ireland
Kenya
Lisbon
London
Los Angeles
Madrid
Mallorca
Marrakesh
Mexico
Miami & Key West
Morocco
New England
New York City
New Zealand
Northern Spain
Paris
Peru
Portugal
Prague
Rome
San Francisco
Sicily
South Africa
South India
Spain & Portugal
Sri Lanka
Tenerife
Thailand
Toronto
Trinidad & Tobago
Tuscany
Venice
Washington DC
Yucatán Peninsula

Dictionary Phrasebooks

Croatian
Czech
Dutch
Egyptian Arabic
French
German
Greek
Hindi & Urdu
Italian
Japanese
Latin American Spanish
Mandarin Chinese
Mexican Spanish
Polish
Portuguese
Russian
Spanish
Swahili
Thai
Turkish
Vietnamese

Computers

Blogging
iPods, iTunes & Music Online
The Internet
Macs & OS X
Music Playlists
PCs and Windows
Website Directory

Film & TV

Comedy Movies
Cult Movies
Cult TV
Gangster Movies
Horror Movies
James Bond
Kids' Movies
Sci–Fi Movies

Lifestyle

Ethical Shopping
Babies
Pregnancy & Birth

Music Guides

The Beatles
Bob Dylan
Cult Pop
Classical Music
Elvis
Frank Sinatra
Heavy Metal
Hip-Hop
Jazz
Opera
Reggae
Rock
World Music (2 vols)

Popular Culture

Books for Teenagers
Children's Books, 0-5
Children's Books, 5-11
Conspiracy Theories
Cult Fiction
The Da Vinci Code
Lord of the Rings
Shakespeare
Superheroes
Unexplained Phenomena

Sport

Arsenal 11s
Celtic 11s
Chelsea 11s
Liverpool 11s
Man United 11s
Newcastle 11s
Rangers 11s
Tottenham 11s
Cult Football
Muhammad Ali
Poker

Science

The Universe
Weather

& MORE

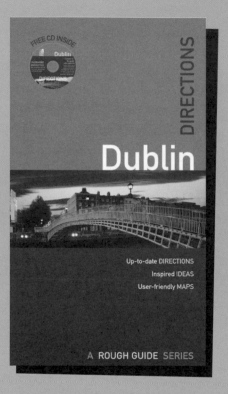

stay in touch!

Rough Guides' FREE full-colour newsletter

News, travel issues, music reviews, readers' letters and the latest dispatches from authors on the road

If you would like to receive roughnews, please send us your name and address:

Rough Guides, 80 Strand
London, WC2R 0RL, UK

Rough Guides, 4th Floor, 345 Hudson St
New York NY10014, USA

newslettersubs@roughguides.co.uk

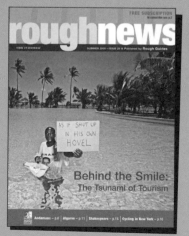

ROUGHNEWS

NOTES

NOTES

Small print and
Index

A Rough Guide to Rough Guides

Published in 1982, the first Rough Guide – to Greece – was a student scheme that became a publishing phenomenon. Mark Ellingham, a recent graduate of English from Bristol University, had been traveling in Greece the previous summer and couldn't find the right guidebook. With a small group of friends he wrote his own guide, combining a highly contemporary, journalistic style with a thoroughly practical approach to travelers' needs.

The immediate success of the book spawned a series that rapidly covered dozens of destinations. And, in addition to impecunious backpackers, Rough Guides soon acquired a much broader and older readership that relished the guides' wit and inquisitiveness as much as their enthusiastic, critical approach and value-for-money ethos.

These days, Rough Guides include recommendations from shoestring to luxury and cover more than 200 destinations around the globe, including almost every country in the Americas and Europe, more than half of Africa and most of Asia and Australasia. Our ever-growing team of authors and photographers is spread all over the world, particularly in Europe, the USA, and Australia.

In the early 1990s, Rough Guides branched out of travel, with the publication of Rough Guides to World Music, Classical Music, and the Internet. All three have become benchmark titles in their fields, spearheading the publication of a wide range of books under the Rough Guide name.

Including the travel series, Rough Guides now number more than 350 titles, covering: phrasebooks, waterproof maps, music guides from Opera to Heavy Metal, reference works as diverse as Conspiracy Theories and Shakespeare, and popular culture books from iPods to Poker. Rough Guides also produce a series of more than 120 World Music CDs in partnership with World Music Network.

Visit www.roughguides.com to see our latest publications.

Many Rough Guide travel images are available for commercial licensing at www.roughguidespictures.com

SMALL PRINT

ROUGH
GUIDES

Rough Guide credits

Text editor: Steven Horak, Amy Hegarty
Layout: Ankur Guha
Cartography: Manish Chandra, Jasbir Sandhu
Picture editor: Jj Luck
Production: Aimee Hampson
Proofreader: Anna Leggett
Cover design: Chloë Roberts
Photographer: JD Dickey
Editorial: London Kate Berens, Claire Saunders, Geoff Howard, Ruth Blackmore, Polly Thomas, Richard Lim, Clifton Wilkinson, Alison Murchie, Karoline Densley, Andy Turner, Keith Drew, Edward Aves, Nikki Birrell, Helen Marsden, Alice Park, Sarah Eno, David Paul, Lucy White, Joe Staines, Duncan Clark, Peter Buckley, Matthew Milton, Tracy Hopkins, Ruth Tidball; **New York** Andrew Rosenberg, Richard Koss, AnneLise Sorensen, Hunter Slaton, April Isaacs, Sean Mahoney
Design & Pictures: London Simon Bracken, Dan May, Diana Jarvis, Mark Thomas, Harriet Mills; **Delhi** Madhulita Mohapatra, Umesh Aggarwal, Ajay Verma, Jessica Subramanian, Amit Verma, Pradeep Thapliyal

Production. Sophie Hewat, Katherine Owers
Cartography: London Maxine Repath, Ed Wright, Katie Lloyd-Jones; **Delhi** Rajesh Chhibber, Jai Prakash Mishra, Ashutosh Bharti, Rajesh Mishra, Animesh Pathak, Karobi Gogoi, Amod Singh
Online: New York Jennifer Gold, Suzanne Welles, Kristin Mingrone; **Delhi** Manik Chauhan, Narender Kumar, Shekhar Jha, Lalit K. Sharma, Rakesh Kumar, Chhandita Chakravarty
Marketing & Publicity: London Richard Trillo, Niki Hanmer, David Wearn, Demelza Dallow, Louise Maher; **New York** Geoff Colquitt, Megan Kennedy, Katy Ball; **Delhi** Reem Khokhar
Custom publishing and foreign rights: Philippa Hopkins
Manager India: Punita Singh
Series editor: Mark Ellingham
Reference Director: Andrew Lockett
PA to Managing and Publishing Directors: Megan McIntyre
Publishing Director: Martin Dunford
Managing Director: Kevin Fitzgerald

Publishing information

This fourth edition published June 2006 by
Rough Guides Ltd,
80 Strand, London WC2R 0RL
345 Hudson St, 4th Floor,
New York, NY 10014, USA
14 Local Shopping Centre, Panchsheel Park,
New Delhi 110017, India
Distributed by the Penguin Group
Penguin Books Ltd,
80 Strand, London WC2R 0RL
Penguin Putnam, Inc.
375 Hudson Street, NY 10014, USA
Penguin Group (Australia)
250 Camberwell Road, Camberwell,
Victoria 3124, Australia
Penguin Books Canada Ltd,
10 Alcorn Avenue, Toronto, Ontario,
Canada M4V 1E4
Penguin Group (New Zealand)
Cnr Rosedale and Airborne Roads
Albany, Auckland, New Zealand
Cover design by Peter Dyer.

Typeset in Bembo and Helvetica to an original design by Henry Iles.

Printed and bound in China

© Richie Unterberger and JD Dickey 2006

No part of this book may be reproduced in any form without permission from the publisher except for the quotation of brief passages in reviews.

336pp includes index

A catalogue record for this book is available from the British Library

ISBN 978-1-84353-658-1

The publishers and authors have done their best to ensure the accuracy and currency of all the information in **The Rough Guide to Seattle**, however, they can accept no responsibility for any loss, injury, or inconvenience sustained by any traveler as a result of information or advice contained in the guide.

3   5   7   9   8   6   4   2

Help us update

We've gone to a lot of effort to ensure that the fourth edition of **The Rough Guide to Seattle** is accurate and up to date. However, things change – places get "discovered", opening hours are notoriously fickle, restaurants and rooms raise prices or lower standards. If you feel we've got it wrong or left something out, we'd like to know, and if you can remember the address, the price, the time, the phone number, so much the better.

We'll credit all contributions, and send a copy of the next edition (or any other Rough Guide if you prefer) for the best letters. Everyone who writes to us and isn't already a subscriber will receive a copy of our full-color thrice-yearly newsletter. Please mark letters: **"Rough Guide Seattle Update"** and send to: Rough Guides, 80 Strand, London WC2R 0RL, or Rough Guides, 4th Floor, 345 Hudson St, New York, NY 10014. Or send an email to **mail@roughguides.com**

Have your questions answered and tell others about your trip at **www.roughguides.atinfopop.com**

Acknowledgments

JD would like to thank his friends and family, in particular his wife Brenna and her sister Beth, and his editors Steven Horak and Amy Hegarty, who contributed much insight, skill, and elbow grease to this volume, and Richard Koss for first getting this edition off the ground with flair and gusto. To Rough Guides photography and layout JD also gives considerable thanks, especially Jj Luck and Simon Bracken, and in cartography Jasbir Sandhu and Katie Lloyd-Jones. JD's Seattle contacts were invaluable, too, especially Arthur Schafer, whose consideration, assistance and pluck were most useful and appreciated.

The editors would like to thank JD Dickey for his always excellent work, as well as Ankur Guha, Manish Chandra, Jasbir Sandhu, Katie Lloyd-Jones, Jj Luck, Diana Jarvis, Aimee Hampson, Anna Leggett, Chloë Roberts, Nikki Birrell, and David Paul.

Readers' letters

Thanks to all the readers who have taken the time to write in with comments and suggestions (and apologies if we've inadvertently omitted or misspelt anyone's name):

Jane Bonner-Morgan, Fabrizio Introvigne, Helen James, Gerry Khermouch, Corinna Laughlin, Silvia Lovato, Lars Osmerg, Heather Wingfield

SMALL PRINT

ROUGH GUIDES

Photo credits

All photos © Rough Guides except the following:

Full page
Washington Park Arboretum © 1999 Evan
    Greger/EcoStock

Introduction
Industrial rockers Filter on stage © Karen Mason
    Blair/Corbis
Coast of Whidbey Island towards the San Juan
    Islands © Thomas Shjarback/Alamy
Puget Sound, Washington © Chuck Pefley/Alamy
Post Alley, Pike Place Market © Chuck Pefley/
    Alamy

Things not to miss
11 Bicyclists ride the Burke-Gilman Trail ©
    Wolfgang Kaehler/Corbis
13 Best Buy Bumbrella stage, Bumbershoot ©
    Bruce Dugdale
21 Visitors at the Experience Music Project ©
    Reuters/Corbis
22 Ferry cruising on Puget Sound © Jeffrey
    Aaronson/Network Aspen

Black and whites
p.141 Boeing 747 jumbo jet airliner production in
    Everett © Mark Wagner aviation images/Alamy

p.197 Gay Pride Parade in Capitol Hill © Michael
    Marquand Alamy
p.203 Bite of Seattle festival © Shelly Oberman
p.215 Display at the Museum of Doll Art, Bellevue
    © Chuck Pefley/Alamy
p.271 Ferry at San Juan Island © Terry Donnelly/
    Alamy

Color insert: Coffee culture
Neon coffee sign at Pike Place Market © Wesley
    Hitt/Alamy
Coffee beans © Natalie Fobes/Corbis
Café au lait © Dave Bartruff/Corbis

Color insert: Green (and blue) Seattle
Seattle © Laura Ciapponi/Getty
Mountain biking © Chase Jarvis/Corbis
Hiking © Bohemian Nomad Picturemakers/Corbis
Mount Rainier and Lake Washington © Chuck
    Pefley/Alamy
Gasworks Park © Morton Beebe/Corbis
Sea kayaker © Paul A. Souders/Corbis
Deception Pass bridge connecting Whidbey
    and Fidalgo islands in Puget Sound © Kevin
    Schafer/Corbis

Index

Map entries are in color.

Map symbols

maps are listed in the full index using colored text

▬▬▬	Freeway	ⓘ	Information office
═══	Main road	✉	Post office
═══	Minor road	⊙	Statue
⊞⊞⊞	Steps	★	Bus stop
━•━	Railroad	♥	Museum
───	Monorail	▲	Mountain
───	Streetcar	℣	Waterfall
▬ ▬ ▬	International boundary	◉	Accommodation
─ ─	Ferry route	▬	Building
───	River	⊞	Church
∽∽∽	Cliffs	▭	Stadium
♦	Place of interest	▦	Park
✈	International airport	⊞	Cemetery

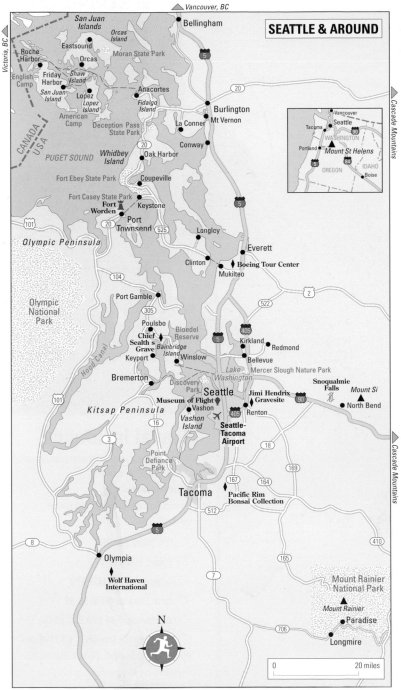

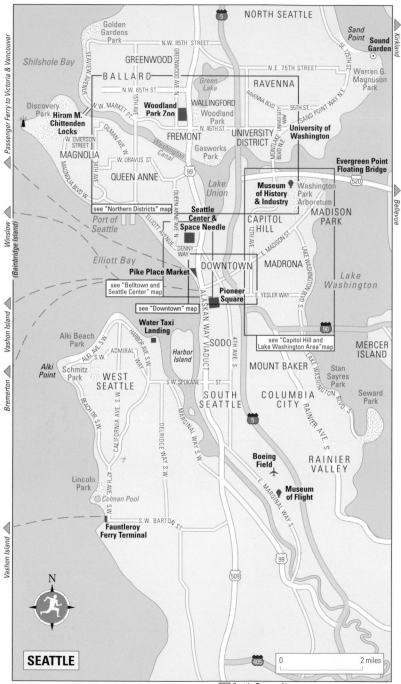

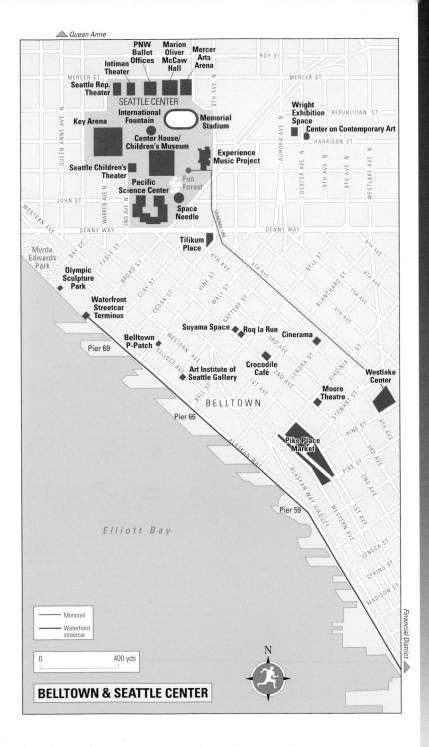

Queen Anne

PNW
Ballet
Offices

Marion
Oliver
McCaw
Hall

Mercer
Arts
Arena

Intiman
Theater

ROY ST

MERCER ST

MERCER ST

Seattle Rep.
Theater

SEATTLE CENTER

5TH AVE

Wright
Exhibition
Space

REPUBLICAN ST.

AURORA AVE N

Center on Contemporary Art

Key Arena

International
Fountain

Memorial
Stadium

QUEEN ANNE AVE N

HARRISON ST.

Center House/
Children's Museum

Experience
Music Project

DEXTER AVE N

8TH AVE N

9TH AVE N

WESTLAKE AVE N

Seattle Children's
Theater

Pacific
Science Center

JOHN ST

Fun
Forest

WARREN AVE N

2ND AVE N

WESTERN AVE

Space
Needle

MONORAIL LINE

DENNY WAY

DENNY WAY

Tilikum
Place

4TH AVE

5TH AVE

BELL ST

9TH AVE

Myrtle
Edwards
Park

BAY ST

EAGLE ST

BROAD ST

CLAY ST

CEDAR ST

VINE ST

WALL ST

BATTERY ST

8TH AVE

7TH AVE

6TH AVE

BLANCHARD ST

Olympic
Sculpture
Park

Waterfront
Streetcar
Terminus

Belltown
P-Patch

Pier 69

WESTERN AVE

ELLIOTT AVE

Suyama Space

Roq la Rue

3RD AVE

Cinerama

Art Institute of
Seattle Gallery

Crocodile
Café

1ST AVE

2ND AVE

LENORA ST

VIRGINIA ST

Westlake
Center

BELL ST

BELLTOWN

Moore
Theatre

STEWART ST

4TH AVE

Pier 66

PINE ST

3RD AVE

Pike Place
Market

ALASKAN WAY

2ND AVE

PIKE ST

1ST AVE

Pier 59

ALASKAN WAY VIADUCT

WESTERN AVE

SENECA ST

Elliott Bay

SPRING ST

MADISON ST

Financial District

Monorail

Waterfront
streetcar

0   400 yds

N

BELLTOWN & SEATTLE CENTER

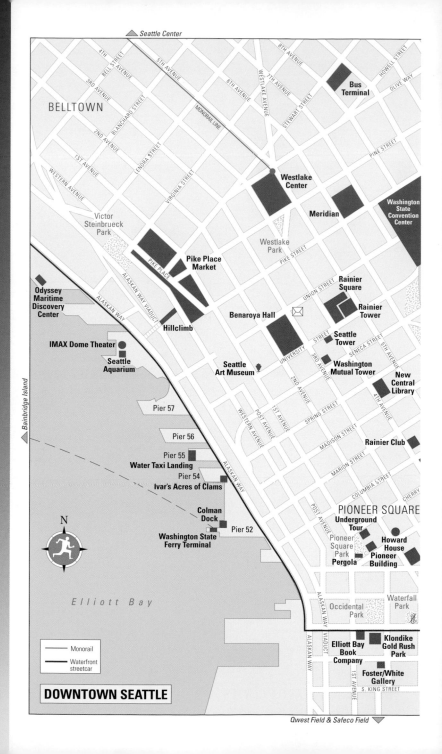

Seattle Center

8TH AVENUE
HOWELL STREET
OLIVE WAY
Bus Terminal

4TH STREET
BELL AVENUE
3RD AVENUE
5TH AVENUE
6TH AVENUE
7TH AVENUE
WESTLAKE AVENUE
STEWART STREET

BELLTOWN

2ND AVENUE
BLANCHARD STREET
LENORA STREET
MONORAIL LINE
PINE STREET

1ST AVENUE
VIRGINIA STREET

WESTERN AVENUE

Victor Steinbrueck Park

Westlake Center

Meridian

Washington State Convention Center

Westlake Park
PIKE STREET

Pike Place Market

ALASKAN WAY VIADUCT
PIKE PLACE
ALASKAN WAY

Union Street

Rainier Square

Benaroya Hall

Rainier Tower

Odyssey Maritime Discovery Center

Hillclimb

UNIVERSITY STREET
SENECA STREET
3RD AVENUE
5TH AVENUE

IMAX Dome Theater

Seattle Aquarium

Seattle Tower

Washington Mutual Tower

Seattle Art Museum

New Central Library

Bainbridge Island

Pier 57

2ND AVENUE
POST AVENUE
1ST AVENUE
SPRING STREET
4TH AVENUE

Pier 56

WESTERN AVENUE

MADISON STREET

Rainier Club

Pier 55
Water Taxi Landing

Pier 54
Ivar's Acres of Clams

ALASKAN WAY

MARION STREET

COLUMBIA STREET
CHERRY

Colman Dock

Pier 52

Washington State Ferry Terminal

PIONEER SQUARE

Underground Tour

Pioneer Square Park

POST AVENUE

Howard House

Pergola
Pioneer Building

N

Elliott Bay

ALASKAN WAY
Occidental Park

Waterfall Park

Monorail

Waterfront streetcar

ALASKAN WAY VIADUCT
1ST AVENUE

Elliott Bay Book Company

Klondike Gold Rush Park

DOWNTOWN SEATTLE

Foster/White Gallery

S. KING STREET

Qwest Field & Safeco Field

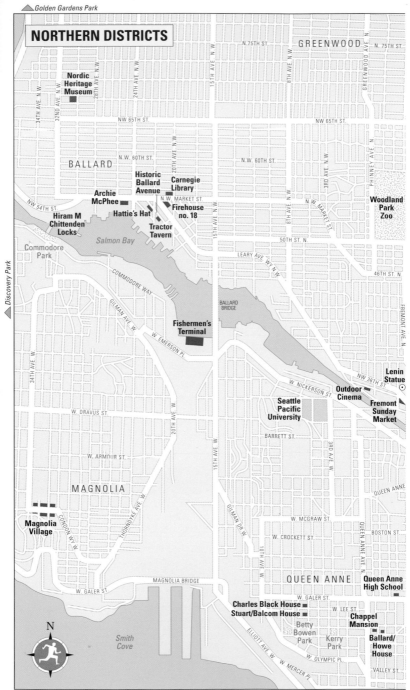

▲ Golden Gardens Park

NORTHERN DISTRICTS

GREENWOOD

N.75TH ST.
N. 75TH ST.

NW 65TH ST.
NW 65TH ST.

N.W. 60TH ST.
N.W. 60TH ST.

BALLARD

Nordic Heritage Museum

Historic Ballard Avenue

Carnegie Library

Archie McPhee

N.W. MARKET ST.

Firehouse no. 18

Hattie's Hat

Tractor Tavern

Hiram M Chittenden Locks

Salmon Bay

Commodore Park

Discovery Park

COMMODORE WAY

BALLARD BRIDGE

Fishermen's Terminal

W. EMERSON PL.

50TH ST. N

LEARY AVE WY N W

46TH ST. N

Woodland Park Zoo

Lenin Statue

W. NICKERSON ST.

Outdoor Cinema

Seattle Pacific University

Fremont Sunday Market

BARRETT ST.

W. DRAVUS ST.

W. ARMOUR ST.

MAGNOLIA

Magnolia Village

W. McGRAW ST.

QUEEN ANNE

W. CROCKETT ST.

BOSTON ST.

MAGNOLIA BRIDGE

W. GALER ST.

QUEEN ANNE

Queen Anne High School

Smith Cove

W. GALER ST.

Charles Black House

W. LEE ST.

Stuart/Balcom House

Chappel Mansion

Betty Bowen Park

Kerry Park

Ballard/ Howe House

W. OLYMPIC PL.

W. MERCER PL.

VALLEY ST.

N

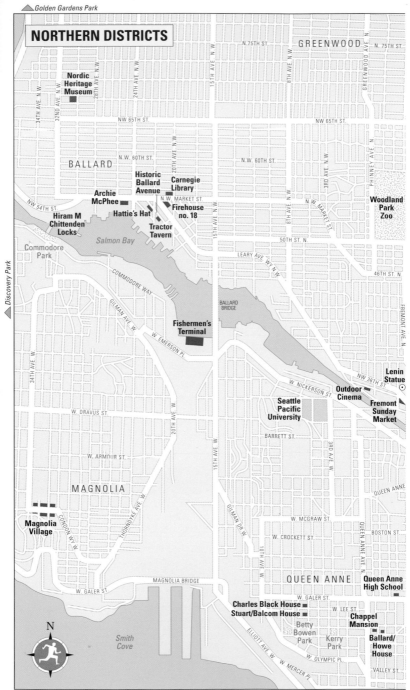

North Seattle
0 500 yds
Green Lake Boat Rentals
Boathouse Theatre
Green Lake Park
Green Lake
GREEN LAKE
Green Lake Reservoir
N.E. 75TH ST.
N.E. 68TH ST.
65TH ST. N.E.
60TH ST. N.W.
Ravenna Park
RAVENNA BLVD
55TH ST. N.E.
Woodland Park
Farmers' Market
Grand Illusion Theater
Seven Gables Theater
UNIVERSITY DISTRICT
WALLINGFORD
Open Books
Wallingford Center
Guild 45th Theatres
45TH ST. N.
45TH ST. N.E.
Burke Museum
University Book Store
UNIVERSITY OF WASHINGTON
Central Plaza
Henry Art Gallery
Suzzallo Library
Allen Library
Meany Hall
University of Washington Visitors' Center
Drumheller Fountain
Sylvan Theatre
Medicinal Herb Garden
Husky Stadium
FREMONT
Fremont Troll
History House
N. 40TH ST.
34TH ST. N.
N. PACIFIC ST.
N.E. PACIFIC ST.
Portage Bay
Waterfront Activity Center
MONTLAKE BRIDGE
Marsh Island
Museum of History & Industry
Bellevue, Kirkland
Gasworks Park
Lake Union
520
Montlake Park
MONTLAKE
Washington Park Arboretum
Louisa Boren View Park
Japanese Garden
Terry Pettus Park
Lake View Cemetery
Ferry Mansion
conservatory
EASTLAKE
Volunteer Park
Seattle Asian Art Museum
water tower
Parker/Fersen House
CAPITOL HILL
Shafer-Baillie Mansion
Center for Wooden Boats
E. HOWE ST.
E. HIGHLAND ST.
E. PROSPECT ST.
E. ALOHA ST.
GALER ST.
HIGHLAND DRIVE
WARD ST.
ALOHA ST.
ROY ST.
WINONA AVE. N.
LINDEN
AURORA AVE. N.
W. GREEN LAKE WY. N.
E. GREEN LAKE WY. N.
WOODLAWN AVE. N.
LAKE CITY WAY
ROOSEVELT WY. N.E.
12TH AVE. N.E.
15TH AVE. N.E.
11TH AVE. N.E.
9TH AVE. N.W.
8TH AVE. N.W.
LATONA AVE. N.E.
25TH AVE. N.E.
21ST AVE. N.E.
50TH ST. N.
50TH ST. N.
E. GREEN LAKE WY.
STONE WAY N.
BURKE AVE.
CORLISS AVE. N.
EASTERN AVE.
UNIVERSITY WAY
MONTLAKE BLVD. N.E.
BRIDGE WAY N.
FREMONT BRIDGE
AURORA BRIDGE
FUHRMAN AVE. E.
EASTLAKE AVE. E.
DELMAR DR. E.
BOYER AVE. E.
LAKE WASHINGTON BLVD
10TH AVE. E.
24TH AVE. E.
QUEEN ANNE DR.
WESTLAKE AVE. N.
TAYLOR AVE. N.
FAIRVIEW AVE. N.
DR.
5

CAPITOL HILL & LAKE WASHINGTON AREA

University District

Marsh Island

Foster Island

SHELBY ST

E. MILLER ST
Montlake Park
LOUISA ST
E. MILLER ST
E. CALHOLM ST
E. McGRAW ST.
LYNN ST.

Museum of History & Industry

Graham Visitors' Center

MONTLAKE

E. BOSTON ST.
E. LYNN ST.
E. NEWTON ST.
E. HOME ST.

Louisa Boren View Park

Washington Park Arboretum

MADISON PARK

MCGILVRA ST

E. NEWTON ST.

Madison Park

Ferry Mansion

Lake View Cemetery

E. BLAINE ST.
E. GARFIELD ST.

E. CRESCENT ST.

E. GALER ST.
E. GALER ST.

conservatory

Samuel Hyde House

E. LEE ST.

HARVARD-BELMONT HISTORIC DISTRICT

E. HIGHLAND DRIVE

E. HIGHLAND DR.

Volunteer Park

Seattle Asian Art Museum

water tower

Japanese Garden

E. PROSPECT ST.
E. PROSPECT ST.

Shafer-Baillie Mansion

Parker/Fersen House

CAPITOL HILL

E. HELEN ST.
E. WARD ST.

Cornish College

MILLIONAIRES' ROW

E. ALOHA ST.
E. ALOHA ST.

Maryland Aprtments

E. ROY ST.
E. VALLEY ST.

Harvard Exit Theater

E. MERCER ST.
E. MERCER ST.

Lakeview Park

Broadway Market

E. REPUBLICAN ST.
E. REPUBLICAN ST.

Denny Blaine Park

E. HARRISON ST.
E. HARRISON ST.

THOMAS ST.

Storey Houses

Viretta Park

E. JOHN ST
E. JOHN ST.

E. THOMAS ST.
E. THOMAS ST.
E. JOHN ST.

E. DENNY WAY

Cobain House

E. DENNY WAY

Egyptian Theater

E. HOWELL ST.
E. OLIVE ST.

Epiphany Chapel

E. HOWELL ST.
E. OLIVE ST.

Jimi Hendrix Statue

E. PINE ST.

Northwest Film Forum

E. PIKE ST.

E. PINE ST.
E. PIKE ST.

E. UNION ST.

E. UNION ST.

Chapel of St Ignatius

E. SPRING ST.
E. MARION ST.

E. SPRING ST.
E. MARION ST.

E. MARION ST.

MADRONA

Madrona Park

Seattle University

E. COLUMBIA ST.
E. CHERRY ST.

E. COLUMBIA ST.

Raymond/Ugden Mansion

E. CHERRY ST.

Lake Washington

CENTRAL DISTRICT

E. JEFFERSON ST.

E. TERRACE ST.

E. ALDER ST.
E. SPRUCE ST.
E. FIR ST.

YESLER WAY
S. WASHINGTON ST.
S. MAIN ST.

YESLER WAY
S. MAIN ST.

Leschi Park

LITTLE SAIGON

S. JACKSON PL
S. JACKSON ST
S. KING ST.
S. WELLER ST.

Frink Park

S. KING ST.

S. LANE ST.
S. DEARBORNE ST.

S. LANE ST.
S. DEARBORNE ST.

S. CHARLES ST.

S. NORMAN ST.

N

S. JUDKINS ST.
S. IRVING ST.

90

S. ATLANTIC ST.

I-90 FREEWAY TUNNEL

I-90 FREEWAY BRIDGE

0   500 yds

Mount Baker & Columbia City

Lake Union

Consolidated Works

Downtown

Pioneer Square & International District

Bellevue Kirkland

Mercer Island

DELMAR DRIVE
BOYER AVE E.
E. INTERLAKEN DR
HARVARD AVE E.
BROADWAY E.
10 AVE E.
FEDERAL AVE E.
BOYLSTON AVE E.
HARVARD AVE E.
BROADWAY
NAGLE PL E.
11TH AVE E.
12TH AVE E.
13TH AVE E.
14TH AVE E.
MAIDEN AVE E.
15TH AVE E.
16TH AVE E.
17TH AVE E.
18TH AVE E.
19TH AVE E.
20TH AVE E.
21ST AVE E.
22ND AVE E.
23RD AVE E.
24TH AVE E.
25TH AVE E.
26TH AVE E.
27TH AVE E.
29TH AVE E.
30TH AVE E.
31ST AVE E.
32ND AVE E.
33RD AVE E.
34TH AVE E.
35TH AVE E.
36TH AVE E.
37TH AVE E.
LAKE WASHINGTON BLVD.
MADISON ST.
MARTIN LUTHER KING JR WAY
GRAND AV.
MADRONA DR
TURNER WAY E.
HILLSIDE DR E.
RANIER AVE S.
BOREN AVE.
8TH AVE S.
12TH AVE S.
4TH AVE
13TH AVE
18TH AVE
20TH AVE S.
23TH AVE
24TH AVE S.
27TH AVE
30TH AVE S.
32ND AVE S.
33RD AVE S.
35TH AVE S.
YAKIMA AVE S.
DELL AVE E.
LAKESIDE
LAKE WASHINGTON BLVD E.